D1585633

Bertolt Brecht: Plays, Poetry and Prose
Edited by JOHN WILLETT
and RALPH MANHEIM

Journals 1934–1955

Brecht's Plays, Poetry and Prose
annotated and edited in hardback and paperback
by John Willett and Ralph Manheim

Collected Plays

Vol. 1 (hardback only)	Baal; Drums in the Night; In the Jungle of Cities; The Life of Edward II of England; A Respectable Wedding; The Beggar; Driving Out a Devil; Lux in Tenebris; The Catch
Vol. 1i	Baal (*paperback only*)
Vol. 1ii	A Respectable Wedding and other one-act plays (*paperback only*)
Vol. 1iii	Drums in the Night (*paperback only*)
Vol. 1iv	In the Jungle of Cities (*paperback only*)
Vol. 2i	Man equals Man; The Elephant Calf
Vol. 2ii	The Threepenny Opera
Vol. 2iii	The Rise and Fall of the City of Mahagonny; The Seven Deadly Sins
Vol. 3i	Saint Joan of the Stockyards
*Vol. 3ii	The Decision, The Mother
*Vol. 4i	The Lindbergh Flight; The Baden-Baden Cantata of Acquiescence; The Exception and the Rule; He Who Said Yes; He Who Said No; The Horatii and the Curiatii
*Vol. 4ii	Dansen; What's the Price of Iron?; Round Heads and Pointed Heads
Vol. 4iii	Fear and Misery of the Third Reich; Señora Carrar's Rifles
Vol. 5i	Life of Galileo
Vol. 5ii	Mother Courage and her Children
*Vol. 5iii	The Trial of Lucullus; The Messingkauf Dialogues; The Exiles Dialogues
Vol. 6i	The Good Person of Szechwan
Vol. 6ii	The Resistible Rise of Arturo Ui
Vol. 6iii	Mr. Puntila and his Man Matti
Vol. 7	The Visions of Simone Machard; Schweyk in the Second World War; The Caucasian Chalk Circle; The Duchess of Malfi
Vol. 7i	The Visions of Simone Machard; Schweyk in the Second World War (*paperback only*)
*Vol. 8i	The Days of the Commune
*Vol. 8ii	Turandot; Report from Herrnburg
*Vol. 8iii	Downfall of the Egoist Johann Fatzer; The Life of Confucius; The Breadshop; The Salzburg Dance of Death
Poetry	Poems 1913–1956; Poems and Songs from the Plays; *Further Poems
Prose	Brecht on Theatre; Diaries 1920–1922; Letters 1913–1956; Short Stories 1921–1946; *Theoretical Writings
Also	Happy End (by Brecht, Weill and Lane)

The following plays are also available (in paperback) in unannotated editions:
The Caucasian Chalk Circle; The Days of the Commune; The Life of Galileo; The Measures Taken and other Lehrstücke; The Messingkauf Dialogues; The Mother

* *in preparation*

Bertolt Brecht Journals

Translated by Hugh Rorrison
Edited by John Willett

Methuen · London

First published in Great Britain 1993
by Methuen London
an imprint of Reed Consumer Books Ltd
Michelin House, 81 Fulham Road, London SW3 6RB
and Auckland, Melbourne, Singapore and Toronto
by arrangement with Suhrkamp Verlag, Frankfurt am Main
based on the original work published by Suhrkamp Verlag
in 1973 as *Arbeitsjournal*
Copyright © 1973 Stefan S. Brecht
Translation copyright © 1993 Stefan S. Brecht
Introduction and editorial notes for this edition
copyright © 1993 Methuen London

A CIP catalogue record for this book
is available from the British Library

ISBN 0 413 65510 5 Hardback
ISBN 0 413 68240 4 Paperback

Typeset by Deltatype Limited, Ellesmere Port
Printed in Great Britain
by St. Edmundsbury Press Ltd, Bury St. Edmunds

Contents

Brecht Between
Two World Systems

Aside from a recently discovered handwritten diary of 1913 (when he was an adolescent), Brecht left two coherent diaries or journals: one for the years 1920 to 1922, which appeared in the Methuen edition in 1979, and the other the present 'work journal' or 'Arbeitsjournal' as it became called, which starts in the summer of 1938 and runs (or in the end hops) until about a year before his death in August 1956. Besides these two contrasting documents there are also a lot of miscellaneous jottings or notes of which a small number were included in the German edition of the first diary and more are expected to see the light in the new thirty-volume 'Berlin and Frankfurt' collected works which began appearing in 1988.

The first adult diary was handwritten and bound in four parts. It is self-aware, self-exploratory, often wildly romantic and exotic, full of poetic and theatrical ideas and insights. It seems to have been written for fun, for the pleasures of language, with little attention to eventual publishers or ordinary readers. Its later and larger successor is much less spontaneous. This is typewritten, recognisably by Brecht himself throughout – no evidence of his collaborators – on loosely filled pages and without capital letters except for the use of small capitals for titles and sometimes for proper names. 'In the last few days', he notes in the winter of 1941/2, when still feeling somewhat lost in the United States,

> i have skimmed superficially right through this journal. naturally it is quite distorted, for fear of unwelcome readers, and i will have difficulty following its guidelines one day. it stays within certain bounds, precisely because bounds are there to be exceeded.

Who were those unwelcome readers, we may wonder? The police, the Nazi invaders of Denmark, the watchdogs of the Communist Party, his household, the women closest to him? About these last he says very little – much less than in the earlier diary – and maybe he meant to control his utterances about politics too, and even about other things, though such matters as his thoughts about Soviet policy and propaganda in 1939/40 burst out none the less. But the possibility of eventual publication, for better or worse, was surely in his mind.

It was not Brecht who used the term 'work journal', and although it certainly contains important reflections about his work, its problems and its progress, there are surprising aspects of his writing about which the journal says very little. About *Mother Courage*, for instance, he says nothing about the original planning and completion in 1939; *Lucullus* too is barely discussed in its first (radio) version; his intentions with *Fear and Misery of the Third Reich* remain unclear; he never mentions that great poem 'To those born later'; and he seems quite to have lost interest in *The Round Heads and the Pointed Heads* after its Danish première. He does however tell us a lot about his fellow exiles, gives vivid glimpses of his own family, comments sharply on Californian life and landscape, keeps an eye on the Second World War and looks around him with his own special mixture of interest and detachment. Repeatedly he says the unexpected thing. Much of this is like a montage, as he cuts from one subject to another, and the scrapbook effect is added to by the insertion of photographs – public or personal – and newspaper cuttings from different sources. There are gaps, sometimes conscious; sometimes perhaps because he is away from his own desk; they become more noticeable as the journal goes on. The year 1946, for instance, is an almost complete blank, and for the last three years or so of his life the material is sparse.

So our editorial notes set out in the first place to comment on what he says, often about little-known individuals and works and sometimes obscure subjects. This has been done separately from the journal proper, not so much in order to preserve its flow as the opposite: i.e. to convey its montage structure, its particular jerky dynamic, not unlike the 'epic' construction of the plays. Generally speaking the pictures and cuttings are as chosen and positioned by him, sometimes with a brief explanatory caption, though he took so many of them from English-language publications that little captioning is needed. We have included some longer notes for the interested reader which set out to resume Brecht's life and concerns during the gaps. And we start the book with a short run-up to the summer of 1938 in the shape of a few self-introductory statements which have not previously been published in this edition. In his maturity he was not generally so introspective.

✽

Now what made him start this journal in 1938? What was happening in his life and writing, and indeed in the world, to impel him? In February he was forty; he was an exile from Germany who had been living quietly in a thatched cottage on a Danish island for four years, stripped of his citizenship and cut off from all the former outlets for his work. In March the Nazis took over Austria, his wife's country; her family were Jewish. In France the Popular Front was already in decline when Léon Blum lost power in April. There and in England the 'appeasers' triumphed that autumn when Hitler's demands were granted under the Munich Agreement. Mussolini and Franco too were doing well. In Russia the purges were under way, powered by the great Moscow show trials of August 1936, January 1937 and March 1938 (with Zinoviev, Radek and Bukharin as principal victims) and their promotion of 'vigilance'. The exiled German writers there were keen to comply, and obediently accused one another. Moscow-based organisations like the International Leagues of Revolutionary Writers (MORP) and Revolutionary Theatres (MORT) had been closed down. Brecht's last piece of immediate Party-Line theatre had had its première in Paris in May, and in the autumn he wrote *Galileo*, first of the new big plays.

By then he had started using the phrase 'the Dark Times', which defined the new climate of his life and art; and it is plain that the darkness was not confined to Nazi Germany, where the Second World War was already being brewed. Three years had passed since his visit to Moscow, when he had met members of the Comintern executive, exchanged views about the *V-Effekt* with Sergei Tretiakov, been honoured by Carola Neher and others with a 'Brecht evening' of songs and poems and discussed various plans for publications and performance; the signs were hopeful. By the beginning of 1938 however Tretiakov himself, the two Comintern members Kun and Knorin and the actress Carola Neher had all been arrested; Ernst Ottwalt (Brecht's fellow script writer on *Kuhle Wampe*) was expelled from the Party, and Piscator advised (by Pieck of the Comintern) not to return from France now that MORT had been 'liquidated'. At the end of the year Mikhail Koltsov of *Izvestiya*, the sponsor of *Das Wort*, the Moscow-based German Communist magazine which Brecht edited with Feuchtwanger and Willi Bredel, was also arrested on his return from the Spanish War. Two months later the magazine was closed down, and with that such small role as had been left to Brecht in Communist cultural policy came to an end.

Brecht saw clearly enough that culture in the Soviet and KPD (or German Communist Party) reckoning was 'Kulturpolitik', an amalgam of its political and artistic aspects as interpreted by 'cultural politicians' approved by the party authorities. He could not say much about the arrests, still less about the deaths which usually followed, though now and again the journal makes a brief allusion; and he was anxious not to weaken the position of what he knew to be his own side in the fight against Hitler. This led him not only to wrap up his criticisms of the USSR in the *Me-Ti* aphorisms which he now resumed writing, and to conceal his bitter poem on Tretiakov's execution in August 1939, but also to hold back nearly all ripostes to the cultural politicians, the self-righteous 'Moscow clique' (as he termed them) of Georg Lukács and other Hungarian critics who dominated the KPD pundits headed by Johannes R. Becher. But entries in the journal were evidently something different, and perhaps this difference was one of the reasons for embarking on it at such a critical time. The result is that the cultural argument gives the whole seventeen years of miscellaneous entries a certain over-arching unity, as we begin with the Moscow view of decadence, decline or degeneration in the arts, and sweep through to the distant climax, where a closely related controversy in East Berlin is resolved, so far as Brecht and his theatre are concerned, by the ironic happy ending, when he goes off to Moscow to get a Stalin Prize.

✳

Brecht was very right, in his introductory remark 'On Progress' (1938), when he said that he 'always needed the spur of contradiction'. He was not by nature a conformist, nor in any sense a right-thinking person, and much of the appeal for him of dialectics was that it left room for disagreement and inconsistency; from such clashes came the 'flow of things'. But if we look back to the start of Brecht's Dark Times, which really does seem to have been where he decided to become a diarist once more, then it is not difficult to imagine how Communist culture might have gone another way. This was the way that had appeared most likely only two or three years earlier, when the newly exiled Brecht, having finished his major work the *Three-penny Novel*, set out for Moscow, Paris and New York. In Moscow he met the leading Soviet directors and Clurman, Losey, Strasberg and Gordon Craig under the auspices of MORT. In Paris he attended the Amsterdam-Pleyel anti-Fascist conference with Barbusse, Gide, Malraux, Gorki, Forster, Aldous Huxley and others. In New York, where he went with Hanns Eisler for the Theatre Union's production of *The Mother*, there was a new League of American Writers headed by Waldo Frank, with Odets, Michael Gold, Langston Hughes and other Leftists. This was to be affiliated to Moscow's MORP.

It seemed like the beginning of a widespread Popular Front culture, encouraged certainly by the Russians and the Comintern, but rooted in France and the Spanish Republic with a strong offshoot in the United States and related branches in Britain, Australia and the Scandinavian countries. Picasso's *Guernica* at the Paris Exhibition of 1937, the films of Jean Renoir and René Clair, the documentaries of Grierson and Ivens, the buildings of Le Corbusier and Aalto, the novels of Malraux and Isherwood, Steinbeck and Dashiell Hammett, the poems of Auden, the woodcuts of Masereel, the music of Stravinsky, Ellington and the young Britten all could be seen as part of an enlightened modern movement which was radically (and not just ideologically) opposed to the simultaneously developing reactionary arts of the Third Reich. This constellation was at its brightest in the years just before the Second World War, and in the democracies it survived in a number of ways – the magazine *New Writing*, for instance, became the (tamer and worse-produced) *Penguin New Writing*; the documentary movement inspired the British Army Film Unit. Later the Festival of Britain in 1951 had something of a postwar résumé about it, Corbusier and Gropius were given the RIBA Gold Medal, and in post-Fascist Italy the whole of this culture got a new impetus through Elio Vittorini's review *Politechnico* and the neo-Realist film. But the slow decline into the mediocrities of Post-Modernism was already under way.

Today this broadly coherent committed culture is studied with admiration and a certain nostalgia, starting with the Left art of the Weimar Republic and continuing through the Popular Front, the New Deal, the impact of the Spanish Civil War and other socio-cultural changes associated with the Thirties and the resistance to Hitler and Mussolini. Part of the essence of this movement was that it was so opposed to the nationalistic, racially-conscious, populist, pseudo-classical art of the Nazis and Fascists, and opposed not just in a philosophically or aesthetically defined sense, but by a recognisably liberal, concerned and forward-looking attitude which appeared to be common to its practitioners across all frontiers. Brecht was not a figure who fitted all that easily into any grouping, but in his individual and sometimes cantankerous way he did fit in here, and his unrealised plan of 1937 for a 'Diderot Society' may show it, with its list of proposed members including Renoir, Eisenstein, Eisler, Piscator, Burian, Tretiakov, Gorelik and Auden. Unhappily names like these were almost as remote from the new Soviet orthodoxy – with its nineteenth-century art models, its Stanislavskyan theatre, its neoclassical architecture, its romantic or folksy music and its Socialist Realist writing – as from Hitler's showpiece House of German Art in Munich. So long as Moscow contained such international arts bodies as MORP, MORT, the International Music Bureau (through which Eisler was hoping to promote serialism) and Mezhrabpom-Film, the Party's artists and writers had some freedom to choose their forms. By mid-1938 these bodies, and with them that freedom, had disappeared.

This then is when Brecht started to say what he preferred not to say publicly in *Das Wort*. What he abstained from dealing with in his opening comments on Lukács's view of 'decline' is the parallel Nazi attack on 'degeneracy' in the visual arts and music as demonstrated in two massive exhibitions around that same time, whose argument closely matched the Moscow rejection of modern idioms. Nor does he take in the political aspect which he mentioned to Walter Benjamin (see Note for 25.7.38). This link between the new Party 'vigilance' generated by the intensive purges of summer 1936 and the anti-'formalist' campaign of the same period emerges from the records of four sessions of the Moscow German writers that September, which were first made public in Germany at the end of 1991. Lukács was only at the opening meeting, but his colleagues Barta and Gabór had leading roles, and Brecht may have heard reports of the mutual accusations and confessions. It is not surprising that from the start of the journal till his departure for California three years later there was no longer any question of his working in the USSR, let alone settling there, while Hanns Eisler had already given up his role in Soviet musical life and was working in New York.

.·.

Unlike his Moscow initiation by Piscator and Tretiakov in 1935, Brecht's New York visit in the autumn of that year had not been a happy experience. It took place just at the beginning of the Federal Theatre Project, and the formal innovations of the Living Newspaper and the Ladies Garment Workers' revues were still to come, but he did see Odets's agitprop play *Waiting for Lefty* and seems to have made something of a disciple of Marc Blitzstein. But with the exception of the designer, Max Gorelik, he alienated virtually everyone concerned with the Theatre Union production of *The Mother*, whose closure in mid-December helped to break the company, and for Brecht their disputes fanned out into a lasting quarrel with John Howard Lawson, the Group Theatre and others now concerned in developing psychological naturalism and the Stanislavskyan 'Method'. During the rest of the New Deal his opponents prospered, till they came to dominate much of the theatre and were richly rewarded in Hollywood as writers and actors. The result was that when he arrived in Los Angeles in the summer of 1941 there were few American friends waiting for him, let alone prospective editors, producers and publishers. Nor did he need to worry about the same sharp-eyed Moscow 'Kulturpolitiker' now that the USSR was at war. His main concerns were personal ones – how to live and work with his wife and children, how to get over the loss of his beloved aide Margarete Steffin, and (more tacitly) how to fit the difficult Danish actress Ruth Berlau into his changed life. For at least a year this was enough.

Roughly half the typed pages of his journal are from America, where he spent just over six years. One quarter is from before he left Scandinavia: mainly from Finland, where he had a particularly fruitful year. Just under a quarter is from his waiting period in Switzerland, where he spent nine months, and from his last eight years in Germany, though it peters out in 1954–5 with over a year left to go. So certainly the American experience bulks large in it, even though he never really settles down in Los Angeles or New York. He starts by mingling with his German fellow-exiles, whether from the world of literature, the films or the old Berlin theatre, or from the broader intellectual-political sphere of the Frankfurt Institute for Social Research. About all of these he is interesting, sometimes (rightly or wrongly) damning, often memorably amusing (see the sketches of Remarque and Emil Ludwig). At the same same time it is they – and for much of the time they alone – who help to give him jobs. He tries to write film stories without much success; these are not on the whole very good. And except in poems like those of Eisler's *Hollywood Songbook* he seems always to be aiming at the conventional American portals to fame: Broadway and the movies. Meantime his real progress is taking place on the other side of the Atlantic, with the production of his big Scandinavian plays – *Galileo* and *The Good Person of Szechwan* – by the anti-Nazi refugees of the Zurich Schauspielhaus, who in spring 1941 had staged *Mother Courage*.

Fritz Lang gives him his big send-off with the resistance film

Hangmen Also Die for which he writes the story and collaborates with the leftist John Wexley on the script. Lion Feuchtwanger helps him with the French resistance play *Simone Machard*, with its flashback Joan of Arc 'visions'; it finds no takers, but Feuchtwanger's novel of their story is sold to MGM. Brecht's old Berlin producer Aufricht commissions an updated musical version of *Schweyk* with Kurt Weill; Peter Lorre thinks of playing in it, but the scheme collapses. Weill himself commissions a 'semi-operatic' version of *The Good Person of Szechwan*, whose script exists but never finds a producer. Elisabeth Bergner and Paul Czinner commission an adaptation of *The Duchess of Malfi*; then Georg Rylands as director scraps all Brecht's work and reverts to Webster's text. Luise Rainer, the Austrian star married to Odets, commissions a *Chalk Circle* which emerges as *Caucasian* rather than Chinese; she loses interest. The *Fear and Misery* scenes are rejigged as *The Private Life of the Master Race*, and only performed once Hitler has been defeated and the play is no longer topical; Brecht disagrees with Piscator's direction, and the result is a flop. All this is émigré stuff, and aimed to satisfy conventional criteria; there is nothing to match the pre-Hitler didactic plays or the music-theatre works with Weill. Only when Brecht gets outside the emigration and finds a new kind of partner does he manage to perfect and realise a work that satisfies him: the Laughton production of *Galileo* in 1947, directed by the Living Newspaper director Joseph Losey.

There were many other threads to Brecht's life in those six years even apart from his private concerns. Thus he began playing a role in postwar planning, and was active in the Council for a Democratic Germany which was started following the establishment of a Free German National Committee in Moscow. A few of his writings began to appear in English, notably the bilingual edition of *Selected Poems* translated by H. R. Hays; there was a tentative plan to take this further, but the publishers changed hands. What really gave him a belated place in the American context was the decision of the House Un-American Activities Committee to examine him in connection with 'Communist infiltration of the motion-picture industry' rather than his relations with the Eisler brothers, whom their sister Ruth Fischer had denounced to the FBI a little wildly along with Brecht. This final association with the 'Hollywood nineteen', which threw him together with just those naturalist writers of whom he was apt to be critical, did not strike him at the time as all that important, and his entry about the hearing is barely longer than his contemptuous critique of the *German Stanislavsky Book* which precedes it. This told him what to expect on his return to Europe a day after testifying. The other would tell him what he was leaving behind.

✻

It was November 1947 when Brecht began his period of waiting in Switzerland. The war against Nazi Germany had been over for two and a half years; the worst of the bomb damage had been cleared from the great cities; the theatres closed during 1944/5 were open again with a mixture of new and old directors; four victorious allies were pushing their own plays. Except in Zurich, where he was hoping to stage *Puntila*, fourth of his Scandinavian plays to have its world première there, Brecht was no longer any better known than in the USA; virtually all his writings since 1938 were unpublished, and anything earlier would have to be brought back into print. Moreover he was not anxious for anything to be performed unless he could direct (or at least supervise) it himself. He wanted to understand the new German set-up, with its four differently administered zones and four sectors of Berlin; nor was it going to be easy for a now stateless subversive to travel, particularly during the Berlin blockade which began in mid-1948. So he had to feel his way with the help of pre-Nazi friends like Caspar Neher; he had to try things out on a modest scale (as with the Chur *Antigone* production); he had to write new texts, of which his theoretical *summa*, the *Short Organum*, was the most pressing; and there were other new possibilities like a revitalised Salzburg Festival to be explored. This was the springtime of his return; as Hitler's fortunes sank, the Dark Times had been absorbed into his poetry, and if he soon enough spoke of 'Bad Times' (in a poem of 1949) or 'Difficult Times' (in 1955) it was no longer with horror but with a certain resignation.

His credentials for establishing himself in the Soviet-controlled third of his country, with its capital in East Berlin, were the support of Friedrich Wolf, the old Communist doctor-playwright who had preceded him as a guest of Theatre Union in 1935, and Herbert Jhering the critic who had promoted him since 1922; then there was the power of *Mother Courage*, in whose Zurich production the new Deutsches Theater Intendant Wolfgang Langhoff had played Eilif; the fact that he had a fiftieth birthday to commemorate (in German culture these dates are important); and of course his anti-Nazi and pro-communist record. So in winter 1949 Mother Courage, unforgettably played by Helene Weigel, came to Max Reinhardt's old theatre, was seen, and conquered; and on that foundation the Berliner Ensemble was built. One of its objectives, certainly, was to introduce and establish Brecht's still unknown plays after *Fear and Misery* and *Señora Carrar*, which had so far been seen as the most acceptable; another was to develop an alternative to the Nazi tradition of high gloss and overheated acting; a third was the extension and reinterpretation of the classical repertoire for a new thinking audience. Brecht realised from the outset that not everything could be done at once, and that the ascetic, didactic forms of his last Berlin productions two decades earlier would be too much of a shock. 'Of course, it is only as epic as they can take (and we can offer) today,' he notes of the success of the Ensemble *Puntila* on 13 November 1949. 'But when will the real, radical epic theatre come into being?'

Whether or not the new Berlin audience, many of whom had been going to theatres under Hitler, would ever have accepted this is a debatable point. But certainly the East German cultural arbiters would not, for they were dominated by reliable ex-members of the 'Moscow clique', with Lukács still as their politico-aesthetic authority, and, in so far as they were reinforced by the locals, these could have changed their political views after 1945 without abandoning Hitler's aesthetic prejudices. As in 1938 'Socialist Realism' was the criterion, and it was not long before *Mother Courage* itself was being attacked as 'negative' and 'defeatist'. Production of *The Days of the Commune* was blocked on similar grounds. The opera *Lucullus* was 'formalist' on account of Dessau's difficult music, and once again pacifist or 'defeatist' in its text; though with the second point, as explained to him in the cold war context by Wilhelm Pieck (another Muscovite who now became the East German President), Brecht rather agreed. The production of *The Mother*, which represented a considerable compromise after the agitprop staging of 1932, was still too heretical to be toured in Poland (though Brecht got this order changed). The Academy of Arts in East Berlin supported Brecht with a special issue of its magazine, but the theatre journal *Theater der Zeit*, now edited by a former colleague on *Das Wort*, pursued the old Moscow line. By 4 March 1953, on the eve of a conference called by the official 'Commission on Art Affairs' to put across Stanislavsky's ideas, Brecht could comment on the Ensemble's loss of any worthwhile public response.

The next day Stalin died, and there are no entries for another five months. This was hardly because of shock, and the Stanislavsky conference, where Brecht left the talking to Helene Weigel, was not all that damaging. But it was followed in May–June by a concerted attack on Hanns Eisler by the party paper *Neues Deutschland* launched by Wilhelm Girnus in alliance with the experienced 'Kulturpolitiker' Becher, Abusch and Rodenberg, with only Brecht effectively standing up for him. The transcript of this unworthy inquest was unpublished till 1991, following the death of Hans Bunge, who had got hold of the material and edited it. The point was to stop Eisler, one of the greatest living German/Austrian composers, from writing his planned opera on the *Faust* theme, whose gist would be that Goethe's divided hero had reneged on his peasant forebears and their struggle against feudalism, and compromised with the rulers so as to frustrate that struggle indefinitely. This was an affront not just to the traditional view of Goethe's play, but also to the very concept of 'the hero' and of the German 'national heritage'; here was the 'German humanist' being presented as a 'renegade', and the so-called 'German Misere' about which Brecht also wrote (for instance in connection with *The Tutor*, another play of Goethe's time) as a national malady rather than a reactionary hiccup. Becher, who had grown increasingly nationalistic, damned Eisler's proposed text as 'antinational'; Girnus repeatedly said that it 'infringed the principles of Socialist Realism'; Ernst Hermann Meyer even cited Stalin's arts henchman Zhdanov. Eisler moved back to Vienna, and wrote to the Party at the end of October to say that he had lost all motivation. Fifteen years later the Berliner Ensemble would plan to give his text a staged reading. The Ministry of Culture advised them not to.

All this was reminiscent of 1938, but at least it was not back to the purges. Just six days after the final assault on Eisler the East Berlin building workers struck and there was rioting on the borders between East and West Berlin. Other East German cities followed suit. Brecht, unlike some more conformist intellectuals, immediately assured the Party of his support, but called for a public post-mortem; by the time of his next journal entry two months later he felt a new confidence in the working class, which had at last made its voice heard. So on the one hand his position as a political artist became greatly strengthened: the Ensemble was at last granted its own theatre, and it could travel triumphantly to Paris in 1954 with *Mother Courage*. At the same time the arts administration was reorganised so as to do away with the 'commissions' that had controlled licences and resources (and had for instance set up the Stanislavsky conference). These were replaced by a Ministry of Culture under the now more tractable Johannes R. Becher, who allowed the 'formalism' argument to wither away.

And yet Brecht was not happy, as the all-round scepticism of that autumn's cycle of 'Buckow Elegies' shows. The Seventeenth of June, he decided, 'has alienated the whole of existence'. And again a year later, driving back from Buckow – itself an elegiac place, in a mistier and more subdued way than Hollywood, where the previous Elegies had been written – he found that he still felt uneasy in his country, whose Nazi past was not all that remote. Like Eisler, and in the end for related reasons, he had too many questions to ask. He was still working, still altering his work when done, still doubting, still enjoying – 'a mouthful of good meat', 'the kindnesses of delightful I. K.', the 'Pleasures' he listed for Käthe Reichel, and finally 'the song of every blackbird'. He could still express these enjoyments in the last poems. But not in the journal. There was no longer time.

Note on the Editing

We are very sorry to have to report the loss of Ralph Manheim, who died in Cambridge (England) last autumn after having worked on this edition and its Pantheon Books precursor ever since the project was initiated by Stefan S. Brecht in New York over twenty years ago. As the leading translator from German in his time he not only supervised the work of American, British, and other colleagues but did much of the translating himself – most recently the large volume of Brecht's *Letters* over five decades. He was still working when the present volume was being prepared. We miss his judgement and his advice.

In planning it we have followed the editor of the forthcoming new German edition, Werner Hecht, in including some material from the 'Autobiographische Aufzeichnungen' originally collected in the Suhrkamp edition of *Tagebücher* (1975), along with the earlier Diary. This accounts for the first four entries, dated 1934, 1935, 1936 and 1938. The journal proper starts with that dated 'july 38'.

We are grateful too to Helene Ritzerfeld and Günter Berg of Suhrkamp-Verlag for answering queries and supplying us with relevant background publications, some of which will be found listed in the Select Bibliography at the end of the Notes.

Throughout the text, phrases in italics marked by an asterisk were written in English by Brecht.

Denmark
1934 to 15 March 1939

1934

i am a playwright.

i would actually like to have been a cabinetmaker, but of course you don't earn enough doing that. i would have enjoyed working with wood. you don't get really fine stained and polished wood much any more, the beautiful panelling and balustrades of the old days, those pale, maple-wood tabletops as thick as the span of your hand that we found in our grandparents' rooms, worn smooth by the hands of whole generations. and the wardrobes i've seen! the way the edges were bevelled, the doors inlaid, the internal compartments offset, and such beautiful proportions. seeing a piece of furniture like that made you think better thoughts. the things they could do with a wooden fork-handle, these craftsmen who have all gone now. even in these times of ours there are good things to be seen. in bond street in london in a shop window i saw a big cigar-box, six plain maple boards and an iron catch, but it looked marvellous. the cigars were a guinea apiece. at a casual glance the unadorned box would have made one think, 'this tobacco is so costly that they can't even lay out a shilling for the packaging, a guinea is the bottom price they can take, and at that the planters are starving'. but on further inspection one could see that the firm had seen fit to provide a case too that would satisfy the expectations of their connoisseurs of fine tobacco.

i am now 36 years old and i have not wasted these years; i am entitled to say this, the more so if i think of the efforts i have made rather than of my achievements, and if i plead in extenuation that i live in times where it is not only easy to waste time, but one is also robbed of it. i haven't lived for myself, but in the public arena, for from the age of 21 i have been known for my literary works and for many enterprises connected with them. i have moreover already attracted followers, and i have advised and given a lead to others. i merely mention this to lend some weight to my statement that 'i don't know everything about life'. not that i am unpractical or live in the clouds; i don't avoid the nuts and bolts of everyday life, i am hardly an 'innocent soul'. i have arranged advantageous contracts that made possible a life that is in accord with my desires, i own houses, a motor car, i maintain a family, employ secretaries, all of this in spite of the fact that no one could call my works marketable. but even if i am unpractical, in the sense that life, as i have said, puzzles me, there are more practical people than me who are equally puzzled.

when i weigh up where abandoning myself to my enthusiasms has got me, and what benefit repeated scrutiny has been, i recommend the latter. if i had adopted the former approach, i would still be living in my fatherland, but by not adopting the latter, i would no longer be an honest person.

1935

years after i had made my name as a writer i still knew nothing of politics and had not set eyes on a book by or about marx. i had written four dramas and an opera which had been performed in many theatres, i had received literary prizes, and in surveys which invited contributions from progressive minds, my opinions could frequently be read. but i didn't yet understand the abc of politics, and i had no more idea of the way public affairs in my country were regulated than any peasant in his isolated cottage. before i turned to literature, i had in the war year of 1917 written an anti-war poem, the 'ballad of the dead soldier', [. . .]. by 1918 i was a soldiers' council delegate and had been in the USPD. but on getting into literature i never progressed beyond rather nihilistic criticism of bourgeois society. not even eisenstein's great films, which had a colossal effect on me, nor the first productions of the piscator theatre, which i admired no less, moved me to study marxism. perhaps this was due to my scientific education (i had studied medicine for several years), which strongly immunised me against influence from the emotional side. then a sort of technical hitch helped me to move forward. for a certain play i needed the chicago wheat exchange as background. i imagined i would be able to get the necessary information quickly by consulting specialists and practitioners in the field. things turned out differently. nobody, neither a number of well-known economic journalists nor any of the businessmen – i followed one dealer with long experience of the chicago wheat exchange from berlin to vienna – could adequately explain what went on at the grain exchange. i gained the impression that the dealings were downright inexplicable, that is, not accessible to rational under-standing, in other words plainly irrational. the manner in which the world's wheat was distributed was utterly incomprehensible. from any angle, apart from that of a handful of speculators, the market in wheat was one huge swamp. the projected drama was never written. instead i began to read marx, and it was then, and only then that i did read marx. and for the first time, my own scattered practical experiences and impressions really came to life.

1936

the experiences i am having at the moment are not without value. i thought i could learn to write for films, but i see that it would take more than just a morning's work; the technique is at a quite primitive stage. however i am learning something different. although kortner treats me as an absolute equal, the nature of the work means that i am beginning to feel like an employee. i have not chosen the subject i am working on for myself, i can't relate to it and i don't know what will happen to my work when it comes on the market. i only have my labour to sell, and what is done with it afterwards has nothing to do with me. my interests are quite opposed to those of my employer. since i am on a weekly wage, it is not good for me if the work progresses quickly, quite the contrary. already i even catch myself taking out my watch as evening approaches; i want to get away, it's time for real life to begin. real life is quite separate, and incidentally quite unappealing. but in 'my own time' i don't waste a single thought on my daily work. i leave with the little englishman who works alongside me as translator and we strictly avoid touching anything that might remind us of work. i feel a sense of total solidarity with him when he refuses to work on sundays. kortner seems to have noticed this incipient class consciousness, for he often says on the phone, when he is cancelling an appointment, that with his job he has work to do – just as any boss might. whenever he can, he makes mock of his employers, points out their inferiority and laziness, whereupon we are both silent.

at lunch – i eat at his place and hanna kortner is very nice – it all stops and i am the great poet once more. i have the privilege of being able to take a nap, but then, after coffee, the situation changes once more. the paper i am using to write this is from work: i pinched it.

1938

ON PROGRESS
it pleased me to think of the progress i have made as having been a rearguard action. every retreat, or almost every retreat, had been preceded by an advance. for example i began with the simplest, most ordinary sorts of poetry, the ballad, the street-ballad, forms which the better sort of poet had not been using for a long time. i retreated to free

verse when rhyme proved inadequate for what i had to say. in the drama i began with a five act play with a central figure, a plot of the most venerable sort (the enoch arden motif) and a contemporary setting. after a while i had moved on far enough to give up empathy, in which even the most progressive spirits believed implicitly. with all my love of the new, i did not give up the old without clinging doggedly to it until it finally ceased to function. when i could no longer make any headway in the theatre with empathy, try as i might, i devised the *lehrstück* for empathy. it seemed to me that if people stopped *merely* empathising intellectually, then that was enough, and something fruitful could be extracted from the old kind of empathy. incidentally i have never had any respect for revolutionaries who put off the revolution because things were too hot for them.

an error?

i have always needed the spur of contradiction.

LOVE OF CLARITY

my love of clarity comes from the unclear way i think. i became a little doctrinaire because i was in pressing need of instruction. my thoughts readily become confused, and i don't at all mind saying so. it's the confusion i mind. when i discover something, i immediately contradict it passionately and to my dismay call everything into question again, when a moment before i had been happy as a sandboy, because at least something had, in some measure, been established for my, as i told myself, modest requirements. such statements as that the proof of the pudding is in the eating, or life is a protein condition, console me uncommonly, until i run into further inconveniences. and scenes that take place between people i write down simply because i can't imagine them clearly unless i do.

BELIEF

i greatly like the proletariat's belief in its final victory. but the proletariat's closely connected belief in various other things it has been told, i find disturbing.

july 38

reading LUKÁCS'S MARX AND THE PROBLEM OF IDEOLOGICAL DE-CLINE. how 'mankind' moves in wherever the proletariat abandons a position. the talk is once again of realism which they have blithely debased, just as the nazis have debased socialism. the realistic writer in an 'age of decline' (our epoch that is; at the outset a few murmurings of 'age of bourgeois decline', then simply 'age of decline' – the whole thing is coming unstuck, not just the bourgeoisie) is relieved of the need to be a dialectical materialist. all he has to do 'is give properly perceived and experienced reality priority over accepted world-views and received prejudices in shaping his material'. since balzac and tolstoy did just this, they reflect reality! all the sholokhovs and thomas manns are thus vindicated, they reflect the world . . . there is no contradiction between the bourgeois realists and the proletarian realists (a glance at sholokhov seems in fact to corroborate this), nor, presumably between the bourgeoisie and the proletariat itself; how could there be, under the banner of the popular front? up with pastor niemöller! realist of the purest water! once again no knowledge is necessary to *shape your material* (for th[omas] mann indeed shapes his material, and it is a fact that he knows nothing). in shaping their material these half-wits give reality priority over prejudice without even knowing they are doing it. it is a process of direct experience: you get a kick, say: ow! he gets a kick, let him say: ow. the simplicity of it! the bold lukács is magically attracted to the problem of ideological decline. it has become his thing. with him it is a case of a kantian developing marxist categories ad absurdum not by refuting them, but by just using them. there is the *class struggle*, a hollow shell, an over-used whore of a concept, burnt out beyond recognition, but still with us, still putting in an appearance. 'among those present were . . .', '. . . also ran'. no more facts, nothing concrete. in the above essay one short quotation from marx. marx praises [EUGENE] SUE's shaping of a figure from the gutter. sue equips *fleur de marie* with beautiful qualities and thus 'slaps the prejudices of the bourgeoisie in the face'. this is concrete if it's anything. there is a slap in the face, a getting to grips with reality, more precisely with the dehumanised condition of fleur de marie. for lukács and his sort the class struggle is a demon, an empty principle which confuses people's ideas, not something that actually happens. it is part of reality and all the writer has to do is depict reality, and he will somehow include it. how this gambit resembles the national 'socialist' manoeuvres, the way these twits launch their formalistic critique with a campaign against formalism . . .

difficulties in CAESAR. he still has to be worked out more as an individual after all. he must rise between the classes. be pushed up between the struggling classes, force himself up. the proletarian revolution (in a country which after the victory had two struggling classes, the workers and the peasants) did after all make rule by one man possible. the equites got c[aesar] above them, at the same time as they got the patres and the plebs below them.

at the end the following tableau: the plebs, constantly renewed from among the slaves, reduced to the standard of slavery, provide a reservoir for the army with which foreign nations are overthrown and held down, as long as they continue to face up as nations, otherwise the armies help the foreign ruling classes to keep down their own proletariats. the plebs under the caesars do not form a proper class any longer. equites and patres are mixed on the basis of an equitable business footing. the senatorial politicians are transferred into the administration. the proletariat, ie slavery, is international, does not get developed as a productive resource. the slave economy has revealed everything it has in it, has reached and already exhausted its potential. oppression is general and embraces all levels of society.

brief, special and short-lived phase under caesar: the peasant plebs are enabled, once the transition to a slave economy in the production of cereals is complete, to participate in the introduction of slavery in the wine and olive oil sectors. this is where the lex julia comes in.

20 jul 38

CATILINA is no doubt the plebs at its lowest level, a nasty piece of work, even after you have scratched away the mud the ruling class slung at him. but perhaps it was just because of this, because certain inhibitions did not operate, that he was able, being totally immoral, corrupt, and devoid of prejudice, to see through the ideological obfuscations that were prevalent, not least among the plebs. there is an attempt here to mobilise the slaves, or perhaps better, a readiness to do so (which was part of his readiness for *anything*). it already contained the whole 'caesarian conception', in so far as it was the city's conception, with its italia programme, its projects for settlements, etc, but there was also the cancellation of debts and of course the appeal to the slaves, all of which was very much against the city. with this the plebs handed their programme to the opportunistic adventurer. it could not be put into effect without the slaves, as this man realised when he tried to implement it. two thousand years of mudslinging by the ruling classes was the result.

22 jul 38

finishing touches to POEMS IN EXILE for the malik edition. the poem TO THOSE COMPELLED TO CONFORM (AN DIE GLEICHGESCHALTETEN) is causing difficulties. it must not be addressed just to the professional ideologists. there are also all the millions of petty bourgeois and non-manual workers who are now politically 'involved' too, the barbers who are active members of SA units, the craftsmen and the small shopkeepers in their many trade associations, not to speak of the teachers, engineers etc. outside germany you imagine the ideological services performed for the regime to be worse than any other kind. this is quite false. the engineer who implements rationalisation and hence increases the physical impoverishment of the proletariat, does at least as much damage. the ideological effect is just the expression of this. the 'manifestations of ideological support' are not the driving force of exploitation and oppression. our ideologists get more excited about the misuse of words than about real damage to the proletariat. the regime's crimes consist of its crimes against the proletarian working class, and *gleichschaltung* switches certain individuals and activities into this criminal activity. the poem however is only directed against their ideological contribution, which it thus castigates as the worst thing.

23 jul 38

writing CAESAR, i have just realised that i must not believe for a moment that things had to happen as they did. that say slavery, which made politics for the plebs so impossible, could not have been abolished. searching for reasons for everything that happened makes historians fatalists. in addition to which slavery in this epoch was already cramping further 'progress'. all this talk of slaves being needed because there were no machines is so superficial and inconclusive! after all another reason they got no machines was because they had slaves. and who are 'they'? did the slaves need slavery because they had no machines? they made up two-thirds of the population of italy. i have to show how the whole of society sinks into slavery in the attempt to keep slavery going. not a single senator or banker in the time of the caesars possessed as much personal security, personal freedom, or potential for political initiative as almost all of them enjoyed in cicero's time. they paid for their fishponds with the loss of all dignity. and no caesar had in effect the power of any one of the many consuls of the republic . . .

24 jul 38

there are concepts which are difficult to defend because they spread such boredom whenever they arise. like DÉCADENCE. there is naturally such a thing as the literature of the decline of a class. in it the class loses its serene certainty, its calm self-confidence, it conceals its difficulties, it gets bogged down in detail, it becomes parasitically culinary, etc. but the very works which identify its decline as a decline can scarcely be classed as decadent. but that is how the declining class views them. on the other hand the FEAST OF TRIMALCHIO exhibits all sorts of signs of formal decadence. and if ELECTIVE AFFINITIES is not decadent, WERTHER is.

25 jul 38

the whole conception of a c[aesar] is inhuman. on the other hand it is impossible to demonstrate inhumanity without having some idea of humanity. and i cannot just describe things from today's position, i have to make the alternative way seem possible from the perspective of those times too. a cold world. a cold work. and yet i can see, between spells of writing or as i write, how low we have come, in human terms.

benjamin is here. he is writing an essay on baudelaire. there is good stuff there, he shows how the prospect of an age without history distorted literature after 48. the versailles victory of the bourgeoisie over the commune was discounted in advance. they came to terms with evil. it took the form of a flower. this is useful to read. oddly enough it is spleen that enables benjamin to write this. he uses as his point of departure something he calls the *aura*, which is connected with dreaming (daydreams). he says: if you feel a gaze directed at you, even at your back, you return it (!). the expectation that what you look at will look back at you creates the aura. this is supposed to be in decline of late, along with the cult element in life. b[enjamin] has discovered this while analysing films, where the aura is decomposed by the reproducibility of the art-work. a load of mysticism, although his attitude is against mysticism. this is the way the materialist understanding of history is adapted. it is abominable.

have been translating andersen nexö's memoirs with grete. i like them in spite of the minute analysis of the soul and the repeated moralising, since there is still raw material there. a respectable proletarianism. but he has beautiful passages depicting the solidarity of the dispossessed.

27 jul 38

the moscow clique is praising hay's play HAVE to the red skies. it is true socialist realism. new, because old. the work of a genius, untouched by the fashions and confusions of his times. what is form? here is content. the play is dismal trash, sudermann is progressive by comparison. 'but here we have flesh and blood characters'. it is a well known (?) fact that for flesh and blood the stage uses cardboard and red ink, which are got up to look like flesh and blood. 'but here we have people with all their contradictions.' the dialectics of the expression 'sixes and sevens'. capitalism is bad in the play because it turns people into money-grubbers. a demon appears in the form of an old witch who leads the whole village, the women that is, to murder, and once, a high point of the evening, performs a demonic dance. according to feuchtwanger she is capitalism. which also leads men to do all sorts of diabolical things. all this you read 'avidly'. 'hay is an innovator. more accurately: the circumstances in which he was working turned him into an innovator in a peculiar sense, in spite of, or perhaps because of – following the old path' (KURELLA). feuchtwanger confirms that for hay marxism 'was not just an idea, but rather filled his entire being, his feelings, filtering deep down into the foundations of the unconscious'. the main thing is of course that marxism did not just remain, or perhaps better, become an idea in this process. the play is 'saturated from the inside with marxism'. dyed then, unfortunately not in fast colours.

3 aug 38

because i am an innovator in my field, there is always somebody or other ready to scream that i am a formalist. they miss the old forms in what i write: worse still, they find new ones; and as a result they think forms are what interests me. but i have come to the conclusion that if anything i underrate the formal aspect. at one time or another i have studied the old forms of poetry, the story, the drama and the theatre, and i only abandoned them when they started getting in the way of what i wanted to say. in poetry i began with songs to the guitar, sketching out the verses at the same time as the music. ballad form was as old as the hills, and in my day nobody who took himself at all seriously wrote ballads. subsequent-ly i went over to other, less ancient forms of poetry, but sometimes i reverted, going so far as to make copies of the old masters and translate villon and kipling. the *song*, which descended on this continent after the first world war as a sort of folksong of the big cities, had already evolved a conventional form by the time when i began using it. i started from that point and subsequently transformed it, though elements of this lazy, vain and emotionally intoxicated form are to be found in my mass choruses. then i wrote unrhymed verses with irregular rhythms. i began, i think, by using them in my plays. there are however some poems dating from about the time of the *devotions for the home*, the psalms which i used to sing to the guitar, which tend the same way. the sonnet and the epigram were forms which i took over as they stood. the only thing i didn't use, really, was certain classical poetic forms which struck me as too artificial.

12 aug 38

we germans have materialism without sensuality. with us the 'mind' is constantly cogitating on the mind. body and objects remain mindless. in german drinking songs all you hear about are effects on the mind, even in the most vulgar songs. the smell of wine-barrels never occurs. we don't like the taste of the world. we have brought a cosiness to love, sexual pleasure has something banal about it. when we talk of taste, we again mean something purely intellectual, the tongue has long since ceased to function, taste is something like having a feeling for harmonisation. think of the combination 'purely spiritual'. with us the spirit sullies itself as soon as it touches matter. matter for us germans is crap, to all intents and purposes. in our literature this distrust of the vitality of the body is to be felt everywhere. our heroes cultivate sociability, but they don't eat; our women have feelings, but no backsides, to compensate for which our old men talk as if they still had all their teeth.

13 aug 38

benjamin maintains freud thinks that sexuality will one day die out completely. our bourgeoisie thinks it is mankind. when the heads of the aristocracy fell, at least their pricks remained erect. the bourgeoisie has contrived to ruin even sexuality. i am helping R[UTH] to put together a volume of short stories entitled EVERY ANIMAL CAN DO IT. 70% of all women are supposed to be frigid. we have good titles (HASTE IS THE WIND that brings down the wooden scaffolding. ALL THE KING'S HORSES AND ALL THE KING'S MEN. then SERVICE etc). the unproductivity of technology. orgasm as a rare fluke.

14 aug 38

from the 5th poem of the cycle TO THE ARC DE TRIOMPHE by v HUGO.

> no, time takes nothing from things.
> to more than one mispraised portal
> his slow metamorphosis has
> given belated beauty.
> on the monuments we revere
> time bestows a severe charm
> from façade to pinnacle.
> never, fracture and rust as he may,
> is the surface he strips
> worth the patina he gives.
>
> it is time that cuts a groove
> in too plain an archstone,
> that passes his intelligent thumb
> over the arid corners of the marble;
> it is he, improving on art,
> who places a live viper
> in the coils of a granite hydra.
> i think i can see a gothic roof laughing
> when from its ancient frieze time
> takes out a stone and puts in a nest.

15 aug 38

FEAR AND MISERY OF THE THIRD REICH has now gone to press. lukács has already welcomed the SPY as if i were a sinner returned to the bosom of the salvation army. here at last is something taken straight from life! he overlooks the montage of 27 scenes, and the fact that it is actually only a table of gests, the gest of keeping your mouth shut, the gest of looking about you, the gest of sudden fear etc. the pattern of gests in a dictatorship. now *epic theatre* can show that both 'intérieurs' and almost naturalistic elements are within its range, that they do not make the crucial difference. the actor will be well advised to study the STREET SCENE before playing one of the short scenes. the aforesaid gests are not to be performed in such a way that the audience wants to stop the scene, empathy is to be sedulously controlled, otherwise the whole thing is a dead loss. the montage, a process that has been so thoroughly condemned, arose here out of letters from dudow who needed something for his little proletarian theatre-group in paris. so the proletarian theatre in exile is keeping the theatre alive. while in moscow maxim vallentin, the one-time director of a berlin agitprop group, has gone over to bourgeois theatre and announced that in art an appeal has to be made to the emotions, which can only mean reason has to be switched off.

16 aug 38

the POEMS FROM EXILE are of course one-sided. but in small works there is no point in having a mix. multiplicity can only occur within a whole, as part of the architecture of coherent works. the overall production plan is however constantly getting broader. and single works only have a chance within such a plan. to THE BUSINESS ACTIVITIES OF HERR JULIUS CAESAR must be added THE TUI NOVEL. to the dramas the *lehrstücke*. when will i be able to start BAD BAAL THE ASOCIAL MAN and LENIN'S ATTITUDES? 30 years would not be too much for what has to be done. for there is also a lot of topical stuff to do as things develop. one thing we do not have is a little realistic novel for the proletarian youth, with a hero, a child would be best, it may be koloman wallisch. meanwhile the housepainter is preparing to conquer the world. yesterday the grand german manoeuvres began, a rehearsal for mobilisation.

16 aug 38

appalling to read poems by shelley (not to speak of ancient egyptian peasant songs from 3000 years ago) in which he laments oppression and exploitation. is this how they will read us, still oppressed and exploited, and will they say: was it already as bad as that?

18 aug 38

by offering only formal criteria for *realism* LUKÁCS, whose significance is that he writes from moscow, is in the final estimate handing readers who are avid to learn on a plate to those famous contemporary bourgeois novelists on whom he has bestowed great, if slightly embarrassed compliments, because they display the said formal features (even if they are not so 'happy', 'pure' and 'creative' as the old masters of the great early period). they become his realists (he allays any suspicion by contrasting them with a form of 'decadence', to which DOS PASSOS and presumably i too belong), whose descriptions exclude the class struggle ('do not not take sufficiently into account', 'do not yet fully encompass'), so that the reader himself then has to unravel the complicated reflections which the 'decadents' incorporate in their books, the very reflections which establish that the events depicted derive from the class struggle. they all display LUKÁCS's hallmarks. HEINRICH MANN presents such a 'tangle' of different human fates in his HENRI QUATRE that nobody can find his way around in it, and doesn't his brother THOMAS unfold the 'whole life of the biblical joseph' in all its ultimate fullness! in HAMSUN we have 'very involved, very indirect relationships' by the dozen. the class struggle is less in evidence in all three, but naturally we can add that for ourselves, for 'in the last resort' everything is class struggle. such obtuseness is monumental.

18 aug 38

the realism debate will gum up production if it goes on like this. LUKÁCS naturally finds a dialectic in the early bourgeois novel, and it is naturally of a different quality from the late novel. the richly 'interwoven pattern of life's paths', the 'rich tapestry of varied, interlinked motifs' etc. in the later examples you either get the complexities combed out, or else you get something which, on the analogy of a kinking of the intestines, we might call a kinking of the motifs. a certain vacuity, a drained, encrusted quality is not merely the fault of the writer, but a failing of 'capitalism' in person. according to LUKÁCS there is in the early bourgeois novel (GOETHE) a 'broad richness of life', and the novel gives rise to the 'illusion that all life has been given shape in its full, unfolded breadth'. follow that! it's just that now nothing unfolds any more and life does not develop in breadth. the only possible advice would be to trample it out flat. trampling flat is something capitalism goes in for anyway, the celebrated iron heel. all we have left to describe are in fact detours, dead-ends, impediments, braking-attachments, faulty brakes etc. but as the quantity increases, a turning point is reached. LUKÁCS, who tends to transfer everything from the world into consciousness, only sees it (with indignation) in the sphere of consciousness. in ZOLA's case a factual complex, money, the mine, etc moves into the centre of the novels. from an organic complexity of composition there develops mechanical linkage, montage, the progressive dehumanisation of the novel! it is from this that he makes a rope to hang the writers who have degenerated from 'story-tellers' into 'describers'. they capitulate. they adopt the capitalist standpoint, they dehumanise life. the protests they add are not allowed to stand. they are post festum, they are laboured afterthoughts, exercises in pseudo-radicalism. but the fact that the dehumanised proletariat puts its entire humanity into protest and takes up the struggle against the dehumanisation of production is something the professor overlooks. the circuitousness of the new ways must not break the mould of the novel. in actual fact he employs a concept of richness (in sentences like 'the richness of this texture') which has quickly worn out. much has become more and there is no longer any trace of richness. calculation has turned into theorising. it no longer occupies the same position, it is no longer located among the 'hero's reflections'. the writer is seeing something new when he watches the proletariat working in abstract terms, and we must be clear about this. the narrative form of balzac, tolstoy etc has foundered on 'soulless' factual complexes, coalmines, money etc. homilies from professors will not refloat it. *all the king's horses, and all the king's men, couldn't humpty dumpty put together again.** GIDE writes his major novel (LES FAUX MONNAYEURS) about the difficulty of writing a novel, JOYCE writes a catalogue of modes of description, and the one great piece of popular fiction of the day, hašek's SCHWEJK, has abandoned the drama-orientated novel form adopted by the early bourgeois novel.

10 sep 38

in literary articles in journals edited by marxists the concept of *decadence* is appearing more and more frequently of late. i discover that decadence includes me. this is naturally of great interest to me. a marxist actually needs the concept of *decline*. it serves to identify the decline of the ruling class in the political and economic spheres. it would be *stupid** for him to refuse to recognise decline in the artistic sphere. eg literature cannot exclude the great shackling of productive capacity by the capitalist means of production. i am restricting myself in the first instance to my own production. my first book of poems, the DEVOTIONS FOR THE HOME, is undoubtedly branded with the decadence of the bourgeois class. under its wealth of feeling lies a confusion of feeling. under its originality of expression lie aspects of collapse. under the richness of its subject matter there is an element of aimlessness. the powerful language is slack. etc etc. seen in this light the subsequent SVENDBORG POEMS represent both a withdrawal and an advance. from the bourgeois point of view there has been a staggering impoverishment. isn't it all a great deal more one-sided, less 'organic', cooler, 'more self-conscious' (in a bad sense)? let's hope my comrades-in-arms will not let that go by default. they will say the SVENDBORG POEMS are less decadent than DEVOTIONS FOR THE HOME. however i think it is important that they should realise what the advance, such as it is, has cost. capitalism has forced us to take up arms. it has laid waste our surroundings. i no longer go off 'to commune with nature in the woods', but accompanied by two policemen. there is still richness, a rich choice of battlefields. there is originality, originality of problems. no question about it: literature is not blooming. but we have to beware of thinking in terms of outdated images. this notion of bloom is too one-sided. you can't harness ideas of value, definitions of power and greatness, to an idyllic conception of organic flowering; it would be ridiculous. withdrawal and advance are not separated according to dates in the calendar. they are threads which run through individuals and works.

11 sep 38

skimmed through BAAL for the complete works. pity about it. it was always a torso, and then it was operated on several times, for the (two)

Barbara (left) and Stefan Brecht, children of Bertolt and Helene, 'in the first year of exile (1933)'.

book versions and the production. the meaning almost got lost in the process. baal the provocateur, the worshipper of things as they are, living life, his own and other people's, to the full. a lot could be got out of his 'do whatever is fun', if handled properly. wonder whether i should take the time. (the lehrstücke about BAD BAAL THE ASOCIAL MAN remain in reserve.)

12 sep 38

in the DZZ something about the late stanislavsky. his cult is a catchment area for everything that is sanctimonious in theatre arts. reason, far from being suppressed in his 'method', is the 'control mechanism'. first of all you 'feel', you bring yourself by means of spiritual ablutions into a state where you can feel (mainly by forgetting that art is a business), and then you allow 'it' to be corrected by reason, or as the expression goes, justified. tuism itself. whether something is 'real' is proved in the feeling. (the antonym would be: right.) as if emotions were not at least as corrupt as the rational functions! a few marxists then spill much ink proving that this is deathless art. 'and now art turns to feeling.' the emotional element is stowed in the 'substructure', the intellectual in the 'superstructure'. people tamely go along with the separation of feeling and reason. if people like me stress the rational, they register the absence of the emotional by the same token. at least they talk (not always with any expression of regret) about an unhealthy separation of feeling and reason in my work. in actual fact there is no sense in talking about feeling in art (except for purposes of criticism), because that would only mean allowing reason free play. every thought that is necessary has its emotional correlative, every feeling its intellectual one. the hypocrisy of the stanislavsky school with its temple of art, its service to the word, its cult of the poet, its inwardness, purity, exaltation, its naturalness which one fears and must fear slipping 'out' of, corresponds to its intellectual backwardness, its belief in 'man' and 'ideas' etc. that is 'real' naturalism, nature is the great unknown, and to imitate it is to imitate its false beard.

25 sep 38

very worth noting for CAESAR the french ruling class's about-turn in the face of hitler's threat of war, the breach of treaty, czechoslovakia wiped off the map, france's position as a great power destroyed. they only wage wars of conquest, they only defend their own conquests. at any time they will sacrifice political power for business reasons when this astonishing choice in fact appears. a war with a forty-hour week? can't be done. these people are a magnificent example of iron logic and immunity to idolas. how to defend their country when it doesn't belong to them?

sternberg here, returning from a tour of scandinavia. from friday to sunday (the night of godesberg) we sit up till three in the morning. there are reports every ten minutes on the wireless in all different languages.

5 oct 38

on *literary value*: what a writer GIDE is, whose beautiful book on earthly pleasures the army of the french popular front carries in its kitbag as it marches! or alternatively keeps on the bedside table and gives marching a miss. and HAŠEK: his great book is shrinking by the hour as the v-zones are occupied by hitler's army. it was the victory report of an oppressed people, the odysseus report. but the victory was too brief. it now stands on a list of suspect books and deals with events that people no longer know.

7 oct 38

the fall of czechoslovakia is remarkable for the way it happened. eg people continue to speak about that country as if it were still the same, and for that reason some of its actions are surprising. people have understood that it has to hand over something to germany, but now it is handing over more, in fact everything as far as everybody is concerned. including the jews and refugees. people forget that this defeat has brought different class forces to the helm, so the state has become a different person in law, one can no longer speak of czechoslovakia. and how did this come about? 'england' could not enter into a war which its russian ally would have won. the russian ally could not enter into a war which the russian generals would have won. france could not enter into a war which the popular front would have won. and none of them, naturally, could lose a war.

23 nov 38

finished LIFE OF GALILEO. it took three weeks. the only difficulties arose with the last scene. just as in the case of ST JOAN, i needed a neat stroke at the end to ensure that the audience had the necessary detachment. even somebody empathising without thinking must now feel the a-effect when he empathises with galileo. with rigidly epic presentation an acceptable empathy occurs.

january 39

koltsov too arrested in moscow. my last connection there. nobody knows anything about tretiakov, who is supposed to have been a 'japanese spy'. nobody knows anything about neher who is supposed to have done some business for the trotskyists in prague on her husband's instructions. reich and asya lacis don't write to me any more, and grete gets no answer from her acquaintances in the caucasus or leningrad. béla kun too is arrested, the only one of the politicians i saw. meyerhold has lost his theatre, but is supposed to be allowed to direct opera. literature and art are up the creek, political theory has gone to the dogs, what is left is a thin, bloodless, proletarian humanism propagated by officialdom. in an official article (THE THEORY OF LENIN AND STALIN ON THE VICTORY OF SOCIALISM TRIUMPHS IN THE SOVIET UNION) a certain vokressensky declares stalin's theory to be that 'the death of the state takes the form of its fortification on all sides' and 'the socialist state is necessary in order (!) to instill the new socialist work discipline in the masses' and 'if the best stachanov-norms in the country were to be made the average norms, the decisive prerequisite for the transition from socialism to communism would be achieved.' workers' switching (between factories with different wage-rates) has been stopped by law, and there are reported to have been strikes. all you hear about political 'democracy' are clichés, and you hear nothing about the social form for the organisation of production. marxists outside russia find themselves in the position marx adopted towards social-democracy. one of positive criticism.

meanwhile capitalism in the form of imperialism and trust capitalism fights out its economic battles in national units. this national form will not disappear before it has done its worst (also to develop the productive forces, which it has now converted into destructive ones).

12 feb 39

translation of nexö's memoirs in three volumes completed with grete. wrote three novellas (THE HERETIC'S COAT, SOCRATES WOUNDED, LUCULLUS'S TROPHIES). a lot of theory in dialogue form THE MESSING-KAUF DIALOGUES (spurred to use this form by galileo's DIALOGUES). four nights. the philosopher insists on the p-type (planetarium-type, instead of the c-type, carousel type) theatre purely for didactic purposes, movements of people (also shifts of the emotions) organised as simple models for study purposes, to show how social relationships function, in order that society can intervene. his wishes turn into theatre, since they can be implemented in the theatre. from a critique of theatre a new theatre emerges. the whole thing so conceived that it can be performed, with experiments and exercises. centring on the a-effect.

february 39

via korsch's MARX, which he roughed out here and which has now appeared in english, i come back to the question of formalism. compared to LENIN's short summary MARX, KORSCH's excellent book is a little formalistic. the method which he extracts tends very much to schematic presentation. it is not shown in application, in action. its historical birthplace is not shown. eg he says: marxism exists not only because hegel and ricardo were inadequate, but, (mainly) because the proletariat existed. this is not however shown. etc.

literary formalism has not been defined politically either, that is, it has not been defined at all. the good LUKÁCS simple-mindedly derives it from decadence. the literary avant garde are bourgeois decadents, end of story. What one has to do is ignore them and look to the classics. nowhere does he deal with the formalisms of the democracies and the fascist state. (cranking up production – of the means of destruction, liquidating the class struggle, instead of the classes etc.) the decline of narrative is viewed as pure decline. *montage* is viewed as a characteristic feature of decadence. because unity is torn apart by it, and the organic whole dies. naturally one could also make a concrete study of *montage*. (in IVENS' film ZUIDERZEE, which shows the reclamation of fertile earth and the parallel destruction of the fruits of the earth in other places.) the other sin is the *inner monologue*. nobody has ever examined this or exposed its actual flaws (you could take the one by the woman in ULYSSES and hitler's from THE SPEECH in [HEINRICH] MANN'S COURAGE). you would not then have extirpated it root and branch as an artistic device, but presumably shown its flaws in concrete terms. for, of course, as pure empathising this must have gigantic potential for error. there is naturally such a thing as an empty self-generated movement of form, a purely formal satisfaction of real needs, a violation of the facts by generalising treatment etc. but you can also treat formal questions formalistically, and this is what happens in the case of the bold lukács. according to these murxists [*sic*] this is how matters stand: the bourgeois realists practised an imperfect realism, still had idola; let us forget about these, and everything will be in order. their facts are accepted, and rearranged. marx is no more equipped with the correct conclusions than ricardo.

sholokhov is balzac with the blinkers removed. in actual fact these sholokhovs don't have an iota of balzac's materialism (a remarkable brew of romanticism, hunger for facts, collector's mania, speculation etc) and have innumerably more blind spots. the recommendation to study the bourgeois realists is utterly formalistic, since it is not connected with any thoroughgoing critique of them.

19 feb 39

the émigrés sleep, but it is a disturbed slumber. there are certain nightmares, that hitler will *not* run out of small change, that the wrong pope will be elected, that churchill will cave in. the little horse people like to put their money on, the favourite, is 'the german people's longing for peace'. chamberlain, who shares this dream, is at least rearming vigorously at the same time (just in case). not that a fear of war does not actually exist in germany, but for the regime that is merely a psychic phenomenon with no sound basis and can be overcome by propaganda. it has good grounds for thinking this, and a handful of aces. from my CAESAR studies i can see how easily the rapidly degenerating roman plebs could be brought to accept wars of conquest. and the working men? they have swallowed a great deal for the abolition of unemployment. *absence* of war means unemployment, the regime will say (and it is right). i see more and more clearly as an old hand in the study of *tuism* that what lends the regime that aura of intelligence is its consistent late capitalism, by taking evasive action it is pursuing a consistent policy, hence its 'instinctive assurance'. hitler's criticism of the social democrats and the frankfurt school (in his last speech) is excellent. without changing production the idiots wanted to change consumption. then they build a gigantic, rationalised industry in a land deprived of political power, and pursue a policy of peace. at least hitler is consistent. the borders that goods cannot cross will be crossed by tanks. which in turn are goods (along with the working men who operate them). the tuis are confused.

25 feb 39

HEGEL's reproduction of the aristotelian theory of art in the introduction to his aesthetics is extraordinarily beautiful. the key sentence seems to me to be: 'thus one adduces as the final purpose of humans living together and of the state, that *all* human potentialities and *all* individual strengths should develop on *all* sides and in *every* direction so as to achieve expression. but such a formal view soon raises the question of the *unit* in which these various formations will be contained, and of the *single goal* which will serve as their fundamental concept and final purpose. as with the concept of the state so also with the concept of arts there arises on the one part a need for an aim that is *common* to particular sides, on the other part for an overriding *substantial* aim.'

LIFE OF GALILEI is technically a great step backwards, like SENORA CARRAR all too opportunistic. the play ought to be completely rewritten, in order to capture this 'breath of wind that/cometh from new shores', this rosy dawn of science. everything more direct, without the interiors, the 'atmosphere', the empathy. and everything based on planetary demonstrations. the structure could be kept, the characterisation of galileo likewise. but the work, which would be fun, could only be done in a practical situation, in contact with a stage. first the FATZER-fragment, then the BREADSHOP-fragment would have to be studied. these two fragments are of the highest technical standard.

26 feb 39

this man hegel's PHILOSOPHY OF HISTORY is a tremendous piece of work. his method enables him not only to see the positive and the negative in any historical phenomenon, but also to make this polarity the cause of further development. amazing how he depicts the formalism of the constitution under the emperors, where wealth was 'not the fruit of industry'. how superb the way the turning points appear in a few concentrated pages. for example, how the gracchi attempt 'to populate italy with citizens instead of slaves'. under the caesars it is *de*populated! and how the inner contradiction under CAESAR is externalised, the empire founded which 'collapsed under the weight of taxation and plundering'. and compare with this the mention of caesar in the INTRODUCTION as the 'managing director of the world spirit'. in those 'spiritual leaders' it is the classes, in this spiritual leader it is the debased senate and the degenerate plebs that irresistibly confront their own inner spirit. and after 'these colossal individuals have emerged from the collapse of the state', the individual characteristics of the caesars become so insignificant, that it can be said that 'under the most brutal and despicable tyrant (domitian) the roman world took a rest'. i was not making any headway with CAESAR, was beginning to think he was incomprehensible. now i am getting visitors. grete's sister, a metalwor-ker's wife, is here from germany. she reads the second book in a single evening and finds it highly interesting. questioned by grete, it appears that she has understood more or less everything. BENJAMIN and

STERNBERG, very highly qualified intellectuals, did not understand it and made pressing recommendations for more human interest to be put in, more of the old novel . . . and then of course there is steff, pressing for the next instalment. that should suffice.

4 mar 39

today i at last realised why i have never been able to produce the little *lehrstück* on the adventures of BAD BAAL THE ASOCIAL MAN. asocial people have no part to play. they are merely the possessors of the means of production and of other sources of livelihood, and that is all they are. naturally there are also their helpers and their helpers' helpers, but they too only as such. it is nothing short of the gospel of the enemy of mankind to say that there are asocial drives, asocial personalities, etc.

5 mar 39

interesting, the new 'realistic' american literature (CAIN, COY, HEMING-WAY). these people protest against the prevailing descriptions of certain milieux, bank heavily on the novelty of 'unbiased' description. it all remains within the domain of the formal. at its inception stands the experience of film (and at the end stands hollywood). film, especially the silent film, needed an unexpectedly large amount of action (consumed a large amount of expression). psychologists at the time were discovering behaviourism, psychology seen through the eye of a camera. literature is now catching up. but with these *hard-boiled men** it is a matter of producing *hot stuff**, they need to arouse emotions because they are part of the great emotions racket. so they use the emotions as driving force, as the path of least resistance. they give a new 10 horse-power engine, complete with the appropriate brakes to the man in the street, to each of roosevelt's new-deal types, garage mechanics, farmhands, reporters. the souped-up petty bourgeois, a romantic character, comes into existence. he is a poor devil who is highly strung beyond belief, has been given a *second spirit** by rationalisation, stands gasping, is threatened by unemployment, and invests his last vestige of strength in competitiveness. he bestrides the stage as hero and muscle-man, and the boards cave in.

15 mar 39

a few days ago i took out the old draft of THE GOOD PERSON OF SZECHWAN (begun in berlin as LOVE IS THE GOODS). there are five scenes, four of which are usable. it is a bit of a charade, what with the costume switches and the changes in make-up. but i can use it to develop the epic technique and get back up to standard again. for a desk drawer you need make no concessions.

interesting how with these thin steel structures the slightest miscalculation takes its toll. there is no mass there to balance out inexactitudes. the *reich* is expanding. the housepainter is sitting in hradčany.

The Brechts' thatched house at Skovsbostrand, Fyn Island, Denmark, where they lived from December 1933 to April 1939.

Sweden
23 April 1939 to 19 March 1940

23 apr 39

travel to stockholm, because of the danger of war. visa arranged by swedish social-democratic committee (branting, ström, etc) in return for lecture at stockholm student theatre. country number three. ruth sees to printing of SVENDBORG POEMS in copenhagen on a subscription basis. wieland [herzfelde's] prague type-formes are lost (along with those for FEAR AND MISERY and the COLLECTED POEMS).

4 may 39

lecture at the stockholm student theatre. EXPERIMENTAL THEATRE. the work seems quite usable. of course no such knowledgeable questions were asked, nor calculated experiments carried out as the lecture might lead people to think. i brought the epic elements 'into the business' ready-made from the KARL VALENTIN theatre, the open-air circus, and the augsburg fair. then there was film, especially the silents in the early days before the cinema began to copy drrramatics from the theatre (chaplin). as difficulties cropped up with didactic theatre this 'style' was there to turn to and had only to be modified. the lecture covers the external development, presents the experiments as leading to reflections, pursuing goals etc. provides a good introduction to the essay NEW TECHNIQUE OF ACTING.

25 may 39

discussions with the german refugee actor greid who is organising theatre groups for the social democrats here, but is close to the communists. he has written a book on dialectics and – optimism. a petty bourgeois with ethical propensities who has taken to thinking. (he himself financially secure on account of well-off swedish jewish wife.) wants to take ethical interests further. 'give these people something.' page-long quotations from engels. 'where is the positive element in marxism?' the search goes on in the ethical sphere. interesting question, when seen in concrete terms. our attitude to petty bourgeoisie utterly pathetic. on the one hand conciliatory; marxists not so bad – as hitler paints them. on the other hand abstains from suggesting any solution. though 800,000 craftsmen have been sifted out in the last year as uneconomic but needed in the factories (where the ten-hour day is being introduced.) the flight from the land is growing constantly. here we could contribute plenty that is positive. the ethical needs of these social strata need not be satisfied ethically. the satisfaction of their material needs is ethical enough. interesting how this man sees the dialectic: all that interests him is the third stage. everything that happens follows the well-known 'spiral' upwards. 3 = 1 plus 2. reconciliation of contradictions with a 'shift of emphasis'. what becomes clear is the petty bourgeois strand in engels's philosophy of nature. in social terms things then look like this; without satisfaction of material needs no ethics, and that is acceptable. but: ethics for the satisfaction of these needs is not acceptable. material needs as ethical, ethical ones as material, this is not grasped. all sorts of material for the book of change.

may 39, whitsun

stockholm. SPEECH TO WORKING-CLASS ACTORS ON THE ART OF OBSERVATION. on the occasion of a meeting to discuss the foundation of an amateur theatre group for social-democratic trade unions.

brooded over the GOOD PERSON. how can luxury be brought into the parable?

and how to avoid the impression of a milkmaid's accounts. the calculated must be paired with the dainty. the girl must be a big powerful person. the city must be a big, dusty uninhabitable place. the drawback is too much action. no room for digression and detour. so everything is much too rationalised. dramatic taylorism. some attention must be paid to countering the risk of chinoiserie. the vision is of a chinese city's outskirts with cement works and so on. there are still gods around but aeroplanes have come in. perhaps the lover should be an unemployed pilot?

15 jul 39

still on the GOOD PERSON. reworked the first scene again. the main thing was to bring some development into bad lao go. then the play got too long. my time-cards for the scenes showed terrible overruns. true, five-hour plays are not too long for the three-hour day, especially if they are epic, ie not taxing. but for the moment two and a half hours are enough.

the house is ideal. it is on the island of lidingö, with firs running right up to it on two sides. the study, previously a sculptor's studio, is 7 metres long, 5 metres wide. so i have many tables.

steff brought a volume of karl sandburg, chicago poems, and translated them from swedish, with relish and skill. good stuff, it has connections with chinese forms.

now and again émigré academics come here. i try to interest them in producing a dictionary of fascist slogans.

august 39

The house on Lidingö Island, off Stockholm. Brecht with Margarete (Grete) Steffin, seated, the Danish writer Martin Andersen-Nexö and his wife and daughter. See 25 July 38.

1 sep 39

at 8.45 in the morning germany warns all neutrals against flying over polish territory. hitler addresses the wehrmacht. in between, the melancholy marches with which german militarists like introducing their bloodbaths. yesterday a british veteran, an officer of course, made an appeal to germans who fought in the great war. conclusion: '. . . otherwise we shall teach the rulers of germany a lesson on how to deal decently and honourably with their neighbours. good night.'

then jazz. on the german side, marches.

The Brechts and their daughter Barbara, outside the new house.

the neutrality pact with the USSR ratified last night. from the english point of view henceforward sacrificing poland no longer means helping hitler's march to the east, but the sacrifice of an ally behind g[ermany]'s back. this was promptly followed by a hardening of the british position and an alliance with poland. they think it will be easier to fight without the USSR (the horse-trading could have been done more easily with a pseudo-alliance). for the dominions and america that is probably true.

hitler's speech on the wireless strikingly insecure ('i am determined to show determination'). the loudest applause when he says that traitors have nothing to expect but death. this is the clique, the gang, the foreign body that begins a war minus god and plus bread coupons. blanquism on a national basis.

in the evening the english wireless was already beginning to discuss the question of war guilt. the germans are permitted to hear (before the iron curtain is lowered), that hitler's 'surprisingly generous proposals' were never actually made.

then on the german wireless more military marches, creating the mood for dying, on the english wireless instructions to the population, the evacuation of 3 million people from london.

grete shakes her head over the 'berliners', who have nothing but sandbags on the landings with which to extinguish incendiary bombs.

at noon lunch for thomas mann at the town hall. (ström, the lord mayor, ljungdal, edfelt, matthis.) mann is opposed to the ussr's support for hitler. erika mann, his daughter, finds the pact logical and comprehensible, but is against the view that it helps the cause of peace.

3 sep 39

only in the evening did the terrible truth dawn on everybody. that was when the english wireless reports on the session in the commons came through. a dreadful spectacle, even if it was only the first act and the mildest one. the german government wants war, not the german people. the french and english governments don't want war, the french and english peoples do, to stop hitler.

4 sep 39

i was pretty convinced the english would draw back at the last minute. but churchill seems to have pulled it off. the question now is whether they will actually fight a war. the machinery will probably be very hard to set in motion. hitler will soon have achieved a fait accompli in the east, at which point they may negotiate after all. the legal position is that there is peace in poland and people are fighting, whereas in the west war has been declared and peace prevails.

5 sep 39 (tuesday)

spooky, this war which isn't being fought . . .in the swedish press there still has not been a word about the fact that not a shot has been fired in the west. four bombs from english bombers off wilhelmshaven, according to german reports. esbjerg bombed 'by an unknown plane'. and an english passenger steamer torpedoed west of the hebrides. the only thing dropped over western germany is leaflets. and from all points of the globe come declarations of neutrality, which appear to isolate hitler, but in fact merely isolate his war of annihilation against poland. the other gangster sits smiling on the axis and plays the neutral, 'to keep the war from spreading'. the war which is quite small. for even the war in poland consists merely of a german advance. poland is not fighting at all. everything is being made to ripen towards a conference: hitler is conquering enough ground to be able to withdraw on his own terms.

7 sep 39

a few people are beginning to realise what a remarkable war it is. the french military command claims to have made contact with the enemy in the vicinity of saarbrücken. the germans issue denials of such horror tales. the english drop leaflets, thereby infringing holland's neutrality but no shot is fired at them. mussolini is silent. but how is one to believe in betrayal when there is no apparent bribe? the germans' statements that the russians are reaching military agreements with them grow more and more definite. this nonsense is gladly disseminated.

the fact is that the russo-german pact makes the air clearer. what we have is a war between imperialist states. we have germany as the aggressor and warmonger. we have aggressive capitalism against defensive capitalism. the central powers need the war for conquest, the western powers need it to defend their conquests. there is enough barbarism to maintain a barbaric situation. for the USSR it would only be possible to enter the war on the western side, it would be more a 'matter of state', would be more akin to the way the social-democratic parties caved in during the great war, would be more like power politics, participating in a reckoning between capitalists, rather than keeping clear of it.

the slogans are now improving, it seems to me. the british labour party now has 'with chamberlain, but not for him'. the germans can have 'against hitler but not for chamberlain', etc. and the USSR can wait until peoples come along with whom they can enter into alliances. instead of just governments. though in fact this involves a great risk. it makes a general agreement among the capitalist states more likely.

9 sep 39

the germans have occupied warsaw. the campaign lasted eight days and the western powers, as hitler forsaw, have not intervened. but hitler is lost if the western powers do not capitulate and conclude a peace (as they will). his war is contained, all he can do is break through or starve. of course chamberlain's leaflets are not going to bring about a revolution in g[ermany]. a childish delusion, were it not plain eyewash. a swedish paper reports that only after reports of victories were people heard in berlin greeting one another in restaurants with 'heil hitler'.

the russo-german pact of course caused great confusion among the proletariat everywhere. the communists immediately claimed that it was a contribution to peace by the soviet union and should be respected. shortly afterwards of course – a few hours afterwards – war broke out, and hitler claimed in major appeals that this pact had made it possible for him to lead the country against poland. now it may be that the soviet union assumed that the western powers would never enter a war for poland's sake. today, on the 8th day, this assumption is still not invalidated. as matters stand the soviet union would now be facing germany alone with poland, for the west is not yet fighting. possible too that poland in that case would not have tried to defend herself. chamberlain's line (hitler is to be directed against the soviet union) would then have triumphed. now however it is more than possible that poland will be subjugated without any great war, and poland is in the east and not in the west. and the union will in the eyes of the proletariat of the world bear the terrible stigma of aiding and abetting fascism, the wildest element in capitalism and the most hostile to the workers. i don't think more can be said than that the union saved its skin at the cost of leaving the proletariat of the world without solutions, hopes or help.

10 sep 39

i dip into goethe's PANDORA and again i am struck by the SHEPHERDS' SONGS. the way the refined and the primitive come together there!

> who will a shepherd be
> long time has he
> let him count the stars that shine
> let him blow upon the leaf

again and again the hand here plunges into the depths, bringing up something, part of which runs off, but something sticks, totally alienated in its new company. the stream's smoothness reveals its depths.

11 sep 39

H. G. WELLS publishes the speech he intended to deliver at the PEN-club congress. really, what a mountain of a philistine! he views hitler and mussolini simply as writers. and he finds them stupid. as if lack of literary talent couldn't prevent the cleverest person from appearing clever in a work of literature. WELLS himself exemplifies the opposite. by means of a modicum of smartness in literary matters he contrives without further ado to give the impression of common sense.

   i am getting bogged down in the work on the *parable*. it doesn't flow properly. much of it is too contrived, the whole is still just so many parts. beautiful, realistic, astute – and so on.

wrote little essay on photos that i had taken while SANTESSON, the sculptress, was working on helli's head. you can see the stages of her modelling. instructive for dialecticians. in fact something oddly good emerges at the end: the head is allowed to keep its contradictions unresolved.

18 sep 39

the soviet russian invasion of poland, preluded by the sensational pravda article in which the military collapse of poland was attributed to the suppression of minorities, awakens fears in the first instance that the USSR could be stumbling into a war on germany's side. this does not seem to be the case. then of course hitler stands to lose a lot. the balkans can be kept neutral. hitler's access to romania is blocked. hungary's neutrality gets some support. italy too is held in check. hitler's war aims in poland can no longer be achieved. in addition to which hitler grows even more suspect for the german bourgeoisie. and the workers more and more become the only partners for the USSR who can sign and deliver, the class that really can seal an alliance. (a war with the USSR would have been terrible. in stockholm the slogan 'the USSR must free the germans from hitler through a war against germany' is much easier to proclaim than in berlin.) but it is still very difficult to get used to the naked reality, with every ideological veil torn to shreds. here we have the fourth partition of poland, the abandonment of the slogan 'the USSR needs no foot of foreign soil', the appropriation of the fascist hypocrisies about 'blood-brotherhood', the liberation of 'brothers' (of slav descent), all the terminology of nationalism. this is addressed to the german fascists, but at the same time to the soviet troops.

19 sep 39

the soviet russian invasion of poland proceeded in a curiously napoleonic form. there was no advance war propaganda of any sort, no preparation of 'public opinion', no councils deciding or approving anything at all. the government decreed. meetings across the country acclaimed the decree. their communiqués are framed to accord with the national tone. in the shadow of great struggles two provinces which formerly belonged to the russian empire are occupied.

diplomatic considerations? before a great army is set in motion, a great empire hears things which only europe, capitalist europe should hear. the text sounds as if hitler had edited it. and yet it snatches *his* war aim away from him. the red army marches into europe.

those communists who discern a comintern conception behind this see first of all the exploitation of divisions in the imperialist camp which has to proceed wholly within the framework of national, state forms. the comintern and the anticomintern are dissolved at the same time. the french and english parties have adduced national and humanitarian grounds for supporting their governments against hitler and are now forced to retreat in haste into total indifference. but one vista that opens up is the destruction of the english empire in the course of the war. we may not have to wait for the warring nations to exhaust themselves for risings among the native populations, they may mobilise instantly and keep going all through the war, in each of its phases.

21 sep 39

the talk one hears everywhere, to the effect that the bolshevik party has changed from the bottom up, is certainly not true. the unfortunate thing is that it hasn't changed. after two decades of exercising power, the russian people is still the 'lever' for all sorts of things. the red army is now showing clear signs of functioning as a lever too. it may be world revolution that is to be set in motion by this lever, it may be less. it is still not the people, the masses, the proletariat that decides, but the government which decides for the people, the masses, the proletariat. stalin finds it impossible to start the war in a revolutionary manner, as a people's war, as a proletarian action, as a mass war (which would be a concretion of *total war*). he has not managed to bring the people so far yet; the people have not developed this or that interest 'yet', or have not 'yet' recognised it.

the meeting of the red and brown armies in poland is now to be awaited with the greatest interest.

7 nov 39

i have completed a radio text for a composer here (rosenberg): THE TRIAL OF LUCULLUS, very quickly it more or less reaches the limit of what can still be said.

start annotating the stories by dr goldschmidt, the chief physician at the rothschild clinic in vienna, who is stuck here. difficulties when he doesn't tell his story (with grete taking it down) but writes himself. writing leaves the amateur in possession of only a single gesture, namely that of writing. odd how much of something like wisdom resides simply in the gest! goldschmidt provides the basic lines of dr koch, the rest will maybe come from my *gederwei* invention (*ged*uld*serwei*terung = extended patience).

the war displays a remarkably epic character, it teaches mankind about itself as it were, reads a lesson, a text to which the thunder of gunfire and the exploding bombs merely provide the accompaniment. it exposes its economic aims blatantly, in that it has direct recourse to economic means. conquests of markets provoke blockades in response, arms build-ups the withdrawal of raw materials. the ideological cover-up has worn so thin that it only serves to throw what is really happening into sharper relief. in contrast to the great war when the classes observed an internal truce in the interests of the national war, national wars now stop for the class struggle. the war is quite literally '*meaningless*'*.

13 nov 39

a few SAP members and syndicalists here see the following picture: the greatest danger for a german revolution is stalin. the proletariats of the western powers must support their governments against hitler, while taking care that germany is neither hacked up, nor, above all, allowed to fall into the hands of russia. russia would make a colony of germany in order to raise the standard of the russian workers and peasants – or if you prefer it of the classes which rule there. the least of all is to be expected from the russian proletariat, the hope of the germans lies with the british labour party and blum's social democrats. should the russians intervene again in g[ermany] at the end of the war against hitler and the western powers, the place for the socialists would be on the side of the western powers.

it can be seen that a repetition of 1918 is being envisaged, except that a new warlike attitude to the USSR has been added.

(everything is then understood and assembled according to this conception, which is incidentally also shared by otto strasser: britain looks like developing in the direction of socialism, the trade unions are getting more powerful, are already exerting control over war production, the french, in contrast to 1914, display no hatred of the germans, and the proletariats of the western powers will be the main beneficiaries from their governments' victories. they will protect germany from all predators and bestow markets etc on her. possibly umbrellas too.)

5 dec 39

you often see the following scenario these days, even in bourgeois newspapers: stalin is prepared to take on the western powers at hitler's side. the dictatorships in the two countries in this case have the sole function of aligning the two peoples with their very different social systems shoulder to shoulder while at the same time preventing really close contact, which is undesirable for both systems. naturally the two partners constantly have to secure their interests against one another. some put this in the following terms: there would be a first phase of progress, when 'state capitalism' and 'state socialism' would jointly divide up the formally liberal and democratic world between themselves. the other scenario you come across is this: stalin is just securing himself against whoever wins the imperialist world war.

naturally each of these scenarios can merge into the other.

7 dec 39

a little german workers' theatre group is rehearsing LUCULLUS. they found it funny and want to perform it with shadows thrown on a screen. my advice: speak the poems in it as poems, poetically, and bring out the characteristics of the figures in it.

here there are constant aesthetic arguments about style and content in the literary pages. they don't understand that you cannot isolate aesthetic effects. they may emanate from the most disparate concoctions. on the other hand they never occur without some admixture of inartistic matter.

scientifically the best solution is obtained when you observe the attitude of the person shaping, narrating, singing, music-making, acting. the relationship, eg the relationship which the narrator has (and thinks he has) with his hearers, the cultural level on which everybody involved in the act of storytelling is standing etc. the notion of the artistic act is in itself very productive. if i opt for a certain narrative stance (perhaps it would be better to say; if i find myself compelled to adopt a c[ertain] n[arrative stance] then only certain quite precise effects are open to me, my subject organises itself in a certain perspective of its own accord, my word-material and my image-material lie on a certain line, come from a certain stock, a certain amount (and no more) of my hearer's imagination is at my disposal, it is open to me to call upon his experiences to a specific extent, his emotions can be triggered along that and that line etc. the attitude is of course not something unified, or constant, or without contradictions.

i have sat down to THE BUSINESS AFFAIRS OF HERR JULIUS CAESAR again, at book IV. grete lent what i have of it (3 books) to some german workers, and the result was pretty encouraging. they are in the main syndicalists, and they grasped everything, even the details. it was really their interest that moved me to start working on it again.

speaking of style; the rarus bits require a bad style, if by that you mean inelegance, slackness, lack of depth. its 'beauties' lie along the architectonic line. nonetheless this prose can be permitted to rise to certain heights *now and again*, namely when it is permissible for rarus to appear involved, or feel committed to composing 'cabinet-pieces'. (description of the battlefield at pistoria and pompey's triumph.) the spicer passages admit of better reflections, and the satirical element becomes more direct, while the architectonic element grows more impoverished. in these terms the first book is 'well written' and the second book 'badly written'.

8 dec 39

i own:
one chinese picture scroll THE DOUBTER
3 japanese masks
2 little chinese carpets
2 bavarian peasant knives
1 bavarian hunting knife
an english fireside chair
copper foot-bath, copper jugs, copper ashtray
little tin bath
2 large panels by neher, THE OLD MAN and BAAL
6 panels by neher DIE MASSNAHME
a couple of prints of THE LORD OF THE FISH by neher
a silver whisky flask
a dunhill pipe
CAESAR in pigskin
LUCRETIUS in an old edition
complete NEUE ZEIT
ME-TI in leather
old wooden bedstead
grey blanket
steel pocket watch
2 volumes of the VERSUCHE
a leica camera with a theatre lens
plaster and bronze casts of my face and head
bust of weigel by SANTESSON
a folder of photos

the manuscripts of SAINT JOAN, ROUNDHEADS, GALILEI, COURAGE
2 volumes of BRUEGHEL PICTURES
a leather pocket notebook
a leather tobacco pouch
a black leather coat
an old round table

9 dec 39

the finnish war can mean that the russians want to protect themselves against the winner of the second world war or just against their ally. 1) can merge into 2). one can hardly see how russia could avoid a military alliance with germany if the finnish war lasted any length of time. this alliance would have little chance, it would be purely an alliance of the regime, which would involve the hitler regime in growing contradictions with the ruling class in germany, without its really moving any closer to the ruled classes. the soviet union would of course have to do all it could to impose as much as possible of its economic system on its ally. hopes in this direction may actually exist in the union, such a scenario not being unthinkable there. indeed all indications point to such a scenario being considered, at least as an expedient.

10 dec 39

the soviet government's two slogans for the attack on finland:
   1) the finns entered the russian border zone, ie attacked. 2) the finnish proletariat is to be liberated. the germans speak of 'the natural expansion of a great power'. the fact that slogan 1) is necessary shows how far the the russians are from being able to produce dialectical slogans. they have to fall back on primitive dramatisations of the facts. The treaty with the russian-installed finnish people's regime runs counter to the notion that the finnish workers and peasants are having to exchange their national freedom for their social freedom, it serves as a pretext and as such it is weak. the law still seems to hold good, that in cases of offensive or preventive war governments move away from their peoples, in the case of defensive war they move closer to them.
   the swedes are very disturbed. war agitation grows daily. the social democrats actively support it, without bothering about the fact that they are thereby undermining their own position, there are already proclamations from the right calling for the resignation of the entire government, and demanding 'able' men, as yet unnamed. volunteer corps are being

formed for finland, which could equally well turn into volunteer corps for sweden and nobody seems to be looking south where the real danger lies.

24 dec 39

it is of great importance for the CAESAR novel to get away from the retrospective angle. a historical researcher naturally always sees the end of his work as his goal, and as he gathers together his motifs he invariably expands the sector he has planned, whether he wants to or not. an example: hitler may have planned the russian pact in order to be able to go to war with the western powers. he was almost certainly planning an offensive for november which the army seems to have vetoed. stalin could have mounted his finland offensive equally safely in the shadow of a gigantic operation like the one through holland, just as he put together the baltic pact while german guns and bombs thundered over warsaw. now he is proceeding with it in a period of relative quiet, and if things were to develop so that the finnish war, by being protracted and uniting all russia's enemies, was to lead to a great reversal, then hitler would certainly be credited with the plan of having concluded the russian pact in order to make peace with the western powers. the USSR for its part used the freedom of movement gained from the pact for a movement which more or less robbed it of more or less all freedom of movement. were the russians afraid of a quick peace treaty? did they conclude from germany's failure to mount an offensive that hitler would soon be replaced by a government of generals? or are they really toying with the idea of conquering the world at hitler's side? is one country not enough to build socialism? that would be madness. at hitler's side only one thing awaits any regime in the world, defeat, nothing else. if it was fear that the capitalist powers would make peace at the USSR's expense, then the question remains as to whether the gain in military security outweighed the loss of the sympathy of the workers throughout the world. was there too little planning – or too much?

1 jan 40

one must always remember that the workers' movement is part of capitalism, said a[ugust] enderle yesterday in his swabian accent. the USSR has nowhere near reached the point in the re-ordering of its productive resources where to lead no longer means to rule. the industrialisation of agriculture is a long way short of the stage where the peasantry merges with the industrial workers. so there are still class struggles in progress which create further state apparatus. the foreign policy of the USSR, though it is the foreign policy of a state which is in the process of building up socialist elements, is not a socialist foreign policy. the finnish campaign, directed towards military goals, may lead to a liberation of the finnish proletariat from the rule of its bourgeoisie, but these socialist goals are secondary to military goals, and are being regulated accordingly. the USSR would no doubt have been happy if it had reached its military goals without social measures. the war will drive the finnish proletariat in large measure over to the side of its bourgeoisie. likewise the russian slogans relating to the conquest of the western ukraine, to the effect that 'the area of socialism in europe has been increased, the area of capitalism diminished', are totally and utterly formalistic, expressions of thoughtless opportunism at a time when the war is raging all around these things. how can it be maintained that the liberation of a few million formerly polish peasants strengthens the socialist sector, if they are purchased at the cost of alliances like that with the fascist clique in germany (not even with the german bourgeoisie)? stalin's alliance with hitler, which in military terms he may need tomorrow, thus weakens hitler vis-à-vis his bourgeoisie and therefore weakens the military strength of his partner in the alliance, for it fails at the same time to strengthen the position of the german proletariat in relation to its bourgeoisie. these are grave political errors which are only explicable in terms of the internal situation in russia.

14 jan 40

helli is working with naima wifstrand in her school for young actors. she is doing studies of shakespeare. they act one scene (MACBETH 2, ii) then they improvise a scene from daily life with the same theatrical element, then the shakespeare scene again. the pupils seem to react strongly to the technique of the a-effect (to be read with astonishment).

15 jan 40

greid the actor has written a tract here on MARXIST ETHICS, utterly amateurish, using the well-known vocabulary. however he does have a naive interest in speculative thinking, and i occasionally go through a few points with him. he is still totally taken up with the question of how men would have to change in order to change the world, so that they could change themselves. he sees all sorts of ethical and pseudo-ethical odds and ends looming in the proletariat, he hears them talking about the inhumanity of their exploiters, about their own animal existence, he sees conceptions of better worlds forming in them, and he sees them going into training for their struggle. we examine a few of these ought-and-may sentences, which relate to social behaviour, which derive from old ethical systems (to get him to accept this plural was difficult) or at least occur in them. in the end i suggest a practical formulation to him. in the interest of the class struggle ought-and-may sentences which contain the expression 'you swine' should be converted into sentences containing 'you ass'. sentences whose 'you swine' cannot be converted into 'you ass', must be extirpated. example: the sentence 'you must not sleep with your mother' was once a 'you ass' – sentence, for in an earlier organisation of society it involved great confusion in the matter of property and production relationships. in this regard it is today no longer a 'you ass' sentence, but just a 'you swine' sentence. when you get down to it the sentence ought to be dropped entirely. the struggling proletariat will however use it in certain circumstances as a 'you ass' sentence, which goes something like this: 'you ought not to sleep with your mother, you ass, because your partners in the struggle have their prejudices and thus you could put your struggle in jeopardy. over and above which the courts will throw you in prison'. it is easy to see how relatively immoral these sentences are, since a peculiar lack of objectivity clings to them, which repels men of ethics. the reason of course is that the matter on which the argument might have been based has disappeared (the property and production relationships) so that the 'matter' has now become ethics pure and simple.

16 jan 40

discussed lagerkvist's VICTORY IN THE DARK. the swedish mystic and symbolist goes right to the frontier of reality and naturalism in this one. 'democracy', in the shape of a minister of state who hates violence, is overcome by confusion when forced to use violence in self-defence. underlying it all, the people's widespread fear of the military and uncertainty about the latter's attitude to democracy. the play is purely phenomenological, it registers in an imprecise, lyrical fashion certain situations which are rendered into primitive exchanges of slogans etc. enderle thinks the play useful here, in spite of its primitiveness, since he believes it exposes the 'shortcomings of democracy' and acts as a timely warning. i think it looks defeatist for democracy, since the nexus of social causality is not exposed, so that no practical definition emerges, and because it is based on the intuitions of the hero, thus giving his failure the character of a natural necessity. the only way to achieve detachment from the hero would be to use an a-effect. the tragedy naturally conceals within it the subject for a comedy. in it democracy has the duty to protect property and in this phase represents better protection for property with its particular nature than does dictatorship, and only as long as it fulfils this duty will the state's instruments of power be at its disposal. since the play is designated as a didactic play (lehrstück) (i call it a lament), scholz draws attention to the distinction between didactic and instructive.

26 jan 40

wrote, without any thought of who might accept it, a little detective story, using a dinner with renoir and koch as setting. can i call it CULTURE?

tombrock working feverishly on large drawings on the subject of FEAR AND MISERY. he has not mastered the a-effect, but my fear is that he would not draw realistically enough if i were to acquaint him with it prematurely. as it is we are getting very valuable drawings with a great deal of documentary detail.

the USSR offers ample subject matter for teaching materialism. there are arguments everywhere between the view that 'that is not socialism' and the view that 'that is socialism'. in actual fact there are very substantial socialist elements of a materialist nature there, with the appropriate superstructure. in some places a certain lightening of man's burden has in all probability ensued, in others, where it might have been expected to follow the freeing of productive capacity, it has not yet emerged, probably because they are too small to be perceptible. few understand this since most take an idealistic view of how socialism works. the one side concludes from the USSR's every action that it lacks socialist convictions, while the others view every action of the USSR as the only possible one for a socialist state. for them socialism is whatever the USSR does, and its nature can be studied in that country's actions.

29 jan 40

tombrock's drawings are in many ways remarkable. he was a miner and a vagrant and never learnt to draw. clever people look at his drawings and say, he'll have to learn to draw first, the elementary things. it is true, he has no grasp of perspective, yet he cannot learn it in isolation, not 'first' and not as something elementary. only in conjunction with other problems that interest him. at the moment he solves all his problems 'by force'. to characterise persons he cold-bloodedly (or hot-bloodedly?) uses shadows, which he draws across faces, the laws of gravity, like those of anatomy, he ignores, his figures kneel on air. occasionally quite wooden figures are found in lively settings, nutcrackers among normal people. but despite all the misfortune, lack of skill, shortcomings and stumblings he will from time to time in a roundabout and pathetic way grasp his problems in a firm grip and make progress. he is now making an oeuvre for the first time, at my instigation. by composing 27 sheets using one and the same technique (pencil) he is setting down the unevenness and inconsistency of his style in all its 'nakedness', so to speak, 'drawing his way up'.

the world situation is getting more and more confused. if the USSR had brought an alliance with the western powers into being, there would have been two ways open: 1) the USSR could support the powers that be and allow them to replace the nazi system with a 'normal' capitalist one, dependent on the western powers. 2) it could force the formation of popular fronts and thus endanger the prosecution of the war. (2) persevered with until 1939 led to the collapse of the alliance. as matters now stand the USSR could find itself in the position of having to support the nazi regime, and how is that to be done even using furnace tongs?

29 jan 40

ljungdal gives me a little essay on the WORLD VIEW OF DIALECTICS. it is cleverly and carefully written, but it has the usual shortcomings: hegel's dialectic is not derived from real history, but from the history of philosophy. and it is not shown functioning in marx, but has the character of a constituent of a world-view.

however, what a lucid little work compared to the HISTORY OF THE BOLSHEVIKS! the author of this history is as it were clear and imprecise, he hews his sentences into shape with an axe and constantly cuts his own fingers in the process of writing. revolutions are derived from metaphysics, they happen because the old yields to the new and because the only thing 'that is irresistible is what comes into existence and develops'. everything is dependent on everything else, and developments happen with miraculous leaps. the identity sentence is valid in the main for 'things in nature', and the ultimate contradictions which must not be whitewashed over, are capitalist conditions. the class struggle must not be hemmed in, but has to be fought out to the end. then one writes memoirs and spares a grateful thought for dialectics. everything is on the way up, the old dies, the new triumphs, it is a matter of 'the transition from an old qualitative condition to a new qualitative condition'. the new is naturally of better quality.

31 jan 40

dialectical thinking corresponds to a differentiated society with powerful productive forces which develop quickly in catastrophic form amid wars and revolutions. the intensified class struggle, the legality of competition, unrestrained exploitation, the accumulation of misery via the accumulation of capital – it all means that dialectics more and more becomes the only possible aid to orientation. such phenomena of a social nature as the progressive isolation of individual social functions, coupled with those same functions' growing dependence on one another, the development of relations among the constituent members and the increased friction this causes, all this sort of thing teaches us how to think dialectically. the proletariat sees nations as people fighting one another, as a unit it sees nations as being against it, the proletariat. only the realisation of their simultaneous unity and disunity enables it to pursue a rational policy. it is the same with the classes; the ruling classes do not form 'a reactionary mass', yet they do just that in one context, when facing the proletariat, in itself a unity. what people must strive for is a formal democracy, of which it is known in advance that it will never become political, only economic. the dictatorship of the proletariat can be conceived as the first form of non-formalistic democracy. the private ownership of the means of production (one owner instead of 50 owners) is on the one hand historical progress, but it soon becomes an anachronism, and production is held up by the individual owner of those means. such observations and experiences are developed by dialectics. – it is high time people began to derive dialectics from reality, instead of deriving it from the history of ideas, and using only selected examples from reality.

10 feb 40

i am reading a lot of macaulay, at the moment LIFE AND WRITINGS OF ADDISON. the english are to be envied for their literature which has a real history and real continuity, because a national life existed and the bourgeoisie came to power at an early stage. and what criteria! when m[acaulay] writes, supposedly in praise of addison, that his best verse is as good as POPE's second best. excellent analysis of the poem CAMPAIGN which glorifies the battle of blenheim. he reminds us that the poem's main claim to fame was noted by JOHNSON, namely '*the manly and rational rejection of fiction*'*. up to then poets had had commanders in the field participating in battles like homeric heroes. now addison compares marlborough to an *angel, guiding the whirlwind**. and he points out that the effect of the simile comes from the unconsidered line '*such as, of late, o'er pale britannia pass'd*'*. england had been ravaged by a typhoon just previously. he stresses 'the advantage which, in rhetoric and poetry, the particular has over the general'. the germans do not have any literature as yet, if one looks closely. one or two tall, spindly champions, entirely unconnected with one another, each with his own criteria, a pathetic particularism in poetry. there was simply no centre, no city like london (or paris or rome). in addition to which education had to be acquired privately, since there were no great schools. even goethe can be classed as an autodidact.

19 mar 40

bedridden 3 weeks with influenza. i am helpless against the clutches of that kind of thing when i have no major work on the go.

in addition to which i cannot work with a temperature.

am considering a little epic work, THE FEARS OF HERR KEUNER, something in the manner of CANDIDE or GULLIVER. herr keuner is afraid that the earth may become uninhabitable if too great crimes, or too great virtues become necessary before a man can make enough to live on. thus herr keuner flees from country to country, since too much is asked of him everywhere, be it self-sacrifice, or bravery, or cleverness, or desire for freedom or thirst for justice, or cruelty, or deceit etc. all these lands are uninhabitable.

9 April 1940. The caption reads 'Germans occupy Denmark and attack Norway'.

Finland
17 April 1940 to 13 July 1941

to finland by ship, leaving behind furniture, books, etc. the locksmith who takes the books that nobody else wants. on the ship the young widow for whom the ship stops, so that she can clamber aboard up a ladder from an ice-floe. in the customs shed at åbo the woman who requisitions soldiers to carry her cases. a quatrain for tombrock, to help him sell a few more pictures.

VILLMANSTRAND: Far har fallit på ärans fält.

Father has fallen on the field of honour.

24

17 May 1940. King Leopold of Belgium capitulates. Retreat to Dunkirk.

6 may 40

got hold of a little empty flat at töölö for a month. helli runs around in a lorry and gets together the furniture we need in two hours, lent by five people we didn't even know yesterday. in the last [week] of april we moved in, and i began to work seriously on THE GOOD PERSON OF SZECHWAN. the play was begun in berlin and taken up again in denmark and put aside in sweden. i hope to get it finished here.

greid the actor was on the ship with us, arnold ljungdal followed later. they come round most evenings, ljungdal explains einstein's theory of relativity to steff. greid's marxist moral philosophy is getting the final, delighted touches. h[ella] wuolijoki very friendly, diktonius, who took a patriotic line in the war that has just ended, now finds the country's chances of staying out of the major war have improved.

finland in a difficult situation, imports cut off, impoverished, burdened with 400,000 karelian refugees.

england's failure to act causes dismay in scandinavia. they comfort themselves with the thought that england always has a bad opening game. the fact is that fascism can only be defeated by fascism or by democracy. for the moment any semblance of a democratic impulse is lacking in england. in addition to which the english lost their monopoly of propaganda this time round when they lost control of the overseas cables. wireless is not amenable to control, and the technical superiority of the combination of bombers and motorised troops over warships completes the picture. those motorised troops went through norway like a knife through butter.

the USSR expressed an interest in sweden's neutrality, and the same presumably goes for finland.

3 jun 40

already people everywhere are talking about the irresistible 'spirit that inspires the german soldiers'. you could equally well, moving from a non-taylorian firm to one that has been taylorised, speak of enthusiasm for work. as if it were hard work that made the conveyor belts move! it is not just that terror has replaced drill, it is, above all, that machinery has made courage etc superfluous. with mechanisation the german general staff has liberated itself from the personal qualities of its soldiers, from the 'spirit of the troops'. the soldier now forms part of the armaments. the engines 'take him with them'. the punctuality of an operation is not assured by a sense of responsibility, but by a stopwatch. the engines have to be tireless. parachutists are dropped like bombs, and bombs do not need courage. the thing that would take courage would be to refuse to climb into the plane in the first place. exposed behind the enemy lines they have to fight for their lives, not for 'the future of germany'. the 'spirit' needed for this can be acquired daily in industry.

Tung tysk luftvärnskanon laddas vid Kanal-kusten.

Loading a German heavy AA gun on the Channel coast.

it is interesting that the war is being fought with men born in the years 1915–1920. in 1933 these soldiers were therefore 13, or at most 18 years old. this is the youth on which nazi germany's future depends. they have no future, but are bleeding to death in france. we will not have to deal with these 'youths who are trained nazis through and through and know no germany other than nazi germany', the nazis will liquidate them themselves. (just as it is not socialism that wipes out the small businessman, but capitalism.)

8 jun 40

speed has become a new characteristic in warfare. the german blitzkrieg has nullified all calculations, in that preconceived moves are implemented with such speed that their consequences are unforeseen. and technology has added another dimension to the theatre of war; the battlefield has become the battle-cube or battle-space. and the poor french can't understand what is happening: they are waging mobile war as if it were trench warfare, trying to prevent their lines of non-existent trenches becoming broken into separate armies. and all the time their only salvation would be to operate in complete freedom and forget about 'front' and 'rear'. the military should have enquired in the city how majority (controlling) share-holdings in companies are assembled and in a general way how money is kept on the move and markets are cornered. the last renderings of the marseillaise are being silenced for ever by german dive-bombers.

11 jun 40

i go through the GOOD PERSON OF SZECHWAN for the umpteenth time, word for word, with grete. i defend my mornings jealously of late, and now that the news has turned so bad i am even considering switching off the early morning wireless. the little box sits by my bed and my last move at night is to turn it off, my first in the morning to put it on.

12 jun 40

cocteau insists that the idea of tank camouflage came from picasso who suggested it to a french war minister before the great war as a means of making soldiers invisible. cocteau also asks himself whether savages don't paint their skins less to make themselves frightening and more to make themselves invisible. that is a good idea. you make things invisible by destroying their form, giving them an unexpected form, making them as it were not inconspicuous, but at once striking and strange.

the germans are marching on paris.

10 June 1940. Italy declares war on Britain and France. Mussolini's speech.

Cocteau's caricature of the Russian designer Leon Bakst in 1912

14 jun 40

in the future it will perhaps be difficult to understand the impotence of the peoples in these wars of ours. their causes are transient. there is the political atomisation, the result of the concentration of gigantic masses by the police and military. there is the phenomenon that, for lack of a better expression, i call the *field phenomenon*. these problems are always perceived and treated by whole peoples as field problems. ie, they are eg regarded as being soluble (and amenable to analysis) only in the capitalist field. this brings about an astonishing neutralisation of the inner contradictions of the peoples, which do not disappear for a moment, yet 'have no part to play in this field'. you can also put it this way: at the helm is this or that class, this or that regime, this or that solution is being pressed, this or that particular direction has been taken etc, and until the real and imaginary possibilities of the field have been framed, tried, exhausted and discredited, no other field arises. the field itself may not satisfy reason (imagination may locate other fields, experience suggest yet others), in the currently functioning field of practice there is still enough reason operating for the purposes of the entire people and for the purposes of justifying what is happening. thus rearmament was in fact the solution of the unemployment problem in the field of capitalism. for the workers there was in it something inherently reasonable, in that it did combat unemployment. war too is the solution to a problem, namely that of germany's having arrived too late for the imperialist carve-up of world markets (caused by the delayed arrival in germany of the bourgeois revolution and with it the creation of national unity). there is plenty there that the individual worker can understand.

The German army enters Paris, a week before the French capitulation.

17 jun 40

HITLER DANCES

FÜHRER DOES JIG FOR VICTORY

Perhaps the most intimate look at Adolf Hitler which the world has ever had is presented in the series of pictures below, taken from a German newsreel. It shows Hitler at precisely the happiest moment of his life. He has just heard the news that France is ready to surrender. The date is June 17. The place is the garden of his headquarters on the Western Front. His German troops have just occu-

pied Paris, overrun Burgundy, reached the Swiss border, isolated the Maginot Line and reduced Metz.

Just before these pictures were taken, Hitler had signed the invitation to Mussolini to meet him at Munich and decide on what terms to allow beaten France. He is in an ecstasy of joy. Keeping his heels smartly together, he clenches his fists and jerks his arms stiffly up and down, grinning in tense,

17 June 1940. 'Hitler dances. Führer does jig for victory.' Introducing a sequence taken from a German newsreel and reproduced in the US weekly *Life*.

prim jubilance. He holds his stomach and says, "It is finished." Still grinning and thrusting out his jaw, he lifts up one foot in a brief Lindy Hop of victory, while his staff beam back at him. This is the face of triumph, frank and unashamed. This is the victory dance, for Hitler's leather boots are hopping symbolically on the prostrate neck of the Third French Republic.

The stooges who surround him are his staff. They are wearing the uniforms of the *Schutzstaffel*, the Nazi Party, the Foreign Office. The round short man among them, at the left of Picture No. 3, is Hitler's official photographer, Heinrich Hoffmann. The tall man nearest Hitler is a Foreign Office underling. After these pictures were taken, Hitler led his staff off with an exaggerated goose-step, giggling

cheerfully. The pictures have been held up by the British censorship.

Hitler's mood that day was reflected in his newspaper which said, "Thirty-nine days . . . not only shook the world, but also brought the collapse of a world of boundless conceit and arrogance, but also a world of real power. . . .We are not revengeful but we have definitely ceased to be goodhearted fools."

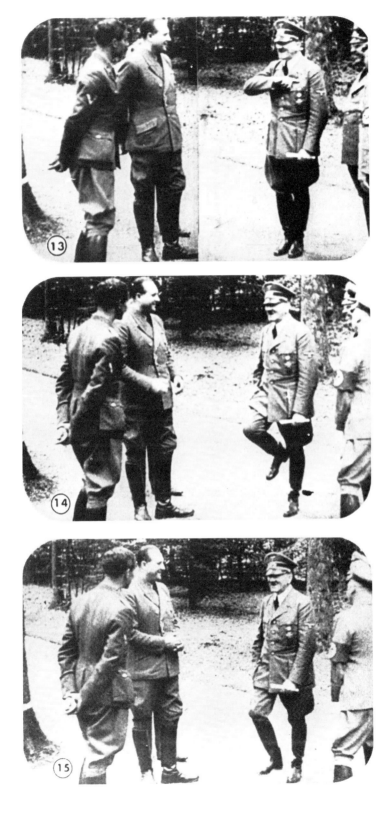

20 jun 40

more or less finished the GOOD PERSON OF SZECHWAN. the material
presented many difficulties, and in the (roughly) 10 years since i first
tackled it i made several false starts. the main danger was of being
over-schematic. li gung had to be a person if she was to become a good
person. as a result her goodness is not of a conventional kind; she is not
wholly and invariably good, not even when she is being li gung. nor is lao

Sgt. Lord Strabolgi: *The peer once known as Lt. Comdr. J. M. Kenworthy served 18 years in the Navy, became its heavyweight champion, then—paradoxically— turned pacifist. Now he is a non-com in Parliament's Home Guard.*

Vansittart

At Churchill's instigation, Robert Vansittart, former head of the Foreign Office, drew up a draft agreement for a Franco-British Union with Jean Monnet in June 1940. It was too late.

30 jun 40

it is impossible to finish a play properly without a stage. the proof of the pudding . . . how am i supposed to find out whether, say, the 6th scene of the GOOD PERSON OF SZECHWAN stands up to li gung's sudden understanding of the social basis for her friend's badness or not? only the stage can decide between possible variants. apart from MOTHER and ROUNDHEADS, everything i have written since JOAN is untested.

DIKTONIUS, the finnish horace, drags me off to a beer hall. he is squat and four-square, as if he had been hewn with an axe from the root of an oak, a peripatetic monument to himself. he has no income from the state and lives off newspaper articles. he always brings something when he comes, a cigar or sweets for barbara. he likes laughing, enjoys making malicious but comic little observations, pithy and well formed. all in all he could be a sea captain.

30 jun 40

appalling, this dominance of the new weapon (whatever happens, we have got the maxim gun and they have not, they once said) of the new brand of state monopoly with its elimination of the cliques of old clapped-out *politicians*. astonishing the dialectic of a moment in time.

the slow war produces the fast one (as the static one did the mobile). but how this tempo changes everything. and for the germans it is not a matter only of the blitzkrieg, but also of blitz-rearmament. and what strength this regime extracts from breaking with all conventions! they combine steamers full of tourists with the most modern warplanes, karl may complements clausewitz. tracked vehicles find petrol behind the enemy lines in roadside filling stations. parachutists drop disguised as priests and commandeer private cars.

1 jul 40

cutting from a newspaper, several years old, perhaps picasso saw the exhibition.

l Berlin har i dagarna öppnats en utomordentligt intressant utställn
av kinesisk konst. Från det mycket uppmärksammade vernissaget in
vi dessa tvenne bilder av en häst från 5 århundradet

The fifth-century Chinese horse was in a Berlin exhibition which may have been held
a decade or more earlier.

nenden Dunkirchen harrt eine unubersehbare Menge franzosischer und englischer Gefangener auf den Abtransport

Dunkirk in the distance, as French and British prisoners of war wait to be taken to camps.

1 jul 40

the world is now changing hourly. i remember how more and more things disappeared one by one. first there were still newspapers, german ones in austria, czechoslovakia, switzerland, the saarland. one after the other they packed up, stopped coming. the wireless went on. but one day vienna was silent, another prague. you could hear warsaw a bit longer. then warsaw was silent, and copenhagen and oslo were restricted to german broadcasts. now paris isn't there any more. of the western democracies only london remains. for how long? steff and i have kept having to look out new maps. poland, scandinavia, then holland, belgium, france. now england lies open.

2 jul 40

we are still mulling over the problem; bread and milk or rice and tea for the SZECHWAN PARABLE. of course there are already airmen and still gods in this szechwan. i have sedulously avoided any kind of folklore. on the other hand the yellow race eating white french bread is not intended as a joke. the london of THREEPENNY OPERA, the kilkoa of MAN EQUALS MAN, these seem to be successful poetic conceptions. point for discussion: how is one to keep in the social anachronisms? industry which threatens the existence of the gods (and of morals), the invasion of european customs. in such cases one is still on real ground. but neither industry nor europeanisation will replace rice with bread. here we have the chinese element as pure disguise, and a disguise full of holes at that! unfortunately i can't clear this up here in helsinki.

'The Widows of Osecha', painting by Hans Tombrock after a poem by Brecht.

tombrock sends photos of a first oil painting (i have hounded him into oil paints). THE WIDOWS OF OSSEG BEFORE THE MAGISTRATES OF PRAGUE. he has made enormous progress, away from romanticism and rags. he has a surprising grasp of the principle of social grouping as a compositional category.

2 jul 40

olsoni the bookseller brings along a literary historian who is working on mallarmé. he shows some of the famous poems which are attacked or worshipped because they 'have no meaning'. of course they have meaning, even if it is very unstable. the way he dislocates normal connections produces little shocks, that's all. it is a mistake on m[allarmé]'s part to mix the words (the seeds of association) too evenly too often, with respect to abstract and concrete. his fear of the banal often results in banalities. he constantly has to accept that certain words or groups of words will be understood in concrete terms, but then he demands in other cases in the same stanza that the reader should not do this. i tried to explain to them how the lyric can be switched over to the gestic. one problem in this undertaking is that the new gests are not theatrical enough (nor carefully enough chosen). then the fall of the drapery is missing – difficult to achieve in the case of overalls.

5 jul 40

drove with HELLA WUOLIJOKI to marlebäk (kausala). she is letting us have a villa surrounded by lovely birch trees. we discuss the quietness out here. but it isn't quiet; it's just that the noises are so much more natural, the wind in the trees, the rustle of grass, the twittering and the sound of water. the white manor house with its two rows each of eight large windows is over 100 years old, built in empire style, the rooms would not disgrace a museum. alongside it lies a huge stone building for the cows (some 80 head) with openings for fodder overhead for the forage lorry to drive to, and handsome water conduits, all in iron and magnificent wood, the reddish pine of the north. the winter in this year of war was very severe, so the cherry orchard froze, and thanks to the lack of rain this spring the vegetables are poorly. there is a small wooden house in which 14 karelians are living, fishermen and their families who were evacuated. they pay no rent and get 10 finnish marks a day. h.w. thinks they manage all right on that. but they can see no future, their fate is being decided by parliament.

we are very sleepy; due no doubt to the unfamiliar air. just the smell of the birches is intoxicating, as is the smell of wood. between the birches is a mass of wild strawberries, and the children are exhausted with picking them. helli is going to have difficulty cooking, i'm afraid, the stove needs to be kept in and the water supply is outdoors. but the people are very friendly and h.w. has an unending fund of stories.

6 jul 40

many now envisage an imminent victory for german fascism, and with it a victory for fascism in general in europe (if not further). a new period of stability, that is. there is naturally not much likelihood of this. equilibrium could only arise if there were german dominance, and if it came to that, many constituent elements of german fascism would disappear again. what is happening in france typifies this. in germany the new structure came as a revolution, in france it comes as a collapse. its 'planning' remains an emergency measure without any productive aspect. pétain is simply a home-grown governor. the country has even escaped from the war. the army and the fleet are lost, and industry is still working for the war, only now it is on behalf of the enemy.

these light nights are very beautiful. i got up at three o'clock because of the flies, and went out. cocks were crowing, but it had not been dark. i like to relieve myself in the open air.

funnily enough i never think about work at such a time. these are not working hours.

7 jul 40

sketch the plan of a play, more to keep my hand in. STREET OF THE MINISTRIES. a blind beggar with a boy sits in the street where the ministries are. from what he sees, minute little events, he draws conclusions about what is going to happen, namely the great war and the great defeat. in this way he is able to give his friends good advice, so that they are able to take themselves to safety. (eg, that the capital will not be defended. so they must not flee but should buy the restaurant opposite which the owner will part with for a song. it is posher than theirs, and soon there will only be posh restaurants left. etc.) a blind man can foresee the end of an empire.

another variant would be: a young french girl in orleans who is looking after a petrol station in the absence of her brother dreams day and night that she is joan of arc and suffers her fate. for the germans are advancing on orleans. the voices joan hears are the voices of the people, what the blacksmith says and the peasant. she obeys these voices and saves france from the foreign foe, but is defeated by the enemy within. (the court which finds her guilty is made up solely of clergymen who sympathise with the english.) the victory of the fifth column.

8 jul 40

it is understandable that people here love their landscape. it is so very rich and varied on such a grand scale. the lakes with their plenitude of fish, the woods with their beautiful trees and the scent of berries and birches. the tremendous summers which burst out overnight after the interminable winters, great heat after great cold. and as the day disappears in winter, so the night disappears in summer. and then the air is so powerful and tastes so good that it almost satisfies your appetite unaided. and what music fills this radiant sky! the wind blows almost non-stop, and since it meets many different plants, grasses, corn, bushes and trees, the result is a gentle harmony that rises and falls, which you hardly hear but which is there nonetheless.

16 jul 40

according to leading circles in germany their french counterparts have now brought in hitler to cash in on the achievements of the people. they are trying to become a kind of post-trianon austria. laval says parliament will disappear, while the parliamentarians will stay. voilà. men of letters will stay, literature will disappear. not a syllable from the great writers during the entire war.

and in england the gentry are running the war, in cahoots with the city. they too are putting their money on big machines (fleet, air force), where the little man is of no consequence.

in the meantime the germans are making plans for a new order in europe, a mighty centropa is being designed. 'the unhealthy power politics of the small states' will be ended.

25 jul 40

steff brought along MELEAGER'S WREATH, translated by august OEHLER. lovely epigrams, reminding me of my sonnet ADVICE TO THE LYRIC POETS OF THE USSR ON INSCRIBING PUBLIC BUILDINGS [Rat an die Lyriker der USSR, öffentliche Bauwerke zu beschriften]. i altered some of them and wrote a few new ones of my own to serve as examples.

when you compare what the weimar writers knew about the greek epigrammists and their problems with the little we know today, you see what a ghastly decline there has been. nowadays we hardly even know anything about the weimarians.

the mood of these greek epigrams is set by their marvellous concreteness, together with their sense of how a specific wind (evening wind, dawn wind, april wind, wind off the snows) will stir the leaves and fruit on a given tree.

an example:

on the threshold of the temple of athene
the master theris's skilled, schooled hand
laid out the rule, the straight yardstick
the stout saw with curved edge
the axe, the plane, and fitting neatly in the hand
the drill as well, all revolutions turned
for all to see, obeying the custom of his craft
once his long industry was at an end.
(leonides of tarentum)

30 jul 40

had a shot at one or two epigrams. (WEIGEL'S PROPS, THE PIPES, LARDER ON A FINNISH ESTATE). quite incapable of working at plays. yet it's so urgent to get the GOOD PERSON finished; only details remain to be done. at such moments of blockage one needs some journalism or work in the practical theatre, neither of which is possible at the moment.

wonderful, these stories of wuolijoki's about the people on the estate, in the forests where she used to own big sawmills, back in the heroic days. she looks wise and lovely as she tells of the ruses of simple people and the stupidity of the upper crust, shaking with perpetual laughter and now and again looking at you with sly winks, as she accompanies the various personages' words with epic, flowing movements of her lovely fat hands, as though beating time to some music that nobody else can hear. (moving from the wrist, she describes with her hand a horizontal eight.) she hauls her great weight over her islands and moors with surprising energy, and her bulk has a chinese quality about it, she sorts out the business of the estate with a light touch, never bosses people around. and she is very human.

2 aug 40

skimmed through the MESSINGKAUF. the theory is relatively simple. it deals with the traffic between stage and auditorium, how the spectator must master the incidents on the stage. the theatrical experience comes about by means of an act of empathy; this is established in aristotle's POETICS. the critical attitude cannot be among the elements that go to make it up, so defined; the better empathy works the truer this must be. criticism is stimulated with reference to the way empathy is generated, not with reference to the incidents the spectator sees reproduced on the stage. not that it is entirely proper to speak of 'incidents that the spectator sees reproduced on the stage' when talking about the aristotelian theatre. story and performance in the aristotelian theatre are not meant to provide reproductions of events in real life, but to bring about the whole theatre experience as laid down (complete with certain cathartic effects). admittedly there is a need for actions recalling real life, and they have to have a certain element of probability to create the illusions without which empathy cannot take place. but there is no need for the causality of the incidents to be brought out. it is enough that it should not give rise to scepticism.[1] it is only the man who is mainly concerned with those real-life incidents on which the theatre bases its playing who finds himself able to treat incidents on the stage as reproductions of reality and to criticise them as such. in doing so he is stepping out of the realm of art, for art does not see its primary task as being the mere provision of reproductions. once again: it is concerned only with quite specific reproductions, that is to say reproductions with specific effects. the act of empathy that produces them would only be thrown out of gear if the spectator were to go into the actual incidents critically. so the question is this: is it quite impossible to make the reproduction of real-life events the purpose of art and thereby make something conducive to art of the spectators' critical attitude toward them? as soon as one starts to go into this it becomes clear that so great a transformation could only be brought about by changing the nature of the traffic between auditorium and stage. in this new method of practising art empathy would lose its dominant role. against that the alienation effect (a-effect) will need to be introduced, which is an artistic effect too and also leads to a theatrical experience. it consists in the reproduction of real-life incidents on the stage in such a way as to underline their causality and bring it to the spectator's attention. this type of art also generates emotions; such performances facilitate the mastering of reality; and this it is that moves the spectator. the a-effect is an ancient artistic technique; it is known from classical comedy, certain branches of popular art and the practices of the asiatic theatre.

[1] In theory it is possible to bring about a complete theatre experience with a completely misleading representation of an event from real life.

2 aug 40

second appendix to the theory of the MESSINGKAUF.

a few points will serve to show what part dialectical materialism plays in the theory:

1) the *self-evident* – ie the particular shape our consciousness gives our experience – is resolved into its components when counteracted by the *a-effect* and turned into a new form of the *evident*. an imposed schema is being broken up here. the individual's own experiences correct or confirm what he has taken over from the community. the original act of discovery is repeated.

2) the contradiction between empathy and detachment is made stronger and becomes an element in the performance.

3) *historicising* involves judging a particular social system from another social system's point of view. the standpoints in question result from the development of society. (incomplete)

note: aristotelian dramaturgy takes no account (ie allows none to be taken) of the objective contradictions in any process. they have to be changed into subjective ones (located in the hero).

2 aug 40

third appendix to the M[ESSINGKAUF] t[heory].

the spectator's need nowadays to be distracted from his daily warfare is continually reproduced by that daily warfare, but just as continually in conflict with his need to be able to control his own fate. among such needs an artificial distinction is made between entertainment and maintenance; entertainment (of a distracting kind) is a continual threat to maintenance, since the spectator isn't led into the void – not into an unfamiliar world but into a distorted one – and he pays for these extravagances, which he regards as mere excursions, in real life. identifying himself with his enemy does not leave him unmarked; it makes him an enemy to himself. surrogates satisfy one's need and poison one's body; the audience want both to be diverted and to be converted – and they must want to be both – because of the daily warfare.

The new theatre is simply the theatre of the man who has begun to help himself. in three hundred years of organisation and technology he has been transformed. the theatre has been very slow to come of age. shakespearian man is helplessly handed over to his fate, ie to his passions. society holds out no hand to him. there is a quite limited radius within which a given type's splendour and vitality is effective.

the new theatre appeals to social man because man has helped himself in a social way, technically, scientifically and politically. it exposes any given type together with his way of behaving, so as to throw light on his social motivations; he can only be grasped if they are mastered. individuals remain individual, but become a social phenomenon; their passions and also their fates become a social concern. the individual's position in society loses its god-given quality and becomes the centre of attention. the a-effect is a social measure.

3 aug 40

appendix to the theory of the MESSINGKAUF.

1) under the aristotelian system of constructing a play and the style of acting that goes with it (the two concepts can be switched round if you like), the audience's deception with regard to the way in which the incidents shown on the stage come about and take place in real life is helped by the fact that the story's presentation forms an indivisible whole. its details cannot be compared one by one with their corresponding parts in real life. nothing may be taken 'out of its context' in order, say, to set it in the context of reality. the answer lies in the alienating style of acting. in this the story line is a broken one; the single whole is made up of independent parts which can and must be compared with the corresponding part-incidents in real life. this way of acting draws all its force from comparisons with reality, in other words, it is continually drawing attention to the causality of the incidents reproduced.

2) to achieve the a-effect the actor must give up his *complete conversion* into the stage character. he *shows* the character, he *quotes* his lines, he *repeats* a real-life incident. the audience is not entirely 'carried away'; it need not conform psychologically, adopt a fatalistic attitude towards fate as portrayed. (it can feel anger where the character feels joy, and so on. it is free, and sometimes even encouraged, to imagine a different course of events, or to try and find one, and so forth.) the incidents are *historicised* and socially *set*. (the former, of course, occurs above all with present-day incidents: whatever is was not always, and will not always be so. the latter repeatedly casts a questionable light on the prevailing social order

and subjects it to discussion.) achieving the a-effect is a technique that has to be taught from first principles.

3) one establishes laws by accepting natural incidents, as it were, with astonishment, in other words, one can only understand their evidence by ceasing to treat them as 'self-evident'. in order to discover the law governing falling bodies alternative possibilities must be imagined for them; among these imagined possibilities the actual, natural possibility will then be the right one, and the imagined alternatives will emerge as impossibilities. the theatre can stimulate the audience to this astounded, inventive and critical attitude by means of its a-effect, but the fact that this is an attitude that also has to be adopted in the sciences by no means makes a scientific institution of it. it is merely the theatre of the scientific age. it takes the attitude adopted by its audience in real life and applies it to the theatrical experience. or, to put it another way: empathy is not the only source of emotion at art's disposal.

4) within the conventions of aristotelian theatre the kind of acting we described above would be a mere matter of style. it is much more. all the same, there is no question of the theatre thereby losing its old functions of *entertainment* and *instruction*, these actually get a new lease of life. the method of presentation becomes wholly natural once more. it can display the various different styles. concern with reality sets the imagination off on the right pleasurable road. gaiety and seriousness revive in criticism, which is of a creative kind. altogether it is a matter of taking the old religious institution and secularising it.

4 aug 40

on the question of *realism*: the usual view is that the more easily reality can be recognised in a work of art, the more realistic it is. against this i would like to set up the equation that the more recognisably reality is mastered in the work of art, the more realistic it is. straightforward recognition of reality is often impeded by a presentation which shows how to master it. sugar as described by a chemist loses its recognisability. that is of course an extreme example, it only demonstrates the (distant) limits. at any rate one must look to see whether the artist is a realist, ie proceeds realistically in his writing, exposes all the veils and deceptions that obscure reality and intervenes in his public's real actions, moreover, you must not stick to form and merely compare the form of one work with that of another and distil from this a realistic form, to do so is pure formalism, even if the form in question is drawn from a realistic work. LENIN's parable of the climbing of high mountains must also be valid as an example of a realistic work of art.

5 aug 40

people often hesitate to call artists like hašek, silone, o'duffy and myself bourgeois writers, but this is quite wrong. we may make the cause of the proletariat our own, we may even for a certain span of time be artists of the proletariat – in which case the proletariat for that span of time has bourgeois artists representing its cause. we for our part may tell ourselves that to be a proletarian constitutes neither an advantage nor positive contribution, and that the struggle is about erasing proletarian features from the face of mankind – nevertheless we demonstrate the limitations and weaknesses of our class, which make us allies in the struggle who must be viewed critically. and, of course, should we transmit bourgeois culture, then it is the culture alone. in certain phases of development, when the proletariat has triumphed, but is still the proletariat, the function of its bourgeois pioneers becomes, as has been shown, formalistic. overtaken by real developments, all they do is go on developing forms for a while. then it is time for new artists and fighters to enter the arena. they then find in the works of their predecessors – our works – not only the most highly developed means of expression, but also elements of the new culture, which always emerge most sharply in the context of struggle. dreams fly ahead of deeds, their very vagueness makes the new field seem limitless, and thus they spur others on. in our works the technique of making a fresh start, developed by people who have tradition at their fingertips, is important, for he who starts again and has not mastered the tradition can easily fall under the domination of that tradition once more. the safest thing is to present us and use us as the dialecticians among the bourgeois artists. in that we stand alongside those bourgeois politicians who have made the cause of the proletariat their own.

9 aug 40

on abbreviation in the classical style: if i leave out enough on a page i conserve for the word *night*, say in the sentence 'when night came', its full value in the mind of the reader. inflation is the death of all economy. it is best for words to dismiss their retinue and face one another with as much dignity as they can muster on their own. and quite false to say that the classicists forget the readers' senses, on the contrary, they count on them. our sensualists are like sclerotics; to get any sensation in the soles of their feet they have to strut like the napoleons. i am reading LYTTON STRACHEY'S essay on RACINE. he too notices how in recent drama racine triumphs over shakespeare. (almost every play is no more than the last act of an elizabethan play) the principle has even triumphed in the novel.

making minor corrections to THE GOOD PERSON is costing me as many weeks as writing the scenes did days. not easy, given the definite objective, to imbue the tiny sub-scenes with the element of irresponsibility, accident, transitoriness which we call 'life'. moreover, in the end there is the basic question to be settled: how to handle the *li gung–lao go* problem. one can either (1) extend the parable aspect, so as to have a straightforward conflict *gods–li gung–lao go*, which would keep it all on a moral plane and allow two conflicting principles (two 'souls') to figure separately, or else (2) have a plain simple story about how *li gung* masquerades as her cousin and to that end makes use of the experiences and qualities which her gutter existence has brought out in her. in fact only (2) is possible unless one is to abandon mrs shin's discovery (scene 7), her conversation with the pregnant lao go and the whole theme of how this pregnancy makes the double game impossible to maintain. the transformation scene before the curtain (4a) is not in any way mystical but merely a technical solution in terms of mime and a song. where the difficulty becomes acute is wherever *lao go* directly addresses the audience. the question is whether he ought not to do this using li gung's voice and consequently her attitude too. at bottom it all depends on how scene 5 is handled. this is where lao go must make some remark to explain his change of attitude. however, he has no confidant, nor can he make a confidant of the audience, not as lao go. what is more li gung's collapse at the end of the scene is harder to understand if the solution adopted is (2) rather than (1). the only possible explanation is that here too she is being addressed as li gung. when you come down to it the elements *good* and *evil* are too segregated for a realistic drama of masquerade. an occasional slip would be unavoidable. the most realistic scene in this respect is the ninth. a further consideration could be that li gung has to make strenuous efforts to play the part of lao go, and is no longer capable of appearing unpleasant when dressed in her own clothes and before the eyes of those who know and address her as li gung. herein lies an important lesson: how easy it is for her to be good, how hard to be evil.

10 aug 40

the ring of iron is closing round britain. the aeroplane, the new weapon, is showing itself to be more terribly new than when it was employed in the last war. and the man who observed that there are no islands any more seems likely to force his way into the legion of *great men*, which would scarcely gain credit thereby. victory will decide, although it will not be for lack of 'greatness' that he will fail. the concept *greatness* is defined by results. he is great who makes the earth bloom, as is he who despoils it. and think what low-grade scoundrels can achieve the latter . . . of course they have such remarkably great support. this is where narrow-mindedness becomes concentration, helplessness the art of attracting gifted people, theft of their reputation the power to curb them. obsession becomes energy, fanaticism becomes single-mindedness, willingness to ignore the rules becomes freedom from convention, murderousness becomes decisiveness, the struggle for power becomes the struggle for an idea etc etc.

16 aug 40

steff is reading about the french revolution and wants above all to know whether it should be presented from the proletarian point of view or from that of the bourgeoisie. would communism have been possible at that time? i explain to him that c[ommunism] is a mode of production which depends on the possibility of collective production of goods, and that the french proletariat was not in a position to develop its productive resources to the extent that the bourgeoisie could. he has difficulty in recognising that the question of whether it was wrong to go for communism at that time is a red herring.

18 aug 40

h[ella] w[uolijoki], over black-market coffee after a sauna, tells the story of the swedish journalist SNELLMANN who was the real founder of finnish nationalism. he was a student of hegel, and it is interesting to see how hegel's influence is to be found in prussia and russia, two countries with a strongly oppressive state bureaucracy and a strong revolutionary movement. s. only got his professorship when the russian governor decreed it. the swedish finns, that is the upper class which had pro-swedish tendencies, sent him to a little country town 1000 km from helsinki. he took the job, convinced as he was that he could get a finnish movement going anywhere 'within three years'. he immediately brought out a newspaper and fought for the introduction of finnish in the schools and the legal and administrative systems. when he confronted the russian governor reason and reality confronted each other and discovered they were related. the governor went to moscow not with s.'s arguments, but with his impression of him and got everything passed. s. saw what power was. he then became finance minister and created the finnish mark. s. was a double traitor for he betrayed the swedes to the finns – one sees here how not only classes but occasionally also nations select their leaders from among their enemies – and the upper class to the lower class. in actual fact industry which was in swedish hands could develop better within an alliance with the russians than if it was dependent on sweden. the russians only occupied political positions in finland, not economic ones. and s. also appeared to betray the upper class to the lower class in the matter of language, though that does not bear close scrutiny either. the deaf and dumb mob is less and less able to serve economic competition as that competition grows more and more acute. the capital of the swedish finns bowed simultaneously under the yokes of czarism and finnish nationalism. in his old age s. became a pillar of reaction.

as i put forward various techniques from non-aristotelian dramatic theory for the play h. w. is planning about s., i am fed little omelettes baked from the blood of young calves, eaten with thyme and sour cream.

19 aug 40

the estate sauna is a little square wooden hut by the river. you go through the changing room into a small dark room dominated by a huge stone stove. you take off the wooden lid and pour hot water from an iron pot that stands beside the stove on round stones the size of your fist stacked directly over the fire. then you climb up a few steps to a wooden platform and lie down. when you begin to break sweat you whip the open pores with birch twigs, then you go out and plunge into the river. when you emerge – the cool water does not seem cold – you leave a trail of birch leaves behind you. at night too, you find some in bed. 'you sleep with the birch' says h. w. finnish soldiers built saunas even in the most advanced positions.

19 aug 40

at present all i can write is these little epigrams, first eight-liners, and now only four-liners. i am leaving CAESAR on one side since the GOOD PERSON isn't finished. when i open the MESSINGKAUF for a bit of a change it's like having a cloud of dust blow in one's face. can you imagine that sort of thing ever coming to mean anything again? that's not a rhetorical question. i should be able to imagine it. and it isn't a matter of hitler's current victories but purely and simply of my isolation so far as production is concerned. when i listen to the news on the wireless in the morning, at the same time reading boswell's LIFE OF JOHNSON and glancing out at the landscape of birch trees in the mist by the river, then the unnatural day begins not on a discordant note but on no note at all. this is all *in-between time*.

BRENTANO, whom i have written to for the first time after a long interval to get news of feuchtwanger, writes back that he knows nothing, hates england, and hopes it will lose its taste in future for casually declaring war on 'us'. it seems to be true that there is great indignation in germany about winston dirtschild instructing his airmen to bomb (according to a plan, it seems) german cultural monuments like goethe's garden-house in weimar or a bismarck mausoleum.

20 aug 40

in the evening i once again take DEVOTIONS FOR THE HOME in my hands. this is where literature attains the stage of dehumanisation which MARX observed in the proletariat, along with the desperation which inspires the proletariat's hopes. the bulk of the poems deal with decline, and the poems follow our crumbling society all the way down. beauty founded on wrecks, rags becoming a delicacy. nobility wallows in the dust, meaninglessness is welcomed as a means of liberation. the poet no longer has any sense of solidarity, not even with himself. risus mortis. but it doesn't lack power.

21 aug 40

BOSWELL's book makes me think of germany. odd how formless the types there are, except where, in the provinces, they are crude and uncivilised. and germany has provinces but no capital city. instant unification drove them wild. there is in fact, if you are looking for a setting for a play, scarcely a single one that is famous, or has a character of its own, scarcely a town that sounds big, or even poetic. it has taken the present regime to create backgrounds, albeit grisly ones, and a certain dark poetry now wafts across the moors with their camps, and the housepainter's deputies give the rhenish towns a shakespearian ring. even munich has taken on a significance with its beerhalls in which the first bloody putsch was launched, the hall of generals, the brown house, and the horse-trading over czechoslovakia. germany makes her entrance as a nation late, and what a nation . . .

22 aug 40

the linguistic clean-up on which i've embarked with the finnish
EPIGRAMS naturally turns my thoughts to the evolution of poetry. what a
decline! that splendid unity, so full of contradictions, collapsed immediately after goethe; HEINE taking the wholly secular line, HÖLDER-
LIN the wholly pontifical. of these the former saw the increasing
dissipation of the language, because naturalness can be achieved only by
small infringements of the formal rules. on top of that it is always a fairly
irresponsible affair, and the effect that a poet achieves by being
epigrammatic absolves him from all obligation to strive for poetic effects,
his expression becomes more or less schematic, all tension between the
words disappears, and the choice of words grows careless: by poetic
standards, that is, for lyric poetry has its own substitute for wit. the
writer stands for nothing but himself. as for the pontifical line, in
[STEFAN] GEORGE's case under the guise of contempt for politics, it
became unashamedly counter-revolutionary, that is not just reactionary,
but actively working for the counter-revolution. george lacked sensuality and tried to make up for it by a refined culinary approach. KARL
KRAUS too, representing the other line, is non-sensual in that he was a wit
and nothing else. the onesidedness of both lines makes it increasingly
difficult to apply one's judgement. in GEORGE we find an extremely
subjective approach which tries to appear objective by adopting classical
forms. for all its seeming subjectivity KRAUS's poetry is really much
closer to the object, contains more matter. the sad thing is that KRAUS is
so much feebler than GEORGE; he would be so much better than him
otherwise. both are in opposition to the bourgeoisie (g. being clerico-
feudal, and his 'paganism' of course a religion; k. a 'radical' critic, but of a
purely idealistic, liberal kind) and this at least brings out in both cases
how bourgeois interests have to be sacrificed if the cultural line is to be
maintained. GEORGE's school only produces results in so far as it sticks
to translation. for this supplies it with the matter which it otherwise has
no way of getting. k.'s poetry is hardly a very good illustration of his
linguistic and poetic doctrines; these should be followed fairly directly.

24 aug 40

i skimmed a small volume of WORDSWORTH in arnold's edition. came on
'*she was a phantom of delight*'* and was moved by this now remote work
to reflect how varied the function of art is, and how dangerous it is to lay

down the law. even such labels as 'petty bourgeois idyll' are hazardous. there are indeed some petty bourgeois tendencies which are directed towards the perpetuation and consolidation of the petty bourgeoisie as a class, but within the petty bourgeoisie there are also other kinds of tendencies that conflict with those. the individual petty bourgeois currently patrolling the fields of england equipped with a shotgun and a molotov cocktail ('as used against tanks in the spanish civil war', so a general assured us on the wireless), has up to a point legitimate enough grounds for blaming his wordsworths; yet it is just in dehumanised situations like these that

'*a lovely apparition, sent*
to be a moment's ornament'*

helps to conjure up other situations less worthy of the human race. certainly ours is a time when the poem no longer serves to '*haunt, to startle, to waylay*'*. art *is* an autonomous sphere, though by no means an autarchic one. a few points:

1) possible criterion for a work of art: does it enrich the individual's capacity for experience? (an individual, perhaps, who goes ahead and is then overtaken by the masses moving in a predictable direction.)

2) it may enrich the capacity for expression, which is not the same as the capacity for experience but more like a capacity for communicating. (perhaps the question is to what extent is the how linked to the what, and the what bound up with specific classes.)

3) poetry is never mere expression. its reception is an operation of the same order as, say, seeing and hearing, ie something much more active. writing poetry must be viewed as a human activity, a social function of a wholly contradictory and alterable kind, conditioned by history and in turn conditioning it. it is the difference between 'mirroring' and 'holding up a mirror'.

27 aug 40

to my great delight i hear from stockholm that feuchtwanger's arrival in lisbon has been corroborated from new york. he has not been out of my thoughts for a single day these last weeks.

tombrock sends etchings for LIFE OF GALILEO which are very beautiful. he has studied BRUEGHEL diligently and intelligently. and these prints too have the lightness and gaiety which are so important for history and criticism.

began a people's play with h[ella] w[uolijoki] for a finnish competi-

Kriegsschauplatz: Die Insel   Angriffe zu Wasser und aus der Luft.

Seit den letzten Tagen der Schlacht in Frankreich haben deutsche Flugzeuger in immer größerem Ausmaße an vielen Orten in England militärische Ziele, Flughäfen, Flugzeugfabriken, Munitionswerkstätten, Hafen-, Transport- und Tankanlagen, Flot- und Scheinwerferanlagen mit Erfolg angegriffen. Ueber die ganze Insel verteilt liegen die Orte, die in diesem Zusammenhang während der letzten Wochen in den Berichten des Oberkommandos der Wehrmacht genannt wurden. Immer heftiger sind seit dem Abschluß des Feldzuges im Besten auch die Schläge gegen die englische Schiffahrt geworden. Bor der Ostküste der britischen Insel ruht sie fast völlig, seitdem die deutsche Wehrmacht dem britischen Zu-
griff auf Standinavien zuvorkam. Das Seegebiet vor dem südlichen England jedoch wird seit der Besiegung der Kanal- und der Inseinorthalb
Atlantikküste zu einem wahren Schlachtseehof. Auf unserer Karte sind die Schiffe eingezeichnet, die in der Zeit zwischen den letzten Tagen der
großen Schlacht in Frankreich und Mitte August vor der englischen Küste lanten. Die beschädigten Schiffe sind auf der Karte nach nicht einmal
berücksichtigt! So spürt England die Folgen dieses Krieges, auch wenn der große Angriff erst noch beginnt.

'War Zone: The Island. Attacks by Sea and Air.' From the *Berliner Illustrirte Zeitung* of 24 August 40.

tion. adventures of a finnish landowner and his chauffeur. he is only human when he is drunk, since that is when he forgets his own interests.

28 aug 40

in ancient greek epigrams man-made utensils are straightforward subjects for lyric poetry, weapons too. hunters and warriors dedicate their weapons to the gods. whether an arrow enters the breast of a man or

The poetry of objects (1) An aeroplane cockpit.

a partridge makes no difference. in our day it is to a great extent moral scruples that prevent the rise of a comparable poetry of objects. the beauty of an aeroplane has something obscene about it. in sweden before the war, when i suggested a film with the motto 'the aeroplane for young workers' – a weapon in safe hands – just wanting to give expression to man's basic dream of flying, the immediate objection was, 'you surely don't want them to be bomber-pilots?'

29 aug 40

greek epigram time again:

> The curved bow here and the quiver
> that launched so many fatal arrows
> now, phoibos, hang here in your honour
> dedicated gifts, donated by promachos
> he cannot offer you the arrows
> for they, gory terror of close combatants,
> still stick in many men's hearts
> gift for the guest and pain of death.
>
> (MNASALKAS, after OEHLER)

> O spear of ash, murderer of men,
> stay in this spot for never again
> your bronze blade wish i to see
> stained horribly with the blood of the enemy.
> here in the storehouse of athens' glory
> in this towering temple make your seat
> and announce the manly virtues and the victory
> of echekratides from crete.
>
> (ANYTE, after OEHLER)

> once i was a pair of horns, flaunted
> by a wild goat, such as escalade
> the lofty cliff, and on my curling hair
> there often lay a crown of green leaves.
> now to make a bow for nikomachos
> a master-turner has joined me neatly
> has smoothed me skilfully and fitted me
> with a bullhide thong which will not snap.
>
> (SIMIAS, after OEHLER)

The poetry of objects (2) Stick grenades for the ordinary man. (Home Guard weapons from *Picture Post*.)

Und zuletzt: Bomben und Granaten in jedermanns Hand.

„Sie sind die Kampfwaffen einer Zivilisten-Armee. Für ihren Gebrauch ist wenig Uebung erforderlich — wohl aber Kaltblütigkeit und gesunder Menschenverstand..." — zu beziehen durch die Schriftleitung der „Picture Post".

2 sep 40

work on PUNTILA. h. w.'s play, half-finished, is a comedy, a conversation piece. (puntila sober is just puntila drunk plus a hangover, and hence in a bad temper, the stereotype of a drinker. his chauffeur is a *gentleman* who had applied for the chauffeur's job after seeing a photograph of puntila's daughter. etc.) but there is also a film of hers, which yields some useful epic elements (the mountain climb, the trip for legal alcohol), what i have to do is to bring out the underlying farce, dismantle the psychological discussions so as to make place for tales from finnish popular life or statements of opinion, find a theatrical form for the master/man contradiction, and give the theme back its poetic and comic aspects. this theme shows how in spite of all her cleverness, her experience, her vitality and her gifts as a writer h. w., is hampered by her conventional dramatic technique. what a gripping epic storyteller she is, sitting on her wooden stool and making coffee! it all comes out biblically simple and biblically complex,

(2) New plan for the
Hermann-Goering
Works in central
Germany. Architect:
Rimpl. Both pictures
come from the *Berliner
Illustrirte* of 19
September 40.

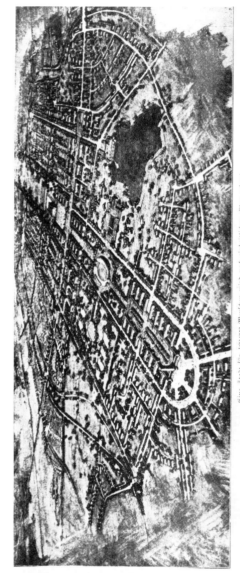

Nummer 38 19. September 1940

22 sep 40

after two weeks at school in helsingfors steff has read faust (both parts) and is very pleased about it. he knows a few lines by heart. further reading: j[akob] burckhardt (since faust has something to do with the renaissance), goethe's translation of cellini, vasari. kafka's trial made a big impression on him.

24 sep 40

h. w. is reading PUNTILA at the moment and seems very shaken. it is undramatic, unfunny, etc. all the characters speak alike, not differently as they do in life and in h. w.'s plays. passages like the conversation between the judge and the lawyer in the kitchen are boring (something the finns are not unused to) and do nothing to further the plot. kalle is not a finnish chauffeur. the landowner's daughter cannot attempt to borrow money from the chauffeur (but can presumably want to marry him, as in h. w.'s play), it's all too epic to be dramatic. there will be plenty more of this, and you can prove logically how unrealistic naturalist stereotypes or popular, family-page psychology are, or faults in construction etc, but proving what is funny or sublime prose is another matter. in addition it is desirable that h. w. should not be discouraged from getting the play ready for the panel of judges, and in the evening we talked about this and i managed to reassure her to a degree. i put it to her that too much suspense did not seem desirable to me, that you can't laugh readily if your stomach muscles are tense, that puntila's richness and vitality need not be put across in a torrent of words and can just as well be brought out gestically, and that even the finns needn't be bored by hearing 'things they know' described. clever and modest and avid to learn as h. w. is, the point i could not get across was that my scenes' gait and garb corresponded to the gait and garb of puntila himself with all his aimlessness and looseness, his detours and delays, his repetitions and frequent indisposition. she wants to bring on the women from kurgela earlier, immediately after they have been invited, so as to make sure the audience hasn't forgotten them. she fails to see the beauty of having them virtually forgotten, not only by the audience but by puntila too, then having them turn up long after the morning of the invitation. nor of the fact that nobody actually expects any sequel when puntila invites them that fine morning, since the invitation was a formality and the actual coming is the faux pas.

weeklies. these poseurs understand the art of epic theatre, giving banal events a touch of the historic.

Die Achſe formt das neue Europa:

Im Arbeitszimmer des Duce im Palazzo Venezia: Nach mehrſtündigem Geſpräch verabſchiedet ſich Reichsaußenminiſter von Ribbentrop vom Duce. Rechts Italiens Außenminiſter Graf Ciano, hinter dem deutſchen Reichsaußenminiſter der deutſche Botſchafter in Rom von Mackenſen, links Italiens Botſchaiter in Berlin Dino Alſieri.

IN ROM

The German Foreign Minister von Ribbentrop taking leave of Mussolini after some hours of talks in Rome.

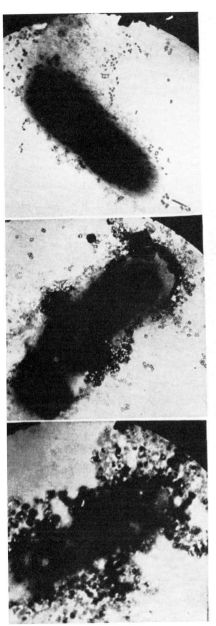

Microphotographs of a bacillus being attacked and destroyed by phagocytes. From the German magazine *Signals*.

10 Oct 40

in SIGNALS (a german propaganda magazine in english) pictures taken with an electric lens.

15 Oct 40

Suffer the old women to come unto me
That they may glimpse, before their graves close o'er them
The man their sons obeyed so faithfully
As long as he had graves still waiting for them.

How cheerfully I eat such simple fare
I who abominate all sensual desire.
Except to rule the world. That's my one care.
Your children's lives – they're all that I require.

16 oct 40

a bookseller here asked me to lecture on theatre to a student theatre, and i suggested the piece ON EXPERIMENTAL THEATRE, which i used a year and a half ago in stockholm. on uttering the title i had the feeling of naming a totally antiquated subject, and not just one that was not topical in wartime. the term 'experimental' now has the same nasty sound it must have had in the era before bacon. the dynamic of events in europe is the running down of the old, the last hectic throes of the obsolete which has nothing of the experimental in its composition. the attempts of a man who has fallen into a swamp to reach firm ground naturally don't count as experiments. to want the new is old-fashioned, what is new is to want the old.

a musician to whom i gave texts from COURAGE, along with some guidelines, for him to set to music composed three pieces, played them to his friends, heard himself copying WEILL and gave up. i tell him in vain that he has only retained the principle, one which weill didn't invent. (i recount to him how i found weill, who was at the time a pupil of busoni and schreker and a composer of atonal, psychological operas, and how i whistled beat by beat for him, and above all recited lines etc.) of course any man who uses a principle for the second and third time has to accept that he will be accused of copying, just like the second and third persons to use the sonnet form. they will also say about me that i was merely repeating myself. people only want things like the THREEPENNY OPERA as a one-off original idea. anyway my works were really never extreme, far less 'modern' than other people's. a few principles were established, and they were always explained and well-founded.

17 oct 40 (see 2 aug 40)

contents of the *first night* of the MESSINGKAUF:

1) the line of experiments in creating better depictions of human interaction runs from english restoration comedy via beaumarchais to lenz. naturalism (the goncourts, zola, chekhov, tolstoy, ibsen, strindberg, hauptmann, shaw) marks the influence of the european labour movement on the stage. comedy turns into tragedy (is this because the point of view is not changed according to class?) more and more inhibiting factors stemming from aristotelian theory emerge. the depictions lack concreteness.

2) the action must contain 'incidents which arouse fear and pity'

(POETICS, IX, 9). the compelling need to conjure up these or similar emotions makes it difficult to depict the incidents in concrete terms. but at least it becomes obvious that to produce these emotions concrete depiction is not *necessary*. all the depictions need is probability. however, the techniques of suggestion and illusion make it impossible for the audience to take a critical attitude to the events depicted. great subjects can only be put on the stage if certain private conflicts can be located at their centre. these ensnare the viewer who is supposed to be being liberated.

3) great theoretical obstacles prevent us from recognising that the concreteness with which life is depicted in aristotelian drama (drama which aims to produce catharsis) is limited by its function (to conjure up certain emotions) and by the technique this requires (suggestion), and that the viewer thus has a stance imposed on him (that of empathy) which prevents his readily adopting a critical attitude to the things depicted, ie prevents him the more effectively the better the art functions.

4) this brings me to a critique of empathy and to the experiments with the a-effect.

17 oct 40

non-aristotelian dramaturgy in principle permits both realistic and idealistic drama. any antagonism between these two approaches is not its concern, since it only affects the interaction of work and audience. to the superficial observer it will not automatically look realistic, since the use of the a-effect is unfamiliar to him and introduces an 'artificial' element into the depiction. the issue is especially obscured by the fact that a superficial observer doesn't know the difference between realism and naturalism. a good example of a non-naturalistic but realistic depiction is LENIN's little prose work ON CLIMBING HIGH MOUNTAINS. realists and idealists alike offer depictions of reality and of thoughts. the idealist however takes an ideal of beauty or art as his point of departure, whereas the realist continually measures ideals against reality and corrects people's conception of it. realism does not merely stand as a contrast to idealism, it implies this struggle. it not only produces depictions of reality, it imposes them against the opposition of idealism. it develops stylistic features as does idealism, it demands convictions in the same way that it does, but at the same time it combats (and it is in this combat that its nature resides) the kind of stylisation in which reality gets lost, as well as convictions that do it violence. it contains an element of relativism. its depictions are relatively realistic, if one can say that, ie if it is understood to mean that it 'drives home' reality.

17 oct 40

greid the actor uses 'objectivise' instead of 'alienate', by which he means performance without feeling. this gives me the chance to correct a possible error. on the one hand the *act of empathy* occurs in conjunction with rational elements, on the other hand the a-effect can be used in a purely emotional way. stanislavsky uses long analyses to achieve empathy, and in the panorama pictures in fairgrounds ('nero watches rome burning', 'the shooting of the anarchist ferrer', 'the lisbon earthquake') the a-effect is pure feeling. in the aristotelian theatre the empathy is also intellectual, and the non-aristotelian theatre employs emotional criticism.

28 oct 40

slight attack of sciatica, unpleasant enough to hinder my working. on such occasions i register just how much good health means to my writing, i write from the top looking down.

    h. w. tells me that paavolainen, whom she thinks very highly of, has declared PUNTILA to be a classic finnish national comedy. he knows of no work where so much is said in such a concentrated fashion about finland. so now i know that the EDDA was written by a jew, and ISAIAH by a babylonian.

1 nov 40

these *concrete depictions* of human events, which the non-aristotelian theatre tries to produce, do not make that theatre purely utilitarian. What is intended is depictions which depict the world not only for the contemplative human being but also for the active human being, ie the world is conceived of as alterable. a moral imperative 'alter it' need not be inherently active in it. it is just that the theatre gets a viewer who produces the world. it must not of course be a matter of handing out a patent solution to the riddle of the world to each member of the audience. only as a member of society is he in a position to take practical action. and the concept *praxis* gets a quite new, powerful meaning. – there is no actual need for the depictions to be 'objective' either.

5 nov 40

snow. and still sciatica.

today america is voting. so an important decision will be made. since the *pact* none has been so important.

in general nobody here seriously believes in a german victory any more, it seems. they are calling dunkirk the marne of 1940. the failure to carry out the invasion is much discussed.

10 nov 40

odd how in discussions about art you find what you are trying to do reported as particularly primitive and retrograde. such as when hagar olsson, the critic, noted as a sign of the backwardness of the public here, that in looking at a picture with a house in it they persist in talking about the house. which is precisely what the most advanced art is trying to achieve afresh.

11 nov 40

i am reading about the life of CONFUCIUS. what an amusing play that would be! at twenty he is rent and tax gatherer for the prince. from his one and only decent job, which resembles goethe's in weimar, he is supplanted by some horses and courtesans acquired by the prince. reminds you of the weimar dog. then he is on the move for 20–30 years looking for a prince who will let him introduce reforms. everywhere he goes they laugh at him. he dies convinced that his life has been a mistake and a failure. – you would have to handle all this in comic terms and interpolate his philosophy quite abruptly, the bits that still seem wise. the scene where he composes the story of lu sticking to the truth would in itself make the play worth the trouble.

MOLOTOV AND RIBBENTROP (NOVEMBER 1940)

Wide W

Molotov, left, now paid a three-day visit to Berlin where he asked for guarantees from the Germans. He is here seen with von Ribbentrop. Hitler thereafter concluded that he would have to attack Russia before any invasion of England, and ordered the Wehrmacht to be ready by mid-May.

15 nov 40

since *non-aristotelian theatre* is usually defined as especially intellectual theatre, which is a bad definition, an attempt should perhaps be made for a change to present it in emotional categories. this is perfectly possible, since in epic theatre the emotional line and the intellectual line remain identical for actor and audience alike. it would be a matter of constructing a range of emotions on the basis of curiosity and helpfulness which would balance the one founded on fear and pity. there are of course other bases for emotions. there is for example human productivity, the most respectable of them all. (even conformity, compliance, patience must be built up on the basis of human productivity.) naturally the individual can only be reached via the masses. yet it is the individual who is subjected to the full tragic force of the horrors of the development of the human race and the classes ('the motor becomes the brake').

16 nov 40

the finnish national theatre is putting on h. w.'s THE YOUNG LANDLADY OF NISKAVOURI. it is the first play in a trilogy about a large farm in tavastland. the trilogy demonstrates how the farm is not there for the people, but the people for the farm; how the property shapes the family and destroys all individual relationships. the newspapers fail to see any of this. reason: the work is written in the naturalist manner, so that all this is only background, it all just happens, it does not come to the fore. the climaxes in the drama don't coincide with the climaxes or pressure points in the subject. (in SHAW the heart of the matter is either a subject of conversation or is dealt with in the preface.)

18 nov 40

gave the lecture on experimental theatre for students (from the local student theatre). nice young people, evidently with no interests, either in studying or in the theatre. shudder at the thought of trying to establish such a thing as non-aristotelian theatre in front of this level of person. my taxi had been announced before one of the girls rustled up the courage to ask a question. was i in favour of theatre with a political bias. i preferred to get into the taxi rather than demonstrate that you can make theatre with or without a political bias in a non-aristotelian way.

the great dramatist here at the moment, and apparently also in sweden, is maxwell anderson.

20 nov 40

again and again you hear in discussions that drama is quite a simple matter, all it needs is a gripping, vivid story, well orchestrated and acted with power and talent, something to make the audience go weak at the knees etc. and you think how remote all this is from being 'natural', how consciously devised and emotionally contrived it is, how it is just another branch of drug-peddling, a standardised product. but the product of an historical phase, complicated and artificial though it may be, always has the surface gleam of a reasonable natural growth, incontrovertible in its own terms. yet inside a contradiction gapes, a disease, something dangerous, no matter how well the product may know that all it is trying to do is combat the danger which threatens the whole. one can only understand the theatre's change of function if it is explained historically.

it was naturalism that confronted the theatre habit with a new social function.

4 dec 40

in the last year steff has spent hours in front of the wireless when it was playing jazz. then i took him along to a german musician who played us a mozart quartet. he liked it and now he goes to a little church every saturday where they play old church music. it was the same with painting. at first he liked whatever was most modern – futurism and surrealism – now he buys folders of dürer and holbein. he is interested in the a-effect too, having got some idea of it leafing through a few pages of the MESSINGKAUF. he has learnt to learn. in the summer he ate lots of greens, although he doesn't like vegetables, and he drank lots of milk since there are times of shortage ahead. now he is toughening himself up, wearing as few clothes as possible. he is extending the areas of his scepticism indefatigably. until recently morality was of great interest to him. i encouraged him to be egotistical, sharpened his distrust of altruistic demands. this took disturbing forms, as one might imagine. i mentioned in the passing that the egotism of the little man is particularly interesting. being not very productive and easily hurt he cannot afford magnanimity and can only maintain his position even in the tiniest things by means of extreme egotism. to support more than one person, namely himself, is beyond him, etc. i can't see the result yet, but his crass utterances have declined. only two years ago he was stealing records from shops and books from libraries like a magpie. i tried to put a stop to it without raising the question of property, by drawing attention to our special circumstances and appealing to his political nous. it was seemingly not without success. his worst fault is a certain vengefulness, he doesn't forget other people's little offences and drops people quickly (and seemingly with glee).

4 dec 40

grete has a high fever; since she has been losing weight for months, great concern. the appendix operation in the spring may have activated the TB. in addition, the saunas in marlebäk were probably a mistake, and now a nasty flu is going round here. added to which, our visas for mexico have arrived and she is not included.

6 dec 40

after the studies in the STREET SCENE other kinds of everyday theatre ought to be described and other examples of theatre in real life identified. in the erotic sphere, in business, in politics, in the law, in religion, etc. we ought to study the theatrical element in customs and traditions. i have already done some work on the application of theatrical techniques to politics in fascism. but in addition to this the kind of everyday theatre that individuals indulge in when no one is watching should be studied, secret 'role-playing'. in this way the 'elementary need for self-expression' in our aesthetics can be sketched in. the STREET SCENE constitutes a big step towards making the art of theatre profane and secular and stripping it of religious elements.

8 dec 40

to object to shakespeare's authorship on the grounds that such an uneducated man could not have written such plays doesn't stand up to scrutiny. how little random knowledge it takes to create an impression of profound learning on the stage. just as an actor, even if he is stupid, can act clever people by simply copying their gests, so the dramatist, if he knows nothing, can display knowledge in his plays. he need not acquire knowledge, he only needs to watch people who have it, and above all, he must not know a single word more than he needs for his lines. what makes me think that a small collective produced shakespeare's plays is not that i believe a single person could not have written these plays because a single person could not have such poetic talent, be versed in so many fields and have such a broad general education. it is just that technically the plays are put together in a way that leads me to believe i recognise the working methods of a collective. the members of the collective need not always have been the same, it may have been a loose arrangement, shakespeare may have been the decisive personality, he may just have had occasional collaborators etc, but the leading ideas can equally well have come from some elevated person who constantly used s[hakespeare] as head of script production. using old plays, the need to build up a repertoire, writing parts for specific actors, the promptbook character of the plays, the parts that are hastily pieced together, the naive love of theatre, the ingenious craftsmanship, the fact that both lyrical and philosophical elements are wholly theatrical and devoid of any independent existence, all this suggests an actor or theatre manager as author.

9 dec 40

the swedish theatre here is interested in putting on MOTHER COURAGE. (?) i took this as an occasion to go through a few scenes with the actor greid. cutting the big scenes up into part-scenes is easy, but greid has not yet been able to come up with a single title. for example scene 2.

G's *suggestion*	B's *suggestion*
MC, selling an item that is already scarce, derives an advantage from the arrival of her son. (2 scenes combined.)	MC profiteering on the sale of foodstuffs in the general's kitchen. (a) c's reunion with her son after a two year separation. she uses his arrival and his fame to force up the price. (b)
eilif reports his heroic deed	she hears how dangerous a soldier's life is for her son. *at the same time* eilif is fêted by the general for his cunning and boldness in robbing some peasants.
MC on bad generals	MC is annoyed at the general because he demands acts of heroism from her son.

etc

somewhat disappointed with this result, i search for methods for devising titles. one could establish a scale for rating degrees of effectiveness and apply it to each scene. poetic, dramaturgical, pertaining to the history of manners, socio-political, psychological (furthering the understanding of man) etc. sentences about these degrees could be devised, which you might find in books on aesthetics, the history of manners, history, psychology. for example the first title in scene 2 can be resolved into the following sentences to categorise the individual degrees of effectiveness.

a) the capon and the praise of its outstanding characteristics are poetic.

b) courage exploits the war for business.

c) the traders pillage their own armies as much as the inhabitants of the hostile country.

d) the interests of the authorities and of the people are not always the same.

e) the art of trading.

10 dec 40

diktonius is financially in a bad way. in small countries the only way to help lyric poets would be by state subsidy. the best thing would be if these were to take the form of state commissions. eg the state could pay for translations of the classics. – commissions of this sort would be part of the promotion of culture in all countries. there would be others too. old plays might be performed without much commentary, new plays without much censorship, if contemporary writers were given the chance to write little plays, comic or tragic, which could be performed after the works in question. no performance of faust without a satire to follow.

11 dec 40

johanson displays great confidence, since he hasn't anything else to show. the romans, who needed the system more than the germanic tribes and who moreover enjoyed it for a decade longer, suffer terrible defeats as a consequence. the last issue of the b[erliner] illustrirte is like a number of *der stürmer*. the germanic tribes seem to have completed a second campaign in poland victoriously. south of lublin there were jewish warehouses which have now been plundered. now we know why there was a shortage of food. however, the battle of lublin shows that the victories continue. and now johanson enters as a big socialist. he has big plans for the workers after the war. mainly cultural, but they will also become affluent. the social barriers are already down, as his own career shows. he has not even studied law and yet he is their leader. he is counting on the workers. even in 14–18 he was struck by the workers. the rich man had every reason to defend his country where he was doing nicely, but what about the poor man? and yet he still defended it. after the defeat j[ohanson] took another look at him, a long cool one. he would certainly do it again, a man like him.

the danube is freezing. the oil-wells of romania are ablaze. america is considering war loans. the balkans are closed. spain signs treaties with USA and britain. france refuses to make peace.

11 dec 40

saw the swedish theatre's HAMLET. what a combination of finesse and crudity! the older play shows through everywhere, yet the clumsy butchery seems doubly clumsy because the intrigues have been cut to make way for philosophical reflections. it is pretty well the crudest plot s. adapted (TITUS ANDRONICUS doesn't count); into this he put his most sensitive hero. his vulnerability constantly leads to wounds. i don't think latter-day interpretations which see the meaning of the play in the presentation of a hesitant intellectual are right – although that may be where his significance lies. hamlet is simply an idealist thrown out of kilter when he collides with the real world, the idealist who turns into a cynic. the question is not: to act or not to act, but to keep silent or not to keep silent, to give approval or not to give approval – nothing is funnier than the serious way our theatres perform shakespeare. he may be theatrical, but he is never ceremonious. our philistines are unable to contemplate naivety and complicity together. s. wrote for a little theatre with a powerful significance, an intimate beer-garden. his greatness is not to be measured with a yardstick. his stage was what we would call surrealistic, without, of course, the shock-effects surrealism goes in for, it is innocent surrealism. (the field-marshal's tents of two opposing armies on *one* stage, simultaneous actions, etc.) HAMLET is a fairy tale even for shakespeare's time, a confused and bloody one, with ghosts, thrusts with poisoned swords, armies on the move etc. the end, though it may be a compromise with kyd's hamlet play, is a piece of amazing boldness from shakespeare's point of view: all that thinking and planning, all the cramped contortions of his conscience finish up uncertainly, fortuitously, in a shambles of intrigue and planlessness. still waiting for corroboration of his suspicions that they are plotting against his life, hamlet dies, with several murders to his own credit. this woeful butchery, devoid of morality, the self-destruction of a clan, only a theatre like the elizabethan could have produced.

the production, being very provincial (ie ceremonious) showed me how much depends on the actor playing the action and not bringing out the exhibitionistic, reflective side of hamlet. this is where most german hamlets fall down.

12 dec 40

H. W. comments on the *new man*, who is constantly being seen or postulated, to the effect that she finds the old man everywhere 'with his perpetual qualities, passions, problems, etc.' i find the postulate itself is a religious one, it is the old new adam. in actual fact the new man is the old man in new situations, ie the particular old man who is best fitted to cope with the new situations, to push the new situations ahead, the new subject of politics. the new modes of acting and reacting constitute the 'new man'; what remains old about him is the very fact that he is human. all postulates about mankind which go beyond the postulates inherent in the situation are to be rejected, such concepts of newness are worthless.

15 dec 40

the golden age of the *tuis* is the liberal republic, but tui-ism is really peaking in the third reich. idealism, having struck rock bottom, is celebrating gigantic triumphs. expressed philosophically (and thus appropriately): consciousness, at the point where it is most utterly enslaved by social existence, has the temerity to attempt to lay down the law to it in the most magisterial fashion. the 'idea' is no more than a reflex, and this reflex appears in the most commanding and terroristic form when confronted by reality.

one small aspect: the quarrel between the democratic tuis and the authoritarian tuis; the former have consecrated the treaties which were imposed through economic pressure and then nullified by means of economic tricks. the latter employ military means. in democratic countries the violent nature of the economy is not exposed (ie is concealed), in authoritarian countries it is the economic character of the violence that is not exposed.

18 dec 40

in assembling the scene titles for COURAGE everything psychological is completely ignored, even the plot is scarcely considered (the niobe-theme). also, it goes without saying, the period features.

19 dec 40

the history of the modern theatre begins with naturalism. this is where the first determined moves towards a new social function were made. the attempt to master reality begins with passive dramatists and passive heroes. the establishment of social causality starts with descriptions of situations in which all human actions are purely reactions. causality is predetermination. typical is the explosion play. clouds have gathered over the heads of certain people, families, groups, then the storm breaks. social milieu has the quality of a fetish, is fate. they only ever play the last act of anything. the new drama begins with the undramatic. two slogans: crudeness (verism) and minimal action. the tragic element is doggedly sustained, though a few trifling reforms could bring relief at any moment. everything decisive happens between the lines, backstage, beneath the dialogue. the active element forces its way in as leading article (speech chorus, song). the agitprop theatre of the proletariat stands in radical opposition; in it reality is only used as illustration.

20 dec 40

clear that the theatre of alienation is a theatre of dialectics. yet until now i have seen no possibility of using the conceptual material of dialectics to explain this theatre: it would be easier for theatre people to understand dialectics by approaching it through the theatre of alienation than the theatre of alienation by way of dialectics. on the other hand it will probably be well nigh impossible to demand that reality be presented in such a way that it can be mastered, without pointing to the contradictory, ongoing character of conditions, events, figures, for unless you recognise the dialectical nature of reality it cannot be mastered. the a-effect makes it possible to enact this dialectical nature, that is what it is for; it's what explains it. even when deciding on the titles that determine the blocking, it is not enough to demand eg merely a social quality; the titles must also contain a critical quality and announce a contradiction. they must be fully adaptable, so the dialectic (contradictoriness, the element of process) must be able to become concrete. the mysteries of the world are not solved, they are demonstrated.

as for the effect: emotions will be contradictory, will merge into one another etc. in every respect the viewer becomes a dialectician. the jump is constantly being made from the particular to the general, from the individual to the typical, from now to yesterday and tomorrow, the unity of the incongruous, the discontinuity of the ongoing process. here a-effects prove effective.

25 dec 40

i thought of writing a play for children to act, and THE LIFE OF CONFUCIUS seems most suitable. it must be about a significant character, as well as one that can stand humorous presentation. all things considered the play need not exactly be designed for an audience of children, but it could be written for one. i have a powerful antipathy to adapting anything to a particular level of understanding. experience repeatedly shows (i am thinking eg of the production of MAN EQUALS MAN by pupils of the neukölln grammar school) that children are pretty good at understanding anything halfway worth understanding, just like adults. and the things that are worthwhile for them are the same. the inner processes of the soul, nuances of atmosphere, tragedies, and the like they don't want to bother about. a biography of confucius would be about something else. you can incidentally, under certain social circumstances, imagine professional child actors. the training for actors should anyway begin much earlier than it does in germany. linking general schooling with work is disastrous only under the present circumstances.

it would certainly not be bad to entrust the acting of the sage to the children. on the other hand precisely this figure, with its big, floppy ears, projecting teeth, boil and bulbous nose offers children great theatrical scope. for rehearsals you could write control-scenes which would project the content of the real scenes into the world of the children themselves.

2 jan 41

leafed once more through a few works on the *world-picture of modern physics* which steff brought home. with a certain shock i see that the new positivism is moving towards a staunch belief in the soul, for if our bodies are thought to be so inextricably bound up with other matter, then the point where all the messages of the senses are received is none other than our old friend, the soul. it is not the case that the external world is denied as some of us believe; it is just that the border between the external world and the 'inner world' collapses, and that our bodies are now transformed into external world too. making material mathematical simply balances material out of existence – in the eyes of those good people for whom a formula means dematerialisation instead of abstraction. light cannot be a particle and a wave at the same time, they say, when they see that it is particle and wave at the same time. it never occurs to them to revise their logic, and they demand the abandonment of logic. the monopolies expand, the individual dematerialises himself. the police find out that observation interferes with the order of things, and must therefore be wrong. it introduces the concept of non-focus into the field of dishonour.

3 jan 41

in the summer H[ELLA] W[UOLIJOKI] told us of estonian war-songs transcribed from the people. she put together a selection as a student. the estonian people does not have a single song expressing enthusiasm for war. she read some, half singing them in the estonian manner. i encouraged her to translate the whole thing. she has dictated it to grete – and, when grete was advised not to write, to me – with an astonishing understanding of german; i have to do very little to turn it into a great poem.

(remarkable contradictory double lines like: my golden home/my silver home/or: barked the grey watchdog/growled the red watchdog. here a dialectical factor strikes you. via a certain breadth and vagueness you arrive at greater tangibility. the singer does not commit himself, just sets imagination and memory going, uses the watchdog at every listener's gate, in mighty epic 'breadth', but at the same time makes a tangible impression on primitive listeners, so that by approaching the object from several sides, by fixing it in a variety of occurrences, a certain congruence is achieved. and there are also a-effects here. at least one could describe these lines in such terms, as long as there is no exact research to hand.)

3 jan 41

ruth stages a little sketch with the children. a small boy gets a uniform for christmas, yet there is no chocolate, no cake, no sugar, no fruit etc. he falls asleep and dreams that these things appear to him and tell him that the war prevents them from appearing to him, except in a dream. the uniform steps out of the wardrobe and tries to order them about, but they will not be ordered. they offer the boy (and the audience) the choice: them or the uniform, since you can't have both at the same time. at the end the child actors sing a song which puts the same choice to the audience. – interesting a-effects. the impersonal delivery of the lines and the gestures (no controlled facial expressions to be seen) the way they stand at ease when it is not their turn. the way they press on regardless. – much desire to do the confucius.

5 jan 41

going over MOTHER COURAGE i am quite pleased to see how war emerges as a vast field akin to the fields of modern physics, in which bodies experience peculiar deviations from their courses. any calculation about the individual based on peacetime experience proves to be unreliable. bravery is no help, nor is caution, nor honesty, nor crookedness, nor brutality nor pity: all are equally fatal. we are left with those same forces that turn peace into war, the ones that can't be named.

8 jan 41

books on steff's table:
den stora engelska revolutionen STAVENOV
changing governments and changing cultures RUGG
from new york to shanghai F. WOLF
atomer og andre småting CH. MØLLER
the origin of the family F. ENGELS
new york is not america F. M. FORD
again the three just men EDGAR WALLACE
nachbarsleute L. THOMA
tampico HERGESHEIMER
magazine NU
the great tradition GRANVILLE HICKS
the life of the gallant ladies BRANTÔME
den moderna fysiken BENNER
från atom till universum KARLSON
om kärnfysiken och dess utveckling TALLQUIST
san luis bro THORNTON WILDER
morkt skratt SHERWOOD ANDERSON
elva årtionden ur finlands historia ESTLANDER
discography 1938 CH DELAUNAY
poems DR J. SWIFT
book of snobs THACKERAY
candide VOLTAIRE
hauspostille BRECHT
miscellaneous contributions to punch THACKERAY

drawings by GRÜNEWALD
atlas of the world
circle (international survey of constructive art)
othello, macbeth, king henry VIII SHAKESPEARE
lady chatterley's lover LAWRENCE
an introduction to problems of american culture H. RUGG
communism, a new civilization? WEBBS
on the wall 7 VAN GOGH drawings, a RENOIR, a MANET, chinese portrait of
   an actor, altarpieces by freiburg masters about 1500.

10 jan 41

the reason why poets like gelsted fail so badly in dealing with politics: to
them, exploitation and the class struggle are not poetic but moral
categories. they have long viewed such things as natural, even if
unaesthetic. now they see them as unnatural, and the unnatural is not a
field for the aesthetic. in poetry morality resides not in indignation, but
in truthfulness. in addition to which these poets like to entrust the
worker with a lofty mission. this fills him with justified suspicion, since
he has no desire to serve as cannon-fodder on ethical missions. his goal is
not morality even if it is moral. he need promise no one anything except
himself.

   these writers are against capitalism because it is not harmless like them.
to the workers they seem cantankerous little souls.

11 jan 41

concerning the role of *empathy* in non-aristotelian theatre: empathy here
is a *rehearsal* measure, it is preceded by the preparation of the role (the
actor sorts out all the speeches, tasks, reactions, so that he feels easy in
them, though at this stage he does not create a particular character, even if
he does fill in one or two general characteristics). now, basically a jump at
a time, comes the creation of the character (here he draws on experience,
copies certain persons, combines features of different persons etc). the
preparation of the role may be concluded by the actor's empathising, in
the first instance with the situations (how he himself would behave in
such a situation). in creating the character he can aim at further empathy,
this time with the person he wants to play, or copy. however this
empathy too is just a stage, a measure which is intended to help him to
grasp a type more fully. it is important here that whatever empathy is
achieved should incorporate no element of suggestion, ie, the audience is

not to be induced to empathise too. this is difficult, but possible. for an actor in the present theatre empathising himself and inducing the audience to empathise (suggestive empathy) are of course identical. he finds it hard to imagine the one without the other or put the one into practice without the other. in reality the two measures occur separately, and combining them is an art in itself. not *the* art. today's actor cannot imagine effects being achieved without empathy, nor effects without suggestion. empathy without suggestion is also practised today, in comedy. it takes an artist to be effective without suggestion.

12 jan 41

in none of these considerations must it be forgotten that *non-aristotelian theatre* is for the moment only one form of theatre; it serves only certain social purposes and has no usurpatory aspirations in regard to theatre in general. i myself can employ non-aristotelian theatre alongside aristotelian in certain productions. in staging say ST JOAN OF THE STOCKYARDS today it may be advantageous to induce (permit, from today's point of view) empathy with joan occasionally, since this character goes through a process of understanding, so that the empathising viewer can survey the main parts of the events from this standpoint. however there will today always be those in the audience who prefer to view this figure from the outside. they are better served by non-aristotelian theatre.

14 jan 41

on *non-aristotelian theatre*: for certain phases of rehearsal it seems desirable that the actor should empathise with the person presented in the play, but not on a suggestive basis, ie not so that the eventual audience would be forced to participate in this empathy. the question whether empathy can be employed without at the same time suggesting that the viewer empathise too is at first answered in the negative by greid and weigel. i point to comedians who – during the performance – empathise with petty bourgeois right-wing extremists and thereby get laughs from the audience. question is, can the preventive techniques used in comedy to avoid audience empathy also be employed by tragic actors. but suggestive acting is something quite artificial. tension in certain parts of the muscular system, head movements executed as if pulling on an elastic band, the feet as if wading in tar, intermittent stiffness, sudden changes, moments of restraint, also monotony of voice, remembered from church responses, all this induces hypnosis, and it can be said that snakes, tigers,

even the support you give to the actor can employ other arguments.
emancipate your orchestra!'

4 feb 41

steff has been working for weeks on a 40-page school essay on the english
revolution in the 17th century. he is trying to analyse the class struggles
on the basis of very bad school books. (the best is by buckle, his cultural
history). he has read a little kautsky and CAESAR. in a postscript he is
conducting an argument with his headmaster by combining a materialist
view of history with a bit of positivism (from books on physics), in order
to combat the metaphysical needs of the pedagogues. all history is a mere
construction, and whether reality bears any relation to it is highly
uncertain, the old tradition being that, in so far as the construction is
logically sound and uses facts, it is true. steff is using the materialistic
method, because it is practical (and elegant), contains certain pointers for
the present time and can be expressed in a graphic contemporary
vocabulary. the single individual follows very imprecisely – so long as it
is expressed as a statistical curve – the movement of the mass of which he
forms part. it occurs to steff that he can therefore treat the king as a mass
(inasmuch as he is dealing with classes, engaged in struggle etc). this does
not disturb him, since the construction which this calls for has its useful
aspects. he is forced to realise that the dialectical method always deals in
masses, always resolves everything into masses, treats the individual as a
part of the masses, even if it does go so far as to convert that part in its
turn into a mass. however he has no difficulty in seeing certain epochs as
units where the various levels of the superstructure have a special
relationship to one another, have quite special significance etc. (religion
in the 17th century was not quite the opium for the people it is in the
20th.) naturally his presentation, excellent as it is, does not make the
grade, since it omits the king in question, charles etc, ie at this point in the
field any king would have done. hence his presentation is colourless,
tasteless and odourless, just like any mechanical model. it will be plain
sailing for the pedagogue to put it down as dead, grey, inhuman.

14 feb 41

a shot at listing his plays, for brecht's birthday 1941, by margarete steffin

I

for weeks i have been swimming on the fever ship. it rocks horribly up and down, i feel so ill, so ill. i want to reach the shore of health, but the ship never docks. i jump into the dark water, they bring me back with nets, with fish-hooks. anxiously i ask if there is any hope of rescue. yes, say the warders, if i can answer a question truthfully. what question? to whom? quick, quick! what question?

come, say the warders, and they lead me into the belly of the ship.

2

mistily i see people waiting on long benches, many people, men and women. i ask a warder: who are these? actors! he says, with a mixture of respect and contempt. and what do they want from me? *their part.*

their greedy eyes devour me. their voices are hoarse with excitement. tell us which is *the* part. then you can go.

3

aha! i breathe again, and the fever loosens its grip on my throat. almost cheerfully i ask: for a man or a woman?

for a woman! yell the women.

for a man! yell the men.

fine, there are enough parts in his plays for you all, i say to comfort them, much as one tosses something to a wolf when he's just about to leap at the sleigh-driver.

and i've no time to think, right away i must start suggesting parts, so i name poor edward and the still poorer queen anne, garga whom i never understood (i supposed he *is* a part?), galy gay, the simple porter from the docks, with his tender soul, who turns into a human fighting-machine on account of a cucumber which he lacked the courage to buy from the whitewashed babylon leokadia begbick. kragler, anna!. . . .

a harsh voice interrupts: ha! so you're not telling us about paul ackermann, or jenny, or the other begbick (who's a leokadia too, is she the same one?)

peachum! i shout, to silence him – i know i'm on firm ground here. mrs peachum! polly!

concealed behind a 'situation'. the *step-by-step*, the *more-and-more*, the *jump*, in short the nature of the process can be followed. innumerable events which passionately interest and move both dramatist and public, have no place in the old theatre. even an examination of the representation of the *error* (as made by the hero) would show the inadequacy of the old type of so-called dramatic principles.

7 mar 41

the great error which prevented my making the little *lehrstück* of BAD BAAL THE ASOCIAL MAN resided in my definition of socialism as a *great order*. it is however much more practical to define it as *great production*. production must of course be taken in the broadest sense, and the aim of the struggle is to free the productivity of all men from all fetters. the products in question can be bread, lamps, hats, pieces of music, chess moves, irrigation, complexion, character, games etc etc.

8 mar 41

on reading DIDEROT'S JACQUES LE FATALISTE: remarkable how we show no signs of a refined sensuality in germany. love there (viz. faust) is something heavenly or something diabolical, a dilemma we escaped from by turning it into a habit. the only names in the field are goethe and mozart, and the latter wisely set his love-dramas on foreign soil. in the lyric there is nothing between the ethereal, hysterical and incorporeal, and dirty barmaid's songs. keller has certain merits, heinrich mann describes only excesses. in the middle ages this is another area of culture which only the clergy seems to have kept up. the german aristocracy was incapable of hedonism, then the bourgeoisie was puritanical in its ideals, and swinish in reality. german students 'did it' after consuming beer in amounts that would have left anybody else incapable of anything but vomiting, whereas they copulated. – it would be hygienic for the germans to get their first love comedy (their mandragola) in the shape say of a LUTHER-AND-KÄTTER drama . . .

10 mar 41

thinking of the american theatre, again struck by the idea i once had in new york, of writing a gangster play, that would recall certain events familiar to us all. (*the gangster play we know.**) i quickly sketch a plan for 11–12 scenes. it must naturally be written in the grand style.

28 mar 41

amidst all the trouble about visas and our chances of making the journey i am working doggedly at the new *gangster-history*. only the last scene is still missing. the effect of the double alienation – gangster milieu plus high style – is hard to predict. as is the effect of guying classical forms, like the scene in martha schwertlein's garden and the wooing scene from richard the third.

steff's knowledge of the ties between the gangster world and the administration are a big help to me.

1 apr 41

in UI the problem was on the one hand to let the historical events show through, and on the other to give the 'masking' (which is an unmasking) some life of its own, ie it must – theoretically speaking – also work independently of its topical references. among other things, too close a coupling of the two plots (gangster plot and nazi plot) – that is, a form in which the gangster plot is a symbolic version of the other plot – would be unbearable, not least because people would constantly be looking for the 'meaning' of this or that move, and would always be looking for the real-life model for every figure. this was particularly difficult.

2 apr 41

after it is finished i have my work cut out to smoothe the iambics in the RESISTIBLE RISE OF ARTURO UI. my treatment of the iambus had been very slack, partly on the ground that the play would only be performed in english anyway, partly on the ground that sloppy verse was appropriate for these personalities. grete calculated that in every 100 lines there were 45 that were flawed. and she thought my two reasons were just excuses. bad iambics would rub off on the translator and seediness can be expressed in ways other than bad iambics. the jazzed up, syncopated iambics i often use (five feet, but tap-dancing) is something quite different and has nothing to do with seediness – it is difficult to put together and is of course highly artistic. but what she mainly meant was that the a-effect would be impaired if the iambics were not smooth. i wonder whether i have managed to give the epic treatment pace – it must not be thought that it has by definition to be leisurely. in principle it is possible to use both slow motion and high speed in the epic mode. and movement, open conflict, the clash of antagonists is naturally just as possible in the epic as in the 'dramatic'. i hope the play shows this.

3 apr 41

a simple presentation of the theory of non-aristotelian drama should always start from the need to deal better (more practicably) with the subjects that affect our times than was possible in the old manner. 'all' that had to be eliminated from naturalism was the element of fate. this step made the whole huge reorganisation necessary. here is the poor dumb peasant. poverty and stupidity treated not as a fact of life but as things which are interdependent and can be eliminated – then we have non-aristotelian drama. the prevalent theatre turned an audience of engineers and revolutionaries into a theatre-going public (of aesthetes, passive hedonists). the new one will turn the theatre-going public (active hedonists) into engineers and revolutionaries.

7 apr 41

grete tortures me with scorpions because of the iambics in UI. for a whole week i have been sitting over them, and she still won't offer any assurances to put my mind at ease. wedekind, she tells me incidentally, could get his meaning into *one* line. the slick (!) iambus is a retrograde step, compared with the syncopated one i usually use. but here it is right, i think.

these are good exercises. yesterday the war between germany and serbia and germany and greece began.

7 apr 41

perhaps one is committing a primitive error if one takes the outcome of a war to be identical with the victory of one of the partners. the shooting at hornberg can be repeated in its totality and in a modernised version. long phases of semi-war can occur. partial pacifications. a degree of exhaustion, which results in the war moving straight into anarchy. the struggles of the monopoly capitalists can become so involved that they leave no way back to the 'peaceful' (unmilitary, economic) forms of the preceding epoch. this would occur if the classical transformation of such wars were *not* to happen, or happened to an inadequate degree.

8 apr 41

remarkable how the tragedy of the small businessman in the face of the trusts is repeated in the tragedy of the small nations. peoples half as big as the population of berlin follow policies which are based on the equal rights of all nations.

people here think the invasion of england has now been superseded by the balkan war. for which – consequently – nobody has an explanation. probably it is the preparation for an invasion. this two-stroke system of attack, with the emphasis on the second stroke, is something we know from last year (norway-france). italy foundered in her task of tying down the english fleet in the mediterranean and thus exposing the atlantic, with japan perhaps also holding america in check. now the germans will have to do it all themselves.

9 apr 41

the world is holding its breath again. the german army is rolling towards salonika just as fast as its vehicles can go. people had imagined a struggle lasting months and it took days. they expected wavell's english army to be there and it wasn't. it was as if there were only one army that could move. it is the only one that is working and it is in command of the battle-cube that has superseded the battlefield. the old armies compete like distaffs against the spinning jenny. valour loses out to good driving, indefatigability to punctuality, stamina to diligence. strategy has turned into surgery. an enemy country is 'opened up' after it has been anaesthetised, then it is swabbed down, disinfected, sewn up etc. all with the greatest of ease.

12 apr 41

apart from the fact that blank verse marries very unhappily with the german language – see the abominations in TASSO – it also has for me something inherently anachronistic, its fatal feudalism. take away the compartmented, involved, formal elements of courtly, official expression and it immediately becomes empty and 'ordinary', an upstart. yet, although the main effect when i make the gangsters and cauliflower dealers act in iambics is travesty, since all that comes across is the inadequacy of their efforts to appear important. what you get, when the blank verse is maltreated, mutilated, stretched and ruined, is new formal material for a modern verse with irregular rhythms which opens up all sorts of possibilities.

12 apr 41

remarkable how the manuscript becomes a fetish, even as you work at it! i am utterly at the mercy of my manuscripts which i constantly paste up and keep up to aesthetic scratch. i constantly catch myself trying to make do with a quite definite number of lines for an alteration, just so that there will be enough room on the page.

12 apr 41

i wrote UI with the possibility of production constantly in my mind's eye; this was a large part of the fun. but now i feel a desire to follow it up with something that would be absolutely and totally impossible anywhere. UI, PART TWO. spain/munich/poland/france.

13 apr 41

there are austrians living above us, a *schutzbündler* and his wife. they are appalled at the rapid fall of salonika. that is where their armies are being beaten, they think.

it is clear that a victory for hitler would open an age of the iron heel. the only question is: does the bourgeoisie have the strength to give the phase of monopoly capitalism its full political expression too? one thing is already clear: that this phase will lead to far-reaching upheavals – the liquidation of small nations, the closure of the free labour market, the suspension of formal democracy, controls on production (without removal of profits) etc – but, naturally, it could be very short. but will it be? from a purely historical standpoint there is still a *fight** to come. there are still resources available. the new forms of organisation and the new weapon are the mark of a new epoch. a victory of one system over the other is possible, and this could usher it in. the mutual desire to annihilate the other that animates both systems contains within it a desire to conserve the system of which both systems are part. – this cripples the other system. and that too makes a 'new' epoch possible, for it inhibits destruction from going too far.

14 apr 41

intellectuals like the critic and novelist hagar olsson are now sinking rapidly back into mysticism and pessimism. their attitude to hitler is characteristically sterile. he is not the high road to c[apitalism] but a byway. he is an anomaly in c[apitalism], it is not c[apitalism] that is an anomaly. he picked a fight at a frontier and started the war, as though there would be frontiers to fight over if there were no property! if i say with relish he is the finest blossom c[apitalism] has produced, the 'last word', the revised, improved edition, which has everything in it, and new material to boot, people look at me as if i were a sad victim of his propaganda.

14 apr 41

spring, a time of dirt and births. the prospect of leaving behind sciatica, bedbugs and nationalism. – subject for a tragedy: setting up a 'sociological experiment' in which a human being lets himself be annihilated to show the apparatus of destruction in action. a teacher, surrounded by his pupils?

15 apr 41

vala tells us about a poem that a young finnish poet has written in recent days. high in the mountains the last troops are fighting. with their backs to the wall they send out a messenger-dog with a request for reinforcements. they do not tell him where to go. there must be aid somewhere, we don't know where, they say. the end of the poem: you must not die, you hound, for with you die all our hopes. – this is the mood of many people here, especially, of course, of many intellectuals who are terrified of the german panzers.

16 apr 41

reading maurois's TRAGEDY IN FRANCE i recall the plan for a play STREET OF THE MINISTRIES (DIE STRASSE DER MINISTERIEN). a blind man sees what is bound to happen. the blind beggar jean savour has his stance on ministry street. from little things he picks up, and information from the doorman at the foreign office, he realises there is going to be a war, and that that war will be lost, and he knows how. he manages to promote his friends' little enterprises.

16 apr 41

in N[EW] M[ASSES] i read a review of GORELIK's theatre book by
H.LAWSON. gorelik, with his theorising, makes the mistake of putting too
much functionalism into epic theatre. what emerges is something
technocratic, and the individual human shrinks to an individual case in a
collective. the great expropriation by late capitalism is presented (or
pilloried) as the ideal of communism. this makes him easy to brush off,
and they attack him with 'full, pulsing life in contrast to symbols and
formulae', when actually all they are offering are illusions. but he sails
manfully into the theatre of illusion, and would make headway, but for
the fact that the only institution he knows which dispenses with illusion
is science.

18 apr 41

it is now, i notice, becoming almost impossible for me to avoid wishful
thinking, ie to practise unblinking analysis of the facts. i keep finding
myself thinking: i'll work that out in the USA.

 i have a desire to write a CASSANDRA. she naturally does not have
second sight, she just uses her normal vision. and her black prognoses
have a practical aim, to stir people up. that dispenses with morbidity and
mysticism at the same time. what is left is the tragic fate of those who
bring bad news. she senses what is to come when she sees how little her
world is prepared for defence; she knows how people will change under
the conditions that are coming, even those close to her. she runs from the
princes to the priests, from the merchants to the fishermen. her mother
exhorts her to be silent. she tries, in vain. she awaits her trial as a defeatist,
separated from her children. she addresses her judges as men doomed to
death. another scene: the expulsion of the pessimists and nitpickers.

20 apr 41

numerous copies of THE GOOD PERSON OF SZECHWAN were sent
months ago to friends (in switzerland, in america, in sweden) and not a
single letter about it has come back. the bayonets of the victors of 1870
may have led 'das kapital' to victory in europe, but the tanks of the
victors of 1940 have buried the GOOD PERSON OF SZECHWAN beneath
them.

 with every report of hitler's victories my significance as a writer diminishes. even olsoni, the bookseller and critic in helsingfors, cannot find the time to read my play. and less and less visitors come. (yet here they find neither desperation nor optimism . . .)

21 apr 41

that these jottings contain so little that is personal comes not only from the fact that i myself am not very interested in personal matters (and don't really have at my disposal a satisfactory mode of presenting them), but mainly from the fact that from the beginning i anticipated having to take them across frontiers whose number and quality it was impossible to predict. this last thought prevents me from choosing any other than literary topics.

21 apr 41

the crisis in the drama is very deep. it is a matter of creating rich, complex, developing figures – without introspective psychology. the normal behaviouristic images are very flat and blurred (if they do not have the clarity of scheme f). even when they include not only biological but also social reflexes, concrete figures seldom emerge. in the same way as c[apitalism] brings about the collectivisation of man through deprivation and dis-individualisation, and as at first a kind of 'common ownership of nothing' is brought into being by c[apitalism], so behaviourist psychology in the first instance reflects only society's indifference to the individual, since the individual is a mere object. on the other hand the destruction, fragmentation, atomisation of the individual psyche is a fact, ie if one identifies this peculiar lack of a centre in individuals, it is not a result of faulty habits of observation. it is just that one is facing new configurations which have to be mapped out afresh. even dissolution does not result in nothing. in addition to which the frontiers of the individual psyche are still clearly visible. even the new configuration reacts *and acts* individually, uniquely, 'unschematically'.

22 apr 41

on the 19th MOTHER COURAGE was performed at the zurich schauspielhaus. today a telegram came from the management and one from giehse, lindtberg and otto saying that the première had been a success. it is courageous of this theatre which is mainly composed of refugees to put on something of mine. no scandinavian stage had the guts to do it.

227. VORSTELLUNG DER SPIELZEIT 1940/41

Freitag, den 25. April, 20 Uhr

Mutter Courage und ihre Kinder

Schauspiel in 11 Bildern von Bertolt Brecht

Regie: Leopold Lindtberg

Bühnenbild: Teo Otto

Musikalische Leitung: Paul Burkhard

Anna Fierling, genannt Mutter Courage	Therese Giehse
Die stumme Kattrin, ihre Tochter . .	Erika Pesch
Eilif, ihr Sohn	Wolfgang Langhoff
Schweizerköbi, ihr zweiter Sohn . .	Karl Paryla
Der Koch	Wolfgang Heinz
Der Feldprediger	Sigfrit Steiner
Yvette Pottier	Angelika Arndts
Ein Feldhauptmann	Hermann Wlach
Ein Werber	Fritz Delius
Ein Feldwebel	Kurt Horwitz
Junger Soldat	Emil Stöhr
Älterer Soldat	Friedrich Braun
Obrist	Willi Stettner
Kaiserlicher Feldwebel	Kurt Brunner
Junger Bauer	Kurt Brunner
Alter Bauer	Friedrich Braun
Alte Bäuerin	Traute Carlsen
Fähnrich	Ernst Ginsberg
Schreiber	Eugen Jensen
Soldaten	Enzo Ertini / John E. Schmid / Hans Wlasak
Junger Mann	Erwin Parker
Alter Mann	Carl Delmont

Technische Leitung: Ferdinand Lange

Die nächsten Vorstellungen

Samstag:	20 Uhr
Der Lügner und die Nonne	
Sonntag:	15 Uhr
Sonntag:	20 Uhr
Montag:	20 Uhr
Dienstag:	20 Uhr
Louis Jouvet «Knock» ou «Le Triomphe de la Médecine»	

Anfang 20 Uhr   Ende ca. 22.45 Uhr
Große Pause nach dem 6. Bild

Programme for the Zurich Schauspielhaus production of *Mother Courage*, which opened on 19 April (world première).

22 apr 41

why is COURAGE a realistic work?
it adopts a realist point of view on behalf of the people vis-à-vis all ideologies: to the people war is neither an uprising nor a business operation, merely a disaster.

its point of view is not a moral one: that is to say, it is ethical, but without being derived from the currently prevailing morality.

the actions of the characters are given motives that can be recognised and allowed for and will facilitate dealing with real people.

the work functions in terms of the present state of consciousness of the majority of mankind.

23 apr 41

figure of comedy: the man who, in view of the badness of the world, is of a mind to be a villain, but can't. after every good deed he is weak enough to perpetrate, he swears he will be tough, but at the next temptation he yields again. he only does good behind his own back. title: THE WEAKNESS OF THE FLESH (DAS SCHWACHE FLEISCH). meaning: how much easier it is to do good than to do bad, to be productive than to be destructive.

(he has an enemy he should hate, but pities, who exploits him and whom he seeks to imitate.)

24 apr 41

when i look at my new plays and compare them – GALILEO, MOTHER COURAGE, FEAR AND MISERY, THE GOOD PERSON OF SZECHWAN, MR PUNTILA AND HIS MAN MATTI, RISE OF UI – i find them abnormally disunified in every way. even the genres change constantly. biography, gestarium, parable, character comedy in the folk vein, historical farce – the plays tend to fly apart like constellations in the new physics, as though here too some kind of dramaturgical core had exploded. and yet the theory which they are based on or which can be derived from them is for its part very definite, in comparison to other theories. one ought perhaps not to forget that different works by an author melt together with time; how else could ROBBERS, BRIDE OF MESSINA, TELL, or IPHIGENIA, FAUST, CLAVIGO find themselves in one basket?

24 apr 41

to equip works to stand the test of time, on the face of it a 'natural' aim, becomes a more serious matter when the writer has grounds for the pessimistic assumption that his ideas (ie the ideas he advocates) may find acceptance only in the long term. the measures, incidentally, that one employs to this end must not detract from the topical effect of the work.

the necessary epic touches applied to things which are 'self-evident' at the time of writing lose their value as a-effects after that time. the conceptual autarchy of the works contains an element of criticism: the writer is analysing the transience of the concepts and observations of his own times.

25 apr 41

my two means of production, cigars and (english) detective novels, are running out and have to be rationed.

29 apr 41

what are the most necessary festivities? *victory day*, the *present-giving night*, the *day of solidarity*, the *day of world struggle, carnival*. carnival would be of great importance. day of disguises and mockery. day of penitence for the most cherished traditions and the most elevated persons.

Heute abend Wiederholung des Schauspiels «Die Mutter»

Die schweizerische Erstaufführung des Schau-spiels ‹Die Mutter› war ein so großer Erfolg, daß das Stück bereits heute Samstag um 20 Uhr im Theatersaal des Volkshauses wieder-holt werden muß. Es sind nur Billette an der Abendkasse, die um 18.30 Uhr geöffnet wird, erhält-ch. Inszenierung und Regie, Darstellung und Ge-innung des Kampfstückes sind durchgehend wirk-um. Niemand, vor allem keine Arbeitermutter, soll ch abhalten lassen, die heutige Aufführung mitzu-rleben.

Unsere Photographie zeigt eine Szene aus dem chsten Bild (Stube des Lehrers Wessowtschikow):

Maria Ostfelden als Mutter Pelagea Wlassowa, Fred Tanner als junger Arbeiter Iwan Wessow-tschikow und Sigfrit Steiner in der Rolle des Lehrers Wessowtschikow, der sich den Arbeitern und Bauern anschließt und ihnen Unterricht erteilt. Bühnenbi'd: Robert Furrer. Vor dem Bühnenspiel, ab 19.30 Uhr, konzertiert, unter der Leitung von Heinz Hindermann, wiederum das flott spie-lende Arbejterorchester der Stadt Zü-rich, wodurch eine schöne Stimmung erzielt wird.

Wir erwarten auch heute abend einen vollen Saal. **Der Bildungsausschuß SP. Zürich.**

«Die Mutter»

Xantippe ohne Sokrates

Aus dem Zürcher Obergericht

K. Wie so das 70jährige, zusammengeschrumpfte Männlein mit dem hilflosen Kinderblick vor den Richtern stand, fielen einem die Worte Therese Ghieses in „Mutter Courage" ein: „ S c h w e i z e r k ä s e , S c h w e i z e r k ä s e , i c h h a b e d i c h s c h o n i m m e r g e l e h r t , d u s o l l s t e h r l i c h s e i n , d e n n k l u g b i s t d u n i c h t".

Während eines ganzen Menschenlebens war auch das Männlein ehrlich. Sein Verteidiger traf wahrscheinlich ins Schwarze, wenn er behauptete, sein Horizont sei von den Dämpfen begrenzt, die aus seinen Kochtöpfen aufstiegen, und sein Geist sei nicht tiefer, als eine Pfütze auf dem Asphalt. Jedenfalls war dieser Chef de cuisine in Kleinformat glücklich, solange er an seinem Herd hantieren durfte, und stellte sonst keinerlei Ansprüche ans Leben. Und das war gut, denn andernfalls wäre er sich sehr bemitleidenswert vorgekommen, weil er eine Xanthippe zur Frau hat, über die bereits Sokrates alles Wissenswerte gesagt hat.

Als er keine Arbeit mehr fand, da begann das Elend für dieses greise Kind! Denn er hatte kein Geld, seine Frau besaß hingegen einen netten Sparbatzen, und er bekam nun Tag für Tag zu hören, welch unnützer Geselle er sei. Mit ihrem ewigen Gejammer machte die Gattin dem kleinen Mann ganz „tuch", und um ihr und sich selbst zu beweisen, daß er doch noch zu etwas gut ist, log er kühn während drei Jahren die Krisen- und Winterhilfe an und gab dort an, er und seine Frau besäßen keinerlei Vermögen.

Der Angeklagte ist jetzt geständig, sich des wiederholten ausgezeichneten Betruges im Betrage von 1900 Franken schuldig gemacht zu haben, wie es in der Juristensprache heißt. Es ist zwar fraglich, ob er auch wirklich versteht, warum sich die Herren vom Gericht so eingehend mit ihm beschäftigen. Jedenfalls ist es unmöglich, dem Männlein verständlich zu machen, daß er zwar zu acht Monaten Arbeitshaus verurteilt wurde, aber, daß die Strafe ihm bedingt erlassen ist. Schließlich begreift er aber, daß er heimgehen darf und gibt allen im Gerichtsgebäude , die sich in seiner Reichweite befinden, freundlich die Hand, wie ein braves Kind, das nicht zu hart bestraft wurde.

estrige schweizerische Erstaufführung des
ngsstückes «Die Mutter», das von Bertold
nach dem Roman von Maxim Gorki verurde, fand vor 1200 mitgehenden Zu-
n einen so großen Erfolg, daß es morgen
. a g , den 3. Mai, w i e d e r h o l t werden
er bekannte Zeichner Lindegger erklärte.
Inszenierung Sigfrit Steiners besser sei
seinerzeitige Berliner Uraufführung unter
Das ganze Spiel ist von einem großen
eseelt. Die Volksschauspieler und die mit-
en kleinen Chöre leisten absolut saubere
die auch von der Berufskritik anerkannt
bt wird. Unser Bild zeigt M a r i a O s t -
als M u t t e r W l a s s o w a . wir glau-
das Porträt mehr sagt als Worte.

opposite 'Repeat tonight of [Brecht's] play "The Mother" [in Zurich].' This was the first Swiss production, by Socialist amateurs in the 1200-seat House of the People.

above Maria Ostfelden as the Mother. The play opened on May Day.

9 may 41

i am reading [andreas] streicher's SCHILLER'S FLIGHT FROM STUTT-GART. note differences in the manner of working which derive from the differences between the aristotelian and the non-aristotelian theories of the drama. s. works out the dramatic scenes, also the monologues, sets great store by 'purple passages' and introduces his effects with care. everything is designed to arouse enthusiasm, to grip you, to delight you, both morally and aesthetically. high-minded characters, tense complications, rhetorical explosions, demonstrations of powerful passions, stimulation of breath-taking controversies, these become irresistible effects. the *misère* comes to an instant end and germany has her national poet. the phenomenon of theatre, newly opening up, with its a-effect, in front of the bourgeois class and the nation, goes through a phase where the presentation of reality is totally subordinated to theatricality (lessing's theatre was still very different in this respect). mankind's vital interest in its own humanity which can find expression in theatre, and forms the basis for all emotions, can be seen at this point to be mainly an interest in theatre, that is, in stage presentation alone. it is, put bluntly, not what is represented, ie what happens between (and within) men, that interests the dramatist, but precisely the emotions that can be aroused by that representation. s[chiller] always takes a long time to find 'subjects' and plots which will 'bear the weight of' his emotions. not that conditions do not interest him, not that he does not protest passionately and offer suggestions – it is just that it is mainly the theatre and the chance to use subjects and emotions for the theatre that makes him write. this gives rise to an art that is in contact with reality and contains reality, but sacrifices reality totally to art.

i can judge how remote i am from this standpoint by the fact that the thought of working out a big scene suddenly seems quite new to me, an interesting experiment. i usually expend great effort on the motivation, keep checking how much of the processes that i have in mind has to be shown, etc, but to my knowledge i have never honed dialogue or tried to make a scene go with more of a swing. i begin with the first sentence and end with the last, without skipping anything, or allotting special importance to any particular part. this is, i suspect, very epic. the epic dramatist views all details with equal affection. i only ever criticise the manner of depiction by way of the subject depicted.

12 may 41

in the evening friends here give us a farewell dinner in a restaurant. hella, diktonius, vala were there. as we leave – we are in high spirits because tomorrow grete has at last been promised a tourist visa by the american consul – the restaurant manager comes and tells us hess has landed in scotland as a refugee. the victory bells from the balkan campaign have not stopped ringing and already the third most powerful man in the victorious state comes limping into a scottish peasant's hut as a refugee. hitler predicts the annihilation of the island, his second-in-command flees there to safety. very epic drama, that . . .

13 may 41

see a german film about airmen (subject: superior officer with rough exterior but heart of gold). the most interesting thing is how completely this military world is cut off from life. in the whole film you only see one non-military setting, the barracks canteen, and only two civilians, the canteen manager, who provides beer, and a peasant girl in a field beside the airfield who provides a sexual organ. apart from this you see how this segregated world is made ready for action. the army is the stake. it is thrown on the grand roulette table, whipped away by the croupier's rake or returned twofold. the players decide. – good how a flying schedule from 1918 can be turned as if by magic into one for 1939, peace is just a truce.

29 may 41 (thursday)

[ON THE DEATH OF MARGERETE STEFFIN]
in the morning i did her packing and helli helped.

she looked for her little ring without finding it. but she was confident she would.

i knew moving her could be fatal.

at midday i went with her in a little ambulance to the 'high mountain' sanatorium in moscow. she had several times to be given oxygen, she looked very changed and tired and often said 'write to me'.

but was it still not certain whether we would get tickets.

i bought a ring and visited her at 5 o'clock. she was very calm, and as usual i was almost happy when i left.

i told her that i was leaving, that i had the tickets. she smiled and said in a deep voice, 'that's good.'

30 may 41 (friday)

was at the sanatorium at 12 with a little elephant, which gave her great joy.

i brought her a pillow. she said, 'i'm coming after you, only two things can stop me, mortal danger or the war.' she was calm again and smiled when i left, without any effort.

she said, 'you have told me things that have made me quite calm.' at 5 o'clock i left for vladivostok.

there was to be no other ship for the whole of june. america's entry into the war was imminent. there were no flights in and out of v[ladivostok] either.

no telegram on the days that followed
on 4 june 1941 at 9 o'clock she died. she had received a telegram at 8 o'clock and was very calm.

i heard about it at 10 o'clock on the far side of lake baikal (4 o'clock moscow time).

13 jul 41 [– 21 jul 41]

in december 40 we were told from stockholm that mexican immigrant visas had been granted for me, helli and the children. grete got none, cables and applications were in vain, and we were told from the USA that we should travel, the new mexican government might annul the visas any day. i therefore applied for american visas, a visitor's visa for grete, since she could not pass the medical for an immigrant visa. the situation in finland quickly turned threatening. we got our american immigrant visas on 2nd may 1941 and our finnish friends pressed us increasingly to leave. german motorised divisions were multiplying in the land, helsinki was full of german 'travellers', the tension between germany and the USSR was growing. finally, on 12th may grete got a visitor's visa for america as hella [wuolijoki]'s secretary. we left on the 13th and were in leningrad on the 15th. in moscow grete, who had done all the rushing around about the manuscripts at the border – only she spoke russian – collapsed. the undernourishment in finland (almost no meat, little fat, no vegetables, no fruit), the fear and excitement, especially the fear she might be responsible for none of us getting away, and on top of all that the journey, had exhausted her completely. only five of the six lobes in her lungs were working. she went into a clinic. when, after a great struggle, we finally got tickets for a swedish ship i tried to change them for a later date; i was told that was not possible. however they said that it would certainly be possible to get a ticket for grete on a later ship if she were fit. since the way was thus open for her (visa and ticket secured) she was very relieved and determined to get better so that she could stand the long trip. i left manuscripts and everything behind with her. she sensed how serious her condition was, but i blamed it all on her heart, and she believed me. on 30.5 we left for vladivostok. the general view was that the USSR would have peace for some considerable time, but that america was about to enter the war. the trans-siberian express took 10 days from moscow to vladivostok. we exchanged daily telegrams. on 1.6: 'on 31st may i felt so-so in the night. on the 1st during the day i felt bad. greetings grete and maria.' maria is maria gresshöhner. on 4.6.41 at 9am she died. she still received my telegram at 8am and was then very peaceful. i learnt this at 10pm on the other side of lake baikal. our little mongolian interpreter translated the telegram for me.

on 13 june we sailed on the 'annie johnson' for the USA. after stopping over for 5 days in manila we arrived at san pedro on 21 july.

wording of the telegram of 4.6 (interpreter's literal translation) taken down verbatim in ulan-ude:

'eight o'clock in the morning grete received your telegram and read it peacefully. at 9 o'clock in the morning she died. with deep sympathy and greetings, yours, FADEYEV, APLETIN.'

wording of a telegram from maria on 5.6.:

'grete did not want to die. she thought only of living. asked for books. thought of you. she wished to get fit and come after you. after the next night she breakfasted peacefully, read your telegram thoroughly, asked for champagne. soon she felt bad, shivered, and thought it was getting better. at this moment the doctor came. a moment later she repeated the word "doctor" three times. died peacefully. at the post-mortem the doctor found both lungs in the last stage. huge cavities, heart and liver much enlarged. a death mask was taken for you.'

1941

TABLE
we were helped by:
from germany
suhrkamp, müllereisert and weiskopf.
in austria
karl kraus.
in denmark
ruth berlau.
in england
fritz kortner
and
in america
jerome.
in sweden
georg branting
naima wifstrand, ninnan santesson
and alwa anderson.

VLADIVOSTOK HARBOR   Sovfoto

America
21 July 1941 to 5 November 1947

21 jul 41

we arrive at san pedro, the harbour for los angeles. martha feuchtwanger
and alexander granach the actor meet us at the pier. elisabeth hauptmann
has had a friend of hers rent a *flat** for us. she herself has a job near NY.

Museum of Modern Ar

ERASTUS FIELD'S AMERICAN MONUMENT
He admitted that it might be faulty.

A fantasy by Massachusetts painter Erastus Salisbury Field (1805–1900).

22 jul 41

feuchtwanger lives in santa monica, in a big, mexican-style house. his personality is unchanged, but in appearance he has aged. he is working for the theatre here on a play about a german astrologer and charlatan. his advice is to stay here, where it is cheaper than in NY, and where there are more opportunities for earning.

AMERICA HAS MUCH TO LEARN from the fate that befell French Democracy. One of our greatest articles was Lion Feuchtwanger's "Lost Souls Limited" in which he pictured the tragedy of France's fall.

Lion Feuchtwanger (centre) in a French internment camp; he was in Les Milles and Nîmes till the capitulation.

1 aug 41

almost nowhere has my life ever been harder than here in this mausoleum of *easy going**. the house is too pretty, and here my profession is gold-digging. the lucky ones pan big nuggets the size of your fist out of the mud and people talk about them for a while; when i walk, i walk on clouds like a polio victim. and i miss grete, here especially. it is as if they had taken away my guide as soon as i entered the desert.

ed bombers destined for the R. A. F. mass at Floyd t Field in Brooklyn. Flown from the hard-working Cal-factory (see previous page), these Hudson bombers will have their wings stripped off, like those at the right, before being shipped. Hudsons are dependable planes, greatly admired by the British. They are being built at the rate of four a day

American-built Hudson bombers waiting to be shipped to the RAF.

MARSHAL TIMOSHENKO (*right*) INSTRUCTING OFFICERS
How genuine was the military culture?

Marshal Semyon Timoshenko (right) addressing Red Army officers.

[august 41]

and now to the survivors! at a garden party at rolf nürnberg's i met the twin clowns horkheimer and pollock, two tuis from the frankfurt sociological institute. horkheimer is a millionaire, pollock merely from a well-off background, which means horkheimer can buy himself a university chair 'as a front for the institute's revolutionary activities' wherever he happens to be staying, which for the moment is at columbia, though, since the rounding up of the reds has started on a grand scale, horkheimer has lost the urge 'to sell his soul, which is more or less what you always have to do at universities', and has gone west, where paradise awaits. so much for academic laurels! – they keep about a dozen intellectuals' heads above water with their money, and these in turn have to contribute all their work to the journal without any guarantee that it will ever be printed. this enables them to maintain that 'saving the institute's money has been their principal revolutionary duty all these years'.

4 oct 41

trying to think of subjects for films i tell REYHER the plan for JOE FLEISCHHACKER IN CHICAGO, and in a couple of hours we develop it into a film-scenario THE BREAD-KING LEARNS TO BAKE BREAD. there is no proper bread in the states and i like my bread. my main meal in the evening is bread and butter. r[eyher] takes the view that the americans are still nomads, and nomads don't know anything about eating. for that you have to study what the soil produces etc. they have no use for real bread because you can't sell it sliced, which it has to be so they can eat it on the move or wherever they happen to be standing. they really are nomads. they change professions like shoes, build houses to last 20 years and don't stay that long, so that home isn't any specific locality. not for nothing has the *great disorder* spread so luxuriantly here.

'Strike [at Bethlehem Steel] began at 9 pm with a mass walk-out.'

5 oct 41

the conflict of interest between various groups in france and britain in relation to foreign policy has rapidly and steadily grown more acute in the last decades. these countries scarcely fight as nations any more. the bank of france switched from the british tories to the german ruhr industrialists (in the middle of the war), because they thought that they could defeat the french people better from the german side. – history really will call this war *the wrong war.*

Sergeant Thompson of Scotland Yard (*right*) has been Mr. Churchill's bodyguard for 20 years. (The Yard assigns a man to every prominent British statesman, in or out of office.) Thompson also serves unofficially as valet, secretary and personal adviser.

Churchill with his police bodyguard Sergeant Thompson.

7 Oct 41

THE GENTLEMAN FROM OMSK
The workers sang: Arise ye slaves!

Hitler hurls 6000 planes, 2 armies against Moscow

7.10.41

This explosive phase of the current controversy coincided with return from Rome of Myron C. Taylor, who is Roosevelt's special emissary to the Vatican, and with some remarks on the subject by Mrs. Eleanor Roosevelt.

Mrs. Roosevelt's reference to the dispute came during her regular Sunday broadcast which is sponsored by coffee interests. She said there never had been any question in Russia of preventing people from getting together to form a church but that the difficulty arose in connection with education, especially education of young men for the priesthood.

She remarked also that there is no real difference in the form of the Soviet Union government today and "the other dictatorship governments."

Father Walsh issued a statement demanding an end to "shadow boxing" on the question of religious freedom and calling on Roosevelt indirectly to compel Stalin to make good on constitutional guarantees.

Anti-Religious Red Paper Quits

MOSCOW, Oct. 6.—(Æ)—The Soviet magazine "Anti-Religionik," bi-monthly organ of the militant Atheist League, suspended publication today.

The magazine served as a guide of the same society which published the newspaper Besbobhnik (Godless), which previously had ceased to appear. The reason given in both cases was to conserve paper.

DETROIT, Oct. 6.—(U.P)—The Ford Motor Co. today announced 20,000 workers in its River Rouge plant and other units would be dismissed tomorrow because of curtailment in civilian automobile production.

It was the motor industry's first major discharge of civilian workers.

The company indicated the men would not be recalled until the firm begins large scale production of defense orders—probably in six months.

Exchange of prisoners cancelled

By JOHN A. PARRIS JR.
Verified.

NEWHAVEN, England, Tuesday, Oct. 7.—(U.P)—British authorities today canceled the scheduled start at dawn of an exchange of British and German war prisoners after a new hitch in the repatriation plans developed over an apparent misunderstanding of the number affected.

"The German government have declared themselves ready to exchange about 100 prisoners," the broadcast was quoted. "These are aboard ship at Nekhaven. With regard to further development of this scheme, diplomatic negotiations still are in progress."

MINER: ★ WAR

CANTERBURY 'PROUD' OF RUSS

LONDON. Oct. 6—(Æ)

The Archbishop of Canterbury told the Canterbury Diocesan Conference today that "we may well be proud of our new ally," Soviet Russia, because of the manner in which she was waging "the battle for world freedom" with "heroic courage and tenacity."

"The true self of Russia has just emerged," declared the archbishop, who is the ranking prelate of the church of England.

"Can we doubt that with this rising up of a whole people there will come a revival of their deep and ineradicable sense of religion?"

The archbishop foresaw "closer relations between, on the one hand, a new Russia, united by affliction and emancipated from the errors of the past, and, on the other hand, the British commonwealth and the United States" after the war.

Cuttings from the US daily press.

8 oct 41

argued with feuchtwanger about the omnipotence of historians. he says, with a mixture of amazement and triumph, that he finds it remarkable how the describers take over history, how horace 'made' augustus, how the prophets in the bible 'built up' the kings. he needs all this to arrive at the notion that *he* will 'in the final estimate' determine posterity's opinion of hitler. our point of departure is caesar's posthumous fame. when i put machiavelli's portrait alongside mommsen's all he can see are writers, individuals, tastes at work. the 'quality' of their formulations is what is then decisive. that machiavelli sees a condottiere, mommsen an enlightened monarch, going along with the middle classes etc, interests f[euchtwanger] little, since it robs the tui of his omnipotence.

Wide World

MUSSOLINI, GÖRING, HITLER ON THE RUSSIAN FRONT

Advancing on Moscow. From the left, Mussolini, Goering, Hitler,?.

20 oct 41

evening at mankiewicz's, who works with o[rson] welles, whose film CITIZEN KANE (about hearst the newspaper tycoon) is much talked about.

BEN HECHT who has come over from NY gives mankiewicz a delicious account of all the NY flops, as a sort of present for his host. 'nobody is writing serious plays any more,' he says. the effect of the crisis in 29 and the new deal seems exhausted, it was too weak to put the drama on its feet. broadway triumphed and demonstrated that it has a stomach like mithridates for minor poisons. the muckrakers have turned into gold-diggers.

21 oct 41

the wrong war goes on. the butchery of the janus-heads. with every week the war is prolonged by a year. the only people who deal with the future any more are the astrologers. in LANG's villa grown adults, refugees, sit and listen to the british court astrologer (a former novelette writer for the berlin illustrated weeklies), a fat booby who identifies the constellation of stars in may 1940 as the cause of hitler's victory over france. he gets very angry if anybody suggests that with hitler's superiority in tanks and planes april or june would probably have done just as well.

BOGGED GERMAN GUNS
Some are in a hurry.

Sticky patch on the Russian front.

the fascist counter-revolution may be sparing the proletariat some very grisly measures in this connection by executing them (in both senses) itself. this is the kind of thing fascist corporations do better than soviets. pity k[arl] k[orsch] doesn't seem to see this.

DNIEPERSTROY DESTROYED

Advancing on the Crimea.

27 oct 41

salka viertel, who wrote many of the great garbo films, tells how, in a film that was to present the life of madame curie, what was originally to be the main scene was cut. in it the curies reject a huge american offer for their method of producing radium, since they, as scientists, cannot turn inventions into monopoly products. the industry didn't want to shoot it, though they had at first been very keen on it. it is immoral to do something for nothing.

27 oct 41

the nazis are pushing into the crimea, threatening the caucasus, leningrad and moscow, the british watch 'with concern', but FEUCHTWANGER shows the utmost astonishment if anybody doubts that the russians can still win. any doubt seems to him to be sheer lunacy. i am very pleased.

27 oct 41

we eat with ludwig hardt, the reciter, and the conversation comes round to rilke or the development of taste at the expense of appetite. here again we have the 'delicacy' of the german bourgeoisie, the delicacy of the upstart whom nobody stirs up. the feudal salon, that school for the bourgeoisie, didn't exist in germany. nor is there a capital, with a central literary market, a forum. art has no life, life is the pretext for art. what you get are not poems with feeling, but poems about feelings. the characteristic example is the 'famous' (there is naturally no such thing as real fame in this context) rilke poem about the panther. enter an oppressed creature, robbed of its freedom: the aristocrat! the beauty of the beast, innocence on a higher plane, nature which is above question. the philistine turns the matter into poetry, declares his own incompetence, asks nonetheless, what must he be feeling, having fallen into our hands? – it is not, of course, the german aristocracy, but the french one, the foreign one.

the conversation then turns to GOETHE, who, when he is delicate, at least doesn't turn everything into delikatessen. his uncertainty in matters of taste is interesting, and, more interesting still, is how his occasional slide into banality, as in the line 'this eternal dying and becoming' in the great hafis poem, lends the whole thing a certain elemental quality.

i nov 41

feuchtwanger tells how COLLIERS rejected an article of his on hitler because it contained 'wishful thinking'. he had presented HITLER as a nonentity, a meaningless mouthpiece for the german army, an actor playing at being the führer etc. in short, h. is not supposed to be a 'personality'. i, though of course i have all sorts of objections to the personality cult, think it important that he is one. but the americans can't see how a man the USA is prepared to spend 40 billion wiping out can be a nonentity. of course he is a personality of a different order from the lavals, daladiers, chamberlains, halifaxes, stresemanns, brünings etc. f. accuses them of judging by success. what else should they judge by? naturally the old nonsense about novelettes being more successful than shakespeare is trotted out. i suppose, when you get down to it the way hitler is judged is only important because for all these he's-a-nonentity-ists it forms the basis for their judgement of the entire upheaval in germany. this makes national socialism a deformity, a wrong turning, a mistake. then how about the healthy part of the body, the straight path, the solution?

1 nov 41

nowhere is writing about theatre more difficult than here, where all they have is theatrical naturalism.

14 nov 41

it is difficult for refugees to avoid either indulging in wild abuse of the 'americans', or 'talking with their pay-checks in their mouths' as kortner puts it when he is having a go at those who earn well and talk well of the USA. in general their criticism is directed at certain highly capitalistic features, like the very advanced commercialisation of art, the smugness of the middle classes, the treatment of culture as a commodity rather than a utility, the formalistic character of democracy (the economic basis for which – namely competition between independent producers – has got lost somewhere). so homolka throws out bruno frank because he gets to his feet and shouts, 'i will not permit the president to be criticised here,' kortner shows up lang as the source of an anti-semitic remark, nürnberg hates lorre etc.

16 nov 41

bought a little chinese amulet in chinatown for 40 cts. think about a play, THE TRAVELS OF THE GOD OF HAPPINESS. the god of those who would like to be happy, goes travelling across the continent. in his wake a trail of murder and outrage. soon he comes to the authorities' attention as the instigator of, and accessory to, many crimes. he has to go into hiding, becomes an outlaw. finally he is denounced, arrested, tried and condemned and about to be executed. he then turns out to be immortal. he reclines happily in the electric chair, smacks his lips when he drinks poison, etc. the distraught executioners, chaplains etc leave exhausted, while the crowd outside death-row, which had come to the execution full of fear, goes away full of fresh hope . . .

16 nov 41

DEUTSCH, THIMIG and KORTNER give a reading in a jewish club. kortner reads most of the german war primer, and the effect is surprisingly powerful. (the audience consists of jewish refugees, mostly well-off.) k[ortner] does not read them as single poems but makes a rhapsody of the whole thing, reading quietly, musically, a little sadly at first, then ending aggressively, a masterly performance.

17 nov 41

korsch's laconic comment on CHILDREN'S CRUSADE 1939 is that there has been a change of tone since the THREE SOLDIERS, but otherwise he is unstinting in his praise. hedda korsch has appended an english translation.

18 nov 41

KORTNER, who is generally feared here as the great thersites who rails with biblical (or maybe lutheran) power and vividness, is quite exemplary in his ability to resist assimilation. he even denounces the climate: the spring breezes which here in god's own country can suddenly turn into tornadoes that lay waste whole swathes of countryside, the 'rare' rain which turns into a deluge, the eternal sunshine which desiccates the brain so that people end up only being able to write hollywood films etc etc. absolutely determined that he will still one day play LEAR at the berlin state theatre, he thought fit in 1940 to join roosevelt's election campaign. he persuaded the columnist dorothy thompson (formerly mrs sinclair lewis) to drop wilkie and back roosevelt, a highly significant turn of events. he wrote speeches and articles for her etc. even the 'stürmer' had a picture of him as a semitic devil, dictating thompson speeches. but he didn't have the fare to go to the white house for tea after the election . . .

STEELMEN PURNELL, GRACE, FAIRLESS

Presidents respectively of Youngstown Steel, Bethlehem Steel and U. S. Steel.

JOHN L. LEWIS & DAUGHTER KATHRYN

The leader of the CIO unions.

20 nov 41

BERGNER has read the SZECHWAN play, helli thought she would like it and told her the plot beforehand. she was very disappointed on reading it and found it 'as boring as it is grandiose'. all very weird and stagey, she could stop reading at any time, nobody would be in the least interested etc etc. i advise her to read it through again. ask her whether she would like to be in a version of heywood's A WOMAN KILLED WITH KINDNESS, directed in the elizabethan style as a choice, exotic morsel. she was not uninterested.

21 nov 41

as a follow-up to the success of the evening in the j[ewish] c[lub] the organiser reuss wants to do an all-brecht evening in december. massary got the 'jewish wife' and max reinhardt wanted to stage it with her. i was against that since helli was much better and SEÑORA CARRAR didn't seem certain. but massary had already refused to appear in a brecht evening anyway; she wanted to do the sketch in a mixed programme, but in the end decided on NAUGHTY BOYS (?). the brecht-evening is in doubt, there are objectors . . .

22 nov 41

the negro CLARENCE MUSE has made an adaptation of THREEPENNY OPERA and wants to do a black production.

2 dec 41

work on a subject for a film comedy with the german actor and compere robert thören. fantastic setting, fantastic methods! he is a writer at metro goldwyn mayer studios, the biggest film company in the world. he has a luxury villa and a chicken farm as a hobby. during breaks in the work he phones all the time, angles for the applause of anybody in the room, poses as charming husband and young father, lingeringly kisses his wife, the daughter of a german painter and hence his lifelong model, and rambles on without a pause, without any plan, carefully avoiding actual thinking (the hero now faces the following possibilities: he can either slap his mother or get her pregnant or ask for money or stick it out or risk his life for her. let's assume he does the first . . . etc). there are no laws of psychology, of common sense, of economy, of morality, of probability. what is right is what has already been shot and is in the can, what is good is whatever gets you a raise in salary. this whole business of guessing the answer, solving the puzzle, showing off, the constant incestuous relationship between those who get paid and applauded and those who get paid and applauded the next time round has gone so far that the simplest comedies (like garbo's new film) cost $250,000 for the script alone, since it takes an army of writers and producers to cobble together a mediocre plot, all of them without inhibitions, like the poor, doped negro who can't help shaking in every limb, not excluding his head, all of them desperate! nobody can bear to listen to a story any more, the big companies simply shoot any old studio rubbish they happen to have, and then they

Admiral Tells of Stalin Visit

'He's Sleepy, Like a Fox,' Says Standley on Return From Moscow Session

LA MESA, Nov. 28.—A friendly little, sleepy-looking man is the dictator of Russia, Admiral W. H. Standley, former chief of naval operations, declared at his home here today on returning from the recent war aid conference in Moscow between United States, British and Soviet officials.

Admiral Standley, who has been on special duty in Washington, returned to La Mesa to enjoy a belated Thanksgiving reunion with his family.

As Stalin moved among the delegates, Standley observed that "he was rather unimpressive, with sleepy-looking eyes—until you took a good look straight into them."

LIKE A FOX

"Then you knew," he asserted, "that he was sleepy like a fox, intelligently alert to what was going on."

The dictator, standing only 5 feet 5 inches tall, is a "friendly little man, without show of pretense and no armed guard," according to Standley.

His major impression of Russia, he said, was that Stalin, rather than attempting to undermine any other form of government, is trying to put his own house in order and is determined to fight to the last man rather than surrender to Hitler.

PLAYED FOR TIME

"Stalin frankly explained that although he had wanted to stand with France and England in the first place, they either ignored Russia or treated her with contempt, and, in playing for time, he had to seek an alliance with Hitler," Admiral Standley said.

"We had a job persuading the Russians that we were not a gang of horse thieves, but really Santa Claus."

check whether it works and maybe scrap the whole lot and start again. mgm's annual profit from all this is $17 million . . .

3 dec 41

at feuchtwanger's with kortner, heinrich mann, l[udwig] marcuse. everybody is irritated at the bad start to the british campaign in libya, which was launched with such a fanfare. feuchtwanger is optimistic, thinks nazi-rommel will be beaten in the end. the british work slowly, without *showmanship**, *without expenses in reason** etc. i myself express the opinion that there is no weapon so new that it can't fail in the hands of a class as old as the british aristocracy. then old heinrich MANN supports me, beaming, when i stress that the nazis' first military defeat in the donetz basin is linked with the resistance of the civil population of rostov, about which the nazis complain miserably. the workers in rostov seem to have wiped out whole armoured units with frying pans on staircases. they take the war as a personal matter, and since they have weapons . . . the nazis are outraged and call this 'a breach of the rules of war' and MANN chortles, 'yes tanks are allowed, but not frying pans.' – each week he goes to pick up his unemployment benefit of $18.50 since his contract with the film-company, like döblin's, has run out. he is over 70. his brother thomas is in the process of building a huge villa.

TIRED GERMAN SOLDIERS
Some are infested.

MUSCOVITES TRAINING WITH SPADES
Their Tientsin, Shanghai, Nanking, Hankow, Canton were gone.

Russia turns back the tide.

RUSSIAN VILLAGE BURNING
A dimension vanished.

4 dec 41

gave fritz lang a god of luck with an epigram:

i, god of luck round whom those rebels cluster
who in this vale of tears stick out for more
am agitator, firebrand, icon-buster
and thereby (turn the key) outside the law.

5 dec 41

lilli laté gave barbara a little white dog some months back, which came straight from the kennels, stood shaking, without looking round, and wriggled along the walls and under the furniture so comically that we christened her mrs wriggles. on the second day i was sitting in the garden with viertel when i heard a menacing bark; wriggles was standing on the doorstep hurling abuse at a big alsatian that had dared to hang around the garden. she was defending her job. when barbara was ill, wriggles was all she had for a while. then wriggles came on heat and we locked her up, since she was too young for the joys of love; wild dogs raged round the house for weeks, then one day steff rushed in: he had been taking wriggles for a walk and had tied her to a tree and a big dog had mounted her and could not withdraw, you could hear his howls of pain from the house. a pail of water separated the lovers, and for a day wriggles was overjoyed, jumped in the air, ran happily in circles and was all over the place having great fun. then she started dragging herself along with an ever-heavier belly, sighing quietly and looking sad, and in the night helli and steff took her to the vet's. she is carrying a litter of dead puppies and is very ill, *but has a fighting chance**. all this has cast a shadow over my day, but barbara is quite cool.

8 dec 41

i was working on a *filmstory** for boyer with kortner when his son came in with the news that japan has begun to attack hawaii. we turned on the radio and it became clear to us that we were 'in the world' again. a giant nation was rising, still half-asleep, to go to war. in the streets drivers were crouched oddly over their radios. in a drugstore kortner saw a young soldier take something out of his pocket (he thought it was an amulet, but it will have been his dog-tag) and hang it round his neck as he was talking, smiling a little.

IT'S WAR!

Hostilities Declared by Japanese;
350 Reported Killed in Hawaii Raid

Berlin Declares Cold Weather Paralyzing All Fighting on Northern Front

From the battlefields of Europe, reduced to secor popular attention because of dominant developments in Pacific, last night came word that the Russian defenders pierced the German lines in two places on the Moscow front. was from London. From Berlin came the declaration that weather had virtually paralyzed fighting on the northern Ru front. From Cairo came reports of a pitched tank battle bet Nazi and British columns which may be the make-or-break b of the Libyan desert.

The dispatches from these fronts told:

Berlin

Nazis Claim Zero Weather Blocks Red Battle

BERLIN, Dec. 7.—(P)—sub-zero weather virtually paralyzed both armies on the Moscow front today, German war reports indicated.

Extremely reticent, the German high command passed in silence both the Moscow front, where the heaviest Nazi push was reported underway yesterday, and the Rostov front, where the Russians were on the offensive.

Musings
They laid him out in his Sunday best,
A pure white lilly across his chest.
She mused as she sat by the candle's light,
"Thank God I know where he is tonight!"
              MINA SHAFER.

8 dec 41

so, in the days when the greatest industrial nation in the world is entering the war, hitler notes that the winters in russia are cold.

8 dec 41

interesting to see whether russia will seize the chance for a *lull**, as britain did this summer; is it going to say that if it intervened it would have to bear the main burden of this war (yet again) and cannot do it? or will it declare war straight away? that would be to heap hot coals on the head of britain, which, sooner or later, would have to be raked out . . .

9 dec 41

FEUCHTWANGER thinks the war was necessary to bring about the closed shop and the 6% profit limit, and also to boost production. there was no other way the 'arsenal of democracy' could have been set in motion.

adolf to hiro: whatever you are going to do, brothers, do it at the weekend! – this relates to the catastrophe in hawaii. it is terrible.

10 dec 41

*blackout** all along the coast of california. japanese landings on the philippines, and a naval battle near there. rumours that two american battleships have been sunk. london confirms that two of the biggest and most modern battleships in the british fleet have been sunk by bombers. hitler has called a session of the reichstag for tomorrow. he has to make a move somehow after the debacle in the east. very possible that the british will regret their six month holiday. if there were a second front in europe, the russians could deploy their forces in siberia quite differently. of course all this is just speculation in the *blackout**.

they have been arresting nazis here too, i hope they got them all.

23 dec 41

the russians have broken hitler's 'greatest army in the world': hitler dismisses his generals and personally takes command. churchill flies to washington to confer with roosevelt.

24 dec 41

read the german manuscript of feuchtwanger's DEVIL IN FRANCE (unholdes frankreich). probably his finest book. remarkable epicureanism among pines, barbed-wire, heaps of excrement, decisions born of laziness and insight, little personal initiative, considerable courage in standing up for his beliefs. in the midst of the assembled horde he remains the master, with one or two servants, and on the occasion of an escape when life was at risk, he does not forget to select the dinner wine carefully. his humanism is soundly based.

25 dec 41

to los angeles yesterday at seven in the morning to get a make-up mirror for helli. grab a four-part frame from a chinese merchant and have mirrors fitted into it. note once again how important it is here to tell workmen why, how and what for, in short to make it a personal matter.

evening, round the tree, elisabeth bergner, czinner, the feuchtwangers, granach, and later lang.

25 dec 41

churchill addresses the senate. most applause when he speaks of russia, long applause when he speaks of china, very short when he speaks of the british in libya. constantly stresses that the war will be very long. all this appears to be directed against wishful thinking, but is itself wishful thinking: status quo ante.

26 dec 41

reyher and the dieterles here. reyher: 'wars do not end because of shortages of material, they end before the material runs out.' he is more afraid of hitler as commander-in-chief than brauchitsch. 'generals turn war into a matter for the manufacturers. only the volume of materials is decisive. the madman doesn't bother about the laws of warfare, which are naturally not binding. in attempting the impossible he is merely doing what generals deem to be impossible.' there is something in this. the french republic really won the great war during the dreyfus trial. it had to defeat its own generals before they could conquer foreign ones. (the generals sent hitler away from the front and spread the rumour that he needed a rest for health reasons. he dismissed them and forced brauchitsch to state that he had a weak heart.) we laugh at the nazis' appeal to the civilian population to equip the army with woollies. even if the things never arrived (they will of course arrive) the hinterland is still being drawn in, made to accept responsibility, involved by dint of knitting socks. did the women of kharkov beat german panzer troops to death on the staircases of their homes? this is the counter-move, petty bourgeois through and through, but apart from that not funny at all.

26 dec 41

on 1 december the russians, we are told, held the first congress of german prisoners of war.

27 dec 41

homolka comes round and we play chess. i tell him about GALILEO. and it is as if i were remembering a strange, sunken theatre in ancient times on a submerged continent. – here all they are concerned about is selling an evening's entertainment. you have to know what is meant here by the concept 'to sell' before you talk about selling. you 'sell' a joke to somebody for example, at first no cash changes hands, the joke has been sold if somebody laughs at it. the buyer is the boss, hard to please, suspicious, blasé or plagued by strange wishes, always ready to shoo away sellers like bothersome flies. whole hierarchies of experts and agents have forced their way between seller and buyer (servant and master), claiming to know the needs and wishes of the buyers; in this way the sellers never get through to the buyers, who in turn never meet the sellers face to face. all they are actually introduced to are the goods, crippled, mutilated objects of suspicion and eulogy, tailored to fit a body that never put in an appearance. every act of selling thus becomes a defeat, either for the buyer or for the seller, depending on whether a sale is made or not. for an author to succeed, his public must fail. the idea that matters of concern to the nation might be treated on the stage is utterly fanciful, since nothing of the kind happens anywhere else in the entertainment business.

28 dec 41

hans viertel, berthold's son who works in a factory in frisco, winge who works in a factory in los angeles and two frenchmen called dacharry all came round. they find the hearst film CITIZEN KANE eclectic and uneven in style. i find that it is unfair to apply the word eclectic to techniques, and modern to use a variety of different styles for a variety of different functions. they are critical of orson welles's showmanship. but he shows things that are interesting from a social point of view, though it may be that as an actor he has not yet turned his showmanship into a stylistic element. Of course the soil here is not conducive to developing talent.

29 dec 41

kortner rings up. somebody has told him hitler is a second napoleon. he was irritated, thought about it, and came up with the real answer: hitler is a second mussolini.

30 dec 41

somebody says: 'we have to leave germany to the russians. why shouldn't it become communist? just one communist country isn't going to interfere with world trade. and as far as hegemony in europe is concerned, why is it always assumed that two communist countries are going to be united body and soul? why shouldn't some kind of equilibrium occur?' possibly the americans in a peace conference nowadays might play the role adopted by the british at the last one.

31 dec 41

new year's eve at bergner's. granach, the feuchtwangers. remarque drops in with a mexican hollywood star, lupe velez. r[emarque] is in a tuxedo and looks like hanns heinz ewers, but his face lacks something, probably a monocle.

6 jan 42

lang disconsolately shows me a book by an american educationalist on the education of young people in nazi germany ('education for death'). It turns out to be the wildest aberration of german idealism. everything that is done derives from the 'spirit'. By the rules of the old school, according to which the spirit cannot perish, this bunkum could go on for 1000 years. in actual fact all that will survive this one year will be the bits for which the nazis have laid actual social foundations, which is very little.

terrible as it is that children are being perverted like this by the million, the practical effect will be nil. this is another germ that can only survive in the medium it was raised in.

Soviet

RED SQUARE
Twenty-four years had passed . . .

7 jan 42

physicists working on relativity make the qualities of space depend on the distribution of matter. i am incapable of reading sentences like these without thinking of something like 'social space'.

8 jan 42

the concept of class too, perhaps because it has come down to us as it was framed in the last century, is used much too mechanically today. there is nothing to be derived from a purely statistical concept of a german working class nowadays; yet such a concept is deep-seated. trade-unions and political parties are accustomed to count members. the political concept is devalued too, since it presupposes organisations and 'democratic forms of state', a 'free interplay of forces' which can be steered by the ruling class. the closure of the labour market in the interests of the war economy has damaged the term 'class' as an economic concept. what remains is the class itself. it, happily, is not just a concept.

Europe

GOEBBELS & RUSSIAN CAPTIVE
What if the captives win?

Hitler's propaganda man.

the fact that wars cannot be waged without the proletariat (as the productive force) does not mean that a war which is disagreeable to the proletariat cannot be waged. a revolutionary situation only comes into being when eg it takes the individual initiative of the proletariat to fight a war that the proletariat favours, or when a lost war can only be liquidated by the proletariat. etc etc.

9 jan 42

write TO HITLER'S SOLDIERS IN RUSSIA after much talk about sending material to moscow radio.

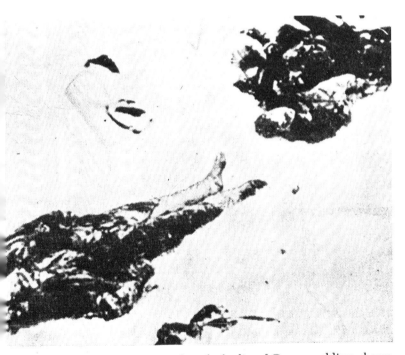

eneral Winter has scored on the bodies of German soldiers, shown in this picture in a snow-covered ditch on the scow front. Cablephoto was sent from London. *Photo by Wide World*

1 feb 42

ruth finds chinese characters very good and suggests a poem about a few of them. *peace* is a woman with a roof over her; *home* is a pig under a roof; *harmony* is a mouth close to rice etc. maybe i ought to draw up a *catalogue of characters* myself. like this:

schön = aufrecht = |

hässlich = gebückt = ∩

herrschen = ein hintern, sitzend auf einen Kopf = Y

verwalten = fluss regieren, also

gut verwalten = abkürzen = ↑

schlecht verwalten = verlängern = ↑

arbeiter = hand weggeben = ⌣

hilfreich = mann = X

mann = mann = 人

schlechter mann = mann ohne arme = ∧

lesen, sehen, hören, verstehen = in hand nehmen = ∪

klug = appellabel (offene tür) = ▢

Translation: beautiful = upright; ugly = bowed; to rule = a bottom sitting on a head; administer = control the flow of a river, so . . . ; good administration = prolong; worker = give a hand; helpful = man; man = man; bad man = man with no arms; read, see, hear, understand = take in hand; clever = on call (open door).

by asking many people you could devise a social script. in the BUCH DER WENDUNGEN discussions about a script might make a good chapter.

7 feb 42

KLINE, who made a film about mexico with steinbeck (music eisler), was here in the evening. he thinks a certain resistance to fascism can be expected from the americans' sense of democracy. leonhard frank and kortner were sceptical. now it is true that there is something here called 'democratic behaviour', probably because the whole of society here was improvised from the start, there was no feudalism and militarism was superfluous. but that only means that the class struggle here goes on without any messing about in drawing rooms, ie that the winner does not go round raising eyebrows to express his contempt for the loser, and that profits are squandered with a certain vulgarity. american fascism would take these forms or the absence of forms into consideration and be correspondingly democratic in the american fashion (the vigilantes didn't do it just for the uniforms either).

9 feb 42

KLINE showed us his film-reports (CRISIS, czechoslovakia 38, spain, britain 39), really grandiose documentary material. difficult to forget how the polish peasants after the declaration of war dug little trenches with little spades, or even with their bare hands, to stop the monster german tanks.

13 feb 42

REYHER invites us to dinner. he went down to the farmer's market for his shopping and made a soup containing every vegetable in the world. he also served a virginian meat-loaf with macaroni. all in honour of the german fleet sailing down the english channel, which he expects to result in a decisive weakening of the tories. of course he predicts the war to end in 1948–50. – he is a good guide to the states when, squatting on his left shin with his right hand scratching his armpit under his shirt and his jet-black eyes sparkling in his foxy yellow face, he explains the peculiarities of that giant baby, america. i casually remark how undignified a great number of american women look, sexagenarians strolling around tarted-up and dressed like *flappers*⁎, forced by the cosmetics industry and the movies to remain sexually competitive unto death. he is quick to dispel my worries with the reply that america has extended women's youth by 10–20 years so they don't just throw 45 year olds on singapore has defended india, in particular against the indians. colonel blimp no longer understands the world. the prospect today is of a long war, waged until the states and powerful classes involved are exhausted. for the tories a short war apparently means their own mobilisation as a kamikaze squadron.

25 feb 42

congress voted to give itself a pension, a movement was started to collect gift-parcels for starving congressmen.

SPOKANE CROWDS WITH DERISIVE PLACARDS LOAD BUNDLES FOR CONGRESS IN TRUCK

A helping hand for the US Congress.

THE GIFTS INCLUDED WERE VEGETABLE (AS ABOVE) AND ANIMAL (A DEAD RA

ITEMS: OLD SHOES, SHIRTS, CORSET, LONG UNDERWEAR, GLOVES, HAT, PURSE AND WIG

GIFTS WERE NOT VERY SUBTLE. EVEN A CONGRESSMAN COULD CATCH ON TO THIS ONE

26 feb 42

being of german extraction, we are enemy aliens, and the fear is that we may have to leave the coast unless an exception is made for hitler's enemies. the japanese fishermen and farmers here are being put in camps. the local american farmers always disliked them, and now the fear is they may be disloyal. exception and rule.

Seek to Till Aliens' Land

The "back to the land" movement is coming back to Southern California now that the Japanese have been evacuated from most of the agricultural country in this area and thousands of acres of rich soil have been left which native American farmers can cultivate without the former difficult competition. Martin Gifford, 26, is shown at left with his wife, Dee, and daughter, Wanda, as he applied for acreage before Howard Wilcox at the county' co-ordinator's office here.

A white Californian family applying to take over farmland vacated by interned American-Japanese.

27 feb 42

feuchtwanger and others cannot come to terms with the phenomenon of hitler because they do not see the phenomenon of the 'ruling petty bourgeoisie'. the petty bourgeoisie is not an independent class in economic terms. it is always an object of politics, at the moment the object of upper bourgeois politics. (the social democrats in exile eg cling to the upper bourgeois classes in britain and america.) this leads to the notion of hitler as a puppet on a string. he is 'merely an actor' who is 'just playing' the great man, the 'nobody' ('anybody else would be just as good'), the 'man with nothing at the centre', precisely because he represents the petty bourgeoisie, which only ever plays at politics. (playing here is both *acting* * and *gambling* *). for the drama this would mean that HITLER could only be presented as a walk-on part (figure-head). this would however be inadequate. for he is 'only' *phoney* * as representative of the petty bourgeoisie's claim to power, not as a person. within the petty bourgeoisie he is not phoney. once you let it collide with the bounds of petty bourgeois possibilities his fate is a real one, and he suddenly becomes a 'character' and a leading role.

Gangster-style caricature of 'Schickelgruber', 'Benny the Fat' and 'The Monk' (i.e. Hitler, Goering and Goebbels). Brecht's comment: 'See "Rise of Arturo Ui".'

28 feb 42

feuchtwanger here to dinner. subject again: *is hitler a dummy?* f.'s view, and that of most of hitler's opponents is that hitler is a wholly insignificant actor whom the reichswehr has retained to see to its business. main argument: the style is the man. no plan, no original ideas, hostility to thought etc. but quite apart from the fact that hitler the *great man* is wholly welcome as far as i am concerned, and that for me the need for a revision of the bourgeois conception of the great man (that is of bourgeois greatness, of what a great bourgeois politician is or might be) seems urgent – for which reason i am willing without more ado to treat H[ITLER] as a great bourgeois politician – apart from all that, feuchtwanger's conception, which is precisely the bourgeois one, seems to make little sense either from the propagandist or from the historical point of view. to present hitler as particularly incompetent, as an aberration, a perversion, humbug, a peculiar pathological case, while setting up other bourgeois politicians as models, models of something he has failed to attain, seems to me no way to combat hitler. just as fascism cannot be combated by isolating it from the 'healthy' bourgeoisie (reichswehr and industry) and eliminating it alone. would people appreciate him if he were 'great'? – the fact is that any penetrating dramatic presentation seems to me to be impossible if it fails to recognise that he is a truly national phenomenon, a 'people's leader', a cunning, vital, unconventional and original politician, and it is only when this is recognised that his utter corruptness, inadequacy, brutality, etc come properly into play. the most hopeless of all classes, the petty bourgeoisie, sets up its own dictatorship when the situation of capitalism is at its most hopeless. the dictatorship is apparent rather than real to the extent that it is established alongside other classes which continue to exist, and thus brings out the 'natural' (economic) weight of the upper bourgeoisie (junkers) particularly sharply and does not rule 'in the interests of' the petty bourgeoisie; it lends a hand, or a fist, but that fist has a certain independence; industry gets its imperialism, but has to take it as it comes, the hitler version. the pathology is wholly class-conditioned. hitler's neurasthenia is the neurasthenia of the post-office clerk. everything that is directed towards an objective is of necessity pure ideology, bad myth, unreal. the beast, very sick, very dangerous, very strong, thinks accurately about detail, expresses itself most cunningly when it expresses itself confusingly (the style is the situation), acts erratically, morbidly, 'intuitively', constantly turns the needs of the moment into virtues, the famous 'thrusts' are merely counterthrusts to the enemy's anticipated thrusts. 'to unsheath your sword' may be ridiculous, against the *tories** it is not ridiculous, but appropriate. nor is anti-semitism something that makes no sense, even if it is abominable. the nation was dealing with a spectre there. the bourgeoisie, which had never achieved power, thereby created a feeling of nationhood ('against the jews' meant 'for our brothers in the sudetenland').

8 mar 42

the grand strategy of the allies, which probably envisaged active support for russia this year, seems to be running into enormous difficulties in britain. letting the german battleships through the english channel, which must gravely hamper operations in the north atlantic and the eventual invasion of norway and finland, and then the bombing of paris, which must bring vichy and its fleet closer to hitler, suggest attempts at sabotage by british tory circles in the army. the delay in according dominion status to india, which means more british troops are needed in the east, is also part of the same tendency, and the british censorship is now permitting reports of american troop-convoys to australia.

Cyrus Wallace, 65, was a farmer in Ohio 40 years ago. He now wants to go back to farming and this is his chance. He is shown applying for a farm at the county agricultural office on North Spring street.

13 mar 42

war, the great dialectician, puts every organ to the test.

Viceroy and Lady Linlithgow

New Delhi, at the time of the Japanese invasion of Rangoon.

15 mar 42

at bergner's for the evening yesterday starting with a discussion of *epic theatre* in the afternoon. she is the most successful exponent of the prevailing theatre, so her reaction is of interest. she likes MAN EQUALS MAN and loathes the notes to it. objects to wedekind who demanded that a father who had something to say to his son should say it to the audience. i attempt to explain that wedekind just needed an a-effect and created it in this primitive way. the main hindrance, naturally, lies in the fact that she does not see the audience as a collection of people with a desire to improve the world, listening to a report about the world. so the basic mood of this kind of theatre is alien to her, the gest of beginning, the enthusiasm for a new millenium, the passion for research, the wish to unleash *everybody's* creativity. she sees the whole thing as a new 'style', a matter of fashion, a whim, and she never recognises that what she does is also just a 'style' etc.

then OBOLER arrives. the most successful american radio playwright, a koltsov type, cracking dirty jokes, smart, not uninteresting when talking about technique.

16 mar 42

i often see GRETE with the belongings which she was always packing into her suitcase. the piece of silk with the portrait painted by cas; the little wooden and ivory elephants from various towns i had been in; the chinese nightgown; the manuscripts; the photo of lenin; the dictionaries. she understood beautiful things, just as she understood beauty in language. when i took her from the hotel to the clinic in moscow, she was lying with the oxygen pillow; but she still got quite worked up about taking her brown finnish hooded cloak, and only calmed down when i showed it to her. i discovered later that, hidden in that cloak, were 15 pounds sterling which she had saved over the years and smuggled across various frontiers: they were to have been her passport to freedom. i loved her dearly when i heard that.

Red troops in white

16 mar 42

i note predictions with a view to checking them later:

the german army is considerably weaker than last year. to start a new offensive will be more difficult, since the lines of communications are longer. the newly-recruited age groups must be more unreliable. a real second front will not eventuate. to embark ten to fifteen divisions you need about one and a half million tons of cargo space as well as a naval escort. even another dunkirk this summer would suffice to drive hitler from the field of combat. but although britain might be prepared for such a risk the tories are not. washington of late seems to want to eliminate london's other inhibitions (defeat of hitler without a british army on the continent) by direct negotiations with the ussr.

hitler will probably occupy iceland first.

1942 will see a decision on whether the war is to be waged in the north or in the south. an allied offensive in the north would threaten berlin, a defensive campaign in the south-east caucasus and iran.

the japanese will have to attack the ussr. this will exhaust their military strength, and only a tory policy in india will open up new resources for them.

17 mar 42

reichenbach's lecture at the university of california on *determinism*. our system of causes is limited by a kind of reproducibility which einstein once expressed as follows: he described very irregular and rhythmically unstable movements with his finger and said, for instance if the stars moved like that, there would be no astronomy. (although they would no doubt have good causes for doing so.) philosophers get irritated by heisenberg's proposition, according to which points in space and points in time cannot be coordinated. even if this had identified a limit beyond which descriptive methods theoretically cannot be 'improved', the philosophers would still be left with the question of the possibility of description, so that their proposition that nothing happens without cause would still stand. the physicists have overturned it by demonstrating its emptiness; they just abandon it. grounds that cannot be established theoretically are not grounds for them at all.

philosophers' inability to imagine *nothingness* naturally no longer prevents physicists from treating *nothing* as *nothing*. all the same, their habit of greeting o as an 'order of magnitude' means that they have a great deal on their consciences. in a system of magnitude o may perhaps be adduced as a magnitude – or rather, it can hardly be designated otherwise. but without some 'feeling' for dialectics it is impossible to make the logical jump from the other orders of magnitude into that of *non-magnitude*. so space as a quality of matter is something philosophers cannot conceive of. they find it uncanny that space should only be that which is occupied by matter.

unfortunately r[eichenbach] does not say a word about all this.

18 mar 42

i like the world of the physicists. men change it, and then it looks astonishing. we can appear as the gamblers we are, with our approximations, our to-the-best-of-our-abilities, our dependence on others, on the unknown, on things complete in themselves. so once again a variety of things can lead to success, more than just one path is open. oddly enough i feel more free in this world than in the old one.

18 mar 42

the random selection of conscripts began yesterday. i had to register on 16.2, since i am not yet 45. this lottery seems somehow strange to europeans, although it comes from europe. this blind choice among millions, this game of chance between state and citizen!

horkheimer and adorno are still ruminating over reichenbach's lecture. the physicists' announcement that they have discovered processes in the microcosm that are not amenable to the causal relationships with which we are familiar, visibly irritates them, because the physicists have also gone over to the attack, contemptuously handing over to metaphysics – with fire-tongs – the postulate that the law of causality might be recognised even where it cannot even be theoretically postulated. the philosophers insist doggedly it is possible to conceive of grounds that you cannot conceive of. the physicists seem to be irritated at the presumption of the strict causationists and have gone over to working with probability theory.

21 mar 42

'nature' is oddly reflected in my works. in BAAL landscape and sexuality are a prey to the great asocial one. in DRUMS and JUNGLE the city is a battlefield. in EDWARD there is a landscape for performance, in MAN morose thoughts, and i stand up to fetch a cigar.

25 mar 42

about 100,000 japanese (incl american citizens) are being evacuated from the coast here for military reasons. wonderful how humanity pulls through despite all these psychoses and panics. in the office where we too had to register as *enemy aliens** i saw an old japanese woman, half-blind, and not looking at all dangerous. she had her companion, a young girl, apologise to the people who were waiting that she was taking so much time to write. everybody smiled: the american officials were very polite. for the first time little people are buying their vegetables from the niseis (japanese born here) something they never did before because they did not think it hygienic; their markets are so empty. now a town is being built for tens of thousands. the military constantly stress that the escorts are only there in case americans molest them. the japanese can police themselves. an outcry in the correspondence columns of the times shows what the authorities have to contend with.

Mad?

What is the matter with this country that we are paying the Japs union wages to build their barrack buildings where they are to be concentrated? When our boys are inducted into the Army at $21 a month and are made to put up buildings, etc., with one saw and one hammer to 150 men, and a superior officer comes around and gives a command to finish it in a week—it's about time the people got mad.
E. JACKSON,
Los Angeles.

26 mar 42

a good counter-play to UI and FEAR AND MISERY might be called THE MARKET OF NATIONS. beneš, who announces with a flourish that he has a plan, and then it turns out to be an aeroplan, and he escapes in it. daladier who has to sell out czechoslovakia because he has sold out the french popular front. the tories send their expeditionary force to france without planes because nuffield the car king wants a monopoly for making bombers. manchukuo, spain, abyssinia are sold out, then france (by frenchmen). running through it all *scrap-iron**, oil, rubber. in munich the soviet union is sold out, finland too in 1939 (to the USSR). next thing daladier is already in prison and chamberlain in westminster abbey, and hess flies to england. the winter in russia is cold, but the weather in the channel is bad for 8 months. fog comes down, and german battleships slip through the channel to threaten the atlantic supply lines. singapore, the police-station of the pacific, falls, the british troops had never held manoeuvres in paddy-fields and rubber plantations. india is only fortified against the north, a thousand million pounds have been invested there. if there were a clearing house for all sales, a few officers' commissions would have been sold to 'second sons' out there.

ny Tightens Control of All Aliens

| 8 P. M. TO 6 A. M. CURFEW |
| The curfew orders forbid the thousands covered by the decree to leave their homes between 8 p. m. and 6 a. m.
During other hours the aliens and the nisei J a p a n e s e may travel between their homes and places of employment or within a radius of not more than five miles of their homes. |

26 mar 42

from PLANCK'S DETERMINISM OR INDETERMINISM (1938):
'so the law governing the reflection of electrons from crystal is a statistical one. it determines the behaviour of large numbers of electrons, but fails when it is a question of the behaviour of single electrons.'
'it is impossible to sound out the interior of a body if the sounding instrument is bigger than the entire body.'
historical materialism also shows this 'imprecision' in relation to the individual.

apr 42

for nearly a year i have been feeling deeply depressed as a result of the death of my comrade and collaborator steffin. up to now i have avoided thinking at all deeply about it. i'm not frightened so much of feeling pain, it's more that i'm ashamed of it. but above all i have too few thoughts about it. i know that no pain can offset this loss, that all i can do is close my eyes to it. now and again i have even drunk a tot of whisky when her image rose before me. since i seldom do this even one tot affects me strongly. in my view such methods are just as acceptable as others that are better thought of. they are only external, but this is a problem which i don't see how to resolve internally. death is no good for anything.

all is not necessarily for the best. there is no inscrutable wisdom to be seen in this kind of thing. nothing can make up for it.

3 apr 42

over a good meal at ludwig hardt's, surrounded by his photos of baudelaire, poe, kafka and heine and his cases of butterflies, we were discussing the evacuation of the japanese from the west coast, and the way democracy survives in its constant struggle against inflexibility, *red tape**, and 'iron discipline', when a german émigré actor says 'in times like these there is just no time for humanitarian considerations'. minds corrupted by goebbels. the old prussian belief that inhumanity pays!

4 apr 42

the papers and radio commentators are getting more and more worked up about the tories who in india would rather lose a subordinate than win an ally.

4 apr 42

i try to interest hardt in a new way of reciting. though he admires WEDEKIND, he sees him as a unique phenomenon, and regards whatever he contributed technically to acting or recitation as his personal style. in his view wedekind's way of reciting was not merely inimitable but also primitive. i point out that, on the contrary, it is open to adoption and development, and is highly sophisticated and full of variety. hardt could only hear the syncopations in the rhythmic pattern; he kept hearing them

The Hanseatic port of
Lübeck after bombing
on 3/4 April – the city
of Thomas and
Heinrich Mann.
Probably the heaviest
RAF raid yet.

without noticing how carefully they had been placed. wedekind was in fact anticipating certain aspects of jazz; complex tap-dance rhythms underlay his recitation of the simplest poems and songs (at that time i was a child of fifteen) i suggested hardt's trying out some poems by goethe along wedekind's lines, maintaining the rhythmic pattern which he would learn by straightforward imitation of the 'unique phenomenon' complete with all his mannerisms, then going on to rid his performance of every truly private element of tone or gest.

5 apr 42

to write poetry, even topical poetry here amounts to withdrawing into an ivory tower. it is like plying the art of the goldsmith. there is something quaint, something oddball, something limited about it. it is like putting a message in a bottle. the battle for smolensk is a battle for poetry too.

AFTER THE BOMBING (SINGAPORE)

International

The silent scream of Singapore. Brecht used this image in his War Primer epigrams and as a model for the Berlin *Mother Courage* of 1949.

8 apr 42

dieterles here. mrs dieterle is hooked on astrology. dieterle, they say, only starts his big films on propitious days. i pick out just two points. if hitler really believes in astrology, it might be possible to forecast from his horoscope what he will do at a given time. (assuming that it is possible for more than one astrologer to come up with the same forecast.) the funniest thing, to me, is determining character from the month of birth, mainly because i hardly ever hear one of the twelve characterisations which doesn't fit me. you just have to listen to these things to realise how incredibly antiquated static characterisation according to qualities nowadays is.

dieterle is always asking about CAESAR'S LAST DAYS, a film subject i once told him about. i outline it for him, though there is no chance. the industry isn't making costume films. it is wary of the nightshirts the meiningers clothed the romans in. in actual fact you could dye the tunics dark colours and have them elegantly cut. the plebs could wear trousers and shirts. the public would come to see this kind of thing since its interest in history and large-scale politics has been awakened. but before you get to the public you have to get past its owners, the distributors and the cinema-owners who 'know' the public. everybody is aware that they are the niggers in the woodpile. this is a really good example of pseudo-democracy.

9 apr 42

and the rain it rained every day
and the sunlight was thin and pale
and in silence they watched the waters rising
up mount ararat

10 apr 42

sir stafford cripps, the great friend of india, returns to the 'capital of the world', having achieved nothing and breathing fire. there was no puppet regime to be found. for the tories the main thing seems to have been to prevent the formation of an indian people's militia. pained astonishment in the press at the ingratitude of these indians towards their liberators. do they really prefer japanese masters to british ones? the indians say no. but they don't believe the british can protect them against the japanese. if

they succeed in unleashing a people's war (against the will of a few tea-
and whisky-swilling blimps in the delhi hotels) then they will have been
able to do both themselves and the allied nations a better service than a
fishy compromise with the tories.

11 apr 42

months ago czinner told me the start of a film (involving hypnosis) and
asked me if i would like to work out how it went on. i worked with him
for weeks, and with bergner as well. in the end i had my story. bergner
told it to a few americans, as she said, to hear what they thought of it.
after that she was doubtful, lost her drive, although she is in dire financial
straits, has debts. then czinner began to help billy wilder (*filmwriter**,
german) making movies, so he had no more time. now bergner tells me
my film has just been sold by somebody else, a friend of wilder's,
complete with all the details of the story, except that the setting has been
changed – without the introductory bit with the hypnosis. $35,000.
much better handled, bergner found it charming. she has read the
*story** . . .

12 apr 42

meanwhile day and night on the snowfields of smolensk the battle for the
dignity of man is raging.

14 apr 42

the döblins here. he has finished the 2nd volume of a novel about the end
of the war in 1919 (more than 1100 pages). no chance of its being
published. one son missing in the french army, another destitute in
marseilles, begging. d[öblin] is as witty and caustic as ever. having long
been extremely anti-russian he has now been converted by books written
by the dean of canterbury and the us ambassador davis. they still talk
french to their son but are again thinking of returning to berlin. he does
not expect the indians to put up much of a fight. they will drive a few
more nails into their bedboards they sleep on

15 apr 42

since WEILL was making difficulties about the negro production of THE
THREEPENNY OPERA, i asked wiesengrund-adorno to write to him. weill

MAXWELL ANDERSON LOOKS FOR PLANES OVER HIGH TOR

FROM THIS TOWER on a hilltop between New City and Haverstraw, N. Y., Maxwell Anderson, the playwright (pointing) listens for enemy planes over High Tor—the hill whose name he gave to one of his most successful plays. With composer Kurt Weill (on steps), his friend and next-door neighbor on South Mountain Road three miles away, he makes the windy, 10-minute climb every other week; watches four hours. On duty, Anderson wears an Alaskan fur cap, little bald Weill goes bareheaded. They haven't heard a plane—not even a friendly one. Photo by Mary Morris. **9** and so their neediness had something classical about it, for people's movements become simplified and ennobled by poverty, just as they do by prolonged hard work. the cottagers and the men bringing the timber down the rivers still reminded you of the shepherds in homer's epics, and in a certain sense their lives have become like part of literature: they live in stories and their lives take courses which are known to themselves and to the village. even the workers in the towns have not become speculators. they fought against mannerheim.

7 may 42

in marlebäk, hella wuolijoki's estate, they used to tell of the following event: the manager and the swiss woman were rowing oxen across the sound on the ferry. for some reason the boat began to sink. to reduce the load the manager pushed the girl into the water. she couldn't swim, so he had to go back for her as soon as he had the oxen on the bank, and she almost drowned in the process. that same evening the two of them cycled into the village to go to the cinema. they were lovers. the swiss girl was not uneducated, she had spent two years at the agricultural school in helsinki.

8 may 42

the finns are still fighting. human patience is enough to make you despair. when i think of the hunger there a year ago! the battle to get my hands on an orange for grete, or an egg – i would bring that orange, or that egg back as if her life depended on it.

9 may 42

eisler does not like the song UND WAS BEKAM DES SOLDATEN WEIB. the sneer in it displeases him. he says, 'and what if i did send my mother a piece of salami from italy in 1917? the generals purloin pianos and carpets, the privates take the chance to buy shoes for their wives. that's what they get out of the war, not much.' – it is a difficult one. i could say that i did not make him send his wife food, just clothes, looted junk. but that doesn't really make much difference, she needs that too. i could say, i would not have written the poem if the widow's veil had come from paris. but the question remains, how can i support the people's claim to lead and at the same time condone its irresponsibility? what i had in mind when i wrote it was probably: and what did the mail bring to the SA-man's wife? that is what it will have to be called.

9 may 42.

eisler quite rightly recalls how dangerous it was when we were putting purely technical innovations into circulation, unconnected to any social function. the postulate then was rousing music. you can hear rousing music on the radio here 100 times a day, jingles encouraging the purchase of coca cola. it's enough to make you call for *l'art pour l'art* in desperation.

when i poured scorn on the unnatural declamation of texts by the school of schönberg, adorno defended them as being brought about by the 'development of music', which required large and abrupt intervals. so it is exclusively constructional, almost mathematical considerations and postulates of pure logic in the assembly of tonal material that force musicians to whinny like dying warhorses . . .

10 may 42

how coldly this war is being fought! you might say, the conduct of the war was icing up. as long as it produces a profit, this huge machinery for annihilating material has as little need for ideological inspiration as the machinery for producing that material. appealing to the lust for revenge would be as superfluous as is an appeal to the joy of creation in 'normal' industry. how stupid these tank battles are in which so much technical intelligence is invested. one formation of tanks rolls towards another and when they meet they shoot at one another; the old hand-to-hand has become machine-to-machine, then in the evening the tanks roll back to have their destructive capacity restored etc etc. the hostility at the top is exactly like the hostility between rival firms thrashing out the conditions for a merger.

10 may 42

the DUNANT theme is throwing up tremendous difficulties. the satirical aspect (in this world humanitarianism is as hazardous for a bourgeois individual as, say, alcoholism) does not open up any way into the timon phase. a problem of warmth. what you have is the transformation of the well-brought-up young man into a ruthless geriatric, the philanthropist-misanthropist dialectic, the opportunistic character of the red cross. the young dunant sets out to capture a concession for mills in algiers and finds himself forced to struggle for a concession for mercy towards the

the parliamentary parties, plus the trade unions. the dissolution of these institutions deprived the working class of organised representation and left it helpless. finding itself too weak to implement its own internationalist policies, it succumbed to the nationalist policies of the bourgeoisie. by eliminating unemployment, introducing a few pseudo-socialist institutions and attracting young people into 'one-nation' organisations, while at the same time instituting a reign of political and economic terror, the bourgeoisie created a field of social existence that will have to be demolished by a war of destruction before the classical structure of society can be reinstated. nevertheless, a comparison between the behaviour of the working class in 1914 and in 1939 shows that the deep field of social being is emitting even stronger impulses now than then. the closure of the free labour market which transferred the central thrust of the class struggle from the economic to the political sphere plunged the working class into confusion, by making its organisations obsolete and outmoded; at the same time it finally forced the working class into the political sphere – with, initially, only negative effect. the complaints of our petty bourgeois coriolanuses that the working class will always 'backslide' into imperialist adventures, and will therefore always form a threat to world order, is of course only valid as long as the plan is to retain imperialism as the politico-economic basis. bourgeois objectors in fact have nothing against this plan, what they fear is that the german masses, having incorporated 'new' components (pacifism, democracy) into their consciousness, might be unable to resist the inevitable appeal of a politico-economic basis similar to the one that existed from 1918 to 1933. of course – and this they neither know nor wish to know – such a basis, policed and split up into regions, would once again produce the very tendencies they are afraid of.

16 may 42

reading singer's SHORT HISTORY OF SCIENCE i discover that i never saw this diagram when they introduced us to the theorem of pythagoras in school. they just gave us it to learn by rote.

Hitler, photographed in conversation with Col. Engel on the Russian Front, seems agitated. He should be—he's not winning.

THESE WELLS ARE AT BAKU ON THE CASPIAN

The Baku oil wells, still hundreds of miles from the fighting.

16 may 42

in SINGER i come on the *magdalenean drawings of a bison with arrows embedded in its heart, from the cavern of Maux on the Ariège**.

these are good examples for concrete definitions in art. if man in the stone age really believed that '*the mere representation of these animals, in the act of being slain, might result in their falling within his power*'*, then that was a readily explicable superstition. knowing, however, where the heart of the buffalo was located, gave the hunter magical powers.

17 may 42

kortner recounts how a negro polishing his shoes while he was having a haircut said, '*I don't like camminism, I like the russian system.*'*

20 may 42

considered how to make a theatrical framework for FEAR AND MISERY OF THE THIRD REICH for reinhardt, who wants to launch a production in NY, a kind of PRIVATE LIFE OF THE MASTER RACE. one could put on stage the classical blitzkrieg vehicle with the steel-helmeted soldiers who are introducing europe to the new order, which the main scenes would then show operating in germany. the vehicle could be treated in balladesque fashion, accompanied by a barbaric horst-wessel march, brutish and sentimental at the same time. reinhardt liked the idea, and also told me for the second time that he thinks WOYZECK the most powerful drama in german literature, and that these scenes remind him of it.

27 may 42

this afternoon spent an hour sitting with feuchtwanger in his beautiful garden. he tells me they now have hormone injections in the army which eliminate all trace of homosexuality (but have to be repeated every few months). so the army isn't any fun even for homosexuals any more.

28 may 42

with lang, on the beach, thought about a hostage film (prompted by heydrich's execution in prague). there were two young people lying close together beside us under a big bath towel, the man on top of the woman at one point, with a child playing alongside. not far away stands a huge iron listening contraption with colossal wings which turns in an arc; a soldier sits behind it on a tractor seat, in shirtsleeves, but in front of one or two little buildings there is a sentry with a gun in full kit. huge petrol tankers glide silently down the asphalt coast road, and you can hear heavy gunfire beyond the bay.

29 may 42

in the evening KLINE and his wife and her brother here when 2 FBI men come to look at my registration book, seemingly some kind of check-up to do with the *curfew**.

30 may 42

eisler brings ODETS, the *white hope** of the american theatre. he sits there, plump and relaxed and says with shining eyes, 'for 20 years i have been watching everything this country stood for collapsing, morals, character, art, personality. today everything is reduced to a uniform level. nobody knows any more who he is, where he stands, what he thinks. he doesn't know his address, his wife, his own jacket. between an actress, a bank director's daughter and a prostitute there is hardly any difference. how am I supposed to characterise a *salesman** on the stage? anybody else could be just like him. that is the only characteristic thing about him. when you come to hollywood, every star you meet says, look, i'm just like everybody else, i'm not corrupted by the money i get, i think what you think, i'm not in the least remarkable, *just nice*.*' i say to him, 'a little bit of fascism and you will have everything you need for a theatre again. above all the differences. and the great personalities. streicher. goering, goebbels, thyssen. and the vast stories. reichstag fire. röhm murders. beer-hall putsch. "you're fired" makes worse iambics than "you shoot yourself dead".' amid all this he lectures on what 'people' in america want; how he wrote a play with several sets which cost $44,000 and flopped, so that now he writes plays with a single set. in short, how the difference between him and any old film scribe has begun to disappear (something that he of course doesn't realise). i recall the great impression made on me by a number of scenes from WAITING FOR LEFTY when they were performed at a meeting in MADISON SQUARE GARDEN. this slender, elegant, intimate structure is wonderfully adapted for mass theatre. (kortner mentions how intimate he finds new york, compared say with hollywood.) the little play used the only form that has any tradition here, vaudeville. odets described this vaudeville with great verve and listened in astonishment as i drew parallels. he is at the moment deep in a psychological play (of the chekhov type). 'i can't write if i don't know what for,' he says. 'write for broadway,' i say like a demagogue, 'but remember that it will soon be at the centre of the world. america has a role in world politics for the first time.'

31 may 42

john lewis is now an interesting figure for the dramatist, being regarded as a large and sinister character. his movements here and there are only reported as hearsay. he is said to be recruiting barber's apprentices, *dirtfarmers** and lumbermen into his miners' union, and many are said to be astonished at the people who call themselves *miners** these days. he was against roosevelt and his daughter was a member of america first, and to date he has made no statement about the war. many call him a gangster, many a fascist, the more cautious people say, '*he is at least too ambitious.*'* they accuse him of being hungry for power. the miners themselves, so they say, don't think he is an angel, but they do say this much for him, that he is defending the interests of the workers tenaciously. the slogan 'down with hitler' must not mean 'down with wages for us' is what they are supposed to be saying. it is probably the case that the american labour movement is too primitive to pursue a dialectical policy. so the leaders represent naked opposites. their opponents in major industry however may well be pursuing a dialectical policy. – from the point of view of the dramatist: if the last act of the gigantic NEW DEAL drama were to be a tragic or a sobering one, lewis would be its fortinbras.

1 jun 42

the city of cologne has been razed to the ground by the RAF. 1000 bombers were over it for one and a half hours. somebody said, if this is the start of a 2nd front then it is a good thing, for it could destroy hitler. of course, if no 2nd front follows, it is not such a good thing, for it will destroy germany.

1 jun 42

'chances': 1) if MGM were seriously to consider filming the THREEPENNY OPERA. 2) if jean renoir were to want to write a film with me. 3) if may wong wanted to do the GOOD PERSON OF SZECHWAN on broadway. 4) reinhardt FEAR AND MISERY.

4 jun 42

anniversary of grete's death,

5 jun 42

lunch at lang's with eisler, odets. we sketch a film framework for scenes from FEAR AND MISERY. odets tries to think of something uplifting. i talk about the tank which gets frozen in; it would have to have a nazi crew that undergoes a psychological change, he says. i suggest: a tank breaks off fighting (during a tank battle). it draws aside and has to be repaired. now come the cold, the partisans and the tightening up of discipline. rate of work is an indicator of psychological condition. when the tank is repaired it goes over to the russians and surrenders. – in the afternoon, at granach's instigation, at the chinese actress anna may wong's, whom he has told about the GOOD PERSON. she acted in klabund's CHALK CIRCLE in london. – evening thören, kortner, eisler, hans viertel, winge. thören tells how a hungarian was trying to sell william tell to a producer here, *'You know, I have written ZOLA. it was a picture for liberty and humanity. now i have written another picture, titled william tell. in this picture there is much more liberty and much more humanity.'*

Russians return to
a recaptured village.

A Russian family comes back home. The Germans had been there and had left—under fire.

5 jun 42

try to sketch a story SILENT CITY with lang. about prague, the gestapo, and the hostages. the whole thing is of course pure monte carlo.

7 jun 42

in the papers more and more articles are to be found which indulge in great expectations for the time after the war. productive capacity, which has been fully employed for the war and is reasonably well planned, now proves to be immense, and technology is developing strongly because of the single goal, at least in relation to that goal. wars are necessary to get our industry rolling, and the nations look on in astonishment at what they might be capable of . . .

8 jun 42

AUFBAU is one of the two german newspapers in the USA (the other is the social-democratic VOLKSZEITUNG). kesten is a novelist, school of josef roth, at one time he was a reader at the de lange publishing house, and his hostile attitude made me refuse to allow him to have a look at my plans for the threepenny novel. the literary characterisation of me which he sketches gives a pretty good impression of the views of the circle round thomas mann.

its line is more or less the same as that of the NY german staatszeitung. interesting how they try to banish certain works of art from literature and lodge them in special concentration camps. the literature of the lowly cannot be high literature.

9 jun 41

a young teacher from UCLA, who wants to publish poems in german and english, called by. at the moment he is working on george's WAR. how presumptuous that high-priest-tone sounds! and these strained borrowings from french and italian literature. plus the not inconsiderable purification of the language – in a morass. posh illustrations (portrait of hindenburg). and what a virtue they make of footnotes!

12 jun 42

thumbed through volumes of poetry by eliot and auden. veritable poetic prophecy. catholicism (or marxism) plus intimate revelations. they observe the flight of the birds – in the dusk – and pick bad omens for the rulers out of the entrails of their sacrifices. otherwise, they only consort with their peers, yet they do not smile when they meet.

16 jun 42

the frankfurt institute opens a seminar at adorno's. adorno, horkheimer, nürnberg, eisler, l[udwig] + h[erbert] marcuse, pollock. horkheimer quotes, with some alarm, a pronouncement of vice-president wallace's, that after this war every child in the world must get 1 *pint** of milk daily. he got almost no *publicity** for his slogan, 'the war is a revolution of the nations, and the century of the *common man** is coming'. but the institute is already addressing the question of whether it might not be a colossal threat to culture if capitalism dispenses (as it is fully capable of doing, according to the economist pollock) so much milk (not only of human kindness). the institute need only look around to see that affluence alone does not create culture, for is there not affluence here, and is there any culture?

18 jun 42

one part of the little garden affords a dignified view, there you are surrounded by greenery, bushes and large-leaved fig-trees (the athletes among trees). if you place your chair right you don't see any of the tarted-up petty bourgeois villas with their depressing prettiness. only a little summer-house, one and a half metres square, meets the eye, but it is dilapidated and ennobled by decay.

18 jun 42

a few hundred paces from here there is a little theatre for rent, very cheap. the wife of henried, an austrian actor who is very successful in films here, can't understand why kortner doesn't just take it and simply 'put something on', since there is a thirst here for *good* theatre. 'the only people who are allowed to go in for art here are the negroes,' kortner explains, 'white men have faces to save.'

it is to us astonishing to see how much you need to do a play. the political environment is just one thing. (only in 4 countries was there theatre after the great war, in the first there was a total revolution, in the second a half, in the third a quarter and in the fourth an eighth of a revolution – the third is czechoslovakia, the last america after the great crash.) but on top of that there is still the tradition which seems to be needed. likewise the material for art must comprise something to be radically transformed. apart from the beauty of a neher design, there was still a memory of what he was not doing; so you could see the innovation.

20 jun 42

somebody tells us: when this woman began to threaten my capacity for work with her egocentricity, i decided to remove myself from her influence. i made the decision as casually as possible, without, as it were, noting it myself, and filed thoughts about her among the questions which are by nature insoluble. i was careful, however, not to think badly of her, on the contrary, i forced myself to think well of her, albeit in an objective and therefore strange fashion, the way you think of people who are not close to you. instead of nursing anger at her fickleness, i found that i could approve of her sporadic friendliness, instead of being pleased at her affection i applauded her independence etc. nothing is harder than to give up somebody without devaluing them, yet that is the only right thing to do.

21 jun 42

as i was standing at the door stroking, or rather scratching, wriggles, i thought i could see something of orion in the haze and i thought: you should transfer the friendliness one feels towards the dead to the living, whether it be to particular persons or to animals. in that way you – for a time – would have the departed to thank for your good deeds.

27 jun 42

it seems the story i am writing with lang (the hostages of prague) has a chance. lang read it to a producer who was impressed. how i hate these little heatwaves that beset everybody as soon as money is in the offing (win time to work, better house, music lessons for steff, no further need for charity).

28 jun 42

rommel seems to be going too far in egypt. understandable in the middle of a war that he should want to ring the till at shepperd's [*sic*] hotel in cairo, now that the RAF has bombed cologne and essen, just to show the americans that it makes sense to send it supplies. but, if rommel does make it to suez, hitler could really find himself stuck with a second front.

28 jun 42

h[erbert] kline, the documentary director, says that more and more people (*'liberals, intelligent people'**) are refusing to distinguish between the nazis and the germans. 'they are all in it together, or at least they are letting it happen,' they say. i ask him whether he cannot name other people for whom this opinion is very convenient; who like to see no distinction being made between fascists and peoples because they are fascists themselves. with their hate propaganda, they are distracting people from the problem of fascism. the soldiers naturally hate nobody, except perhaps these people. hatred is not even particularly necessary for modern wars. it neither harms nor helps the war effort. nor need the workers in a factory love their work. it is unnecessary. – i propose the following formula to him: fascism is a form of government which enables peoples to be subjugated to such an extent that they can be misused to subjugate other peoples.

VICTORIA IN VALLETTA
Like Malta, still respectable.

Malta and its harbour at Valletta were being heavily attacked by the Luftwaffe.

them. hitler and hunger killed her. hitler is still alive, and hunger rules the world. my efforts to save her were defeated, and i was not able to make it easy for her. you should forget your successes, but not your failures.

30 jun 42

the tories are hoarding american tanks under the mattress. and the peoples are bleeding to death. everywhere the vague suspicion that the military policy for a second front is a continuation of diplomatic policy at munich.

1 jul 42

hong kong and singapore have fallen without a fight, burma is lost, leaving china encircled and cut off. rubber and oil fall into japanese hands. german warships sail through the channel to threaten the northern supply line. india is not allowed to arm herself, and troops are being taken from libya to defend india against the japanese. for years during which britain has not been fighting, although (some say because) hitler's armies (300 divisions) are fighting on the eastern front, three german divisions have been stationed in africa, and now they are moving forward into egypt; tobruk has fallen without a fight and the frontier fortifications have been overrun, likewise without resistance. the tory parliament, strengthened by the labour bosses, gives a 'tumultuous ovation' to the war leadership.

At the end of the desert road.
Both men were replaced in August.

Gen. Sir Claude Auchinleck, commander-in-chief of British Middle East forces, left, talks to the 8th Army's leader, Maj. Gen. Sir Neil M. Ritchie. They now are trying stop Rommel from reaching Suez.

2 jul 42

in the *'information bulletin, embassy of the USSR'*⃰ i read, *'in the near future we shall also see* the face of fascism, *based on short stories of the well-known German anti-fascist writer Bertolt Brecht.'*⃰

3 jul 42

you hesitate to refuse when a dog wishes to be scratched, because you are afraid it might cease to have such wishes, and this would permanently disturb the whole reasonable relationship between man and dog – its making itself clear and your recognising your responsibility.

5 jul 42

while i dictate the story, lang is negotiating upstairs in the studio with the money men. the figures and the agonised screams can be heard below, like in a propaganda film, '$30,000.' – '8%.' – 'i can't do it.' i go out into the garden with the secretary. gunfire out at sea . . .

6 jul 42

from the expression *'they overdo it'** or *'they overact'**, kortner has derived a new expression for the germans – *'they overfight'**.

8 jul 42

there has been a report in the press recently that london circles see the serbian insurgent army, now that they have been 'recognised' by the 15-year-old king peter in exile, as the second front all sorts of people have been calling for.

9 jul 42

Emil Ludwig

macht die deutsche Bevölkerung voll mitverantwortlich und erklärt in den New York Times: "Wir können uns gegen die Kriegsleidenschaft des deutschen Volkes nur schützen, indem wir ihm drei Dinge aus den Händen nehmen: Waffen, Erziehung und Regierung. Die Erziehung soll von Nichtdeutschen ausgeübt werden, die die deutsche Sprache beherrschen." Der Vorschlag bedeutet nach Ludwigs Umschreibung keine Bestrafung, sondern eine zeitweise Erklärung der Unreife für das deutsche Volk.

11 jul 42

kortner cannot get any part. eisler recounts that the people at RKO laughed out loud when the screen test was shown: he rolled his eyes. real acting is frowned upon here and only accepted from negroes. stars don't act parts, they step into 'situations'. their films form sort of comics (a novel of adventure in instalments), which show a fellow in tight corners. (even the accounts of the story in the press say things like: gable hates garbo, but as a reporter . . . etc.) but his very unemployment forces kortner to act much more, even in private life, than he ever did on the stage. i watch him with a mixture of amusement and horror as he recounts a simple tale of inconsequential events with a plethora of expression and gesture.

12 jul 42

the so-called gallup *poll tests** play a particular role here. using a certain system to assemble a representative selection of different social groups, they sample the views of the population (on political problems, but also on the casting of films based on popular novels). this is considered to be a democratic institution. in actual fact it is a test of the efficacy of publicity and propaganda.

    a man with a glass of water walks up to a man dying of thirst in the desert: which brand of drink do you prefer?

13 jul 42

it is not true that the tories do not want to distinguish between hitler and the german people. only that when they say german people they mean the industrialists and the generals.

15 jul 42

gorelik here with candel, also homolka. gorelik talks about the difficulties with the theatre union in 1935, how they thought the MOTHER lacked a climax and how he came to meet us outside the theatre: we 'humbly' begged him to get our hats from the theatre, the hostility had got too much. i described the production of PETROLEUM to them that we did with piscator. they need something like that here, and i would like to do SCHWEYK again with scenes from THE LAST DAYS OF MANKIND interpolated, so that you can see the ruling powers at the top and, at the bottom, the soldier who survives their grand plans.

16 jul 42

now we have a chance to get rid of this terrible lower middle-class villa with its tiny garden. my room is 11 foot by 12 foot. it is stuffy and has pink doors. since there are tables against three of the walls and a chaise-longue by the fourth, i can only take three paces when i am working. there is something indescribably cute and ignoble about the place, which can't even use its smallness to effect. my black military chest, an epic piece, which dominated the house in the woods at lidingö and the harbour barracks at helsingfors, seems devalued in this place, and is just *'not a nice thing'*.

18 jul 42

talk comes round to d'annunzio. it is impossible for me to listen to his name being taken in vain in the proximity of people like werfel, hecht, odets. his aim in life was not after all just a weekly cheque from l.b. mayer. he conquered fiume, eleonora duse and a property on lake garda, not just a movie credit. he was a charlatan, but a charlatan who wrote pastoral poems which will not be forgotten, and his charter for seamen will remain an interesting document for a long time. even his provocations could be given opus numbers and published. his vanity is vastly superior to the habitual hollywood smugness, so is his taste, even if that is a little too disparate, together with his whole style of living, which gives not only his work but also his personal excesses something positive. he also heads them in terms of earnings, and this is what must impress them most. though he has to put up with being compared with them, albeit favourably

20 jul 42

with lang all the time, working on the hostage story to earn my bread. supposed to get $5000, plus $3000 for further collaboration.

26 jul 42

eisler tells me he has finished setting the last of FINNISH POEMS. ending with THE CHERRY THIEF and TODAY, EASTER SUNDAY MORNING. he says how much the poems gained the more he worked on them. i see his setting in the same way as a performance is to a play: the test. he reads with immense precision. in the last of these poems he took exception to the word 'work' and wasn't happy till i had substituted 'poem' or 'verse'. in the poem IN THE WILLOWS BY THE SOUND he cut the words 'über die herrschenden' [about those in power], on the grounds that this made the poem cleaner; i'm not sure resultant cleanliness isn't open to criticism. it might mean the poem losing its historical self-sufficiency. he also attacked the third poem FOG IN FLANDERS, in the cycle '1940', as being unintelligible, and was not satisfied till i had renamed it FLANDERS LANDSCAPE 1940.

27 jul 42

this journal alone has many entries which show the dire straits i am in, dropped at the very centre of world drug-trafficking, amidst the ultimate tuis of that trade.

   what an infinitely dismal fabrication this hostage film is that i have to occupy myself with these days. what a load of hackneyed situations, intrigues, false notes! the only respectable part of it is that i have confined myself strictly to the framework of a bourgeois-national rising. and now there is the cast on top of it all. i looked at a book with photos of all the actors we can have, or rather who are on the books here – faces from the programme at the municipal theatre in ulm.

28 jul 42

here i personally experience how ridiculous and impertinent it is to tell a working man he should read great literature. i can't even read it myself here, in this environment.

28 jul 42

settings in russia are now all the rage here. it is possible to put a love story in a tank. guerrillas are a substitute for wild west films – wild east films.

12 aug 42

moved to 26th street, santa monica. the house, one of the oldest, is about 30 years old, california clapboard, whitewashed, with an upper floor with 4 bedrooms. i have a long workroom (almost 7 metres), which we immediately whitewashed and equipped with 4 tables. there are old trees in the garden (a pepper-tree and a fig-tree). rent $60 per month, $12.50 more than in 25th street.

in the afternoon a party at homolka's. eisler, who had eaten nothing since morning, got drunk on the peach punch and was in grave danger of telling all the home truths he has been suppressing for months in the interests of getting a job. in the evening the döblins came round. somebody said that toch the composer had wept when he saw the film of MRS MINIVER. (this film shows the 'new style england' with great success: for years a duchess has been winning first prize for her roses, but the year after dunkirk she lets the prize go to a little man who actually deserves it.) eisler mounts a defence of toch, excuses him comprehensively on the grounds of unworldliness etc, and concludes, 'he is just a child, and a dirty one at that.' he praises döblin as the poor man's doctor from the frankfurter allee, but he also describes his petty bourgeois flat, especially a desk with ornate carving and cabriole legs, and a brandy he was given there. we laughed until our ribs ached.

13 aug 42

at adorno's horkheimer, pollock, adorno, marcuse, eisler, stern, reichenbach and steuermann discuss HUXLEY's 'brave new world'. huxley is disturbed at certain modern phenomena. he establishes a certain lowering of cultural needs. the more *iceboxes**, the less huxley. when physical needs have been satiated (vice-president wallace has already held out the prospect of a glass of milk a day for all mankind) spiritual needs suffer. suffering has been created by culture; so is barbarism likely to ensue if they put a stop to suffering? dr pollock, the economist from the institute for social research (formerly frankfurt, now hollywood) is convinced that capitalism can rid itself of crises simply by means of public works. marx could not predict that governments would one day just build roads. – eisler and i, somewhat tired of the way things are going, lose patience and then 'get across everyone' for lack of anywhere else to get.

14 aug 42

today, for the first time, i actually feel halfway all right here. i am alone downstairs, it is one-thirty in the morning. i can even go into the garden without going through anybody's room. from my desk i can see automobiles going down the street. i am still working on the MESSING-KAUF.

16 aug 42

reyher talks about japanese film technique. while we put close-ups after actions and only use them to show reactions, it seems that the japanese put the close-ups first, set them in motion (a sequence, with one after the other) and only then go into the action. ('we act,' says reyher, 'then we reflect on what we have done – they think first, and then act.') according to him japanese films are more exciting than ours.

17 aug 42

the house is very beautiful. in this garden it becomes possible to read lucretius once more.

19 aug 42

at the office in hollywood every day. i drive the 12 miles at eight-thirty in the morning. breakfast in the office about 1 o'clock with sandwiches from home and a swig of californian white wine. it is hot but we have fans.

grudges against kortner, who once said unpleasant things to him in company when he was defending freedom of opinion in democracies, eg that he was talking with his weekly pay-cheque in his mouth. lang seemingly has less against homolka, mainly the fact that he is a good actor. last week kortner was virtually sure he had the part of litvinov in MISSION TO MOSCOW and then homolka got it, following an unsuccessful screen test, allegedly only because of the intervention of his father-in-law, one of the most influential men in washington. in fact kortner sometimes met homolka here, since homolka, making use of the curfew, was always coming round. now k[ortner] is talking about an 'atmosphere of millions, intrigues, and so on', which he says he can't stand. lang, who refuses to give him a part, he calls a murderer, and naturally i am working hand-in-glove with him . . . it's tricky. the dinghy, which might save us . . .

now there is something problematic here, if you like. for me an actor is often something outside morality; he derives his morality exclusively from his attitude to what he produces as an actor. his self-centredness amuses me when it is given physical expression; characteristics which are asocial in themselves, like cowardice, sycophancy, brutality, once they are aesthetically formulated, instantly enrich me. homolka amuses me immensely when he talks about the character he is playing as 'my brother', and, with a contagious pleasure, digs out all his weaknesses, illusions, effrontery and slyness. he transforms me instantly into an audience, ie into somebody who has nothing to fear from his attacks.

18 oct 42

if i could continue the VERSUCHE, i would take the epigrams and the short poems in the manner of the kriegsfibel and print a few scenes from the script for TRUST THE PEOPLE along with them. say the first scene, before the attempt on his life, in which heydrich shows the czech industrialists the leaflets with the tortoise *slowdown** sign that have been found in the munitions factories. this is an intelligent presentation of a modern tyrant: the terror is set in motion because czech workers are sabotaging production destined for hitler's war in the east. thus the german terror has the same impersonal character as the czech assassination. -- then there are several scenes with the hostages where class differences in the camp are shown. just five minutes before the nazis take the hostages for execution, there are displays of anti-semitism in their midst etc – the film is constructed in the epic manner, with three stories that succeed one another, the story of an assassin, the story of a girl whose father is taken hostage and who knows something, and the story of a quisling who puts paid to an entire town. that eg is not bad; nor is the bit about the underground movement making mistakes which are corrected by the broad mass of the people etc etc.

19 oct 42

interesting how a person falls apart if one function is closed down. the ego becomes formless if it is no longer addressed, approached, ordered around. alienation of the self sets in.

during the work i was occasionally hard put to it to avoid getting involved in solving their grubby little problems, like finding those slick, smart '*lines*'* and the transitions from one pointless situation to another, and writing gush in general, all of which i left to others. that kind of thing can seriously damage your handwriting, at least that's how i felt.

20 oct 42

what i enjoy doing is sprinkling the garden. curious how all such everyday occupations are affected by one's political awareness. why else should one mind about the possibility of some part of the garden getting neglected, the little plant over there might not get enough or get less, that old tree might be neglected because it looks so strong. weed or not, anything that is green needs water, and one discovers so much green in the soil once one starts watering.

22 oct 42

i now notice that this work on the film has almost made me ill. these 'surprises' which consist in impossible things happening, these 'moments of suspense' which consist in withholding information from the audience, these underground leaders who stand bleeding behind the curtains while the gestapo searches a house, these indignant shouts of 'why should i give the line to a worker whom i am paying $150 when there is a professor standing beside him whom i am paying $5000!', these effects from the rose theatre anno 1880, these eruptions of a tainted imagination, of sentimentality which reeks of money, of deep-seated reaction triumphant, the persistent wild resentment at having supposedly to make a great film when in actual fact you are just part of a composite production . . . and then they blur the images you took such pains to work up, the characters get distorted and revert to the old types and they build stout pillars into the structure where there is nothing to support, the clever become stupid, the progressive reactionary, the noble mean, the mean

4 nov 42

between the german and british governments there is a serious legal conflict about the fettering of prisoners. that kind of thing makes for bad blood. tactlessness in the middle of a war.

LEWIS BROWN, a lecturer, was here. he recounts quite horrifying episodes among the small-time los angeles fascists. they are struggling with bitter poverty. once they needed $14.50 for a very important pamphlet, which was supposed to incite the people to subject themselves to a führer. they could only raise $12. thus they suffer for their bloodthirsty ideals, and the greatest crimes may just possibly remain uncommitted, simply for lack of financial support.

5 nov 42

winge went to the *us employmentservice** to find out about openings in the *defence industry**. the official in the industrial division, a thin, quiet man in spectacles with a rather worn collar looked at his card, said to him, '*you're a refugee? see, our defence industry is owned by big money, got me? and big money doesn't like people who don't like hitler, got me? and big money doesn't like a certain racial minority either, got me? and so they are not taking people like you.*' winge got him.*

15 nov 42

high hopes of the second front in africa. though the political arrangements are a little surprising.

work with feuchtwanger in the morning on JOAN OF ARC FROM VITRY, occasionally pop into the studio. when lang sets up a fight between the gestapo commissar and the heroine's fiancé something that almost looks like art emerges, and the work has the dignity and the respectability of craftsmanship. it is technically not uninteresting to see the precision and elegance with which a jackboot deals a kick, first to the chest and then in the ribs of a man on the ground. naturally this fight is inserted here, and not at the nobler point we had suggested, when the kitchen staff of a restaurant prevents the gestapo from capturing an underground cell . . .

16 nov 42

read the soviet drama RUZA FOREST by konstantin finn. rarely do you find such gloss and glitter as in this 'naturalism'. the partisan camp in the depths of the forest reminds one vaguely of fra diavolo or the gipsies in carmen. the portrayal of the german army on the russian model is touching. a major who speaks like a sergeant-major and his lieutenant, who, though a nazi, is actually more like a political commissar. the main effects are derived from the conflict between the constant officialese spoken by all russians and the 'individual traits' ('comrade commissar, i beg to report, i have liquidated my canary'). borchardt's decline of the world as a consequence of unnatural speech is, let's hope, merely the decline of literature. pathetic how this literature stands on its toes to hold a mirror up to the proletariat.

Women From Nazi-Occupied Nations

A Danish actress, formerly of the Royal Theater, Copenhagen, broadcasting from the O. W. I. Overseas Branch studio in New York Herald Tribune—Rice

Collect and Broadcast Facts for O. W. I.

Ruth Berlau at the microphone. She had been taken on by the Office of War Information as a broadcaster to occupied Denmark, and was now based in New York.

17 nov 42

wriggles had two mongrel sons some months ago. in feeding she preferred one of them; he got round and fat, and we grew angry about her partisanship. but then it turned out that johnson, the fat one, was weakly. he became lame in his back legs and could only drag himself along. but he was a fighter. hampered by his lameness he struggled after his lively little brother and offered to fight him, and he liked fighting with me too, never biting, just snapping. then his mother began to treat him. she licked his weak back legs and almost seemed to chew them. and she kept poking him in the rear with her nose to make him run. he often fell over, but he did manage some movements and was now just half dragging himself and half running; his fights got easier. now he has healthy back legs, and we don't want to give him away because he is such a trier.

19 nov 42

henried the viennese actor has had a rapid career in films here, and we ate at his new house, a spacious building in the cottage style. his wife, daughter of glück, the art-historian, whose brueghel book i have dragged round half the world, has been buying up old californian furniture with helli who has a nose for these things. wonderful old tables with astonishing treatment of the wood and copper spittoons which have been converted into lamps. it really seems as if america once *was* a nation with a culture . . .

20 nov 42

rhymeless verses with irregular rhythms seem to have been useful here:

PUT A WAR SAVINGS STAMP ON EVERY
CHRISTMAS CARD YOU SEND

This Christmas, Americans will send their families and friends
More than one billion Christmas cards.

A ten-cent War Savings Stamp on each of these cards
Will fill 20 million War Stamp Books, and start a million more!
Enough to put more than 100 million dollars in the U. S. Treasury!
Enough to buy 500 long-range bombers!
Enough to buy 2,500 fast fighter planes!
Enough to buy 1,000 sixty-ton tanks!
Enough to buy 3 heavy cruisers!

In this year of war, there is only one thought in our minds,
Only one hope in our hearts...
To win the Victory that will bring our boys home to us,
And make possible, once again,
"Peace on Earth, Good Will to Men."

So, in this year of war
Let's add a Victory note
To our customary Christmas greetings...
Let's put a War Savings Stamp on every card we send!
On every Christmas card to our families and friends;
On every Christmas message we've planned to send to customers;
On every Christmas card and letter we address
To every Soldier, Sailor, and Marine!

Yes, this year, let's all join in
And make a *Christmas Card Crusade for Freedom!*
For every War Savings Stamp we buy and send
Will help bring Victory nearer... will help create
A vast reserve of buying power which,
Unleashed by Peace, will bring prosperity and jobs
For all our boys when they come home.

A SUGGESTION FROM CALVERT

HOW YOU CAN JOIN IN...AND HELP TO WIN THIS CHRISTMAS CARD CRUSADE FOR FREEDOM!

Paste the Stamp directly on the greeting card. It may then be cut out or steamed off and placed in a War Stamp Book.

Stationery and drug stores can help by having Stamps for sale at card counters and displaying reprints of this message.

Business organizations can help by putting a War Stamp on every greeting card they send to employees, customers, and associates.

Department stores can aid by displaying this message in advertisements over their own names; and by selling War Stamps at card counters.

Factories, schools, theatres, can help by displaying this message (reprints without our name free on request) on their bulletin boards.

Organizations or companies desiring reprints of this message suitable for their own signature are invited to communicate with Calvert Distillers Corp., 1500 Chrysler Building, New York, N. Y.

24 nov 42

the particularly crude manner in which lang went back on our strict agreement to give weigel the role of a vegetable woman in our film – he insisted the part should have no foreign accent, declared one or two superfluous sentences wexley had added to my almost wordless construction of the figure to be essential, made a hasty voice test, promised a full screen test, made her wait and work for it, then simply filmed the first scene with somebody else without even letting us know – raises the question of how you take this kind of thing. the old obligation to react violently to unscrupulousness in personal relations must, in the light of prevailing conditions, be regarded as void; such mutual instruction has been terminated as pointless. even a friend quickly reaches a point where he no longer has any right to moral indignation. where artists are concerned, the conditions are such that every inadequacy of talent demands and produces its own weight in unscrupulousness. on the other hand indignation, socially a most productive emotion, cannot be directed against the conditions alone, since this would totally depersonalise the conditions, denude them of human participation and treat them as out of reach and no longer alterable.

RED ARMY SKI TROOPS
The possibilities are immense.

War Artist's Exhibition Depicts Heroic Defense of Leningrad

Yar-Kravchenko Reaches High Degree of Mastery In Portrayals of Men and Events During Epic Days of War

From Moscow News Correspondent

SVERDLOVSK, RSFSR (by mail)—What is undoubtedly one of the most glorious pages in the annals of this war rises vividly before you as you walk from drawing to drawing at the exhibition of the work of Lieutenant Anatoly Yar-Kravchenko opened recently at the local House of the Red Army. On display are 100 sketches, depicting the heroic defense of Leningrad from the air and Red Air Force men operating on this sector.

The drawings cover a wide range of themes; flyers joking over a game of dominoes in their dugout after a hot engagement with enemy aircraft; men on a flying field in the midst of a Russian winter's raging blizzard; a heated discussion at a meeting in a frontline dugout; burning planes hurtling earthwards in a power dive that will crash them into the heart of an enemy tank column; a Soviet pilot skillfully ramming a Nazi air raider, and portraits upon portraits of young flyers, the artist's comrades-in-arms.

STYLE CHANGED

One of the things this exhibition shows is that the war has brought about a definite change in Yar-Kravchenko's style and technique. He used to work slowly, unhurriedly, weighing each detail in his mind's eye dozens of times before setting it down. But now his time came in short snatches between combats and raids; time and again he had to discontinue work on a portrait when the flyer sitting for him was called out on an urgent assignment.

Now that the young artist's work has passed through the crucible of war we find it tempered to that great degree of expressiveness which makes itself felt in simplicity of line and form, in the economy of means characteristic of true mastery.

Not that Yar-Kravchenko was an indifferent artist before the war. A recent graduate of the Leningrad Academy of Arts, he had earned a reputation as a portrait painter already during his student days. His first major effort, a lithograph showing Stalin smiling down at a dark-eyed little girl was published in a big edition. Copies of his diploma work, an oil painting showing Maxim Gorky at home reading a story to Stalin, Molotov and Voroshilov, were made by 60 museums and art galleries.

Comparing his work then and now we find that his drawing has taken on greater clarity. His group composition has improved, while the faces of his portraits show a much greater individuality and character.

When the war broke out, Yar-Kravchenko had to lay his pen and brush aside for a time. Weeks of intensive military training followed. In September, however, portraits of flyers defending Leningrad, drawn by Lieutenant Yar-Kravchenko, began to appear in "Attack," a frontline newspaper put out by one of the air units.

HERO OF THE SOVIET UNION A. SEVASTYANOV. Portrait by Anatoly Yar-Kravchenko

"POWER DIVE." Drawing by Anatoly Yar-Kravchenko

From *Moscow News*, undated.

25 nov 42

working regularly on the jeanne d'arc play, now THE VISIONS OF SIMONE MACHARD, from 11 to 2 at feuchtwanger's house on sunset. working exclusively on the structure, for which f[euchtwanger's] dogged defence of naturalistic probability is very useful. his outmoded 'biological' psychology holds us up a little. as for marx's laws of the class struggle, they are valid, but only for the classes, ie not for the individuals. he holds out longest against the hiding of the petrol (simone saves the petrol from the nazi tanks, negating its character as property), he pleads for it to be set on fire instantly by simone. the innkeeper initially benefits from this, because the local people patronise his inn (on account of his patriotism), but as soon as patriotism ceases to pay he turns away from simone. since it is impossible to make him see that the inn's profits aren't an adequate source for the innkeeper's patriotism, he finally goes for the power instinct. the argument clarifies much and is very beneficial. f[euchtwanger] is pretty well reconciled when in the second week, mainly because i can't motivate simone's patriotism, i suggest making her a child.

Wait for Me

By Konstantin Simonov

Translated by Nathalie Rene

Wait for me, and I will come,
Wait, and wait again.
Wait when you feel sad and numb
And dreary is the rain.
Wait, when snows fall more and more,
Wait when days are hot;
Wait when others waited for
Yesterday were forgot.
When from places far away
You receive no mail
Wait, when others, waiting, say
They tire, they fail.

Wait for me, and I will come.
Give no kindly thought
To those so sure that I am gone,
That waiting brings back naught.
Should even mother and my son
Believe that I'm no more,
Should weary friends with waiting done,
Turn from the empty door,
And pledge my soul in bitter wine,
A friend, grown somewhere chill...
Wait still and let it be not thine
The last-come glass they fill.

Wait for me and I will come,
Mocking many deaths,
So let them say—and there'll be some—
"What luck. He came out best."
Could they ever comprehend,
Those who did not wait,
How your waiting to the end
Saved me from my fate!
How I came through hell on earth
Just you and I will know,
You who waited as no one did
Through rains and winter's snow.

This cutting from a Moscow paper must have stuck in Brecht's mind. See note.

2 dec 42

the whole play is clarifed as far as plot is concerned, two thirds have been constructed but i am as yet unable to formulate a single sentence for simone. the approach f[euchtwanger] suggests, via her psychology, is no help, i don't need it, i need stylistic elements, literary tones for the voice. they ought to be latinate tones, highly developed language treated sensuously; this is needed for the exhibitionist urge, which in the theatre replaces the urge to be ethnographically faithful.

Associated Press

GERMAN OFFICER & CAPTOR
Rommel made a faster getaway.

Most highly organized are the British officers' camps in Germany. One typical camp has a library of 16,φo books; courses in 70 different subjects, including 23 foreign languages, all taught by prisoners; regular self-staged theatrical and musical shows; flower and vegetable gardens; painting; woodwork; a sports program; bridge drives, spelling bees and debates. "One debate," reports Y-man Strong, "was: 'Resolved, That in the opinion of this house it would be better to be married to Ginger Rogers than to Mrs. Beaton' [the British Fanny Farmer]."

There is also great interest in religious services by captured chaplains which has resulted in over 7,000 acts of Communion from Anglicans, Presbyterians and Roman Catholics in a six-month period. Ten candidates for ordination are studying under an Anglican chaplain.

Among the supplies this camp asked for: 50,000 gramophone needles, conjuring tricks, roulette wheels, daffodil bulbs, water colors, saccharine, 10,000 sheets of examination paper (British universities are giving credit for these prison courses), cricket equipment, cigaret holders, 100,-000 razor blades, Communion wine and bread, 50 dice.

as far as simone's figure is concerned, i am toying vaguely with the idea that her childishness must be accompanied by an a-effect, perhaps by showing how the thirteen-year-old is sent out to work before her time and forced to do a grown-up's job, forced likewise to speak, think and behave like an adult; this makes her childlike features appear as painful inadequacies, as the unhelpfulness of someone who will actually still be in need of help for some time to come. she is, as it were, wearing the skirts of a fully fledged servant which are much too long for her.

2 dec 42

a great discovery: the need to buy vitamins here in the form of pills. i was already clearly aware how badly my brain was functioning, how quickly i tired, how low one's vitality gets, and so on. five days of taking vitamins and i was fit again. what striking proof of the social origin of the proletarian 'inability to think'!

7 dec 42

we eat at homolka's, by the fireside, looking out over the autumnal garden with the oil derricks in the distance, and construct a play based on the remark that in mexico the practice of religion is actually illegal. we introduce a vast black market in religion. in dark alleys touts whisper 'confession?' in the ears of passers-by, and crucifixes are smuggled in disguised as machine-guns. neighbourhoods are divided up among the bootleggers who stage wild battles among themselves. the most successful of them can only be brought to book on charges of income-tax evasion. not a single religious object is to be found in his house. the better-class elements suffer terribly. they are incapable of going down to the stock exchange without their habitual shots of religion etc . . .

8 dec 42

we have got the structure and i've begun to write, first the second real scene, which seems to be the most difficult.

the difficulty is I'm writing the scene with no picture of the principal part, simone. originally i saw her as a somewhat ungainly, mentally retarded and inhibited person; then it seemed more practical to use a child, so I'm left with the bare functions and nothing to offset them with in the way of individuality. maybe it would be better to do THE ANGRY WOMAN after all?

10 dec 42

reading trotsky's little book on LENIN (published in 1924) with great pleasure. beautiful the way lenin shows the young man 'their' westminster. thus he speaks of german artillery, french aircraft, the abundance of information in the 'times', as things 'they' understand, have achieved, managed to do. ' "will they agree to a compromise?" asked lenin, looking penetratingly at me. i explained that we deliberately gave reassuring information in the press, and that it was just a stratagem for the moment when we launched the general attack. "now that's go-ood," said lenin, savouring the sound of the words, full of delight. he rubbed his hands excitedly and began to pace up and down the room. "that is ve-ery good!" ilyich was especially fond of cunning stratagems. taking in the enemy, pulling a fast one – what could be better?' then the tragic part: 'once, at a particularly difficult moment in 1918, vladimir ilyich said to me, "a workers' delegation came to see me today. after i had talked to them one of them said: it's easy to see that you too, comrade lenin, are on the side of the capitalists. do you know, that was the first time i had heard that kind of thing said. i confess i was confused and didn't know what to answer. if that man wasn't ill-disposed – wasn't a menshevik, then it is a disturbing symptom."'

11 dec 42

the papers say that jhering has become director of the hofburgtheater. for a refugee that makes him a nazi director. on the other hand, for ten years now this whole people, drawn into an immense war by the ruling scum, has been living through this phase like any other, and the difference between nazi bakers and nazi theatre directors is probably less than we are inclined to think. rolls do less harm than johst's plays, ie the theatrical profession is more dangerous. at any rate i can't say i feel anything like shock. i can't stand tarred-with-the-same-brush judgements, people like jhering – if we are talking tar-brushes – are not, i take it, the main enemy. any judgement must be an internal one.

12 dec 42

feuchtwanger has agreed to write an essay on OVID for emil ludwig, for a book by exiles about exiles, and, in spite of my objections to writing for l[udwig], who wants to have the german people educated by american teachers for several decades, f[euchtwanger] can't bring

basis of false evidence from the staff of the hostelry) and then be put in a house of correction by mme mère and capitaine letain for disorderly conduct. the version for performance must fudge this; simone's conviction for arson out of hatred for her boss means that she will not have to face a german firing squad. in this version i can only count on the effect of the last dream scene, which is in clerical garb and raises the issue of authority (the voice of god is the voice of the people and is overridden by the voice of the church).

20 jan 43

the sight of spiritual mutilation makes me ill. it is scarcely possible to stand being in the same room with these spiritual cripples and moral invalids. a session of the screenwriters guild, whom i had to call because pressburger and lang gave me no credit for my work on the screenplay – wexley was against it. he sat there with half a hundredweight of manuscripts and maintained that he had hardly spoken to me. – the credit would possibly enable me to get a *filmjob**, if things get really bad.

12 feb 43

arrive in new york. train was full of soldiers, mostly other ranks, really *nice boys** with very good manners, playing cards, drinking beer and lemonade, listening to the radio. they turned off the radio instantly whenever a news bulletin started. among them old ladies with badges, always with two or three young people around them at their beck and call, making conversation, smiling. mother harpies. the toilets are the only place to escape from them. you imagine they serve to uphold morality (the old ladies' morality). – arizona and texas remind you very much of siberia, seen from the train. the grey two-storey wooden farms and the people look very poor.

14 dec 43

just managed to catch korsch who has to leave tomorrow. he has got fatter, speaks with still more footnotes, is really quite changed in type. though he was always a big man, he managed to seem rather haggard and had those deep blue eyes under dark eyebrows. now he is fleshy, thick-set, his eyes smaller, almost cunning. he lives off the institute's $100 and works on his essays. that has not changed, he says again that he composes his scientific papers like poems whereas i make my poems as a cobbler makes shoes. at the moment he is interested in geopolitics.

16 feb 43

in the evening K. A. WITTFOGEL comes with his wife and LANGERHANS. w. too, who was always a somewhat stooping schoolboy, is now somewhat *stout**, has married money, made a name as a sinologist and runs a kind of salon. besides which he is an anti-stalinist, a job that keeps him occupied full-time. stalin consciously planned hitler's rise to power, destroyed, sacrificed and got rid of the communist party and all its organisations. radek said to w. in 32, 'then the german workers will just have to put up with this for two years.' the betting from the outset was that there would be a major war between the western powers and germany. w. has the fieriness and the trauma of the disappointed troubadour ('and *she* lets herself be fucked by the groom'). – L. is as pleasant as ever, talks about the concentration camp, where they once got a full season of theatre going. 'you went to hut 32 in the evening to see the captain of köpenick, or to another hut to see suchandsuch a revue.' in brandenburg prison he heard an inmate reciting my poems about the housepainter. my style of moritaten and sketches served as a model everywhere. land of culture. – the song of the peat-bog soldiers was known and permitted in all the camps. he didn't like it there, it seemed too much of a song for slaves. as for the negative in the last chorus '*no* more with the spade on the moor', everybody waited eagerly for that 'no' and stamped when the 'no' came, so that the hut shook.

GERMAN PRISONERS IN TUNISIA

march, april, may 43

meet many people. hauptmann lives with bärensprung, the former social-democratic police president, and doesn't have much spare time, though she would like to work again. grosz is the same old grosz, rather disappointed with america; i see his exhibition, and his still lifes impress me, because they introduce a grandiose materialistic, sensual element into german painting. he sells almost nothing, however. wieland [herzfelde] is running a little stamp shop; he doesn't complain and is planning a new publishing venture and designing letterheads, while his son contributes to the family income as a figure-skater. graf, who has not learnt a single word of english, is fat, underhanded, and obsessed with his local clubs and he believes there will be a reactionary period lasting decades. sternberg can't write books for writing articles, but pustau is still working on her autobiography, which is interesting. a new acquaintance, kurt lewin who is working in iowa, teaching 'leadership' to scouts and workers, and invites me to visit him, interested in BAAL THE EVIL AND ASOCIAL. weill has a big broadway hit, but is no longer so sure about his future here. aufricht arranges for us to meet. weill wants to produce the szechwan play, and we plan a schweyk. lenya helps me with the recording of the 'song of a german mother' for the office of war information, music by dessau. the german desk sabotages it. lenya also sings 'what did the mail bring the soldier's wife' and songs from the 'threepenny opera' in public; records are made at aufricht's instigation. he also wants to set the 'children's crusade' to music. lorre and bergner read poems. both have forgotten nothing, their techniques have remained completely fresh. i am adapting webster's 'duchess of malfi' (with hofmann hays) for bergner. i stay with weill for one week in new city, where i make a version of szechwan for here.

27 may 43

back from NY yesterday. tell steff something of the plan for schweyk. he immediately says the original schweyk would hardly bother about baloun's difficulties, would be more likely to advise him to join the german army and would hardly frequent a bar like the CHALICE in its present form. these are in fact things that have got harsher since 1914. nevertheless i decide on the spot to build this apolitical attitude of s[chweyk's] into the plot (*the rescue of baloun the glutton*). reading the old schweyk in the train, i am again overwhelmed by hašek's grand panorama and by the genuinely unconstructive attitude of the people, which, being itself the only constructive element, cannot take a constructive attitude to anything else. under no circumstances must schweyk become a cunning, underhand saboteur. he is just an opportunist specialising in exploiting the little opportunities that remain open to him. inasmuch as he approves of any kind of order, he honestly approves of the existing order, destructive as its consequences are for him, even a nationalist order which he only experiences as a form of oppression. his wisdom is devastating. his indestructibility makes him the inexhaustible object of maltreatment and at the same time fertile ground for liberation.

28 may 43

eisler criticises SIMONE (he has written a wonderful piece of music for the angel's first appeal) for being too much of a 'natural patriot'. he wants to see the role of the *book* expanded. she is the victim of a patriotic education. she ought only to carry out what is required of her; she obediently saves france (the possessions of the possessors) by defending it against the germans, then she fails to save it (as possessions of the possessors) by handing it over to them. for the ending he wants all mention of the *free french** eliminated. simone is reduced to the ranks, she has to give back her book and her apron and joins those with the big heads. her friends are no longer allowed to say anything, they are defeated.

29 may 43

ON SCHWEYK: classical works have an element of imitability within them. a classical work is extraordinary only to the extent that it improves on similar pieces which inspired it and made it possible. – spoke with LORRE about schweyk. he is opposed to the scene where schweyk slaughters a stolen dog and brings it to the landlady at the chalice so that his friend baloun can have a decent goulash. lorre of course has a grisly past in horror films to live down, so the moment he appeared with a parcel everybody would see the dog's skinned carcass, the skeleton in the brown paper bag as he calls it. but the errors that arise from that kind of thing are productive. so at the same time he is very enthusiastic about schweyk's being a dog-lover. which schweyk of course isn't, being a dog-dealer.

8 jun 43

hear the last act of DON GIOVANNI on the radio in the night. this peak has never again been scaled, and it rose up at the very beginning!

9 jun 43

complete the first act of SCHWEYK. in the evening kortner, eisler, viertel here. viertel tells how they persuaded a director who complained about something during a take to drive to a restaurant. when he got back he had been replaced, and he had difficulties getting his hat back. a well-meaning producer recommended to kortner that if he wanted to help somebody up there in the studio he should not describe him as *brilliant**, but as a *swell guy, easy to work with**. – eisler has set 'one stormy night', 'german miserere' and 'march of the sheep' to music beautifully.

24 jun 43

SCHWEYK largely finished. a counter-play to MOTHER COURAGE. in contrast to the schweyk which i wrote for piscator in about 27 – a straight montage from the novel – the present one (in the second world war) is considerably sharper, corresponding to the change from the established tyranny of the habsburgs to the nazi invasion. – the lang film (now called HANGMEN ALSO DIE) has given me enough breathing space for three plays. (THE VISIONS OF SIMONE MACHARD, THE DUCHESS OF MALFI, SCHWEYK).

25 jun 43

eisler has written two magnificent cycles for the HOLLYWOOD SONG-BOOK, poems by anacreon and hölderlin. this opens up a possibility of achieving dramatic choruses, since the compositions are now totally gestic.

US miners' strike
lasts six months
(May to end October).

George Strock

MINERS' BOSS

Internotionol

THE MINERS WALK OUT
They did not realize where their leader had led them . . .

26 jun 43

half past nine in the morning: anna seghers is lying in a coma in a mexican hospital, having been found lying in the street yesterday after being run over, or, as the police are assuming, thrown from a car.

28 jun 43

weill here, to cast a revue. his judgement in dramatic matters is good. eg he misses the survival element in schweyk, which i had included in the short outline. – i map out the meeting with the dog for this purpose.

3 to 6 jul 43

at lake arrow-head with the writer-producer e[rnest] pascal and lorre to discuss a film, THE CROUCHING VENUS. an artificial mountain lake set

600 m up in the hills with pines, property of a private company with little red notices saying *sold*⁑ on some of the trees. lorre rides, swims, drives a *speedboat*⁑, shoots clay pipes and is generally nice, somewhere between my patron and my student.

7 jul 43

reading WARD'S HISTORY OF ENGLISH DRAMATIC LITERATURE. the elizabethan theatre was a similar set-up to hollywood in many respects. collective writing, rapid writing on commission, repeated re-use of the same subjects, no control for writers over their own products, fame only among other writers, then the passion-filled action, the plots, the new settings, the political interests, etc. support by the aristocracy is over and the *box-office*⁑ becomes decisive; class differences become more acute, the public is made up of irreconcilable classes, the highest and the lowest (the middle group is tied up in business between 2 and 5 in the afternoon). even shakespeare's curious retirement to run a public house resembles the escape to the ranch that everybody here is planning.

9 jul 43

a chinese author and actor, TSIANG, on piscator's recommendation, invites me to the performance of two one-acters in a specially rented hall. the acting is extraordinarily interesting, the attempt to combine asiatic forms of expression with our own, with a little stanislavsky in there somewhere, yet T[SIANG] greets me solemnly as the '*founder of the epic theatre*'⁑. then he comes out here and demonstrates a few points to helli and me. he shows how the chinese, using a stick as a gun, simply take the stick as a symbol for the gun; he treats the stick as a gun, stresses how heavy it is, brings out the roundness of the butt etc. up to this point it is the technique of illusion à la stanislavsky, but then he agrees with me that the real art begins when the gun itself is treated as a stick being treated as a gun, ie where the gun itself is alienated. so it is not a matter of the gun's appearing to be be no more (if no less) than a gun, but of the gun's having something said about it (recounted, raised for discussion, exposed to associations if you like). like, say, when a sentry is shown to be influenced by a gun, or when a civilian is transformed into a soldier by a gun. the soldier's well-drilled, almost objective way of killing to standard commands, the bearer of weapons, the servant of weapons can all be expressed in this way and so on.

10 jul 43

farrant's theater in blackfriars must have been a small room 'not over 25 feet in width'. burbage's in blackfriars 66 feet by 46. the fortune: outside measurements 80 feet each way. interior a square of 55 feet. 3 galleries, 12, 11 and 9 feet in height and 12 feet 6 inches in depth. width of the stage 43 feet, it extended into the yard 40 feet.*

11 jul 43

talked to LORRE in the evening about a-effects. he finds that in my productions (he mentions the production of THE MOTHER in berlin) the matter of the actors' technique was neglected, except when they could manage it anyway, and he advises me at least to mention the need for technical maturity. it is true that i was content to use amateurs alongside real professionals in order to show that the new techniques had general application. in effect how to *behave* on the stage, how to project text and other things across the footlights is something that can be taught to the lower and middle ranks. however what i want to do is base the actor's interestingness on the interest he brings to the social phenomenon with which he is concerned in his acting.

12 jul 43

on SCHWEYK: the language of the play is essentially different from the language of the german translation of hašek's book. south german elements have been worked in and the gest is in many ways different. for that reason it would eg be false to do this play in a czech accent, ie the intonation is not to be czech.

17 jul 43

at feuchtwanger's meet lawson, who has written on dramatic theory (reactionary stuff, 'back to gustav freytag') and represents the views of new masses. murrow of the CIO has grown in stature and is nowadays much more *'statesmanlike'** than he used to be; green (AFL) is supposed to have spoken out strongly against the anti-labour laws passed by congress etc. in europe liberal governments will be installed, the mood of the american people precludes anything like a north african policy. the soviet union will, they say, not wish to clash with the democracies over socialist states.

18 jul 43

i think the german army will once again be defeated on foreign soil. the germans' notoriously bad nerves have been made worse by fascism, generals are going straight from HQ to lunatic asylums. if they find they have not got everything they need for their military operations they capitulate on the spot. hagen and volker have made themselves experts on 'the chances of carrying on with the slaughter', and militarism is so in-bred, that the 30 ss divisions will probably hide in attics if headquarters sues for an armistice. the italians, who have been exposed to fascism for twice as long, are already too far gone to be able to collapse.

18 jul 43

there are now supposed to be over 60,000 german prisoners of war in the usa; they 'maintain discipline under their own officers, sing the horst-wessel-song etc'. at least they are being preserved for the postwar era in a state of pure nazism. there are very few accounts of this, and the few there are tell of their belief in hitler's final victory.

19 jul 43

read souvarine's depressing book on stalin. the transformation of the professional revolutionary into a bureaucrat, and of a whole revolutionary party into a corps of officials is placed in a new light by the appearance of fascism. for its attempt to create state capitalism the german petty bourgeoisie has borrowed certain institutions (plus ideological material) from the russian proletariat which is endeavouring to create state socialism. in fascism socialism is confronted with a distorted mirror-image of itself. with none of its virtues and all of its vices.

20 jul 43

from time to time i think about a cycle called SONGS OF THE GOD OF LUCK, a thoroughly materialistic work praising 'the good life' (in both senses). living in a house, eating, drinking, sleeping, loving, working, thinking, all the great pleasures.

20 jul 43

the hearst press is fulminating about the foundation in moscow of a committee for the liberation of germany from fascism, made up of refugees and prisoners of war. its programme, as far as you can judge from the papers, contains nothing more than professor tillich (and probably brüning too) would demand.

21 jul 43

every time a work has been finished in these last years there has been a soul-destroying interlude to be endured as it lay in an unnatural state of non-use. the expelled stone-carver, clinging to habit like an addict, has turned another lump of rock into a statue and now sits beside it, resting, he says; waiting, as he fails to say. as long as nobody comes by everything is tolerable, it is only when they come by and look up that it gets bad. and works of art do not travel easily, being pieces of rock, transformed . . . in 10 years i have written the following plays:

the round heads and the pointed heads
fear and misery of the third reich
life of the physicist galileo
the good person of szechwan
mother courage and her children
mr puntila and his man matti
rise of ui
the visions of simone machard
the duchess of malfi (adaptation)
schweyk

not a bad repertoire for a defeated class.

25 jul 43

during vice-president wallace's speech in detroit (beginning of the *new deal** campaign for the presidency) under the slogan: *for private enterprise and full employment!** the programme on the radio is interrupted: prime minister mussolini has resigned.

here in the evening: kortner, tsiang, winge, viertel, steuermann, eisler, kaus. we hear on the radio: the socialist benito mussolini, who 20 years ago . . ., has now fallen back into the gutter he came from.

years have changed Hitler. Left, he is shown addressing his followers shortly after his ascension to power on i. 30, 1933. Right (picture taken last November), he is shown trying to explain what has been happening to his nies in Russia. Note, among other things, the difference in waistline. *Photo by Wide World*

Hitler then and now.

26 jul 43

hamburg is being destroyed. there is a column of smoke above it twice as high as the highest german mountain, 6000 m. the bomber crews need oxygen apparatus. there have been raids every 12 hours for 72 hours.

28 jul 43

that hitler could not get the generals to defend fascism in italy is proof of the increasing weakness of his position. on the other hand he will probably now derive another brief benefit from the troubles in italy. – at eisler's i took the opportunity to ask adorno and another tui from the institute for social research what will now become of their economist pollock, who was expecting a century of fascism, believed in the german bourgeoisie's planned economy, etc. they said the fall of mussolini proves nothing. in addition they are all astonished at the casual ease with which the italian bourgeoisie dismissed its 'dictator' and dissolved all the 'all-pervading' fascist institutions, etc. when, a year ago, i expounded my idea that what they had in germany was nothing more than a superficial war economy with very little real coordination, and very tenuous state intervention in the economy, there were raised eyebrows everywhere.

29 jul 43

there is of course such a thing as 'german servility'. there are historical reasons for it (but explaining it does not put an end to it). nonetheless the puzzle of how the germans manage to hold out (two winters in russia, now again in sicily, but also in the anti-fascist factories of germany herself) can hardly be explained to non-dialecticians. fascist concentration on one goal is a totality which can only be diverted sporadically into a totality of a different sort. (only the upper hand is ever visible, never the lower hand. indeed the upper hand steers the under hand.)

1 aug 43

an evening gathering at the viertels: TH. MANN, H. MANN, FEUCHT-WANGER. BRUNO FRANK, L[UDWIG] MARCUSE, H[ANS] REICHENBACH and me. in four hours the following proposals were adumbrated:

At this moment, when the victory of the Allied Nations is approaching, the undersigned writers, scientists and artists of german extraction deem it their duty to declare openly:

We welcome the declaration of the prisoners of war and émigrés in the Soviet Union, calling upon the German people to force its oppressors into unconditional surrender and to fight for a strong democracy in Germany.

We too deem it necessary to distinguish clearly between the Hitler regime and the classes linked to it on the one hand and the German people on the other.

We are convinced that there can be no lasting world peace without a strong democracy in Germany.

> Thomas Mann Heinrich Mann Lion Feuchtwanger
> Bruno Frank Bertolt Brecht Berthold Viertel
> Hans Reichenbach Ludwig Marcuse.

TH. MANN wrote the first sentence. he had reservations about the mention of the soviet union. the last time i saw him, in february, he said, as he juggled with a plate of *sandwiches**, 'i should like the russians to be in berlin before the allies.' afterwards i discovered that on that afternoon he had recorded a speech of congratulation for the red army at the russian consulate and had then been wined and dined. now bruno frank persuaded him that not to mention the moscow committee would just be odd, and the discussion turned to the notion of 'classes linked to it', for which th[omas] suggested 'guilty by association' and h[einrich] 'trusts'. in the end everybody agreed to the above formula, and th. went down and read it to the women with visible satisfaction.

German fliers taken captive by the Red Army. Luftwaffe men are, in the main, of better appearance and morale than German foot soldiers (top).

Luftwaffe prisoners taken by the Russians.

2 aug 43

and this morning TH. MANN calls feuchtwanger: he is withdrawing his signature because he is 'feeling low'. we are making a 'patriotic declaration', which amounts to a 'stab in the back' for the allies, and he would be unable to call it unfair if the 'allies were to punish germany harshly for ten or twenty years'.

once again the single-minded cringeing of these 'pillars of culture' momentarily stunned even me, the odour of decay that the frankfurt parliament gave off is still strong enough to immobilise people even now. if the hearst press takes them up, they will agree with goebbels's assertion that hitler and germany are the same thing. aren't the german people, they are saying, guilty of servility at the very least for falling for goebbels in the same way as we are falling for hearst? and were the germans not militarists even before hitler? th. mann remembers how he himself and 91 other intellectuals approved of the kaiser's attack on belgium in 1914. such people have to be punished! as i said, for a moment even i considered how 'the german people' might live down having tolerated not only the crimes of the hitler regime but also the novels of herr mann, specially when you think that the latter don't have the support of 20–30 armoured divisions behind them.

7 aug 43

hitler's position must be difficult in the extreme, with the war in the east lost, italy cracking, mussolini doomed, no defences against air attacks. he could topple any day.

8 aug 43

in the afternoon gorelik and tsiang here, winge too. to my dismay even the sceptical, left-wing gorelik supports vansittart's line. 'why haven't the workers in germany protested against the atrocities in russia?' (it is the custom here for highly-paid scribes who poison the minds of the american masses to sign protests against one thing or another.) the degree of fascist and especially nazi persecution is unimaginable here. they cannot grasp the 200,000 inmates of concentration camps at the beginning of the war, the transformation of workers into technicians which dissociates work from its purpose etc. then there is this terrifyingly dogged fighting spirit which is totally abstract, killing for the love of order, this fury which operates according to a law of inertia. gorelik points to the poor fighting qualities of the italians, tsiang explains that the germans (and japanese) will also fight their masters better when the time comes. the idea of freedom is not a 'natural' idea. and the knaveries of a regime are seldom seen by that regime's subjects as their own, or indeed as something they might be held responsible for, since they are in fact the victims of many of the knaveries in question.

9 aug 43

last sunday when THOMAS MANN, with his hands in his lap, leant back and said, 'yes, they are going to have to kill half a million in germany,' it sounded absolutely bestial. it was a stuffed shirt speaking. no fighting was mentioned and none would be required for these deaths, it was a matter of punishment in cold blood, and why not revenge when even hygiene as a reason would have been bestial (for this was the resentment of an animal)?

9 aug 43

'o sprinkling the garden, to enliven the green'. and, 'my native city, however shall i find her?' but a lyrical œuvre must have an (inner) history, which may chime harmoniously with or stand in contrast to external history. i think of things like painters' 'periods' as seen in our day in picasso. no matter how disordered the impressions, no matter how wilful my sallies in these years, the poems i have written always have the character of experiments, and the experiments are ordered in a certain relationship to one another, and reading can scarcely produce adequate pleasure if a poem like the first one cannot be enjoyed as an innovation within my complete production, as a domesticum.

10 aug 43

on the question, 'why do they fight?' – if the organisations and means available to an oppressed class are destroyed ('re-functioned'), then all that is left is for the individual is to look out for signs that the dictating class's organisations are cracking up. only when the new units into which it has been forcibly organised begin to break up (local sections of the labour front, front-line combat units etc), can it proceed to form units to meet its own needs, mostly with the function of taking over the more general tasks of the collapsing units, that is, those not related to the class struggle. – the accusations connected with the atrocities in the east that are being levelled at the former socialists fighting in hitler's armies, amounting mostly to the fact that they tolerated them, are painful; probably they are confronted with comrades who are embittered by the guerrilla war being waged by the civilian population, which is something new. – people on the left are allegedly already saying, 'these german workers won't be able to object if they have to rebuild what they have destroyed in the ukraine.' now, if it is not a matter of reparations, and if they have to rebuild under the conditions which we expect to obtain in germany (trade unions etc), then they can have no serious objection.

14 aug 43

helli organised a party for DÖBLIN's 65th birthday. heinrich mann greeted him with a wonderful speech, kortner, lorre, granach read from his books. blandine ebinger sang berlin songs, steuermann played an eisler theme on the piano, and at the end döblin made a speech against moral relativism and in favour of fixed standards of a religious nature, and in doing so hurt the irreligious feelings of most of the guests. an awkward sensation came over the more rational of his listeners, something like the sympathetic horror felt when when a fellow prisoner succumbs to torture and talks. the fact is that döblin has been dealt some very severe blows, the loss of two sons in france, a 2400-page epic that no publisher will print, angina pectoris (that great saver of souls) and life at the side of an incredibly stupid and philistine woman. the reciter hardt made a revealing slip. he was reciting 'zoroaster's prayer' by kleist, and, instead of saying 'may i have the strength to disregard the errors and idiocies of my life' he substituted 'wife' for 'life' in the solemn plea: döblin and his wife had just spent the weekend at hardt's house.

when döblin started to describe how, like many other writers, he too was to blame for the rise of the nazis ('did you not say, mr thomas mann, that he's like a brother, albeit an evil one,' he asked of the front row), and then went doggedly on to ask why that was, for a moment i had the childish conviction he would go on and say, 'because i covered up the crimes of the ruling class, discouraged the oppressed, fobbed off the hungry with songs' etc, but all he did was to announce stubbornly, without repentance or regret, 'because i did not seek god.'

15 aug 43

tsiang was here in the evening, a young american actress, an american actor, granach. i asked why they acted. the americans say: to express themselves, to use their creative faculties etc. (the first answer, 'to make my living; is rejected out of hand.) tsiang acts because he loves and hates people, and in this way he can either put them forward for approval or discredit them. granach takes the opportunity to consume the whole of a human life in three hours, becoming about 300,000 years old in the process.

in the states where we have as much and as little theatre as in ancient rome, the problem is not that it is nothing but entertainment, but that it is very weak, casual, inconsequential entertainment. escapism, but only enough to take you as far as the elevator, an aphrodisiac, but only enough for a flirtation, etc.

20 aug 43

there are reports of strikes, not only in milan but in berlin. occasionally, for a brief moment, the battlefields, theatres of war, the geographical contours of europe appear populated. there are people in milan and in hamburg . . .

24 aug 43

the great crimes are only possible because they are incredible. ordinary fraud, simple lies, unabashed racketeering, these are things that take many people unawares. the more subtle spirits refuse to believe such primitive fraud, and when they do get suspicious, they look for too much, expecting meticulously planned crimes of masterly complexity. they indignantly refuse to 'confound' statesmen with horse-thieves, generals with stock-exchange speculators, and so they fail utterly to understand horse-thefts and speculative trading. of course they are right to look for cunning in great men, but it is a low cunning whose use is limited to criminal activities. the blows they deliver are not always fatal. they pull the wool over the people's eyes with fine speeches designed not to make their victims unfit for work, but merely to turn them into idiots.

25 aug 43

interesting how little is actually said by gorelik's report on epic theatre, the only one in america and maybe in the whole world. he restricts himself almost exclusively to the intellectualisation of the theatre, and sets up a romantic cult of the machine. very little about the new subjects that have to be dealt with, or the new social functions of the theatre. he pays no attention to the fact that it is addressing a new public that has come or ought to come, not to see the world interpreted, but to see it changed. the american theatre, in the brief span following the economic collapse of 29 when it became a sort of political institution, got no further than a kind of patching-up, and this means that gorelik can only make valid aesthetic points when *he* is describing the european theatre.

27 aug 43

horrific lessons: if wars last long enough, plain folk end up recognising the inhumanity of their governments and the imperialistic nature of war, but at the same time they learn that the enemy too is pursuing imperialistic goals. – following an article in 'american mercury' on the government's intentions with regard to germany the journalist kingsley smith, who is supposed to be close to the state department, has now written one on italy. kingsley smith imagines germany and italy as being governed more or less like india. the first result would be indian famines. few (of the not so few who condemn such brutal and domineering plans here) can see that fascism not only provided the maximum possible but also the minimum necessary police control to preserve the predominant system of production. And then on top of that the war was necessary for these regimes.

28 aug 43

article on the war economy in germany (the economic journal): towards the end of 42 the trusts, via the war ministry, finally gained the whip hand of state control. rationalisation, specialisation and standardisation further increased production. the trusts can, it would seem, no longer be broken up by the bourgeoisie, yet it has become impossible to bring them under state control.

29 aug 43

the heart stands still when one reads about the air-raids on berlin. since they are not linked to military operations one can see no end to the war, just the end of germany.

30 aug 43

budzislawski has reformulated the declaration of 1st aug to avoid referring to statements by the prisoners of war. tillich advises dropping it altogether.

2 sept 43

from the 'economic journal', volume LI, dec. 41, here are some statistics without which developments in the USSR are scarcely comprehensible:

	1928	1929	1930	1931	1932
number of workers and salary earners (millions)	11.6	12.2	14.5	19.4	22.9
from which:					
large-scale industry	3.1	3.4	4.3	5.5	6.3
building and construction	0.7	0.9	1.6	2.5	3.1
transport	0.3	0.4	0.8	1.6	2.4
yearly average wages (rbls)	703	800	936	1127	1427
yearly agefund (milliard rbls)	8.2	9.7	13.6	21.4	32.7
total number of population (millions)		154.3			165.7
gross output of large-scale industry (milliard rbls 1926/27)	15.8	19.9	25.8	32.2	36.8
production of consumer goods:					
cotton-textiles (million meters)	2742	3068	2351	2272	2417
woollen textiles	93.2	100.6	114.5	107.9	88.7
raw sugar (thousand tons)	1.238	823	1.507	1.486	827
gross output of agriculture (milliard rbls 1926/27)		14.7	14.0	13.9	13.1
gross yield of crops (million quintals)	733.2	717.4	835.4	694.8	698.7
number of cattle (millions)	70.5	67.1	52.5	47.9	40.7
pigs	26.0	20.7	13.6	14.4	11.6
sheep & goats	146.7	147.0	108.8	77.7	52.1
import of consumption goods (million rbls)		394.2	455.0	222.5	250.5
export of agricultural products		1572.1	1899.0	1499.1	803.4
national income (milliard rbls 1926/27)	25.0	28.9	35.0	40.9	45.5
national income on basis of current prizes (milliard rbls)	30.0	32.6	40.7	43.8	
revenue of state budget	6.6	8.2	12.8	20.3	30.6
state expenditure on financing the national economy	3.8	4.8	7.7	16.5	24.8
state independents	1.4	2.0	2.6	2.9	6.2
yearly average of money in circulation	1.7	2.3	3.5	4.8	6.6

4 sept 43

alfred kreymborg has translated SCHWEYK. the only thing missing is the song of the moldau. oddly enough i can't write it. i have the content and i have the lines, but together they don't work. now and again i have a glimmering of the agonies of the untalented.

5 sept 43

what a waste this working out stories for the *pictures** is, the great roulette-wheel. and the worst thing is that you can never foresee any moment when you will be materially secure for a reasonable length of time. i have been unable to finish the caesar novel and even to start the tui novel. the messingkauf lies in disarray. i would like to do the JOURNEY OF THE GOD OF LUCK, a piece that is half poetry, half prose, at least in the chapter about the discovery of the joy of creation. etc.

6 sept 43

two days with the swedish consul, lochner and frischauer about wuolijoki who has been arrested in helsinki. georg branting cabled us to send statements as evidence.

7 sept 43

Cost of bombing Berlin . . .

BERLIN WIPING OUT COST SET AT $18.75 TO EACH AMERICAN

DETROIT, Sept. 6. (*AP*)—Secretary of the Treasury Henry Morgenthau Jr. told a Labor Day War Bond rally here today that "we want to blast the city of Berlin off the face of the map." and estimated that it would cost possibly six times as much to do this as it did to crush Hamburg.

He placed the total cost of preparation, equipment and bombing of Hamburg at $346,000,000.

"Say it costs six times as much to bomb Berlin," the Treasury Secretary said. "That will be pretty close to $18.75 for every man, woman and and child in the country —the price of a $25 bond.

september 43

. . . as compared with Hamburg

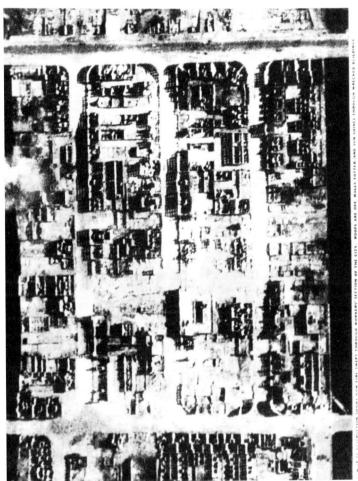

9 sept 43

THOMAS MANN, so first-hand reports tell me, is going around saying 'these lefties like brecht' are carrying out orders from moscow in trying to get him to make declarations about the need to distinguish between hitler and germany. that reptile cannot imagine anyone doing something for germany (and against hitler) without orders from anywhere, and spontaneously regarding germany as something other than a lucrative audience. the perfidiousness with which the manns – his wife is very active in this area – spread these slurs, which they know full well can do a great deal of harm, is striking.

20 sept 43

ISHERWOOD comes to dinner, small, gentle, tough, patient, and trying. he has read THE GOOD PERSON, makes a few polite compliments and says he is not happy about the gods. i explain to him how they, as agents for moral prescriptions that have become fatal, decline both outwardly and inwardly during their tour of inspection, until finally, starving and in a state of total disillusionment, they can even stomach the shabby fraud in the last act etc. he laughs now and then, but recovers his composure and drops the subject quite quickly – i had hoped he would be interested in translating it. then viertel arrives. they are old friends, from london. the conversation turns to english upper-class writers, himself, AUDEN, HUXLEY. 'india has done for you', says VIERTEL. 'it has infected you with its leprosy,' i say, to broaden the attack. in fact, isherwood is a buddhist (a little ersatz monk standing barefoot in a habit amid the incense in a hollywood monastery that is in point of fact a boarding-house), auden an anglo-catholic, huxley a deist of the vaguest sort. isherwood, who is a very close friend of the latter, allows me to 'take the mickey out of' his witty, subtly nuanced, elaborate descriptions of the spiritual agonies of parasites, but when i say he has been 'bought' he looks at his watch and stands up. one doesn't talk about that kind of thing, waiter, bill please! i have the feeling a surgeon would have if the patient stood up during an operation and walked away: all he has received is a wound.

25 sept 43

the capture of smolensk by the russians has totally changed the world situation. the setting up of the german committee of prisoners of war and exiles is now revealed (like the congress of the russian catholic church that seems to be aimed at the balkans) as part of the final offensive.

26 sept 43

am making the poems i've written here into a collection. ('landscape of exile', 'children's crusade 1939', 'to the german soldiers in the east', 'what did the mail bring the soldier's wife?', 'on a stormy night', 'german miserere', 'the mask of evil', 'of sprinkling the garden', 'homecoming', 'aurora'.)

27 sept 43

really surprising, the way politics have gone to the dogs in every way in highly civilised industrial states like germany and italy so that history is written in the style of a cheap novelette. these classes *scratch the bottom**. gangsters at the head of 300 motorised divisions. the pope in his hide-out shoots the brother guarding the gate.

DUCE & RESCUE SQUAD

Dirty Gertie was fond name given this dilapidated dummy by Sergeant V. M. Gemelli who rescued her from wreckage of a Bizerte shop. Dummy did not inspire famed song.

30 sept 43

BORCHARDT'S THE CONSPIRACY OF THE CARPENTERS has appeared in english. i note a violent aversion among the refugees, who find the work confused, religious, reactionary, a scandal. now borchardt, being, like many moralists, malicious, is a provocateur through and through and is, as a satirist, professionally addicted to exaggeration, etc etc. but it should not be forgotten that his works tower above those of werfel and his consorts, since they treat the social struggles of our times with passion and precision. in fact it is almost only in a religious context that one finds any parallel to these social struggles in the bourgeois camp. you just have to compare thomas mann with tillich. something like religious socialism exists, and exerts itself against clerico-fascism. I have not yet read b[orchardt's] book.

october 43

LIFE magazine is printing recent soldiers' songs, ie the printable ones.

Dirty Gertie from Bizerte
Saw ze capitaine, made ze flirty.
Captain think she veree purty;
Lose his watch and lose his shirty;
Call ze general alerte.
Ze gendarmes look for Dirty Gertie
From Casablanc' to Gulf of Serte.
Has anyone seen Dirty Gertie?

Bless all the blondies and all the brunettes.
Each lad is happy to take what he gets.
Cause we're giving the eye to them all,
The ones that attract or appall.
Maud, Maggie or Susie;
You can't be too choosey.
When you're in camp, bless 'em all.
Bless 'em all, bless 'em all
The long, the short and the tall

Take me somewhere east of Ewa
Where the best ain't like the worst
Where there ain't no Doug MacArthur
And a man can drown his thirst.
Where the Army takes the medals
And the Navy takes the Queens
But the boys that take the rooking
Are the United States Marines.

Chorus:

Hit the road to Gizo Bay
Where the Jap fleet spends the day.
You can hear the duds a-chunkin'
From Rabaul to Lunga Quay.
Pack a load to Gizo Bay
Where the float-plane Zeros play
And the bombs come down like thunder
On the natives 'cross the way.

I wanted wings till I got the goddamned things.
Now I don't want them any more.
They taught me how to fly and sent me here to die.
I've had a bellyful of war.
You can leave all the Zeros to the goddamned heroes.
Distinguished Flying Crosses don't compensate for losses
Oh, I wanted wings till I got the goddamned things.
Now, I don't want them any more.

Oh, the pilots all drink
The airplanes stink
And the navvies don't know where they are
The bombardiers couldn't hit
A target when lit.
Oh, Colonel, we've been here too long.

These B-26's they rattle and roar,
I don't want to fly over Munda no more.
Take me back to Brisbane,
Where the brass hats clamor in vain.
Oh, ma, I'm too young to die.
I want to go home.

This bloody town's a bloody cuss,
No bloody tram, no bloody bus.
But nobody cares for bloody us.

Chorus: *Bloody, Bloody, Bloody.*

All bloody clouds, no bloody rains.
All bloody stones and no bloody drains.
The dust gets in your bloody brains.

Chorus: *Bloody, Bloody, Bloody.*

1 oct 43

a struggle is raging in the senate over the calling up of fathers. senator wheeler, who before pearl harbor often sided with hitler, demands a law to exempt fathers from the draft. if more soldiers are needed, they ought to be recruited from government offices. in general people follow the call of the government very submissively. i find it agreeable that there is none of the revolting hypocrisy that in european countries would prompt statesmen or demagogues at least to make startling protests on behalf of those who are not deemed fit for military service.

2 oct 43

meet renoir at eisler's. he complains about the destruction of naples. 'it can never be rebuilt, it had no style, it just grew up among civilised people.' the conversation comes round to french architecture. 'the age of the hand is giving way to the age of the brain. the most dangerous animal that exists is the architect. he has destroyed more than the war has.' it is funny, almost exciting, to watch monsieur renoir eating a sausage. there is nothing wrong with *his* senses.

3 oct 43

if hitler cannot hold the dnieper it is easily possible that the german generals might do what the italian ones did. the russians with their committee have prepared the ground for this by recognising the generals as negotiating partners, probably counting on the fact that in destroying their own mass base the most they can achieve is to buy a stay of execution for themselves. roosevelt and churchill however seem concerned, since in the meantime they have come out in favour of extirpating the military caste in germany – probably for the first time. the russians, on the other hand, will point to the difficulties of the italian campaign and the fact that the allies could not see their way to start operations in western europe. the fact is that the italian campaign seems to promise more for the war in asia than for the european one.

10 oct 43

ADORNO was here. this frankfurter institute is a goldmine for the TUI NOVEL. the counterparts of the 'friends of an armed rising' are the 'selfless admirers of the idea of materialism'. 'marx is not interested in things, only in relationships between people, which are reified in things.' very amusing to read statements like, 'robert walser is very significant, since he reflects the decline of bourgeois society.' too bad this bourgeoisie then declined into panzer divisions and ss-squads.

12 oct 43

recipe for success in writing for films: you have to write as well as you can, and that has got to be bad enough.

15 oct 43

no matter what papers you read, what conversations you hear – what a grey, dismal, hollow mood there is everywhere. during the first months, when the country was still poorly armed and even the west coast was thought to be under threat, there was some sort of impetus, now it has completely disappeared. the memory of the great war depresses people's spirits. the new script reminds people of the old one in almost every move, and what a wretched ending that one had.

15 oct 43

ALEXANDER GRANACH, the actor, has written his 'memoirs'. the child of poor galician jews, a baker's apprentice, then an actor who had his legs broken in an operation to straighten his knock-knees so that he could play in tights. i remember him as shylock in munich about 1920, impertinent, importunate, shouting loud enough to make the chandeliers shake, very colourful. the galician anecdotes are good, if not quite as true as they sound, but the way he describes his profession! at the end, as the climax, he describes reinhardt's deutsches theater as just like hollywood (quite true). what a disaster, what confusion! has his legs broken to straighten them, then his spine to make him supine.

In the Ruins (continued)

Children's vaudeville is presented in a natural theater in London's Aldgate. Irene
Yasheim, who used to live in it, is putting across *As Time Goes By*. Notice curtain.

16 oct 43

reading a controversy among soviet literary historians about great
writers of the past, printed here in 1938. are the shakespeares and
tolstoys to be treated as apologists for their class or for mankind? lifshitz
and nusinov write rather bloodthirsty stuff. lenin says of tolstoy, and
nusinov has the temerity . . .? the public prosecutor is called in to put an
end to the allegations that shakespeare wrote for the bourgeoisie. no
proper examinations actually take place, or they take the form of trials.
the tone is terrifyingly unproductive, spiteful, personal, authoritarian
and servile at the same time. clearly it was not an atmosphere in which a
lively, combative, flourishing literature could prosper. the fact is that not

only are there no significant novels, but even trashy novels like alexei tolstoy's are considered good. and there is no drama, no single figure in a drama, either comic or tragic, not a philosophical quality in any play, and all this in spite of a highly accomplished theatre. findings like these normally serve to expose deep-seated faults, to prove 'that something must be rotten'. For the moment all that need be said is that the bolsheviks had no idea how to develop a literature. there is no need to assert that their methods in this field were a failure, it is maybe enough to say that the methods they chose to employ in this field failed. the situation was certainly unfortunate. the proletariat's seizure of power took literature by surprise.

a dialectician would find no difficulty in the dispute about whether the great bourgeois writers represent mankind or the bourgeoisie, since they were members both of mankind and of the bourgeoisie at the same time, and thus contradictory creatures. they represent mankind as members of the bourgeoisie, and the bourgeoisie as members of mankind in general.

17 oct 43

the politics of art of the working class. both to win the struggle for power and to keep power, the working class needs realism in thought and deed, and this is nothing special, the bourgeoisie needed realism and still needs it. tarted-up war reports are harmful for the commanders themselves, and doctored reports on the political situation are harmful to people on the stock exchange. in accordance with their respective situations the bourgeoisie needs secret realistic reports, and the proletariat needs open ones. so what is realistic art, say in the theatre? illusionism? sensualism? everything in colloquial prose, with atmosphere, as impenetrable as life itself? so plausibly done that we are left with the impression that things are so and can only be so? and man is always the victim of conditions, of the climate, of property, of passion, of the way things are? in that case the truth is always in there somewhere, but nobody can get at it. realistic art is art that leads reality against the ideologies and makes it possible to feel, think and act realistically.

28 oct 43

'helli, do you think somehow in the management of this hectic day you could do my hair?' says barbara at her birthday table.

1 nov 43

max reinhardt died in new york. in berlin at the beginning of the twenties i saw almost all the rehearsals for 'dream play' at the deutsches theater. the stylistic elements in his case aged just as quickly as in other cases in our era, with its yawning gulf between art and life, so that there is little art in life and little life in art. there is nothing natural in art when life itself is something artificial.

5 nov 43

a good play for the germans would be one where you could demonstrate how one man perishes thanks to their servility, ie is glad to accept it in the first instance in his capacity as führer and then later goes down with them as a result of their lack of independence. peasants' war.

10 nov 43

döblin brings I[NTERNATIONALE] L]ITERATUR] 1943, iv, containing GERMAN DOCTRINE, an article by becher which stinks of nationalism. again hitler's nationalism is quite naively accepted; hitler just had the wrong brand whereas becher has the right one. a 'type' of 'new german national literature' must be 'created'. ('literature will be national in this sense, or it will not exist.') he demands that the 'weaknesses of so-called literature of the left' shall be overcome, weaknesses which presumably consist mainly in its being of the left. appalling, opportunistic drivel, reformism applied to nationalism. the 'national front for peace and freedom against hitler' is of course an obvious tactical position to adopt, since catastrophes on a national scale can only be caused by nationalism. there must be opposition to nationalism's penchant for fragmentation and 'deindustrialisation'. but is this gigantic, philistine superstructure necessary? even in schiller, goethe, hölderlin the nationalistic element is intolerable to us. how philistine this 'ur-german element' in götz! 'we must show german figures that embody everything we conceive of as representative of the new german man.' i read, 'it is a new sense of community that is being formed, in order that germany's will be done, and that we should be the agents of this, and it is the highest thing of all that guards over such a common weal, the genius of an eternal germany.' pass the sickbag, alice!

11 nov 43

in '*19th century and after*'* a report on the extermination of the jews in poland. i really wish no more would be said or written about 'german man' (pronounced cherman), so as to save us from having to ascribe these qualities to every one of us. all these expressions coined by smart salesmen that peddle 'german scholarship', 'german spirit', 'german culture' lead inexorably to 'german atrocities'. we are the race who have to set an example by calling our country country number 11, and leaving it at that. germany must emancipate itself not as a nation but as a people, more precisely as a working class. it is not a case of 'never having been a nation', it was a nation, ie it played the nation game for a stake in world power and developed a stinking brand of nationalism.

11 nov 43

steff is collecting old records of once famous jazz pieces. here was a type of folk music which began, scaled a few peaks and went to the dogs, all very quickly. these are fields where nobody and nothing comes to anything. writers are lured to hollywood after their first slim volume and squeezed dry. they write for nobody. they all drink. it is a strain to see döblin and heinrich mann in such surroundings. they are nothing short of failures here. h. m[ann] has no money to call a doctor, and his heart is worn out. his brother in that house he built, with 4–5 cars, literally lets him starve. nelly, just 45, vulgar and with a coarse prettiness, worked in a laundry, has taken to drink. the two of them sit, among cheap furniture and the few books mann managed to salvage, in a stuffy little hollywood villa with no garden. and one day, talking about his return, he says, 'will we be able to take our belongings, won't it be too expensive? i don't want to have to start again from scratch at my age. i'd rather stay here.' but now he knows he can't stay here if he doesn't want to starve. 'if i see another ebert greeting the undefeated army at the brandenburg gate, i will fire a revolver, which needn't necessarily be loaded.'

7 jan 44

the american communist party offers the heroic red army a little compliment in the form of a harakiri.

mid-november 43 to mid-march 44

in new york at 124 east 57 st. working with hays and bergner on DUCHESS OF MALFI. not quite completed since bergner has little time. – COUNCIL FOR A DEMOCRATIC GERMANY founded. mainly on the intitiative of budzislavsky and tillich. – saw OUR TOWN, directed by J[ED] HARRIS, a progressive production, ROBESON as othello, bad in a terrible production, a musical, which was good. – negotiated with harris about GALILEO, came to an agreement with WEILL for the SZECHWAN PLAY as a semi-opera. contract with broadway for a CHALK CIRCLE, fixed up by luise rainer. began the play. – in the meantime feuchtwanger has signed for a film of SIMONE (i'm to get $20,000). buy new trousers.

6 apr 44

JED HARRIS, the producer-director who did a very good production of TH[ORNTON] WILDER'S OUR TOWN, is interested in GALILEO. so i took another look at the moral which i have always found slightly worrying. precisely because i was trying here to follow history and had no moral interest, a moral emerges, and i am not happy about it. g[alileo] is as little able to resist blurting out the truth as wolfing a tempting dish, it is a form of sensual pleasure. and he builds up his personality with the same passion and wisdom as his view of the world. in actual fact he collapses twice. the first time when he keeps silent about the truth, or recants because his life is in danger, the second time when he carries on and disseminates his research in spite of the danger to his life. his productiveness destroys him. now, to my dismay, i am given to understand that i thought it right for him to recant in public in order to carry on his work in secret. this is too cheap and shallow. g[alileo] destroyed not only himself as a person, but also the most valuable part of his scientific work. the church (ie the authorities) defended the biblical doctrine simply in order to maintain itself, its authority, its capacity to oppress and exploit. the people were interested in g[alileo's] astronomy only because they were suffering under the rule of the church. g[alileo] jeopardised true progress when he recanted, he let the people down, astronomy reverted to being just another scientific subject, the domain of experts, apolitical, isolated. the church separated the 'problems' of the heavens from those of the earth, consolidated its rule and then accepted the new solutions without further objection.

10 apr 44

mainly working on THE CAUCASIAN CHALK CIRCLE. interesting how much is destroyed when you are squeezed between 'commission' and 'art'. i dramatise unenthusiastically in this empty, aimless space.

29 apr 44

laughton, who has gone overboard in a big way for SCHWEYK (which he read in the rough translation) tells bitterly of the contempt in which actors are held in england. his grandfather was a butler, his father a hotelier, he himself came to the theatre when he was 28 and was famous inside a year. a bond street tailor only agreed to make suits for the international filmstar if he kept it secret since otherwise his tory customers would stay away. here, he says, they don't have any esteem to offer, but at least they have money. where else could an actor live like this he asks, pointing to the antique furniture, the park with its lawn and its mexican granite snake's heads, it's really something. here i can study shakespeare. he reads MEASURE FOR MEASURE for us at our place, and THE TEMPEST at his place. he sits cross-legged on a white sofa in front of a magnificent bavarian baroque long-case clock so that all you can see is his buddha-like belly, and he reads the play from a little book, partly like an actor, laughing at the jokes and excusing himself here and there for not getting a scene quite right. his reading leads me to see prospero like that remarkable portrait of napoleon on st helena, wearing a straw hat, with a yellow complexion and looking like a dutch planter. he reads caliban with pity.

producer-writer called auerbach, an american of whom he thinks highly. winge tells them the plot of the c[AUCASIAN] c[HALK CIRCLE]. g[orelik] asks what it means, and then they set out to criticise the structure. where is the conflict, the suspense, the flesh and blood etc? i try to expound the complex and audacious structure of hamlet. so what, so hamlet ain't builded (the way moss hart would understand builded). as they get into the car with winge, they say, 'he'll never be a success. he can't create emotions, he can't even get identification, so he goes and makes up a theory, he is crazy and he's getting worse.' the prostitution of these 'artists' is total. the whore sells the bare 'effect' and for that she gets highly paid, since her clients are impotent. the interest the public takes in life is that of the usurer, it should be called the 'dividend'.

6 jun 44

i came back from seeing MEMPHIS BELLE (flying fortress mission to wilhelmshaven) with homolka and karin, and was playing chess again when eisler called to tell me the invasion of france had started. the radio was spewing out news; an eye witness was talking from normandy.

barbara says the social science teacher didn't even mention the invasion; steff scarcely heard anything at university either. winge reports that a man had said to him, 'it's only foreigners who are getting excited about it and people with relatives in the army over there.' this is a natural response and displays a certain freedom even if it is in 'bad' form according to hegel.

Associated Press

BREWSTER STAY-INS
Who was to blame?

TRANSITION
The First Cutback Crisis

Some 8,500 men & women reported to work as usual at Brewster Aeronautical Corp.'s Long Island factories—and discovered that 4,500 had been fired that day. The sudden shock of this news stirred angry questions to which all U.S. labor wanted an answer: Was this to be the pattern of cutbacks and reconversion? Where were Washington's well-laid (or at least well-trumpeted) plans for painless transition to peacetime production?

Brewster employes dramatically forced an answer. At the urging of their union (C.I.O. United Auto Workers), all but 200 of the day shift stayed at work, even after the night shift came on. Since there was too little work for two crews, some workers played ping-pong and shuffleboard, danced to the music of piano, brass and drum. The union sent in enough sandwiches, pies, doughnuts, coffee and soda pop for a five-day siege. Some of the stay-ins crowded out on the balconies, hanging signs: "We've Got the Tools. We've got the Ability . . . but We Ain't Got the Work." Below, women pickets carried placards: "Is This What My Husband Is Fighting For?" The union proudly proclaimed the first strike-to-work in U.S. history.

ster workers knew that cutbacks—and shutdowns—were inevitable. Brewster's contract had been canceled because the Navy no longer needed so many Corsairs, and because the Navy considers Brewster, harried by bad management and long strangled in one of the most rigid labor-union contracts in the U.S., the least efficient producer. (The Navy said Corsairs cost $72,000 at Brewster; $63,000 at Chance-Vought, and $57,000 at Goodyear, for identical planes.)

HEMINGWAY

THE U.S. v. SEWELL AVERY

CHURCH FOR THE FRONT

The Archbishop of Canterbury is here shown blessing one of the first two motor churches ever designed for British troops at the front. The trucks, supplied by the War Office, were fitted out in spare time by members of the Royal Electrical and Mechanical Engineers, and the Auxiliary Territorial Service. Interiors are lined with polished oak; altars and hangings are red and blue, shoulder-patch colors of the 21st Army Group to which the churches are assigned. Each chapel-truck can accommodate twelve worshipers inside, carries an amplifying system.

Pope Receives Irving Berlin

ROME, June 17. (AP)—Gen. Sir Harold Alexander, Allied commander in Italy, and song writer Irving Berlin were among those given private audiences today by Pope Pius.

The Pope also received 3000 more Allied soldiers in a general audience.

Berlin's show, "This Is the Army," is now playing in Rome.

POOR PAT! POSTWAR JOB OUTLOOK BAD

A SECRET AMERICAN AIR BASE IN WESTERN CHINA, June 17. (U.P.)— Rugged 1st Lt. Pat A. Chance of 4303 Griffin Ave., Los Angeles, one of 26 American Army engineers who supervised construction of the huge B-29 bases, is worried about his postwar future.

"When the war is over," he lamented, "I know what will happen. I'll ask for a civilian job and they'll hand me a form to fill out. There'll be a dotted line— 'Past experience and size of job handled'—and my answer'll have to be:

"'Built air base with 65,000 coolies and little else.'

"Then they'll shake their heads and whisper: 'Poor old Pat. He's been away too long.'"

Communist Party Quarters Raided

ROME, June 17. (AP)—American Military Police operating under the Allied Military Government entered headquarters of the Communist party in Rome June 7, searched the premises for firearms but found none, party officials said today.

There were no arrests. The Communists said the soldiers at first "acted roughly," but that an officer later expressed regrets.

Tito Drives Nazis From Three Towns

LONDON, July 17. (AP)—Marshal Tito's Partisan forces have driven the Germans out of three Western Bosnia towns—Prozor, Bravsko and Kljuc—with heavy losses, and the Nazis are rushing up reinforcements to stem the drive, said tonight's Yugoslav communique recorded by the Ministry of Information.

The war bulletin said 800 Germans, Bulgarians and Quislings were killed as the Partisans pressed their Serbian offensive, and that much material was captured.

FEET HURT?

Get Relief THIS

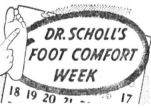
thoughts for D-Day.

6 jun 44

finished the CAUCASIAN CHALK CIRCLE yesterday and sent it to luise rainer.

PAY CORPS CARRIES CASH TO INVADERS

LONDON, June 9. (U.P.) — Today is payday for the British troops on the beaches of Normandy, the British radio, quoting a report of the London Daily Herald, said.

The broadcast said men of the royal army pay corps struggled ashore with the rest of the troops on D-Day morning, "clinging to their tin money cases as if nothing else in the world mattered."

12 jun 44

told gorelik he had changed, and gave him a few theses. he came back with 'the drama needs suspense, climax and identification' again, and claimed he couldn't understand if he couldn't empathise. it was like talking to a brick wall when i explained how little understanding is involved in empathising with a victim. there is no way of weaning him from his interest in 'selling the story'. and in selling shocks and emotions.

International

PIUS XII

Und Feuer flammen auf im hohen Norden
Auf stille Küsten stürzt der Lärm der Schlacht.
›Ihr Fischer sagt, wer kam da, euch zu morden?‹
›Der Schützer tauchte auf im Schutz der Nacht!‹

The quatrain reads: 'Great fires are blazing in the arctic regions/ In lonely fiords the clamour's at its height./ "Say, fisherman, who launched these deadly legions?"/"A gunman who loomed up at dead of night." '

there are now about 60 quatrains, and along with FEAR AND MISERY OF THE THIRD REICH, the volumes of poetry, and perhaps FIVE DIFFICULTIES IN WRITING THE TRUTH, the work offers a satisfactory literary report on my years in exile.

25 jun 44

horkheimer recounts how, for his broadway hit X AND THE COLONEL, saint frunzis of hollywood, gschwerfel of that ilk, used a poor refugee's story and didn't pay the man a cent. 'i have made an eternal monument to you, is that not enough?' he told him.

3 jul 44

the C[AUCASIAN] C[HALK CIRCLE] uses the fiction that the singer stages the whole thing, ie he arrives without actors; the scenes are just representations of the main episodes of his story. nonetheless, the actor must act as if he were the director of a company: he strikes the floor with a little hammer before entrances, makes it clear that at certain points he is supervising the proceedings, watching for his next cue, etc. this is necessary to avoid the intoxicating effects of illusion.

21 jul 44

when snatches of information about the gory goings-on between hitler and the junker generals trickled through, there was a moment when i had my fingers crossed for hitler; for who, if not he, is going to wipe out this band of criminals for us? first he sacrificed his SA to the herrenklub, now he is sacrificing the herrenklub, and what about the 'plutocracy'? the german bourgeoisie with its junkers' brains is having a stroke. (the russians are advancing on east prussia.)

30 jul 44

laughton reads the first three acts of LEAR to us (the feuchtwangers, tsiang, winge, dessau, gorelik, steff). he brings out the lear of the first act excellently, insisting on 10 pounds of filial love per 1000 square metres of land. then, after he has relinquished his power, the refusal to give up its appurtenances. he contrasts the empty, formal appeal to supernatural powers beautifully with simple, realistic utterances and genuine feelings. – gorelik then objects to the play in much the same terms as he did to the

10 aug 44

KORTNER and HOMOLKA, and to a much lesser extent LORRE, judge this country by its theatre, in which conventional evening entertainment is sold by speculators. kortner was once, to a very limited extent, 'politically conscious', homolka was totally apolitical. but now both criticise eg the americans for not being political. both nurture a myth of the german theatre in the weimar republic, bad as it was.

14 aug 44

i still, as i have done for years, keep a map of europe on the wall by my typing table, and on it the conquests of the nazis stand out in lobster-red. now this army is going down like ninepins. the generals are deserting, abandoning their war to its own devices with the cry that the corporal has bungled it. what a rabble! the fact is simple: they have lost it comprehensively.

15 aug 44

but what about the question why the germans continue to fight? well, the population has the ss on its back, and besides it is without a political will in any direction, robbed of the few parliamentary institutions it had, questionable though they were, and economically under the heel of the possessing classes, as it always has been. its soldiers are fighting for their lives in the context of strategic and tactical operations, while supplying their labour to the machinery of destruction, with as little concern for the results of their work as if they were toiling at the machinery of production. in a word, the germans are still fighting because the ruling classes are still ruling.

16 aug 44

in the evening edward steuermann, in a private recital, plays a mozart rondo, one of bach's english suites, some schubert variations and beethoven's hammerklavier sonata. even as a boy when i heard the st matthew passion in the barfüsser church, i decided never to go to a thing like that again, since i abhorred the stupor, the wild coma, into which one became lulled, in addition to which i thought it was bad for my heart (which had been enlarged by cycling and swimming). i can now listen to bach, i believe, with impunity, but i still don't like beethoven, that surge to the sub- and supernatural with all its (for me) attendant kitschy effects and 'confused emotions'. it 'breaks all bonds' like mercantilism, it has the sentimental vulgarity of the rabble, with its 'o ye millions, freely gather', whereby the millions have a double meaning (as if it went on 'let all the world have coca cola!').

20 aug 44

took a look at 'l'immoraliste' by GIDE, the man who is a style in himself. the description of how the immoralist cures his tubercular body is somewhat hectic and the narrator himself somewhat breathless, every-day things are infected with tuberculosis, the immorality has no vigour, sees itself as perversion – and yet the book, which is itself in a state of disintegration (which is something more than just conducive to disinte-gration) gives a foretaste. what a literature there might be in an age in which the state has gone into liquidation and morality (or rather moralising) has been dissolved. of course literature might by then have dissolved itself too . . .

24 aug 44

romania capitulates. fall of paris.
    the way the nazis were driven out of paris will soothe the fears of the possessing classes. in the end the fascist gendarmerie went on strike, then it fortified the ile de france in the seine. nothing is said about fascists, from which one concludes that a few officials, compromised as collaborators, have fled. france has been liberated and is taking a look at its liberators.

28 aug 44

last night a great chunk of laughton's garden, about which i had started a poem ('*garden in progress*'*) fell away in a landslide. he rang about noon to see if he could come over this evening, and when he came he excused himself for bringing his worries to people who haven't had a real roof over their heads for a decade. he began right away to read chapters of the life of david which he is preparing for some records he is going to make (at my instigation, he says), and he read very beautifully about david and jonathan. he had also brought along a couple of volumes of shakespeare and read (or acted) osric from HAMLET, jacques from AS YOU LIKE IT and

On a Paris street, a wounded Nazi . . .

. . . who disarms him . . .

. . . is pounced on by an F.F.I. woman . . .

News of the Day International, Associated Press
. . . then helps carry him off.

16 sept 44

there is nothing surprising about the german military defeat in france. no reason why hitler should let the anglo-american armies in before the russians. there is undoubtedly a great deal of treachery on the part of the generals. if they have any will to fight at all, it is to defend their little places in east prussia against the russians. and the way they deal with a conquered country. a dismal picture.

17 sept 44

german art is difficult. precisely in these times, some of the most dreadful in history, it should learn to be easy, not of course by running away, but by depicting the times and their dreadfulness. so the normal must assume the character of the never-before-known, and things that have never before been known must take on an ordinary character. the man acting blood and sweat must not sweat.

i realise this when i draw the attention of barbara, who is tap-dancing in the next room, to her drops of sweat, and advise her to do less than she could rather than to attempt more than she can before she can do as much as she can.

18 sept 44

steff drafted into the 26th army. he decides to take a look at the country and is travelling to san francisco, saint louis, new orleans.

160 10=NEWORLEANS LA 12 1204P

1944 SEP 12 AM 10 50

:ERT BRECHT=

1063 20TH ST SM=

:BED. NEED THIRTY FIVE TODAY ANKLE WRENCHED OTHERWISE ALL

HT=

STEFAN.

20 sept 44

essay by a certain bruno bettelheim, '*behaviour in extreme situations*'* about the behaviour of prisoners in concentration camps. confirms borchardt's observation that prisoners assume the bearing and manner of speaking of their torturers. one interesting thing is the rapid (galloping) loss of personality experienced by those who are only able to reject the treatment meted out to them because they perceive in it an illegal use of the law. another interesting thing is the group treatment of prisoners by the gestapo. (a group gets maltreated because an appeal has been made on its behalf.) such descriptions ought to interest people who cling to the liberal concept of the personality and react particularly violently to the suppression of personal freedom in the USSR. there the criterion for measuring the personality is the ability of the person to swim against the current. this criterion is, as it happens, specially valuable before and during revolutions. for then the collective freedom of the group takes precedence over the freedom of the group (which is complicated during the class dictatorship by the need for self dictatorship).

26 sept 44

took steff to the streetcar-stop on ocean on a misty morning, since he has been drafted into the army. yesterday evening conversation with eisler, helli, steff about a brilliant and reactionary preston sturges film and the prologue to CHALK CIRCLE. steff would like to see the conflict between the villages more real and tougher, because the goat collective is really getting a raw deal.

Stefan S. Brecht, aged 20.

5 oct 44

talked to dessau and winge about a subject for an opera, THE JEW'S WHORE MARIE SANDERS. particularly about the choral parts. the composition of the chorus shouldn't be rigid, a collective person. the choruses to be formed of main and lesser characters, depending on the particular situation. even incomprehensibility should originate in lack of comprehension. etc.

18 oct 44

the great dialectic is unfolding more and more. the russians take the finnish nickel mines. iran refuses them the use of the oil-wells in north iran which they have occupied. spanish loyalists are concentrating in western france among the *maquis*, and they say american troops are going to occupy the pyrenees. de gaulle is preparing massive reforms designed to ruin the *comité des forges*. the big polish estates are to be broken up on 12th december. italy is vegetating as a british crown colony, greece, breathing fire, awaits its king. the vatican is propagating a new munich based on clerico-fascism.

19 oct 44

eisler recently read GIDE's 'paludes' and MANN's 'tonio kröger' and has been talking about how badly the latter comes off. (he also tried to read 'joseph', that encyclopaedia for the half-educated.) when you get down to it we really don't have a literature. the bourgeoisie prepared its revolution in literary form and then sold it. any style that crops up later is pretentious.

21 oct 44

i am listening to schönberg's 'theme with 7 variations' on the radio when the doorbell rings. an anaemic, prematurely aged young woman on the doorstep asks, '*can i ask you for a busfare?*'* i hastily give her 10 cents and go on listening to the romantic work with its pre-stabilised harmony.

21 oct 44

SCHÖNBERG is saving classical music to destruction. eisler always calls it

– with profound respect – totting up music's household account. for me there is something circular about this music, the movement isn't going anywhere, the logic only satisfies itself.

october 44

at a farewell party for kalatosova who performed the 'jewish wife' in leningrad for front-line troops i get into conversation with odets. i praise spencer tracy's acting in the SEVENTH CROSS for a few almost sublime expressions which are otherwise thin on the ground here. odets hadn't noticed and was annoyed when i advised him to see the film again. he kept clutching his chest and insisting that he hadn't noticed anything. for him the cinema is a kind of electric-shock machine and he just registers its discharges. impossible to make him understand that you can go into a cinema and watch carefully to see whether some reflection of reality might not pop up on the screen, buried under childish plots, hidden in 'stock characters'. characteristics that are very easy to miss.

22 oct 44

conversation with several left-wing jews at GORELIK'S; it seems there is a new communist policy: the american jews are to organise themselves as a national minority. someone laments, 'the jews know nothing of their culture!' scholem asch is a literary figure of world class. if heine had written in yiddish it would have been better from the jewish point of view. attempt in vain to object that neither yiddish nor hebrew is a fully developed modern language like english, russian, french, spanish and

MR. O'MALLEY, BARNABY AND GORGON
Miracles are promised but not performed.

certain asiatic languages. that schönberg, einstein, freud, eisenstein, meyerhold, döblin, weigel represent not jewish but other cultures etc etc. to my knowledge there is no evidence of 'jewish' culture to rank alongside jazz or negro sculpture or irish drama. what the jews need, just as in marx's time, is to emancipate themselves from capitalism (commerce) and not to retreat into their 'old culture'.

end october 44

dinner at schönberg's with dessau and the eislers. the astonishingly lively, gandhi-like schönberg in his blue californian silk jacket, a mixture of genius and craziness. for example, he complains at the shortness of copyright for intellectual works. ('my son, when he is 45, won't get another cent,' he says, as if he were speaking of a monstrous injustice.) then again, partly, but only partly, to tease, he says that, in contrast to other composers (not all that many of course) he sometimes finds that his own works sound awful. after he has written them he finds it hard to understand them and has to study them laboriously. a string in me 'vibrates sympathetically' when he complains that in music there is no purely musical conceptual material. form, as an example, he defines as follows: it is the repose between two forces acting on one another. (seemingly a field concept.)

29 oct 44

wanted to fetch steff home on leave yesterday. had prepared everything on friday, new tyres on the car, permission from the district attorney etc. then i was supposed to call steff between 7 and 9, but the camp was not accepting calls. so we didn't know whether he would get leave. the frischauers, who have often been to camp roberts, claimed the trip was impossible with my old car (260 miles each way); since the new piston-rings are new i was only supposed to do 25mph, there was thick fog along the coast, my wiper had packed in, the lights failed intermittently, so i didn't go and had all saturday and sunday to ask myself whether it hadn't just been self-indulgence, failure to make a special effort. suddenly i began to see this leave as a desperate escape into private life, into the human domain, which it probably was, and i saw steff going back to the 4 others whom he had wanted to bring along (in the little car whose tyres would almost certainly have burst).

6 nov 44

frequent conversations about music (connected with the GOLIATH OPERA) with eisler and dessau who is much less developed and seems tied up in routine. modern music converts texts into prose, even verse texts, and then poeticises that prose. it poeticises it and at the same time makes it psychological. the rhythm is dissolved (except with stravinsky and bartok). for the epic theatre this is useless.

7 nov 44

roosevelt is being elected again. at pascal's in the evening with laughton (barbara was there too in a black evening dress). groucho marx and chaplin there. helli, chaplin and i were the only ones by the radio.

15 nov 44

took out the REFUGEE CONVERSATIONS again and read a few chapters to winge and dessau and to brainer, the austrian worker who came over with us on the 'annie johnson' and works on the southern pacific. their reaction discourages me a little. the intention was to situate philosophical discussion on a 'lower' level, but the lack of elegance still distresses me. with us germans such a gulf separates the live and realistic from the elegant. in addition to which i am always working for the theatre where so much is a matter of chance and everything, in a literary sense, is in disorder.

17 nov 44

now and again i forget a german word, i, who only now and again recall an english one. when i try to find it what comes to mind is not high german words, but dialect expressions like *dohdle* for godfather.

27 nov 44

it is about eleven o'clock at night. i am sitting with a whisky (i don't often) and reading GIDE'S JOURNAL 1940. it is quiet and it is pleasant to sit isolated like this, but then i can't resist switching on the radio for the news although there won't be anything new in it – i listened at half past nine and half past ten. the fact is that there is no reasonable rest except what our surroundings (in the broadest sense) offer. to cut yourself off from the world is to immerse yourself in the raging torrent of the void. so i am writing this now as i listen to the radio and then i shall carry on reading gide as i listen.

28 nov 44

i have been given ARTHUR WALEY'S TRANSLATIONS FROM THE CHINESE as a present. since the american publisher has stuck cheap chinoiseries between the poems i have to paste bits of paper over them. i notice to my amusement when i have done my patching that the value of the poems has gone up for me; i had proved their value for myself by investing my own labour!

astonishing what an ass this excellent sinologist waley is! he cannot grasp that for PO CHÜ-I there is no difference between didacticism and amusement. no wonder we find that learning, practised as the quick purchase of knowledge for resale purposes, arouses displeasure. in happier times learning meant a pleasurable absorption of the arts (in the baconian sense). literature, in didactic as in other works, manages to enhance our enjoyment of life. it sharpens the senses and transforms even pain into pleasure.

29 nov 44

PO CHÜ-I: RESIGNATION [english by Arthur Waley]

keep off your thoughts from things that are past and done;
for thinking of the past wakes regret and pain.
keep off your thoughts from thinking what will happen;
to think of the future fills one with dismay.
better by day to sit like a sack in your chair;
better by night to lie like a stone in your bed.
when food comes, open your mouth;
when sleep comes, then close your eyes.

free translation:

> denk nicht vor: hast du kein glück
> kannst noch lange schauen
> denk um himmels willen nicht zurück
> erinnern ist bedauern
> besser, du sitzt tagaus, tagein
> wie ein sack in deinem gestühle
> besser du liegst in der nacht wie ein stein
> unbewegt auf dem pfühle
> ist's das essen, auf das maul!
> ist's der schlaf: zu die augen!
> hockst du im wagen, schafft's der gaul;
> muß zu etwas taugen

translation in irregular rhythms without rhyme:

> halte deine gedanken von allem, was aus und basta ist
> denn das denken and die vergangenheit weckt bedauern
> halte deine gedanken von allem, was kommt und nicht kommen mag
> denn das denken an die zukunft weckt unruhe.
> besser du sitzt am tag wie ein sack in deinem stuhl
> besser du liegst bei nacht wie ein stein in deinem bett.
> wenn essen kommt, dann auf mit dem maul
> wenn schlaf kommt, dann die augen zu

30 nov 44

nothing worthwhile to do and the old russian headache. so i am doing a little translating.

> THE HAT GIVEN TO THE POET BY LI CHIEN [english by Arthur Waley]
> long, long ago to a white-haired gentleman
> you made the present of a black hat.
> the gauze hat still sits on my head
> but you are already gone to the 'nether springs'.
> the thing is old, but still fit to wear;
> the man has gone and will never be seen again.
> out on the hill the moon is shining tonight
> and the trees on your tomb are swayed by the autumn wind.

> lange zurück, ein weißköpfiger herr
> machtest du zum präsent einen schwarzen florhut.
> der florhut sitzt noch heute auf meinem kopf

du aber gingst schon zu den 'unteren quellen'.
das ding ist alt, doch ganz präsentabel
der mann ist gegangen und kommt nicht wieder.
draußen am hang scheint der mond heut nacht
und um dein grab die äste schwanken im herbstwind.

10 dec 44

now working systematically with laughton on the translation and stage version of the LIFE OF THE PHYSICIST GALILEO. – remarkable how difficult it is to solve even the tiniest problems (like, say, a new transition) when they present themselves separately. when you are writing continuously you miss out the problematic bits; that is where the adroitness of thought lies, and this not getting involved is not a decision to capitulate, on the contrary. you just don't dig your oar in too deep, or too shallow, for moving on is all that matters. on a purely 'external' level, when my concentration drops beyond a certain point, i reach for my crime novel, since i don't trust my thought processes any further.

12 dec 44

the eislers, kortner, the henrieds, the thörens, kaus. the attitude of the french refugee artists to de gaulle and vichy comes up for discussion. they say rené clair and renoir are anti-semitic. eisler: 'not anti-semitic, they just can't stand jews.' these unfortunate intellectuals! are they dangerous? they are dangerous, like cigars cut up in the soup.

18 dec 44

letter to steff:
    the frankfurt sociological institute (which inspired my TUI NOVEL) has now consolidated its shaky financial basis: the new york jews are financing a comprehensive project of research into anti-semitism for them. horkheimer and adorno have already worked out questionnaires, to identify the fascist type methodologically and on a strict scientific basis. this is the type who is potentially anti-semitic, and from now on it will be possible to diagnose the condition at a non-virulent stage (and eventually treat it). questions such as: do you believe that natural disasters – plagues, earthquakes, etc – are linked with the world war?' – 'do you consider syphilis to be incurable?' i brought the conversation round to a little piece by K.M[ARX] on the jewish question, only to be

told yet again that it is out of date (and anyway it is by the *young* m[arx]). m they say fell for goebbels's distinction between creative and rapacious capital. my malicious question as to whether the new york jews would in their opinion be financing the marxian standpoint if m had not been wrong, or if the institute could prove that he had been right after all, fell on deaf ears. (i am almost certain that adorno would not include these points in his questionnaire.) m took the jew in his historically 'existing form', shaped by persecution and resistance, with his economic specialisation, his forced reliance on liquid cash (the need to buy oneself free, or to buy oneself in), his cultivation of ancient superstitions etc etc. and m advised him to emancipate himself (and himself demonstrated how). adorno *can't* make a long face, which is a handy failing for a theoretician. so i had to go a little further. i suggested that he attack capitalism for liquidating haggling. which eliminated all the imagination, all the humour, all the amusing conflict, in short all the wit from trade. i describe to adorno the contempt the chinese (far better hagglers than the jews) reserve for western traders who simply pay the asking price and take the goods away without any human interaction, any contest of minds, taking place. if the presence of the seller is as superfluous as that, why not just break in and steal the stuff in the first place? –

massive preparations for christmas are going on in the house. helli is sewing innumerable jackets, nightshirts etc and baking innumerable christmas stollen. barbara is taking on loans that will keep her a slave for 50 years. we are all hoping very much that you will be here to get a noseful of the smell of pinewood downstairs combined with the chemical stench upstairs.

20 dec 44

explaining the political usefulness of non-aristotelian drama is child's play; the problems begin in the aesthetic sphere. a whole new artistic experience in the theatre has to be put across. it is a question of taking away the metaphysics, of earthifying the artistic experience. man is no longer the pawn of supernatural forces (the fates, who still control the *plot** on broadway today,) nor of his own 'nature'. the new theatre creates (and derives its life from) the joy of conveying human relationships.

december 44

working systematically with laughton on the version of galileo. he translates sentence by sentence, writing down my clumsy translation first then his own one, or rather ones. we make alterations at the same time. the biggest difficulties are with galileo's speech about the new time in scene 1, especially the sentence 'because it is so, it need not stay so'. associations in english are so different, likewise the arguments and the humour. to replace the biblical quality of 'for where faith has been enthroned for 1000 years, doubt now sits' we are trying to use blank verse, '*blind placed faith deposed by healthy doubt!*'* – at least that gives it a scholastic quality. the element of blasphemy is naturally lost.

besides that, making photographic experiments with r[uth] with a view to setting up an archive of my work on film. innumerable experiments, once even with the help of reichenbach. it is amusing to discover what sources of error there are in the kinds of papers, the types of film, the lighting equipment, the lenses etc. first result POEMS IN EXILE. then i go through the STUDIES again to the same end.

POEMS IN EXILE contains:

THOUGHTS ON THE DURATION OF EXILE	from the SVENDBORG POEMS
THE SNOWSTORM	from the STEFFIN COLLECTION
THE CHERRY THIEF	,, ,,
THE DEATH-BIRD	,, ,,
1939: LITTLE NEWS EMANATES FROM THE REICH	from the SVENDBORG POEMS
QUESTION FROM A WORKER WHO READS	,, ,,
THE ANSWER	from the STEFFIN COLLECTION
THE DOOR	,, ,,
HOLLYWOOD	(new)
READING WITHOUT INNOCENCE	(new)
ON READING THAT A MIGHTY STATESMAN HAS FALLEN ILL	(new)
READING THE PAPER WHILE BREWING THE TEA	(new)
THE MASK OF EVIL	(new)
GERMAN MISERERE	(new)
I, THE SURVIVOR	(new)
HOMECOMING	(new)

when you come down to it, the poems are written in a kind of 'basic german'. this in no sense corresponds to a theory. reading through such a collection i'm conscious of the lack of expressiveness and rhythm, yet when i am writing (and correcting) every uncommon word sticks in my craw. poems like LANDSCAPE OF EXILE i'm not putting in, they are already too rich.

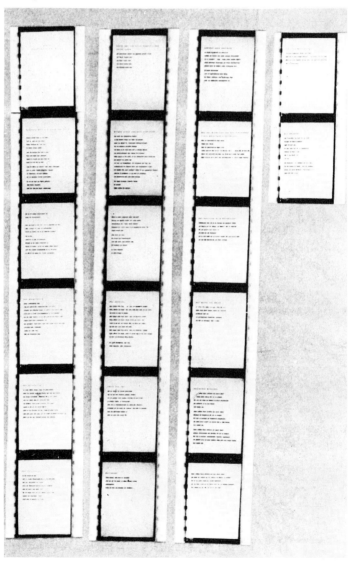

Contact prints of the *Poems in Exile*, 1944, Brecht's first collection since 1940.

22 dec 44

the reactionaries have found a popular long-running bone of contention in the polish question. without bones like that politics is hard going, since not all disputes can be popular. churchill instantly threatens to rat on his polish friends if roosevelt rats on him in greece. – the left is confused. the warsaw rising, which was armed, was at first encouraged by the russians, and then, when the reactionary bor began to dominate it, it was coldly handled (even if you take into consideration that it evidently came too soon for the russian strategy, so that this precious assistance by the people was wasted in order to give the owners of poland in london a *claim**). the left is now saying that the russians in poland were afraid of the difficulties the british had in greece, and that it makes no difference when you are eating fish whether you have your knife in your left hand or your right.

15 jan 45

MAX GORELIK, who gave an account of epic theatre in NEW THEATERS FOR OLD, has drawn more and more theoretical gaps to my attention: i can see where he goes wrong. gorelik's efforts to convey the picture give off a peculiarly puritan odour, reminiscent of the laboratory. the aesthetic side shrinks into formalism. (the theatre for a scientific age becomes scientific theatre.)

16 jan 45

[in] GALILEO, with its interiors and atmosphere, the structure of the scenes, which is taken from epic theatre, has a remarkably theatrical effect

19 jan 45

meet s[IDNEY] HILLMANN of PAC and the CIO at dieterle's. he has just come back from a trade union conference in london, a fox who has left many a tail in the jaws of an iron trap. the general feeling in london was, he says, that they have to be extremely careful this time, having been disppointed by the german social democrats in 1918. they had read in konrad heiden's book that these people worked hand in glove with the general staff. i corroborate this fact but warn him against heiden. the

SPD, i try to explain, only had as much power as the allies and the german imperialists allowed them. – 'and why didn't they seize more power?' he asked. – 'there was a certain fear of revolution,' i said. – 'we don't want any more war,' he said. – 'then you must do away with the system that means war,' i said. – 'oh,' he said, 'we can at least prevent germany from starting another war in a hurry.' – 'if you get rid of the system there, that is,' i said. – 'we haven't heard anything about a german resistance movement,' he said. – 'no,' i said, 'i haven't heard anything about a german resistance movement being liquidated either.' – again and again it is impossible to rectify people's ideas about conditions in germany if they haven't been told of at least two of the principles of dialectics, the sentence concerning contradictions that look unified, and the principle about the leap from quantity into quality.

20 jan 45

from time to time dessau rings me up and plays me a new quatrain over the phone. he sounds like a man from another planet.

POLISH PEASANTS DIVIDING THE LAND*

Warsaw had fallen to the Red Army two-and-a-half months after the suppression of the Warsaw Rising.

21 jan 45

after his *basic training** at camp roberts steff is going to the university of chicago to learn japanese. we are very pleased.

23 jan 45

begin the opera, JOURNEYS OF THE GOD OF LUCK.

24 jan 45

steff, on three days' leave, has a party. fetching a girl, he runs over an old man who was crossing the street. MPs, ambulances etc. he doesn't tell the whole story that evening, brings eisler and brainer to his party. eisler says next morning that he was in high spirits, but then he comes along with the stuffing rather knocked out of him. it is possible that the accident could cost him his time in chicago.

28 jan 45

still nothing from upper silesia about the attitude of the workers.

11 feb 45

since LAUGHTON has to work on a pirate film for eight weeks i look around for work to do, and decide to set myself a little task and put the manifesto into verse, in the manner of a lucretian didactic poem, the decision being influenced a little by the possibility of producing little photographic editions which not only give the illusion of miniature books, but also promise critical correspondence. the manifesto as a pamphlet is itself a work of art; but it still seems to me that today, a hundred years later, and given new, armed authority, it would be possible to revitalise the propaganda effect by removing its pamphlet character.

20 feb 45

i use my mornings for the poem. (in the afternoon i help r[uth] to produce the archive.) i work standing at a high desk on which i have placed my typewriter, so that i can walk about, since the difficulties are great. i have photographic prints of the original text lying all over the place.

25 feb 45

all the while the lack of any uprisings against hitler in g[ermany] – source here of such angry comments – is perfectly comprehensible to me. for the first time i can see possibilities (from afar) when i hear that the reich is caught between a shortage of labour for the munitions industry on the one hand and unemployment on the other because raw materials are running out, the transport system is cracking up and the factories have been bombed. in st petersburg in 1917 the workers in the putilov works rebelled when the bourgeoisie shut them out of the munitions factories.

3 mar 45

feuchtwanger tells me the hexameters are bad. that means a great deal of polishing. the fact is i know too little about it.

4 mar 45

party at the eislers' place. CHAPLIN did a wonderful impression of a chopin film with muni. chaplin says he used to do a particular trick muni did with a handkerchief when he was eight: he was playing an unhappy old man in music-hall – the easiest thing in the world. then he told us about a bluebeard film he is planning. a middle-aged man, a rather stuffy family man, murders women because it is hard for a middle-aged man to make a living. chaplin intends to abandon the charlie of the classic films. it is not just a question of how charlie should speak now that all films are talkies. charlie was in every sense speechless. the typical lumpenproletarian has fallen victim to the *new deal.* *the new deal took care of him.*

5 mar 45

KORTNER, who was also watching chaplin yesterday, is disappointed with the muni impression. it showed that character actors are out of date, just that. kortner would, rightly i think, naturally formulate it like this: character actors have survived here in an out-of-date form.

Service Song

The Marines still are having a field day in PM's daily service song column and will until some Army and Navy songs come in. Here's one called *Bloody Rabaul*, from the South Pacific:

Once down to Sydney from Guinea
*   I strolled*
From a place called Bloody Rabaul.
I met an old sergeant, he said,
*   "Pardon me please,*
You've blood on your tunic and
*   mud on your knees.*
Da-de-ah, Da-de-ah,
You've blood on your tunic and
*   mud on your knees."*

Now listen here, Doggie, you
*   bloody damn fool*
I just got back from a raid on
*   Rabaul*
Where shrapnel is flying and com-
*   forts are few*
And good men are dying for bas-
*   tards like you*
Da-de-ah, Da-de-ah,
Where good men are dying for
*   bastards like you.*

10 mar 45

between the DIDACTIC POEM and the terrible newspaper reports from germany. ruins, and no sign of life from the workers.

Brecht and Feuchtwanger at Pacific Palisades.

20 mar 45

we hear that industry's capacity for rebuilding itself is great, but this only applies in relation to the goods produced, and only so long as the basic machinery is not destroyed. as long as furnaces are working, tractor ploughs are quicker to make than wooden ploughs, but what if they aren't working? as for culture, it decays with amazing rapidity (as would the artificial flora of california, planted as it is in the desert, if it were not watered). even great nations in tight circumstances are no longer willing to pay even a dozen great minds the salary of a minor official. it was naturally not the military defeat that enabled marxism to brush aside proudhonism in the war of 1870: the more progressive people triumphed and with them the more progressive theory. the proletariat has progressed further in france than in germany. but the commune's glorious struggle left the working class almost ruined.

2 apr 45

i am working with GORELIK on an american play, THE VINEGAR SPONGE. one scene is to show how a young man, trying to get a job, has to put an older worker out of work. the young man has to say why he needs the job. 'we mustn't have any talk of money, that's anathema on broadway,' says gorelik seriously. it is a fact that money is never mentioned in the commercial theatre, just as you don't talk about cancer in front of cancer sufferers. a possible motive for his search for a job would be if his father died without insurance, a natural catastrophe in other words. it would be impossible, however, for him to find his mother with her head in the gas oven because she hasn't got $12 for the beauty salon and her boss has threatened to sack her – she might be a waitress. utterly impossible is the truth that the young man needs the money to keep body and soul together, and will lose his girlfriend if he can't afford tickets for the movies.

3 apr 45

discuss film for german prisoners of war in the USA with DIETERLE. we go through WHAT DID THE MAIL BRING THE SOLDIER'S WIFE? and a discussion of possible misunderstandings develops. it is not a denunciation of the soldier for looting. What he sends home is trifling, and that's all the people are going to get out of the war. the theme is that wars of conquest are not worthwhile; all the campaigns and atrocities won't produce enough to dress the woman, and they rob her of her man.

12 apr 45

ROOSEVELT dies. with the death of the enlightened democrat the leadership of the democracies passes to churchill. winge's girlfriend reports that many of the women in her factory wept.

GANDHI sent mrs roosevelt a telegram; condolences on the death of your husband. congratulations that the man of peace does not have to see peace being murdered.

end of april 1945

AUDEN must unfortunately return to england before his work (on the C[AUCASIAN] C[HALK CIRCLE]) is finished.

laughton is not in the mood to start working on GALILEO again.

in NY they want to put on MASTER RACE for a CIO audience.

2 may 45

The *Herald Tribune* of April 3 reports a Russian radio broadcast of a statement by the Soviet-appointed mayor of the German town of Landsberg on the Warthe. A former member of the German labor movement who had been arrested twice by the Nazis for his political views, the new mayor, Paul Schulz by name, urged all Germans to "follow our example and liberate yourselves from Hitler." He described the aid given by the Russians in rehabilitating the captured town. Under Soviet direction, he said, the waterworks had been repaired and factories reopened to supply the 25,000 inhabitants. "Fifteen bakeries are working for the benefit of the population. New household and bread-ration cards have been issued. The labor office, the housing office, and an office for the care of refugees are busy promoting reconstruction work. Streets have been cleared up. A hospital, two maternity wards, and a children's home have been established." The military commandant of the town, Schulz emphasized, was helping the population in every way.

On 2 May Berlin surrenders to the Red Army.

3 may 45

help LAUGHTON to rehearse the story of the creation for a record. his ear is attuned to the familiar, international parsonical tone, which spoils everything, since his voice seldom follows his gest and is clumsy when it does, ie has little mobility. i advise him to do a few exercises and we go to a recording studio and record the following: a) the creation as recited by a frenchman like jean renoir, b) by a yorkshireman (laughton's home), c) by a cockney (*at the beginning mr smith created the heaven and the earth**), d) by a planter trying to make the natives believe he created the world, e) by a butler (*in the beginning his lordship created . . .**), f) by a soldier '*in the foxhole*'* (with '*so what*'* and '*much good did it do us*'* between the acts of creation. now the whole thing sounds like a primitive fertility rite or phallic dance.

8 may 45

nazi germany capitulates unconditionally. the president makes a speech on the radio at six in the morning. as i listen i contemplate the californian garden in bloom.

12 may 45

discuss two films that could be made for germany: DR LEY and the story of a peasant woman who struggles for two days with herself and her family (including a son on leave) as to whether they should slip half a loaf to a starving prisoner. she does it and brings her son, the soldier, bound with cattle ropes, to the allies (and safety) in a hand-cart.

14 may 45

with LAUGHTON on GALILEO. we add some really good things, like the disputation with ludovico in the sunspot scene.

mid-may 1945

and then when it was the month of may
a thousand-year-reich had passed away.

and down the street called hindenburggass'
came boys from missouri with bazookas and cameras

seeking the way and what loot they could take
and one single german who thought world war II a mistake

field marshals were rotting along the pavement
butcher asked butcher to pass judgement.

the vetches flowered. the cocks were quietly moping
the doors were closed. the roofs stood open.

june to mid-july [45]

in new york for a performance of the PRIVATE LIFE OF THE MASTER
RACE. a $6000 job. originally piscator was going to direct; he cast it with
students and émigrés (the SPY with the bassermanns) and wanted a new
framework. i brought in viertel and we put the production together in a
few days' rehearsal. the press attacked the production, spared the play.
nobody discussed the content. anything technical is so expensive in a
broadway production that it can only be hired for musicals.

broadway reflects the intellectual life of the states adequately. a wholly
modern actress, TAYLOR: her acting is epic.

negotiate with two publishers about a complete edition in english.

wieland herzfelde sets up aurora publishers (and prints FEAR AND
MISERY).

then i finish DUCHESS OF MALFI in rough with BERGNER (latterly in
vermont)

read the DIDACTIC POEM to schreiner, walcher, duncker. surprising
impression.

back on 18th july, after meeting steff in chicago. he is in hospital for
constant headaches and expects to be discharged from the army.

20 jul 45

EISLER came to NY with me to write the music for MASTER RACE and keep
an eye on things. in NY there was a telegram waiting which said he had to
get back to the studio straight away. he returned in unseemly haste,
considering that he had been given leave of absence; he wrote the music
while waiting for his ticket. it was film kitsch, and at my insistence he
wrote it again. this time it was brilliant theatre music. – now DESSAU is
complaining that e[isler] called him when he got back to hollywood, said
his nerves were bad and asked him to write some 12 minutes of film
music for the studio. it was agreed that e. would split the cheque ($1000)
with d[essau]. d. wrote 4 minutes, but by then e. had recovered and
decided d.'s music was not usable. d. naturally insisted on his money
nonetheless (to e.'s astonishment). he was due $200 (usual price) but
contented himself with asking for 100. 4 weeks went by. d. was in dire
straits and needed the money, and e. knew it. sitting in my study, with d.
in the kitchen, e. complained that hollywood music was ruining his ear.

3 sept 45

LASKI REPROVES ITALIAN SOCIALIST

Says Nenni Loses Confidence in Democracy in Advocating a Merger With Communists

By Wireless to The New York Times
ROME, Sept. 2—Prof. Harold J. Laski, chairman of the British Labor party's executive committee, came out today for a republic in Italy in the first article of a series written for the Rome political weekly Nuova Europa.

The article, under the headline "My Advice to Nenni," strongly advised Pietro Nenni, Vice Premier and leader of the Italian Socialist party, to carry out a program aimed at ending the monarchy at socialization and dissolution of the concordat with the Vatican through democratic methods in the Constituent Assembly.

At the same time Mr. Laski declared that Signor Nenni, having "lost confidence" in democracy, was heading toward the foundation of a one-party state through a merger of the Socialists with the Communists.

While paying tribute to Signor Nenni's honesty, Mr. Laski warned him against dictatorship, which, he said, would mean "mass arrests even among those who fought against * * * Mussolini."

Mr. Laski's intrusion in Italian politics got the Italian press worked up, but more in terms of Signor Nenni than of Mr. Laski.

While no paper found it worth the comment that the chairman of the Labor party executive had taken sides on the institutional question, at least to the extent giving assurance that "the United Nations will support the popular choice of a republic," nearly all went to work either for or against Signor Nenni along the lines of a crisis of the Socialist party.

Signor Nenni denied that he has "lost confidence" in democracy and the two most serious are the Murray so-called Full Employment insisted that the movement anticipating a merger of the Socialists and Communists was not a prelude to a new dictatorship. On the contrary, the Vice Premier wrote that the danger of a counter-revolution in Italy would continue "as long as the monarchy is spared."

While the Christian Democrat paper Popolo said that Signor Nenni might feel somewhat less enthusiastic over the British Labor victory than on the day it was announced, the independent paper Momento noted the coincidence of warnings the same day by Mr. Laski and Premier Ferruccio Parri against the solution of Italian political questions by other than strictly democratic methods.

Signor Parri, speaking in Milan at a convention of the Committees of National Liberation of the North, declared the coming elections must be conducted along democratic lines and asserted that he would be the first to "annul any election influenced by violence or the threat of violence."

The basic theme of the Laski and Parri remarks is emphasized by the incessant campaign being waged by Allied authorities, notably United States Ambassador Alexander C. Kirk, for the retention of American forces here on the ground that they are required to "stabilize" the situation this winter.

Italy whose progress toward democracy has been publicly acknowledged by the highest spokesmen of the United States, Great Britain and France, has at least the seeds of internal dissensions by which all of what has been gained can be lost.

Letters to The Times

The New York Times

ECONOMICS AND FINANCE

'Fighting Inflation' by Price Control

By HENRY HAZLITT

Endless estimates are being poured out day after day, by both Government and private soothsayers, telling us exactly how many jobs or unemployed we are going to have six months a year or two years from now; exactly how large our national "income" or "gross national product" is going to be; exactly how many automobiles, houses and television sets are going to be produced, and so on. Most of these figures, unfortunately, are worthless. For the simple truth is that nobody knows what our future national income, employment or production is going to be unless he knows first of all what political and economic policies we are going to follow. We can run into full production or disorganized production, full employment or mass unemployment, depending upon what those policies are.

In some segments of our economy, the war controls have been removed with surprising swiftness. To that extent business has been encouraged to go ahead. But many obstacles to quick reconversion and full production remain. Of these the two most serious are the Murray so-called Full Employment Bill, described by President Truman as a "must" measure, and the retention of rigid and unrealistic price control policies by the OPA.

* * *

The "fight against inflation," in fact, seems to have come down to a policy on the part of the Government of prolonging the basic cause of inflation while trying to prevent or conceal the symptoms. The basic cause of inflation is the Federal deficit, which creates new monetary purchasing power through an increase in bank credit and in currency. Instead of trying to put the Federal budget into manageable shape, when through the end of the war it is at last in a position to do so, the Administration is now actually demanding a bill which proposes to achieve full employment by means of "compensatory" Government spending; that is, by means of chronic deficit financing. The whole objective of reducing or even stabilizing the huge national debt of $263,000,000,000, the whole objective of balancing the budget, the whole objective of Government economy, or of reducing Government expenditures to a point where it might be possible to reduce the unparalleled load of taxation on enterprise, seems to have been forgotten.

This drive for the Murray Full Employment Bill, of course, can only increase inflationary fears in the free market economy.

the country. On top of this the former controls over industrial wages are being allowed to lapse. There is substantial support in Congress for increasing national minimum wage rates. The unions are about to bombard industry with demands for higher wage rates. But with all this prospective increase in purchasing power and in the cost of producing goods, where they are. The patient's fever is being increased, but everything is to be made to look right by holding the thermometer down to normal.

To the extent that this policy is not evaded by a growth in black markets, it means that profit margins will be cut or wiped out, that reconversion will be delayed, that production in many lines will be discouraged, that unemployment will be created by governmental policy. It appears probable, for example, that the display and sale of new automobiles will now be held up for weeks because of the red tape involved in the complex pricing formula of the Office of Price Administration. If this sort of thing were to grow, the next step, presumably, would be for the sponsors of the Murray bill to claim that private enterprise has once more failed to provide full employment and to insist that the Government step in with more Government spending or direct work relief.

We can avert these consequences only by a return to prudent Government spending, accompanied by revised tax rates that leave an incentive for risk-taking and production, and by an orderly but rapid withdrawal from price control. It is true that, when we withdraw from price control, the general level of prices is likely to rise because of the huge wartime inflation of bank credit and currency that has already taken place. But the only safe way to bring this inflation and price rise to a halt is to stop the heavy deficit financing that is its primary cause. To try to stop it by price control, while its fundamental causes remain, must lead either to one of two results. If wages also are controlled it must lead to rationing and allocation of material and labor and so into a completely totalitarian economy. If wages are not controlled, private enterprise will not be able to operate, and the result will be mass unemployment. Our only solution, in brief, is a return to a free market economy.

Congress Is Urged to Give Attention Also to Needs of Industry

TO THE EDITOR OF THE NEW YORK TIMES:
At the hearings now being conducted before the Senate Banking and Currency Committee, as reported in THE NEW YORK TIMES, much is being said as to what the Government ought to do for labor and as to what the Government ought to give to labor during the forthcoming period of reconversion unemployment. Little is being said as to how to speed the reconversion period and enable industry to reabsorb those who have been or will be released from war work and those who presently will be taking off their military uniform.

That unemployment of sizable dimensions would be inevitable during the change-over period was obvious to any seeing eye. Yet the press and radio are now playing up this angle with extravagance, and pressure groups are making demands on Government accordingly.

During the Nineteen Thirties our Government was more social-minded and did more for labor than ever before in our history. However, despite the billions of debt that it piled up, in peacetime, mind you, there were still some seven to nine millions unemployed in 1939 when war came to Europe.

Capital Handicapped

During those same years there was generally an atmosphere of estrangement between Government and business. Name calling was indulged in. Did it ever occur to our lawmakers that business makes jobs under our capitalistic system of free enterprise, and that business, requiring the investment of risk capital, which, by its very way, oftimes is lost, will only operate and take risks when the atmosphere is friendly and opportunities for profit, all things considered, seem present?

As long as we adhere to the capitalist system in preference to any form of totalitarianism—and it's a system that has made us the richest and mightiest nation in the history of the world—why not try to lessen the work on all eight cylinders, instead of putting hindrances and obstacles in its path? All new proposed legislation ought to be examined with this thought in mind. Of what use will it be to hand out another two billions in unemployment insurance if in the process risk capital be again forced into hiding?

Ready to Go Ahead

Industry in this country today is raring to go after a brief period of change-over to peacetime production. It has the working capital. It has the plant. It has manifold new products and improved old products to put on the market. The pent-up demand for a variety of goods that have gone unsatisfied these many years is huge both here and abroad. Let's give business the right-of-way, subject, of course, to the standing rules and regulations. Let's remove any barricades that exist, certainly not erect new ones. Let us encourage enterprising men to enter business in search of profits. They will create jobs and produce goods and services in the process.

Labor has a stake in seeing that our present economic system function well and survive, as well as capital. Labor need only compare its lot here, under the capitalist system, with that prevailing under any other system anywhere else in the world.
A. Y. COWEN.
New York, Aug. 30, 1945.

aus einer Times-Nummer

'From *one* issue of the Times,' says Brecht's pencilled note.

MONDAY, SEPTEMBER 3, 1945. **FINAN**

1945.

ARCHBISHOP CUSHING ASSAILS COMMUNISM

BOSTON, Sept. 2 (AP)—The Most Rev. Richard E. Cushing, Archbishop of Boston, declared today that it would "be a brutal tragedy if totalitarianism and materialism —or the blending of these two which is atheistic communism— should take over the peace." .

In a sermon preached at a special mass at the Cathedral of the Holy Cross in anticipation of Labor Day, the Archbishop said:

"We are beginning once again to detect the efforts of false friends of labor to divide working men from their spiritual leaders, Catholic people from their heirarchy, 'the proletariat,' as these false friends would call them, from those whom the same group would call 'the prelates.'

"These false friends of labor have made slow progress in the United States, because working men and the American hierarchy were of the same blood families."

In all the American hierarchy, he declared, "there is not one Bishop, Archbishop or Cardinal whose father or mother had been graduated from college."

"Every one of our Bishops and Archbishops is the son of a working man and a working man's wife," he added.

"That is one reason why it has been so difficult a task for the saboteur to divide our people from us."

WEALTH OF BRITAIN FOUND HELD BY FEW

Ownership of 55 per cent of private property in Britain is concentrated in the hands of 1 per cent of the adult population over 25 years old, according to the International Federation of Trade Unions, which has its headquarters in London.

Official statistics for 1943 and 1944 show, the federation says, that 8,600 persons at the top of the income scale had a total income of £180,000,000, or an average of £21,-000, while 1,755,000 persons in the lowest brackets earned a total of £2,355,000,000 or less than £250 (about $1,000) on the average.

"A factor of the utmost significance for the so-called 'war fluctuation' is that the share of the salaried persons in the total income fell from 27 per cent in 1939 to 22 per cent in 1944 while that of wage earners in spite of bonuses, overtime additions, etc., remained approximately the same at 42 per cent," the federation says.

Steel Industry Seeking Price Rise of $7 a Ton

By The Associated Press.

CLEVELAND, Sept. 2—Steel mills, used to operating in the black during recent lucrative war years, are seeking to stay financially solid through further price relief, the magazine Steel reported today.

Confronted with rising production costs and shrinking income as a result of cancellations of war orders, the steel industry seeks an overall ceiling price increase of $7 per ton, or a flat $7.50 per ton increase on carbon steel products, the trade publication reported.

Steel asserted that details are lacking, but it quoted authoritative trade circles as saying that a resolution was adopted by the steel industry advisory committee on Aug. 24 asking relief from the Office of Price Administration.

E NEW YORK TIME

CHURCH HELD FR OF FRANCO BOND

Continued From Page 1

the Primate commands as la
church following as Pedro (
nal Segura y Saenz of Sevil
still has the most powerful o
church position in Spain, and
is no doubt that the pastoral
will have a tremendous effe
the political situation here.

Criticizes Foreign Critic

Formerly Bishop of Salm
Dr. Pla y Deniel, member
wealthy Catalán family, was
nated as primate by Ge
Franco in 1941 and appoint
the Vatican in the same yea
has been a close friend of Ge
Franco since the civil war, wh
loaned the general his Bi
palace at Salamanca. His
Miguel Mateuy Pla, former M
of Barcelona, is now chief o
Spanish mission to Paris.

In his pastoral, the Bishop
that some foreign critics of
and of the present regime in
the Spanish Church in their
cisms. "The Spanish ecclesia
heirarchy has not been, and
not be, the slave of anyone, nc
it defended, nor will it defen
ther a statist or totalitarian
ception."

He added that during his
as primate he had had almo
obsession in insisting agains
enslavement of the church to
political regime.

The recently enacted Spanis
of rights is commended by th
mate as "orientation of Chr
liberty as opposed to state t
tarianism."

Finally, the Primate decl
"The past civil war and cr
was an armed plebiscite, whic
an end to religious persec
None wants any unnecessar
vision that would bring new
war, with great damage to
and great dangers to the pea
the western nations of Europ

5,000 Plastic Eyes Made by Army
The Army Medical Corps has
made and fitted more than 5,000
plastic artificial eyes, The Associated Press reports.

Spanish Primate Denies Church Serves Under Bondage to Franco

By PAUL P. KENNEDY

By Wireless to THE NEW YORK TIMES.

MADRID, Sept. 2—A denial that the Spanish church has been en-slaved to Generalissimo Francisco Franco is contained in a pastoral letter issued by Dr. Enrique Pla y Deniel, Archbishop of Toledo and Primate of Spain, which was pub-lished here this morning. Dr. Play Deniel openly endorses the Franco regime but he denies the accusation that the church favors totalitarianism and also disclaims any church responsibility in the affairs of State.

All Madrid morning newspapers carried the letter on the front page, but only Arriba, official Falange organ, commented edito-rially, declaring:

"This time it is not the propa-ganda organ of this or that re-gime, but the church primate, who has spoken on behalf of per-manent truths, which transcend all strictly political considerations."

Early in his pastoral the primate declared that when there is close concord between church and State, as in the case in Spain, one should not confuse the activities or re-sponsibilities of the church with those of the State. "We affirm solemnly that the church in Spain has kept perfect neutrality," he said.

Praying that another civil war would not set Spain in flames, he added that while all wars are ter-rible, they are just when necessary and when they are "for the re-establishment of international or-der."

"None likes peace more than the Catholic Church, but do not fall into the error of some heretics who condemn all wars as unjust."

While there is some doubt that

---

the atom bomb, in which atomic energy makes a timely first appearance, strikes 'normal folk' as simply awful. to those impatiently awaiting their sons and husbands, the victory in japan seems to have a bitter taste. this superfart is louder than all the victory bells.

(for a moment LAUGHTON fears quite naively that science might be so utterly discredited by it, that the birth of science – in GALILEO – could lose all sympathy.' *the wrong kind of publicity, old man.*'*)

20 sept 45

most of the time we are still working on GALILEO, which laughton's audience in the military hospital listen to with quite extraordinary interest. the atom bomb has, in fact, made the relationship between society and science into a life-and-death-problem.

in between times i am making a COPY OF MACBETH for a film with lorre and reyher. the great shakespearian motif, the fallibility of instinct (the lack of clarity in the inner voice) cannot be renewed. from it i take the little people's defencelessness against the ruling moral code, which limits the criminal potential of their contribution.

25 sept 45

we hear that the THREEPENNY OPERA has been performed to packed houses in berlin, but then had to be taken off, at the instigation of the russians. the BBC (london) reported that the ballad 'food is the first thing, morals follow on' was the reason for the protest. personally, i would not have permitted the production. in the absence of any revolutionary movement, the play's '*message*'* is pure anarchism.

25 sept 45

the labour victory in britain fills me with very mixed feelings. the mass protest against tory rule will probably lead to a confused tolerance of rule by the social-democratic party machine. the 'western bloc' is turning pseudo-progressive.

2 oct 45

considering a PROMETHEUS. the gods are ignorant and malicious, ingenious in extracting sacrifices, they live off the fat of the land. prometheus invents fire and quite criminally hands it over to the gods. they capture and fetter him, to make sure he cannot deliver his invention to mankind. for a long time he hears nothing about this fire of his, then he sees conflagrations on the horizon: the gods have used it to scourge mankind. the gods appear only as a chorus.

5 oct 45

FEUCHTWANGER is being pressed by AP, the biggest US press agency, to cover the nuremberg trials for them. not as a journalist – they have dozens of star reporters there – just 4000 words a week. he turns it down. 'i'm no good at that kind of thing,' he says. 'then just do it as best you can, you're the only one they've asked,' i say. 'they overestimate this trial,' he says. 'for the first time in recent history a government is on trial for its crimes,' i say. 'they don't mean it seriously,' he says. 'that's why you ought to go,' i say, 'to see that a government's crimes against its own people are remembered too.' 'you are so subjective,' he says, 'just try to understand my reasons.' – 'quite by chance you are in the happy position of being invited to represent the german anti-nazis, you have no right to be getting on with your novel,' i say, 'speak badly, stutter, let them gag you, but at least get out there.' – 'you know it isn't cowardice,' he says. 'there are worse things,' i say, 'it's the easy way out.'

HEINRICH MANN at 75, when i report this to him, says he would go like a shot. but of course nobody asks him.

10 oct 45

driven on by his theatrical instinct, LAUGHTON plugs away relentlessly at the political elements in GALILEI too. at his behest i have worked in the new 'ludovico-line', and the same goes for the reordering of the last galileo scene (handing over the book first, then the lesson that the book must in no way alter the social condemnation of the author). laughton is fully prepared to throw his character to the wolves. he has a kind of lucifer in mind, in whom self-contempt has turned into a kind of hollow pride – pride in the *magnitude* of his crime etc. he insists on a full presentation of the degradation that results from the crime which has unleashed all g[alileo's] negative features. all that is left is the excellent brain, functioning in the void independently of the control of its owner who is happy to let himself sink.

he brings this conception out most clearly one evening when they had shouted 'scab'* at him as he went through a picket line in front of the studio. this wounded him deeply – no applause for him here.

15 oct 45

fiat mundus, pereat justitia! the only way de gaulle's courts can get rid of laval is by judicial murder. this profoundly treacherous class is publicly strangling one of its own, the tiger which bears its class sins. laval, remembering that he drew up the rules of the game himself, breaks them all. he is not standing 'before his maker', he is standing before his creation. at the end he shouts 'long live the bank book', that is to say, 'vive la france'.

28 oct 45

EINSTEIN is demanding that the atom bomb should not be handed over to other countries, especially russia. he uses an image: a man who wants to enter into a business partnership with another man must not hand over one half of his capital at the outset, since the other might become his competitor. the 'world government' demanded by einstein seems to have been created in the image of standard oil, with managers and managed. – a brilliant brain in his own subject, housed in a bad violinist and eternal schoolboy with a penchant for generalising about politics.

it is dawning on the other scientists who are involved in the production of the atom bomb (their remarks about the outside world are vague – one doesn't have to understand the world to destroy it) that freedom of research may be considerably restricted if the new source of energy is treated as a monopoly of the military. their own country's first step towards ruling the world is to place a policeman at their side.

29 oct 45

'the expected military advantages of uranium bombs were far more spectacular than those of a uranium power plant . . . such thoughts were very much in the minds of those working in this field . . .' (OFFICIAL REPORT by H. D. SMYTH)*

20 nov 45

EZRA POUND has been arrested in italy and is being brought here as a traitor. an element of feudal dignity clings to people like GEORGE, KIPLING, D'ANNUNZIO, POUND. historical figures when all is said and done, not exactly to be found in the market place, more in the temples – on the fringe of the market place.

beyond the immediate damage that was done. the very fact that they are inclined to draw up accounts is a bad sign; and in future they will be more sparing with credit and will thus diminish their prospects of improving people.

17 dec 45

LAUGHTON caught up in the machinations of his agent is an instructive performance. he read the play indefatigably to soldiers, millionaires, agents, friends of the arts. not a single response, it seems, was negative or even cool. then the question of a production arises and his agent says, not before the autumn, stressing the danger of the summer break. (he wants to be involved in the financing himself, which takes time.) WELLES agrees with me that spring would be better politically (interest in the struggle between the scientists and the state, atom bomb, etc); since he couldn't then be the producer (he can't raise the money that quickly), he puts it as follows: he couldn't take the responsibility vis-à-vis the backers if it were

Brecht and Charles Laughton, in the latter's garden in Pacific Palisades.

to be spring. CZINNER has the theatre and the money and is prepared to take the risk in spring. l[aughton] '*hates the sight of that man*'* but is prepared '*if necessary' to swallow him*'. a summer break would mean earning nothing during these months, at least not in films. he would like to have me along, but i may not be here in the autumn, but his agent says . . .

5 jan 46

the british fascists who publicly supported hitler ('lord haw-haw' and john amery son of the minister for the colonies) go to the gallows with great dignity. they are convinced that the british bourgeoisie has betrayed 'western civilisation'. and the fact is that all churchill has to show is a three-year delay in the invasion . . . the record of the french bourgeoisie is equally dismal; they have proved that they would rather live under the prussian elite than the french mob, and in the most shabby manner possible . . . all in all the european bourgeoisie ought quickly to cancel its one new creation, namely fascism, and thereby abandon all hope of surviving another 30,000 years. nuremberg: the counter-revolution is devouring its own children. the russians do what the bourgeoisie has omitted to do, they introduce agricultural reform. and the big thing is: they have not been destroyed. they are more indestructible than ever. so the hangover is a sizeable one.

20 feb 47

in SONNTAG, a berlin weekly, for 5 jan 47, BECHER writes a leader headed DEATH AND RESURRECTION which begins 'when luther on 31 october 1517' and it goes on, 'it is inconceivable that those of us whom destiny calls, who must watch over this new, this infant germany, those of us in whom lives the people's will to be born again – it is inconceivable that we and others like us should fail in this task.' and 'the end of the first half of the twentieth century must bring germany's tragedy for ever to an end.' and 'let us bethink us of generations to come, of the beginning of the year two thousand, of the generation which, as the century turns, will weigh all our aims and all our achievements in the balance.' and 'the thirty years of suffering and death, the flower of german youth fallen in the great war, millions of lives laid down in the second world war, all this will have been as nought unless we, by responding to the needs of the people and the reich, by creating a new liberal germany, give a meaning to the untold suffering and the nameless dying. then shall the bells ring for a resurrected germany. then we shall we be able to sing: now praise be to god . . .'

the pied piper of hamelin must at least have known how to whistle.

Margaret Bourke-White-LIFE

RUHR MINER AT WORK
Weak and unwilling

Photograph from *Life* by Margaret Bourke-White.

Leaders Again Disturbed by Surplus Farm Crops

One of the most important economic problems facing the United States today is the disposal of surplus farm products, Albert S. Goss, master of the National Grange, told members of the Wilshire Chamber of Commerce yesterday at their luncheon meeting in the Chapman Park Hotel.

"Since 1939 food production in this country has increased 35 per cent while consumption has increased only 15 per cent," Goss said. "This leaves a surplus to be disposed of without upsetting the economy of the farmer and of the nation as a whole."

Three Plans Proposed

Four major plans to solve the problems are under way, he said. Three of them are being proposed by agencies in Washington, and he doesn't think much of them. They have to do with what he calls artificial methods of establishing production, prices and distribution.

"The law of supply and demand still rules," Goss declared. "If it is not followed, it will break us just as the farmers went broke in 1920."

The fourth plan, backed by the Grange, is an international organization of agriculturists which held its first meeting last May to establish regulations for what foods shall be raised throughout the world. Under its regulations a world-wide agency would establish minimum and maximum prices and buy or sell on the open market to keep them within prescribed ceilings.

Could Be Sent Out

Surplus products purchased to bolster prices would be canned or otherwise saved, or distributed to hungry populations in various countries which would have to set up credits in the form of other types of exchange goods which they could furnish at the time or later.

Thus, he said, no surpluses would be destroyed, as has been the case in this country in the past.

"Never forget," Goss told his audience, "the farmers of the world comprise 80 per cent of the purchasing power. We must keep up that purchasing power if business is to flourish."

Goss, whose headquarters are in Washington, is in Los Angeles on a brief business trip and will return to the capital today.

WAITING FOR THE RED CROSS (IN RUMANIA)
Food for the poor, stability for the bewildered.

15 MILLION GRAVES
MARK NAZIS' TRAIL

Russians and Poles suffered
most among 9 nations invaded

20 mar 47

finish THE ANACHRONISTIC PROCESSION. a kind of paraphrase of shelley's 'the masque of anarchy'*.

24 mar 47

read zhdanov's 'errors of certain types of soviet literary journals'. this is the kind of thing that is always used by intellectuals as balm for their consciences when they have opted for their jobs. under the dictatorship of the proletariat literature ceases to function as a safety valve; it is no longer partisan in the way it is under the anarchic expansion of productive forces by the bourgeoisie. the compulsory dissolution of the monopoly in education creates a kind of vacuum; for a certain time literature (inasmuch as it continues to be practised as a profession) has to confront the uneducated masses' hunger for education. its most progressive methods, marked by the contradiction between productive forces and mode of production in the bourgeois era, are on the one hand corrupted both by police censorship and by the censorship of taste exerted by the 'free' market, but on the other hand represent the sole result of past developments and cannot simply be abandoned. the soviet union, in instantly turning the bourgeois revolution into a proletarian one, compelled the available progressive writers to make a leap whose effect in many cases was to break their necks, or at least a leg. in a kerenski-style russia ehrenburg would have become a major figure in world literature. for a great number of writers the condition which mayakovsky experienced as freedom was a state of severe repression. they made mayakovsky pay for that.

24 mar 47

completing THE COAT (after GOGOL) as a scenario for lorre. no prospects for it in hollywood, am thinking of switzerland. i have sent THE TWO SONS to dudow in berlin. – very impressed by two films i saw in recent weeks: STORM OVER ASIA and CHAPLIN'S MONSIEUR VERDOUX: the latter was to have been called 'the provider'*.

26 mar 47

intoxication with war. in the vast people's armies of the great bourgeois wars it is often pseudo-communism one finds among the youth of the petty bourgeoisie – the grand task on a national scale, the gigantic collective, economic security, public denunciation of profit, physical labour, contact with machinery, hygiene, etc. – in the case of germany it would be rewarding to make a serious effort at some stage to trace the socialist elements that national-'socialism' has put into operation in a perverted form. in no other way can its success with the masses be explained.

27 mar 47

saw MALRAUX'S MAN'S HOPE*, the film on spain which contains excellent dialectical elements, is marvellous aesthetically and can be regarded as a good contribution to the theme of 'the progress of the hollywood technique'. the peasant flying in the bomber who does not recognise his own fields down below is magnificent. saw EISENSTEIN'S STORM OVER MEXICO, assembled here without eisenstein from an enormous amount of material. what an eye the man has!

29 mar 47

receive an exit and re-entry permit to go to switzerland.

30 mar 47

the difference between realism and naturalism has still not been cleared up.

naturalism	*realism*
society regarded as a piece of nature	society regarded historically
segments of society (family, school, military unit etc) are 'little worlds on their own'.	the 'little worlds' are sectors of the front in the great struggles.
the milieu	the system
reaction of individuals	social causality
atmosphere	social tensions
sympathy	criticism
events are supposed to 'speak for themselves'	they are helped to become comprehensible
detail as a 'trait'	set against the whole
social progress is recommended	taught
copies	stylisations
the spectator as fellow man	fellow man as a spectator
the public addressed as a whole	the whole is exploded
discretion	indiscretion
man and the world from the standpoint of the individual	of the many

naturalism is a surrogate for realism

3 apr 47

we called on a writer who repeated the well-known thesis that the american worker rejects marxism because he has been bribed by prosperity (created by the 'cultural imperialism of the bourgeoisie') – which is why we have to turn to other strata. 'through our films, newspapers, radio-operas, we have made him what he is.' what interests me in this tirade is the 'we'; first he said it was the editorial we, then he said he wanted to put his own complicity on record. my impression was that this was another of the well-known appearances of 'the nation'. 'do you know that our workers speculate on the stock exchange and gamble on horses, and do you know how much is spent on liquor in this country? i knew a button-maker in NY who bought up buttons in 1917 and then committed suicide in 1929 because he had lost a million on the stock exchange!' at the moment he is trying to combat the anti-semitism of the gentiles with the philosemitism of the jews. they ought to study

WORLD STRENGTH OF COMMUNISTS

All the Communist Party members in the world could not elect a U. S. President. Figures released in London, at a congress of the British Communist Party, showed that Communist and other parties that "base themselves on Marxism" have 18,692,000 members scattered through 57 countries. That total is 6,000,000 less than the vote cast for the winning candidate in the 1944 U. S. presidential election.

The Worldgraph reproduces these figures on Communist Party strength. An added column shows the percentage of the total population of each country that its Communist Party membership represents.

The figures bring into sharp relief a cardinal difference between Communist and democratic political organization. Russian Communists rigidly limit the size of their party, set an annual quota for the admission of new members. Thus, the one and all-powerful political party includes only 3 per cent of the country's population.

Under similar organization, Czechoslovakia's 7 per cent of Communists is far in excess of the proportion needed to rule the country. A dozen other countries, including France and Italy, equal or exceed the Russian ratio of party strength. In general, this strength is highest in states neighboring Russia, falls off to one tenth of 1 per cent in Britain, one twentieth of 1 per cent in the U. S.

Date and source unknown.

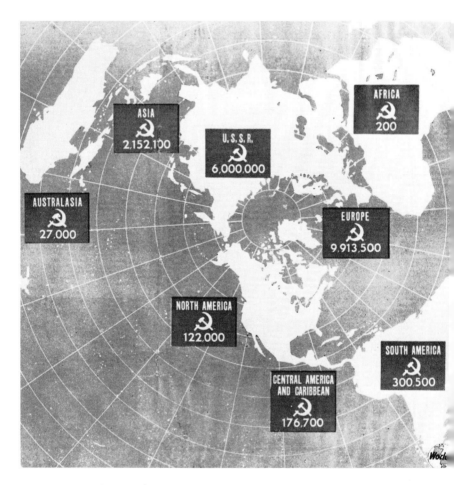

Date and source unknown.

and stress their cultural distinctness. 'the german proletariat was the best
organised in europe and it was indoctrinated with marxism, yet it fell
victim to anti-semitism and followed hitler.' when we germans talked
about the role of disunity, except in the context of parliamentarianism,
or of defeatism in the question of unemployment, we were 'romanticis-
ing' the german worker.

15 sept 47

reading THE GERMAN STANISLAVSKY BOOK (ottofritz gaillard, vallentin). they are now putting this into practice in an acting school in weimar.
one can of course imagine that it has a relative value; here in the states too
stanislavskyism represents a protest against the commercial theatre, a
handful of serious actors are building a temple, but, as it happens, on the
market place. the remarkable thing is how the germans were able to
conserve the system of the progressive bourgeoisie of the czarist era
intact, in its entirety. among the exercises (enacted situations) i have yet
to discover a single example from the class struggle. (bride is making up
at her dressing-table, a letter is delivered . . .) the realism is peculiar.
'reality' is turned into an elaborate cult. it has, in the main, to do with
subjective emotions which are screened from the influences of the
external world while they are being worked out in exercises of a loyola-
esque type aimed at auto-suggestion. nowhere is observation recommended, unless it be self-observation. the external world is reflected
exclusively in sensory perceptions. instincts, compulsive psychic reactions are never questioned. it all has to do with acts of creation, the actor
creates out of himself, it all reminds one greatly of ernst mach. no

Brecht and his son Stefan in New York.

(1) Santa Monica 1063 26th Street (1942–7). (2) October 1947. Packing the suitcase. Both photos by Ruth Berlau.

SMOKE SCREEN is thrown up by cigar of German-born Writer Berthold Brecht, an acquaintance of Communist Gerhard Eisler. His thick accent mystified the committee, which excused him after he denied being a party member.

Brecht before the House Un-American Activities Committee. Two days later he returned to Europe.

dialectic. (a definition of 'dialectic': term for a concept in the dialectics [the art of arriving at the truth via statement and counter-statement] which were elevated by the philosopher HEGEL to a system, can be found under 'thesis').

30 oct 47

morning in *washington* before the *un-american activities committee**. after two hollywood writers (LESTER COLE and RING LARDNER JR) had answered the question whether they belonged to the communist party by saying that the question was unconstitutional, i was called to the witness stand, followed by the lawyers for the 19, bob kenny and bartley c crum, who were not permitted to intervene in any way. about 80 pressmen, two radio stations, a newsreel cameraman, photographers, in the public galleries theatre people from broadway as friendly observers. as had been agreed with the other 18 and their lawyers i, as a foreigner, answer the question with 'no', which also happens to be the truth. for the prosecution stripling reads from DIE MASSNAHME and has me give an account of the plot. i refer them to the japanese model, define its content as dedication to an idea, and reject the interpretation that the subject is disciplinary murder by pointing out that it is a question of self-extinction. i admit that the basis of my plays is marxist and state that plays, especially with an historical content, cannot be written intelligently in any other framework. the hearing is excessively polite and ends without an indictment; i benefit from having had almost nothing to do with hollywood, from never having participated in american politics and from the fact that my predecessors refused to give evidence. – the 18 are very pleased with my statements as are the lawyers. i leave washington immediately, along with losey and hambleton, who had come over. – in the evening i listen to parts of my hearing on the radio with helli and the budzislawskys.

31 oct 47

in the morning i meet LAUGHTON who is already going around in his galileo beard and is pleased that it isn't going to take any special courage to play galileo, there being, as he says, no *headlines** about me. – in the afternoon i take off for paris.

1 nov 47

uneventful flight. at le bourget i meet ella winter and donald ogden stewart at the airport. we move into adjacent hotels. i decide to wait for anna seghers who is expected on monday.

paris is shabby, impoverished, one big black market. invited to a fabulous meal with the stewarts. meet joe forster, the friendly editor of *new masses**, who wants to talk to picasso.

3 nov 47

monday. in the evening 'the trial' after kafka by andré gide at barrault's theatre. flashy production, lots of tricks, instead of a representation of confusion just a confused representation; an attempt to convey fear to the audience. de gaulle ante portas.

4 nov 47

anna seghers, white haired, but her beautiful face fresh. berlin is a witches' sabbath where they don't even have any broom-handles. she is visiting her children who are studying in paris, and she also wants to recuperate. in order to safeguard her mexican passport she is not living in the russian sector, so she does not get the privileges without which it is impossible to work. she wants her books to be read in the non-russian zones too. she seems to be perturbed by the intrigues, suspicion and spying.

    i encourage her to write the 100 novellas she promised me 12 years ago.

5 nov 47

wednesday. leave for zurich in the morning. meet CAS[PAR NEHER] in the evening.

Switzerland
16 December 1947 to 20 October 1948

mean they will be taken as adequate to have caused the unfortunate state of affairs. the graffiti which appeared in italy a year after the execution of mussolini with calls to 'give us back the stinker!' were characteristic of such moods. national socialism must be regarded as the socialism of the petty bourgeoisie, a crippled, neurasthenic, perverted popular movement which produced or promised to produce a surrogate for what was being demanded from lower down the social order, one which would not be too unnacceptable to the ruling class. the pseudo-socialist beginnings must therefore be compared with the real thing and not with 'democracy'. the criticism of nationalisation for purposes of war should not be levelled at nationalisation as such, but at its purpose, namely the war, which perverted it. youth, right down into the proletariat it would seem, was captivated by the socialist features which tend to take a powerful hold on the imagination in undertakings such as war, if only because there is a common aim and economic 'freedom' is suspended.

25 dec 47

HÖLDERLIN's language in antigone deserves deeper study than i was able to give it this time. it is of astounding radicalism.

'süß mahl den vögeln, die auf frasses lust sehn' or:
'so steht es dir und gleich wirst du beweisen ob
  gutgeboren . . .' etc.
then the swabian popular gest:
'und die sache sei/nicht wie für nichts.'
'denn treulos fängt man *mich* nicht.'
'treibt sein' verkehr er, mit dem rossegeschlecht.'
'hochstädtisch kommt, unstädtisch
  zu nichts er, wo das schöne
  mit ihm ist und mit frechheit.'[1]

i wrote the bridging verses in hexameters, largely to test whether i had learnt anything from the MANIFESTO. in fact it is now easier, above all it can be done faster.

---

[1] Gloss: 'sweet meal for the birds, anticipating devouring's pleasure' or: 'thus it behoves thee and thou prov'st now, whether well-born . . .' etc. 'so be the matter not as for naught.' 'for *me* they shall not disloyal trap.' 'consorts and dallies with the race of steeds.' 'from high town, no town comes/ to naught where the beautiful/ is with him and with impudence.'

bear
shou
  all
to e;

13 ;

as fc
exce
gera
bou
brur
and
and
east

15 ;

befc
wo·
w[a
soft
han
but
a kr
'ha\
can
selli

20

rea(
naz
nee
it w
unl
and
of t
cau
'th(
gra

25 dec 47

on christmas eve CAS and ERIKA come round. we work on the
ANTIGONE. first we twiddled the radio knob but the only german station
we could find was broadcasting endless lists of names of missing soldiers,
and the nehers' son is missing in the USSR.

26 dec 47

reading LUKÁCS's 'the schiller-goethe correspondence'. he analyses how
the german classicists assimilate the french revolution.
    still being without one of our own, we will now have to 'assimilate' the
russian one, i think to myself with a shudder.

1 jan 48

this is precisely the solution proposed by existentialism. all you have to
do is to end the sentence 'that only death, voluntarily procured, delivers
the human being from torment', a little differently, namely, 'delivers the
human being from being a tormentor'.

Shoots Himself to Prove Belief in Existentialism

BOLZANO, Dec. 29 (A.P.).—Armando Berasi, twenty-two-year-old son of the director of the local branch of the Bank of Italy, locked himself in his room here today, police said, and shot himself.
  Afterward, police arrested his close friend, Livio Zanetti, twenty-four, and charged him with responsibility for the suicide. The reason the police gave: Existentialism.
  According to the police, they found in Berasi's diary entries showing that Zanetti had urged him to commit suicide to prove his belief in the Existentialist theory—as Zanetti explained it—that only death, voluntarily procured, delivered the human being from torment.
  Zanetti accompanied Berasi to his room, the police charged, waited outside to hear the shot, and went off to report to other Existentialists that he had committed suicide.

18 aug 48

more or less finished with the SHORT ORGANUM FOR THE THEATRE; it is a potted version of the MESSINGKAUF. main thesis: that a certain form of learning is the most important pleasure of our age, so that it has to occupy an important place in our theatre. this way I was able to treat the theatre as an aesthetic enterprise, which makes it easier to describe the various innovations. this means that the critical attitude to the social world no longer suffers from the blemish of being unsensual, negative, inartistic, as the ruling aesthetic would have it.

19 aug 48

the effect of bourgeois propaganda is overpowering here. many know that it is phoney, but lies are after all just twisted truths, and since you need the truths but can't find them anywhere, you just twist the lies around; the problem is how far to twist. even those who regard the USSR

Hannah, Brecht's actress daughter by his first marriage, had married Dr Joachim Hiob-Sproessner in July.

as a socialist state and are pro-socialist seem to compare the men who lead it with one of those gangs of crooks that american trade unions employ in their struggle with the bosses – not of course without themselves being ripped off and tyrannised in the process. a journalist said to me, 'they can't help fighting their private feuds as affairs of state and their political feuds as private matters. the power is there and won't disappear; if one lets go of it someone else will pick it up.' the bourgeoisie froths at the mouth at the condition of the humiliated and oppressed in the soviet union. it is absolutely forbidden to write that freedom prevails there. etc. if you appeal to objectivity they suspect you of being an agent of stalin. the russian suggestion of de-imperialising germany and then withdrawing the occupying troops is not popular here. where in all this, they ask, is any guarantee that one can do business?

1 sept 48

reading SCHILLER'S PLEASURE IN TRAGIC OBJECTS with some amusement. he begins, as i do in the ORGANUM, with pleasure as the proper business of theatre and defends himself against theories that harness the theatre to morality (thereby ennobling it), but then he sets everything to rights again by stating that he cannot imagine pleasure without morality. ie the theatre does not serve morality adequately by just providing pleasure, but cannot give pleasure unless it is moral. the moral elements must not therefore be pleasurable to find acceptance, but the pleasure has to be moral to be admitted to the theatre. actually i do something very similar with learning, by simply pronouncing it without more ado to be a pleasure of our times.

3 sept 48

the nuremberg doctors' trial shows how a state can be killed off by removing its contradictions. and yet all the bourgeois state does is to make people forego their individuality in the practice of medicine, just as in the field of labour.

25 sept 48

on looking at CÉZANNE'S GUSTAVE GEFFROY: 'the old masters take the utter reality into account as a matter of course and clearly differentiate between the human face, landscape and still life. the peculiarly collectivising aspect of cézanne's painting combines faces, landscapes, still lives within a single painterly convention while keeping them differentiated ... an astounding alienation takes place between model and portrait ... an emotionally animated face turns into an architecture of colour, into a complex of modulations ...' (hausenstein and jedlicka). cézanne, *humble et colossal*, is supposed to have said of himself, 'i didn't realise my potential'. but did he use too many or too few alienations? (the face as *still life*, cf ORGANUM paragraph 67.)

12 oct 48

reading STRINDBERG's essay on the one-act play. it seems to me possible to construct a technique of alienation for depicting states (of a more or less naturalistic type); even if in the first instance it turns out only to be fruitful for plays with a real plot. the naturalists had to choose between actions involving states and princes or the bourgeois 'intrigue', and they rejected both. and poetry, fantasy and music to boot. in a general way it would be worth adopting their achievements (in the field of observation, particularly of the psychological complex) for the play with a story – but, as has been said, other types of plays are conceivable, with descriptions of states.

17 oct 48 (sunday)

departure for berlin. at the station hirschfeld, barbara, lerski, the young mertens who let us have their summer house for a whole year, as well as helping with my work. – evening salzburg. erika neher (cas is in vienna), von einem, the composer.

18 oct 48

salzburg. discussion with von einem on the russian anti-formalist campaign which is seemingly rejected by most musicians simply as a constraint, not as a compulsion to anything undesired or undesirable.

here 'you can get anything', ie on the black market. you pay more and you don't need food coupons. strict democracy for those with no means, ie the working population, each gets equally little.

city has a clapped-out, exhausted feel.

19 oct 48

arrival in prague.

no exhaustion here, but that condition which looks like poverty and is usual after upheavals. society is compelled for the first time to put its productive elements on the table for all to see and it turns out to be too little. it finds itself caught in the act of producing shortages and stops washing, everything gets run down. no black market here, at least not on any significant scale; once, when food coupons were stolen in bulk, there were executions. the judicial system is undemocratic: when people with money are caught, they are punished more severely than the poor. prices are kept low. there seem to be enough potatoes and bread, in spite of a bad harvest last year. little fat, milk only for children. total consumption higher than in beneš's republic. landowners with more than 50 hectares expropriated. evening at burian's d 48.

20 oct 48

of 37,000 jews 800 came back after the hitler occupation. we visit the jewish cemetery. it was reduced in 1903 to make room for a polytechnic. the gravestones were moved and left in a disorderly heap. but in the old part too the gravestones are quite indecently crammed together – even the synagogue, the oldest in europe, was only permitted to be 9 m wide and 15 m long. the stones are ugly in shape, but covered with writing, and many tell of persecution. scholars have grapes as their insignia.

Berlin
22 October 1948 to 18 July 1955

22 oct 48 (friday)

we leave prague early and are at the frontier by noon. schrecker fetches us with a car. he lets the car taking our luggage overtake us on the road: 'have you brought anything with you, i'm hungry.' chewing bread and sausage he tells us that we are in power but face great difficulties. a meal with speeches in a suburb. present: renn, theatre people, party people – very nice and very hungry. photo-call as in the USA and in broadcasting. the party chairman points out that nowadays it is 'morals the first thing, food follows on'. a car takes us on towards berlin. the driver, who has a thin jacket and shrapnel in his lung, tells us how hard life is, no shoes for his son, they eat two slices of bread in the morning and drink ersatz coffee, then potatoes at midday and in the evening, the russians have imported soya-oil which helps. autumnal woods, here and there a bridge which has been blown, rusting tanks at the roadside. at the zonal border the papers for the car are missing, i go into the german police station and phone the deutsches theater in berlin. we are fetched by a few cars, abusch of the kulturbund. becher, jhering and dudow are at the kulturbund club. the press was at the station so they are off our backs for the moment. we are housed in the adlon.

23 oct 48

last night we could just make out the ruins of the friedrichstrasse when we arrived in the dark. at six in the morning i walk down the wilhelmstrasse to the reich chancellery. to smoke a cigar down there, so to speak. a few workers and rubble-women. the rubble bothers me less than the thought of what people must have gone through while the city was being reduced to this rubble. a worker shows me the way. 'how long before this looks like something again?' 'there will be a few grey hairs before that. if we had some financiers it would be different, but we don't have any financiers any more. so? . . . good morning.' to me these ruins are a clear indication of the former presence of financiers. – morning kuckhahn, weiss the publisher and others. evening first night of hay's HAVE at the D[EUTSCHES] T[HEATER]. appalling performance, hysterical and stilted, totally unrealistic.

right then: afternoon reception for us in the kulturbund house. jhering and langhoff speak. i have arranged with becher that i won't be called upon to speak. clever little speech by dymshitz, the soviet cultural officer.

24 oct 48 (sunday)

kulturbund peace rally. zweig is there and speaks. i don't speak. i've decided to find my feet and not make public appearances. afternoon at jakob walcher's, who talks about the difficult situation, very sober and positive as usual. evening at otto's, who looks worn out by the apocalyptic years.

An der großen Friedens-Kundgebung des Kulturbundes am Sonntag in Berlin nahmen eine Reihe hervorrag *...*ischer oder soeben aus der Emigration zurückgekehrter Schriftsteller und Künstler teil. Von links nach rec*...* *...*, Bert Brecht, Arnold Zweig, Hanns Eisler, Louis Fürnberg. *Fotos:*

In Berlin for the Kulturbund's peace manifestation. Left to right: Julius Hay, Brecht, Arnold Zweig, Hanns Eisler, the poet Louis Fürnberg.

25 oct 48

among the workers, i hear generally, the panic caused by the raping and plundering after berlin was overrun is still rippling below the surface three years later. in the working-class quarters they had been looking forward to the liberators with desperate joy, arms outstretched, but the meeting turned into an assault which spared neither the seventeen-year-olds nor the twelve-year-olds, and in public at that. they say that during the house-to-house fighting the russian soldiers, bleeding, exhausted, embittered, had ceased firing to let women fetch water and allow the hungry out of the cellars to go to the baker's, and had helped to dig out people buried under the rubble, but after the fighting hordes of drunken soldiers stormed through the houses, hauling out women and shooting men and women who resisted, raping women in front of their children, standing in queues in front of houses etc. kuckhahn saw a seventeen-year-old shot after being raped, and he saw a commissar shoot down two soldiers who had been looting and had attacked him when he challenged them. after all the material destruction caused by the nazi armies in their country, the russians will now have to face the psychological havoc that hitler's marauding armies have wreaked on the czar's dehumanised 'muschiks' who had only just been exposed to the process of civilisation.

d[ymshitz] recalls that there is something specially tragic in all this: it was difficult for the soviets to get their army to take the offensive. the socialist solutions and the construction of a new economy without competition had made the masses peaceful. then suddenly they had to be taught to kill; old instincts had to be reawakened, especially in the backward soviet nations – the regiments that ran amok were mostly peasant regiments from beyond the urals.

26 oct 48

frisch, when he came back from the peace conference in breslau where formalism had also been discussed, told the story of how PICASSO has said he too was against formalism, the other side's formalism.

they say he is now making pots. and it would seem to me to be a good idea to form an academy of artists and pay them to design objects for use, cutlery, playing cards, chessmen and boards, chairs, containers, type lay-outs for books, coffee machines, tobacco pouches, lamps etc. all this for mass production.

27 oct 48

berlin, an etching by churchill after an idea by hitler.

berlin, the heap of rubble outside potsdam.

above the silent streets of ruins the freight planes of the airlift drone in the night.

the street-lighting is so faint that the stars in the heavens can be seen from the streets once more.

goethe, even if he doesn't see the 'act' as so noble. what a work, this *hamlet*! the interest in him that has persisted for centuries derives from the fact he is a new type, perfectly finished, who steps wholly alienated into a medieval environment that has not been tidied or tampered with at all. the scream for revenge that was dignified by the greek tragedians and then invalidated by christianity, is still loud enough and infectiously enough reproduced in *hamlet* to make his new doubts, tests and plans disconcerting.

25 nov 48

we have to alter the first scene of COURAGE, since it has in it the seeds of what enabled the audience at the zürich production to be moved mainly by the persistence and resilience of a being in torment (the eternal mother creature) – which is not really the point. now courage loses her first son because she lets herself be drawn into a little deal, and against this there is only her pity for the superstitious sergeant-major, which represents a weakness deriving from business which she can't afford. this is a distinct improvement, it was suggested by young kuckhahn.

26 nov 48

as long as by realism one understands a style and not an attitude, one is nothing other than a formalist. a realistic artist is one whose works of art adopt an attitude that brings results. (one part of an artist's reality is his public.)

9 dec 48

everywhere in this great city, where everything is always in flux, no matter how little and how provisional that 'everything' happens at the moment to be, the new german *misere* is apparent, which is that nothing has been eliminated even when almost everything has been destroyed. powerful impulses are coming from the russians, but the germans elect to frolic in the backwash which arises when the other occupying powers try to stem this movement. the germans are rebelling against the order to rebel against nazism; only a few hold the view that an imposed socialism is better than none at all. the proletariat's takeover of production coincides with (and to many seems to be designed for) the hand-over of goods to the victors. socialised factories which had rigged up production lines from all sorts of bomb-damaged machinery have *several times* had their machines confiscated as reparations. and the workers never reflect that hitler's war of destruction against the soviet union was waged without their being consulted, though not without their participation; and the jobs created by rearmament met with the acclaim of a great number of them. huchel tells how, when a blast furnace which had just been patched up could not be fired, a worker handed back 3 drums of oil he had purloined for the black market, thus losing provisions when he was starving and at the same time risking being reported to the police. his motives were not political, and that's the tragedy of it. then of course there are the mistakes which happen because the russians and the germans are at such different stages of development. there is the principle of performance which the russians apply because they think the most recent discovery is always the best. felsenstein once put all the pajoks in his theatre together and divided then up equally; the russians discovered this and cancelled all his pajoks for two months. the russian view was that unequal rations improved production, felsenstein's that equal rations did so. and it is not just that the german workers at the moment do not realise that their own dictatorship is 'inside', but that they do not really seem ready to take it over. people's rule in the form of dictatorship (inwardly and outwardly) doesn't make sense to them. (in contrast, the bourgeoisie, viewed as individuals, were prepared at the drop of a hat to safeguard their own economic rule by submitting to dictatorship.) in a curious way a 'german experience' is repeating itself: the bourgeoisie had to be forced to take over power by napoleon, and then shared it instantly with the aristocracy; and the proletariat is acting in exactly the same way in relation to the bourgeoisie – but this is not the whole truth.

10 dec 48

i put in 10 minutes epic rehearsal for the first time in the eleventh scene. gerda müller and dunskus as peasants are deciding that they cannot do anything against the catholics. i ask them to add 'said the man', 'said the woman' after each speech. suddenly the scene became clear and müller found a realistic attitude. the next day she went on strike when all i wanted was the peasants' misery, the 'mangle' the little man goes through, an almost theatrical attitude behind (and not in) which lies fear. she wants to feel the misery, which she has long been unable to do, being as she is a crater exhausted by an excess of eruptions.

Return to the Berlin stage. Rehearsals of Mother Courage at the Deutsches Theater, with Weigel as Courage.

11 dec 48

if it turns into another catalaunian battle of the spirits, if the conflict is shunted into the field of culture, this cannot be done without somebody's help. this battle at least must be waged in the whole of germany. literature cannot withdraw behind the elbe and assist in the construction of a model province under the military (and police) protectorate of the russians. the rest of germany cannot be brought to revolution by being offered samples as at a trade fair. literature must commit itself, it must join the fight all over germany, and it must have a revolutionary character and show it, and externally too, in its forms. formalism in this situation is what dissipates its revolutionary content.

12 dec 48

langhoff and i work out a project for a *studio theatre* to be attached to the DEUTSCHES THEATER. first year: involvement of top émigré actors through short guest appearances (giehse, steckel, lorre, homolka, bois, gold). build up a company in conjunction with them.

three or four plays, say GALILEO (with kortner) or SCHWEYK (with lorre); SCHELESNOVA (GORKY) with giehse and steckel; a lorca or an o'casey. development of epic acting through demonstrative children's theatre. themes; FERDINAND THE BULL (peace not attainable by peacefulness); THE STRUGGLE AGAINST YELLOW FEVER (work and struggles of scientists) and STEFFIN's children's plays which, it is to be hoped, have not been lost.

own plans: ROSA LUXEMBURG and ARES'S CHARIOT.

12 dec 48

begin cautiously introducing the epic mode in rehearsals. the scenes begin to fall into place of their own accord once the fulcrums become visible. BILDT immediately grasps that it is about preventing total transformation. KUCKHAHN improves the constant interpolation. 'said courage' by making it 'courage is supposed to have said'.

13 dec 48

actors are constantly trying to make it loud, as if loudness were strength, and all that then remains is the gest of shouting at one another. if you bring them back to normal volume they make it seem restrained and thereby retain the tension.

14 dec 48

the excellent danish cabaret artist aase ziegler, from whose place i phone ruth (currently in copenhagen), lets me have a quick look at the british club. the ballroom is empty, with an old-fashioned string trio playing waltzes. a few officers and ladies are clustered round the bar. they stand stiffly, very drunk, conversing. each guest an empire unto himself.

14 dec 48

as we are coming out of the 'möwe' on to the street after an exhaustive conversation with jakob walcher and his wife on the shortcomings of the german workers in '18, '20 and '23 a very young, drunk russian officer is lurching between the exit and walcher's car, aiming a revolver at walcher, then stopping helli and brandishing the revolver in front of her. he has the pale, desperate expression drunks have and is sunk deep in the realm of inarticulate gestures, incapable of making himself understood either with them or with his two revolvers. finally he steps back gesticulating with both arms, indicating he is 'about to go' and leaving the way free. but the 'möwe' has just turned out the lights and neither the doorman nor anybody else takes any notice of what is going on.

15 dec 48

the lieutenant forced his way into the 'möwe' last night too. they phoned the town commandant and he was arrested. – otto recounts that several patients told him that a russian commandant in one of the suburbs has gone to the hospital and apologised to a man who, for no reason at all, was bayonetted by a soldier; this was commented on favourably all round, and provoked the remark that the russians didn't bomb civilian targets either. people even thought that the soldier must have felt threatened by the hostile attitude of the inhabitants . . .

17 dec 48

allow myself to be inveigled into buying a first edition of hölderlin's poems and a second edition of 'hermann and dorothea'. this is something to show the printers. what taste! what a sensitive response to the poems!

overall and in detail. the printer is constantly letting the poems present difficulties for which he finds bold solutions. and this is neither handmade paper for the affluent nor cheap stuff for the masses. of course time in those days did not mean profits.

18 dec 48

i usually get up at 5.30. then i make tea or coffee on a primus stove, read some lukács or goethe (the COLLECTOR). when i look up i see a large print of brueghel's peasant dances on the wall, walk around a bit on the red carpet and sit down at my table to work. it only gets light outside about eight, the ruins emerge (the ss set fire to the adlon hotel the day after hitler's death in the bunker, only one wing on the courtyard has been renovated).

after 8 kuckhahn comes. he orders my breakfast and we prepare the courage rehearsals. at 9 i am in the theatre in my office, and kasprowiak is waiting for me to dictate my letters. rehearsals begin at 10 o'clock.

20 dec 48

at the first run-through of scenes 1 to 8, jhering notices variations in weigel's portrayal of courage that we had not observed when we were looking at the individual scenes. the variations are therefore of the right sort, they can only be seen in long sequences. BILDT, today undoubtedly the greatest actor in germany, even notices new difficulties; he has not been working inductively enough, ie he has been trying to arrive at a character too soon, instead of just doing what the situations required, and now he has a character with no development.

21 dec 48

we really need four months of rehearsals. in these circumstances it isn't possible to make it epic. you cannot burden the actors with the process of lightening everything in so short a time.

21 dec 48

made a little song for the FREE GERMAN YOUTH (SONG OF RECON-STRUCTION). not happy that the 'new state' comes into it, but it has to be there to link the material and the political reconstruction. however i ignore the officials' objections to the last stanza ('and no führer leads out of *this* pickle'). work with dessau on the musical setting and insist on fast tempo and the 'demelodising' of the refrain. would like to achieve the quicker march of the french.

22 dec 48

write the SONG OF THE FUTURE, since education here is all too parochial (and the red flag is pretty well in disrepute, a point that is being looked into).

interesting how berlin has become the cynosure of the world's eyes while in asia huge developments are impending which the americans simply haven't noticed.

SATURDAY DECEMBER 18 1948

CHINESE DESTINY

Now Peking itself is reported to be isolated and the northern holding of the Government's forces is shrinking like the last patch of snow in hot sun. The outsider is puzzled to know what to make of it all. He remembers that after the end of hostilities with Japan large Chinese Government forces were equipped by the Americans on a scale lavish by comparison with what they possessed during the world war or in the earlier years of opposition to the Japanese. Where has all this equipment gone to? If the enemy has taken it—and it is clear that a large proportion has gone that way—how has it come about that the Communists, equipped mainly with small arms, mortars, and grenades from the Manchurian arsenals, could wrest tanks and artillery from the hands of their opponents?

The answer can perhaps be found in the old Clausewitzian contention that war is but an extension of politics. This is true of all wars, but it has been particularly true of Chinese wars. The conduct of the belligerent, and above all that of the belligerent whose fortunes are on the downward grade, is governed by what he feels and expects to happen rather than by what he has the physical means to accomplish. The fighting is but a demonstration of the sentiments of the fighters. British soldiers are taught to " think a move ahead." The Chinese commander of the war-lord era used to think half a dozen moves ahead, and it would seem that the habit has not gone out of use. The Chinese are, in a sense, too subtly intelligent for the business of war. If the vision seen six moves ahead is seen as inevitable—and discouraging—then the logical man must shape his course accordingly. It has not been lack of weapons but lack of fighting spirit that has brought about the defeats of the Government's forces. Nanking's failure to grapple with corruption and inflation has carried disillusionment and disappointment to the masses, including the rank and file of an unfortunate army which has been fighting for nine years without seeing any end to campaigning; the same feelings would appear to have taken hold of many in high places, civil and military. They shape their course towards what they see as the preordained future, and that future for them is the downfall of the present régime and a regrouping of the forces which together shape the destiny of China.

29 dec 48

eisler here for four weeks. he has now sublimated his antipathy to the vulgarity and primitiveness of the marching songs by absorbing the united front song symphonically, ie as a folksong in formally strict pieces. naturally, i immediately try to coax him into new vulgar excesses by lumbering him with the song OF THE FUTURE. he, however, gives me an ODE BY MAO TSE-TUNG, written during his first flight over the great wall, a wonderful poem which i am adapting. my expectation of a renaissance of the arts, triggered off by the rising of the far east, seems to be approaching fulfilment earlier than one might have thought.

1 jan 49

dear dessau, i'm writing you this partly to get a certain item straight in my own mind. it seems that in the present ruined state of the theatre our SONG OF THE HOURS can't be done. you yourself had doubts, before i had mine. the text is good, and the music, i think, is full of meaning, in fact it is one of your best pieces, but even if the actor didn't lack the hardness and subtlety, even if the general artistic standard of the production were higher and it were possible to use the new alienation technique, we'd still be forced to doubt whether the audience would accept it – cf. the misgivings of jhering and engel – even though kuckhahn, who is younger, is in favour of using it. in some of the plays you have 'rescued' a good deal by quick accommodation to the available means, and even created new beauty – i admire this more than you may think – but in the present case even that wouldn't help. so we shall probably have to put the song aside, but whenever the play is revived a discussion of whether or not the 'song of the hours' can be performed will be a clear indication of how high or low theatrical standards are at that time.

2 jan 49

in the matter of the RECONSTRUCTION SONG for the FDJ (FREE GERMAN YOUTH) the leader of the berlin group asked me to reconsider the line 'and no führer leads out of this pickle', since nobody is the slightest bit interested in hitler any more, he's old hat (but old hats can easily turn into old laurels when nobody is watching), and what we would have then would be the party as führer. i can't help him, the stanza is constructed round the motif of self-leadership, as indeed is the whole song. in my EPITAPH FOR ROSA, which dessau is setting to music, the line 'a jewess from poland' is reported to have been criticised by the berlin radio people. (presumably to spare 'the sensibilities of a wide range of people in this regard'.)

3 jan 49

when i asked, walcher told me that the headstone set up for karl and rosa in a suburb (in the russian sector) which the nazis had destroyed, has not been rebuilt; pieck apparently told him it had been decided that nothing be done about this. – the germans have no sense of history at all, probably because they have no history.

3 jan 49

would like to bring out the poetry volumes printed differently from usual, at least here in the eastern zone. smaller, so that they will go into the pocket, just like the editions of 1820. but in old face and not of course in the *biedermeier* style.

6 jan 49

am fetched out of rehearsals and taken to the mayor of berlin (N), where my theatre project (re bringing in great émigré actors) is discussed in the presence of langhoff and wisten, hitherto intendant at the schiffbauer-damm theatre. the mayor said neither hail nor farewell, didn't address me once and uttered only one sceptical sentence about dodgy projects which destroy things that are already in place. the representatives of the SED (ackermann, jendretzky, bork) suggested the kammerspiele for the project, along with guest appearances at the deutsches theater or in

The opening night. Helene Weigel takes her bow . . .

of the fighting – the last sitting of the commune was held next day – a decree handed over the private theatres to the artists' collective.

7 may 49

it being the *goethe year*, i see a few of his plays. interesting, those last act compromises in TASSO and FAUST. there is always enough dissatisfaction to make a play necessary, and always enough crawling to enable it to be put on. yet the theatre can do so much, since there is after all plenty of lively material there. not too difficult to play the cathedral scene as, say, gretchen's spiritual and physical execution by the church, that is, first and foremost a moral execution – this is where she is put up to murder.

what an hodgepodge of medieval mystery play and modern revue is fused into an organic whole here. and now that your german philistine has made himself at home in it, this immense, rambling structure would be a real shambles even if it hadn't been built that way. the young faust is still with us today in the young men who research, learn, try to develop themselves, but only themselves, nothing more.

A New House

Back in my country after fifteen years' exile
I have moved into a fine house.
Here I have hung
My Nō masks and picture scroll representing the Doubter.
Every day, as I drive through the ruins, I am reminded
Of the privileges to which I owe this house. I hope
It will not make me patient with the holes
In which so many thousands huddle. Even now
On top of the cupboard containing my manuscripts
My suitcase lies.

9 jun 49

pushkin celebration. lyric poets in other languages are a problem, since translations are usually so bad. the thing at the moment is naturally to thrust russian literature into europe's cultural consciousness along with p[ushkin's] political activity.

9 jun 49

DEFA the film company in the eastern zone has all sorts of problems finding subjects, especially contemporary ones. those at its head list significant themes: underground movement, distribution of land, two-year plan, the new man etc etc; then writers are supposed to devise stories that interpret the theme and its associated problems. this naturally often goes wrong. i suggest sending out people just to collect stories.

11 jun 49

if all morality is to be derived from productivity, and if the ultimate aim is to develop the productivity of the whole of mankind on a grand scale, then the spell of mere existence must be broken, as must our resistance to putting what is available to use. i love: i make the person i love productive; i build a car: i make the driver drive; i sing: i ennoble the hearer's hearing etc etc. but then society must have the knack of utilising all things productively, it must have such a 'capital' of ready-made things, such a superfluity of goods on offer, that the individual's production is, as it were, something else, something unexpected. if productivity is the highest thing, then the strike too retains its honour. (in the realm of aesthetics this is already the case. the asocial man is also a source of pleasure; it is regarded as satisfactory that he 'produces himself'.)

18 jun 49

national prizes are being awarded, unfortunately first, second, and, i think, also third. official candidates have been nominated without any of them being asked whether they wanted to be considered. i hear there are only two first prizes for literature, and they intend to give them to heinrich mann and j[ohannes] r becher, with, i'm sorry to say, a second prize for me for COURAGE. so helli advises them to count me out, since i would consider that kind of classification harmful and would have to turn down the prize. you have to look at these things quite impersonally, and sharply distinguish the useful from the harmful and prefer nothing at all to nothing much. why should people devalue what they have by attributing a lower value to it, just because they can't afford the higher price?

8 mar 50

am having some scenes transposed into the form of stories by the assistants, so that the actors can read their lines in the third person, with descriptive insertions. as they read they then do the moves and the main gestures. this clarifies the content and gait of the scene, and geschonneck, who is so excellent in the naturalistic mode, gets a feeling for the epic style for the first time and becomes 'transparent'.

2 apr 50

ruth has now recovered and saw in schwerin, where they used her leipzig model, how difficult it is to transfer humour and grace. her model is like a straitjacket, which of course greatly hinders its appeal to the public.

23 apr 50

evening with a member of the new academy, also hofer the painter. they discuss old french carpets about which i know nothing, though, as with so many things, i wish i did. then hofer praises the COURAGE production and dismisses the idea that a photographer could take good pictures of it. i tell him that for the black and white film i have asked havemann, a chemist, to mix an emulsion which would give the film the character of a daguerreotype, and hofer admits that by weakening the colour tones in the middle range you can get artistic pictures. colour film is, however, for the moment hopeless, since only the translucent colours and not opaque ones (ochre, white, earth) can be made.

28 apr 50

CAS and WAGNER-REGENY years ago started a comic opera from 1001 nights and can't find an ending. it is called the DER DARMWÄSCHER. we analyse the scenario and deduce an ending on a mathematical basis. add a few arias.

29 apr 50

meet von einem at blacher's in zehlendorf. blacher has an opera ready and talks very pessimistically about the future. since 1912 (rosenkavalier) no opera (nor any major piece of music) has really caught on. the public manages fine with older works. i argue that these fulfil the old function of opera better, and a new function has not been found. the revolutionary bourgeoisie's operas (DON GIOVANNI, MAGIC FLUTE, FIGARO, FIDELIO) were inflammatory; opera has made no efforts in that direction since 1912.

30 apr 50

after our terrific success with the press we were apprehensive about how the volksbühne public would take to the play, but there seems to be no difference, evening after evening there are 30 curtains – the general public loves its caviar. and the scenes at halle with reference to kant come in for applause too.

1 may 50

glorious day. watch the demonstration at the lustgarten from the stands. at the front the FREE GERMAN YOUTH with blue shirts and flags, and companies of the people's police. then an hour-long procession of machines, wagons, exhibitions of clothes etc on lorries, pictures and banners. the demonstrators amble along, as if they were going for a walk and stop briefly in front of the stands. as the chinese participant is speaking doves are released. (not far away an american helicopter circles over the counter-demonstration beyond the brandenburg gate.) an astonishingly big number of districts of west berlin are represented, in spite of the pressure over there. the BE rolls by on its lorry, barbara sitting in courage's waggon and waving a red flag. helli is greeted in every street, women hold up their children. 'that's mother courage!'

25 may 50

at ILYA EHRENBURG's with anna [seghers] and tchesno. during dinner there is applause and marches are played on the shawm outside the guest house: the FDJ is greeting the chinese delegation. we talk of how literature subsides in impotence in the face of auschwitz. ehrenburg tells of a woman hiding her jewish husband during the german occupation. soldiers are to be billeted in the house. she makes a hole in the roof of their hovel so that the snow comes in and the germans don't occupy it. but she also makes a hole where her husband is hiding to let in some light. her child tells the mother there was an eye looking through the hole. she says it was a rat's eye. but then ehrenburg goes on to tell how a soviet jewish officer, whose whole family has been wiped out, came into a german village as commandant. e. met the officer with his arm around a little orphaned german girl who had been picked up. e. himself didn't see anything special in this, nor in the fact that he saw to it that she was put to bed, but he couldn't restrain his tears when the officer later jumped up and asked whether they had given the little girl a potty. as i listened it was difficult for me to hide the fact that i saw nothing special in this either. of course, what crimes the nazis committed, if even a man like ehrenburg was confused.

26 may 50

the FDJ's whitsun meeting has completely changed berlin. like an abstemious little old shopkeeper's wife getting drunk, the city is joyful and can't understand itself. in the evening on the squares a sort of naples breaks out. you hear little bands everywhere. people sit on the grass in the open air watching films. slogans have been put up for them in the huge gaps where buildings were bombed.

8 jun 50

when it comes to planning in the arts, you have to proceed very carefully. the techniques – and one needs techniques – cannot just be separated from the social functions which they have. and you rarely get master-pieces from people who are keeping their heads down – yet masterpieces are what is needed. naturally a party can begin to work on artists from the inside, but only in relation to what they are actually capable of. the most important thing is the mobilisation of the new reading masses. they too must have instruction from the party, they must present their problems to the artists. presenting the artists with problems is like throwing sheep to the lions. on the whole the less said about stylistic matters the better. and, if the artists are to be won over, it is better to show that you do not understand them (even if you are prepared to learn), than to attack them. in the arts as in sleeping together, need is the seducer, but, just as when you are sleeping with someone, there must be no hard words.

10 jun 50

writing children's songs in little posies for eisler. silversmith's work.

10 jun 50

read a work on gorki and me, written by a working-class student in leipzig. ideology, ideology, ideology. nowhere an aesthetic concept; the whole thing is like a description of a dish in which nothing is said about the taste. the first thing we have to do is institute exhibitions and courses to develop taste, ie for the enjoyment of life.

FUTURE AIR war on the northern roof of the world will be carried on by warriors dressed like this U.S. soldier, who, looking like a man from Mars, is wearing clothing specially designed for service in the Arctic.

You women back in Pittsburg and Texas
D'you really want your sons to look that way?
You know your sons are being sent to us –
Are we to be attacked by beasts of prey?

beginning of august 50

drive to ahrenshoop, helli with the children, ruth and i in the steyr. there are a few old fishermen's houses, which look good, even when painted dark blue, or dilapidated or even renovated for the tourist trade, maybe because you interpret their age as meaning that they have been well maintained here; the new ones look impudently assertive, basically unattached, scorned by the landscape.

it is pure nazi territory and, until now, nothing much has happened, nothing could happen; there are too few places where you could make a start. the little tourist entrepreneurs feel hampered everywhere by measures against the black market, and being peasants they have to hand over their produce etc. since the area is under the kulturbund, it is visited in the summer by people who belong pretty directly to the new government.

5 aug 50

the laughter the a-effect produces: laughing at what is strange, at negroes, hippopotomuses, townspeople in the country etc. higher stage: laughing at children, very old cars, etc.

2 sept 50

with r[uth] in the steyr to munich. overnight in pegnitz on the pegnitz. the view from the 'weisses lamm' inn on the market square in the early morning light is like a delicately, powerfully coloured brueghel and is equal in beauty to the view from a flea-ridden hotel on the old harbour in marseilles.

4 sept 50

begin building and blocking rehearsals for COURAGE with giehse. set by otto.

3 oct 50

director's assistants for COURAGE: ERIC BENTLEY, EGON MONK, RUTH BERLAU, BENESCH (of the vienna SCALA), set TEO OTTO. (since he has fallen ill, ZNAMENACZEK is helping out.)

october 50

evening at DESCH's who has got a few young authors together. take ruth and SCHUMACHER along. no knowledge of the GDR. tell of land distribution, workers' and peasants' universities. the FDJ's whitsun meeting, and explain why socialism is for peace, capitalism for war: that their existence depends on the SED's difficult struggle in the east. they listen politely.

october 50

travel to LORRE in partenkirchen along with ruth, geis, burri. he has jaundice. offer him hamlet.

6 oct 50

VON EINEM in munich. agree with him that salzburg can do the CHALK CIRCLE. directed by viertel, with käthe gold and homolka.

8 oct 50

sunday. première of COURAGE in the evening. the moves based on the model are triumphant. giehse, domin, blech, wilhelmi, lühr, lieffen, quite different from berlin and excellent. during the entire rehearsals not one dispute. giehse is quite admirable in the way she completely revamps the moves she had used with such success in zürich and vienna.

9 oct 50

go over the adaptation of BIBERPELZ AND ROTER HAHN with hirschfeld. he agrees with me and will press my line with the hauptmann heirs. agree with BURRI and GEIS to make a film (with lorre) of THE OVERCOAT after gogol and with burri to make the COURAGE FILM at DEFA. negotiate with a manageress of the GROUP THEATRE in London for a production of courage. (BROOK, the director, is supposed to be coming to berlin in a few weeks to see the production.)

10 oct 50

travel back to berlin in the steyr with ruth.

29 dec 50

dip into lorca's poems in beck's mediocre translation. i read with pleasure, but stop at various places to think how this pleasure might be made available to our workers, and whether it ought to be available to them. you could argue that our situation, the phase we are at, doesn't permit it. no drunken orgies on mountaineering tours! but mountaineering tours cause their own type of intoxication, as does literature, and a few other arts.

[notes broken off.]

Died. Kurt Weill, 50, German-born composer of topflight musicals (*Lady in the Dark, One Touch of Venus*), who collaborated with Playwright Maxwell Anderson on the current Broadway smash hit, *Lost in the Stars;* of heart trouble; in Manhattan.

10 jan 51

first (private) performance of the MOTHER by the BE in the DEUTSCHES THEATER. neher's sets now meet with general approval. partly because the principles have by now been established – eg by their being the subject of wretched imitations. the figure of vlassova as performed by weigel couldn't be bettered. but busch's worker too is wonderful. the audience, which is average volksbühne, takes it in its stride. about 40 curtain calls, several times with the safety curtain. our more relaxed handling of the old model which berlau reproduced excellently (and strictly) in leipzig just last year seems successful.

15 jan 51

spoke to dessau in the morning. the chorus rehearsals for LUCULLUS have started, but now the ministry for popular education has asked again for the score, and dessau would prefer to postpone the performance until the autumn. i am against this. the subject is important just at this moment, when the americans are issuing such hysterical threats. dessau is naturally afraid of attacks on the form, but even these, if that is what they really intend, will be less drastic if the content is so important. in the end both dessau and i are convinced that the form of the opera is its content. in addition to this you must never be afraid of criticism; you either refute it or you put it to constructive use, that's all. why should we assume that the situation will be more favourable in the autumn if we haven't made the effort in the spring? the paralysis induced in the musicians by this contact with new classes of listener must be overcome. you have to commit yourself and then wait and see.

after[noon] visit to hüdepohl in saint hedwig's hospital.

started discussions with burri. report to him on the plan to achieve the character of daguerreotypes in the photography by changing the film emulsion, which would enable us to write more poetically. – one of the main things with the COURAGE FILM will be to retain enough of the audience's detachment from courage, so as to enable it to wonder at her, since you can't feel with her, only about her.

10 feb 51

enjoyable rehearsals in the new rehearsal building (among the ruins on the reinhardtstrasse), even little things count for a lot, such as clean walls with no daubings from previous plays, and the fact that nothing is going on except the rehearsal. and once we get it established that rehearsing is done in daylight ... (places that are in the intoxication business – churches, breweries, theatres, don't have any windows). THE BEAVER COAT AND THE RED COCK is beginning to look good.

25 mar 51

about the postponement of LUCULLUS: it is evident that during upheavals of these dimensions the arts will run into trouble even where they help to show the way ahead. the backwardness of the arts clashes with the backwardness of the new mass public in their protest against bourgeois aesthetics (and the bourgeois art business). some artists have developed new forms. now they are being told from the proletarian side that these are not the forms for the new contents. this is sometimes right, and sometimes it is wrong. sometimes people demand the forms they are used to because the new contents have not fully permeated the class which has come to power, and people erroneously think that new

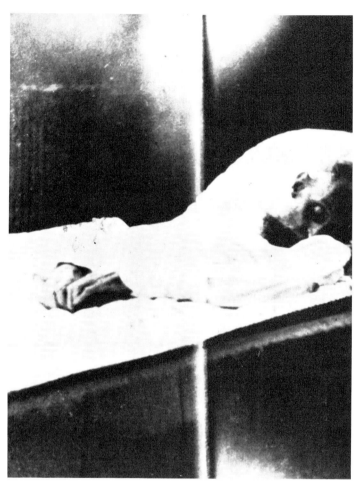

Considered 'decadent' by Nazis *and* Stalinists: Ernst Barlach (d.1938).

26 jun 51

first preview of the revival of COURAGE with WEIGEL, HURWICZ, LUTZ, BUSCH, GESCHONNECK. the play has to stay in our repertory, if only because it contains one of WEIGEL's two big classical roles. two leading actors from the DEUTSCHES THEATER had defected to the west, the cook and the chaplain. we are still able to cast the parts, as well as all the rest.

29 jun 51

burri has finished the script for the COURAGE FILM and gone back to munich. good collaboration. terrible how much talent is lying around unused in germany.

30 jun 51

busy with ruth's courage model-book. these models, and the revivals which expand and tidy up the models, are so necessary because the arts, as a consequence of the cultural sell-out in late capitalism and in spite of the emphatic adoption of the arts by the new class, are, at least from time to time, threatened by rapid decay. even under capitalism a few people made an effort to save our heritage from the putrefaction spread by the declining bourgeoisie, and tried to prepare the arts for the new class, but the new class, for all its good intentions as it assumes power, has artificial and perverted taste. the political task is pressing and the arts, weakened by mercantilism etc, will not be allowed much time to recharge themselves. they are accustomed to submit more easily to possibilities than to necessities.

1 jul 51

last week a discussion with students from the workers' and peasants' faculty in an FDJ hall. poor understanding. predominant wish to have day to day problems dealt with, which they, however, only articulate lamely and in a wholly unproblematic fashion. in addition to which the young people suspect scepticism when faced with somebody's demanding standards. their crash course, conducted by inadequate teachers, is not at the outset producing a scientific attitude, not even in the new social sciences. thinking stays rudimentary where products of thought are learned by rote. things are particularly bad when it comes to describing phenomena, and without that, no kind of intervention is possible. even artistic works are not really studied, in particular their artistic component is given a wide berth. but these are only teething troubles, nothing worse.

3 jul 51

wrote the text for dessau's cantata HERRNBURG REPORT for the world

22 aug 51

yet again literature must manage without any resonance from the nation. and the resonance it gets from the working class is drowned out by abominable background noise.

ADDRESSING PRE-ELECTION CROWD IN GERMANY

Dr. Kurt Schumacher of the Socialist-Democratic party, campaigning for votes in Frankfort, prior to the balloting next Sunday.

The New York Times (Frankfort Bureau)

GERMAN UNIONISTS END LABOR SURVEY

U. N. GROUP VOTES MINUTE OF SILENCE

The leader of the West German SPD (from the *New York Times*).

5 jan 52

morning rehearsal for THE BROKEN JUG. discussed 2–3 costumes with palm. 3pm see barlog at the schillertheater about the lorca play for giehse. quick bite to eat. then dessau played his appeal in the rehearsal building, text by skupin of the ensemble. evening PUNTILA press night with bois, geschonneck, lutz, giehse. (i read PETER I at home and have reports phoned through.)

6 jan 52

worked all day on a children's play by skupin and martin pohl, midday therese [giehse] for lunch. busch here in afternoon, about his production of the chimes.

7 jan 52

jug rehearsal.

1 feb 52

the barlach exhibition in the akademie der künste was attacked so violently in the TÄGLICHE RUNDSCHAU and in NEUES DEUTSCHLAND that the few surviving artists were cast into lethargy. i made notes, bringing out the positive values and the exemplary quality of the work, defending it against their completely abstract demolition using social-critical weapons. in doing so, however, i established how right, ie pointing in the right direction, social-critical arguments are, even in the weakest and most incompetent hands, and i made my notes accordingly.

2 feb 52

discussion with PALM, NEHER, HILL, MONK about the URFAUST which monk is supposed to be doing. cas has suggested the age of werther for costumes etc, but i plead for dürer's middle ages, so that the devil, the magic and the whole business of the old puppet play can be presented naively, while goethe's 'modern' bits, the gretchen tragedy and the students in auerbach's cellar appear alienated. (it doesn't work the other way round, for the old has too little value beside the theatrical.) the contradiction between old and new is to be brought out strongly and to the cathedral scene the character of a funeral mass, since you have to assume time for the pregnancy between the handing over of the poison and this scene. only in the prison scene does gretchen confess guilt for the death of her mother. before the conversation about religion there is the scene at the well with lieschen's chatter. the conversation about religion thus becomes dramatically important: gretchen, who has already surrendered her innocence, is showing unease and testing her lover's morality. although he is evasive, she still commits herself more deeply to him. faust however disappears after the murder and leaves gretchen alone and pregnant. faust's parasitic love, ruthlessly aimed at pleasure, is more sharply drawn. the pact with the devil totally deforms this love. the whole first part of the tragedy will never come to life without this sinister note.

> Sequence of scenes:
> gretchen at the spinning-wheel
> on the market square ('now tonight?' – 'what business is it of yours?' – 'i get my fun out of it too.')
> at the well
> discussion of religion
> funeral mass in the cathedral (followed by valentin scene)
> you who have suffered so, mistress of suffering, turn your face to me
> an outcast driven to despair
> night. open field.
> prison.

15 jul 52

house and surroundings in buckow tidied up enough for me to be able to read a bit of HORACE. the fact that in the satires, which are too carefully written to be intended just for contemporaries, he so obviously praises weak poets quite shamelessly shows how much he feels he can rely on posterity, or does he think that the quality of his eulogistic verse extinguishes the praise?

22 jul 52

STRITTMATTER brings the new version of the second act of KATZ-GRABEN. the last few pages are written in iambics. he got into this rhythm, it seems, as a cow treads in a hole. only he enjoys it more. i am not sure how putting it in iambics will affect the comedy, but i don't have the heart to spoil his fun. – less than 14 days ago georg lukács said in the pavilion out front that you should use elevated forms for contemporary plays too.

25 to 30 aug 52

eisler here with his FAUST. we go through the whole thing, tightening it up, bringing everything into focus as far as possible, which is often no small task, given the wilfulness of the work. were it not for eisler's artistic sensibilities, this would be a hodgepodge of stylistic elements. for example the transformation of the little (and dramatically questionable, incidentally) *orpheus ballet* in act three comes out well. faust is not only hooted down by his hearers (students); he also adopts their judgement and so turns back of his own volition from his return to antiquity ('what is orpheus to us?'). the aria itself gets quite a different impetus when hanns discovers in my horace that orpheus charmed not only animals but people as well. what a feat of artistry – and interesting for our arts administration – he achieved there with singing alone, and not, as it happens, with singing about humanity.

30 aug 52

ORPHEUS itself is a subject for opera, if the antique work is cleaned up and not tarted up as by cocteau.

30 aug 52

CORIOLANUS and KATZGRABEN

   outside my door is a corner formed by a demolished greenhouse and another wall. there are grass and pines, wild roses climb the walls. i have managed to find a thin café-table and a bench, with iron legs and the remains of white paint, very elegant. but horace's satisfaction displeases me more and more.

2 nov 52

rehearsal of TRIAL OF JOAN OF ARC in the rehearsal building.

in this we may not yet have extricated ourselves from bourgeois thinking, where persons are only formed by contradictions with their environment.

(1) Käthe Reichel as Jeanne d'Arc in Anna Seghers' play.

17 nov 52

from anna seghers' radio play TRIAL OF JEANNE D'ARC we made a two-hour play which we have now staged. mainly following the original minutes and quotations in anatole france's book. interesting type of play, very light, thin arches with the changes in the people and the heroine as tender interludes.

(2) Brecht (centre) rehearsing it.

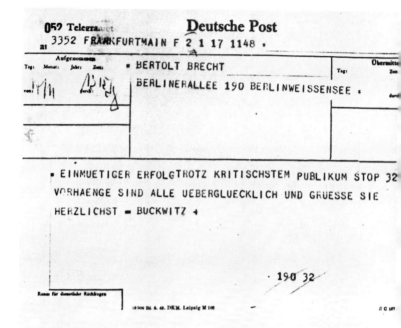

German première of *The Good Person of Szechwan*, Frankfurt. Director reports great success.

26 nov 52

we are looking for folk art, and naturally, in a highly industrialised country like germany you have to go a long way back in time. the mistake we make is to look for folk art only among the established arts like painting, music, dance etc. that's just where everything has been ruined by these same arts. instead we should be looking to arts like furniture-making, wrought iron, theatre costumery etc. arts that are decaying before our eyes for lack of appreciation.

28 nov 52 (?)

discuss subjects for statues in the stalin-allee with henselmann. *the three rubble women. the confectioner's apprentice, kohlhaas with the horses.*

suggest for downstairs in the big housing blocks reliefs showing an activist who worked on their construction.

about 1952

from time to time i feel a certain spiritual unease and cut myself off, go away into a kind of cave and read my crime novels. this is of no significance, my relations with the outside world are not changed, except temporarily. it is not within my control.

by nature i am a difficult man to control. any authority which is not rooted in my respect i reject with annoyance, and laws i can only consider to be provisional proposals for the regulation of human interaction, subject to constant modification.

6 dec 52

with schumacher from munich who is writing a doctoral dissertation on my early plays; talked about JUNGLE. the play deals with the impossibility of contest, here taken positively in the sense of sport (within capitalism, which doesn't emerge, ie has been overlooked). to that extent it is in the same line as GALILEO, where the impossibility of uncontrolled research, and CHALK CIRCLE where the fatal results of motherhood are treated – in which cases capitalism is not concealed. – the play represents a great step forward for drama, in spite of its weaknesses; it had to 'assimilate' hegel's idealistic dialectic before it could progress. like all the other dramatists i had never read a line of hegel. i just wanted to write something as dramatic as the ROBBERS and discovered,

[notes broken off.]

15 dec 52

saw SCHREINER again. he is suffering from his old headaches and inoperable gallstones, but works on without interruption. shakes his head over DEFA's thälmann film. it seems that during the hamburg rising they made him into a general with his own headquarters, whereas in fact he was riding from factory to factory on his bike, sought by the police and hiding in the crowd. an 18-year-old leader of a group of 100 was killed, and his mother told schreiner that she asked him in his last night what he would do if he caught her, his mother, stealing a loaf: 'then i would have to shoot you and me.' schreiner knows dozens of these stories, but DEFA isn't interested.

25 dec 52

i have, as far as i can recollect, never written a single line when i wasn't well, physically. all this healthiness gives you a sense of being on top of things which you need if you are to write. you have to write from the top downwards, you have to sit above your subject. of course, conversely, this kind of well-being more or less sets in when i sit down at the table with the typewriter.

25 dec 52

if you look soberly at what i have called epic acting, it is a type of acting that brings out the contradiction, which is there in the nature of things, between the actor and the character he is acting. the actor's (social) criticism of the figure, to whom he must naturally give full expression, comes into play. the opinions, passions, experiences, interests of the character are not of course those of the actor, and the latter have to come out in the acting. (that always happened, in the natural course of events, but there was to my knowledge little consciousness of it.)

in this, as in various other matters, the entry of dialectics into the theatre triggered a perceptible shock among those who accepted dialectics in other areas.

27 dec 52

am translating the murder of CORIOLANUS. feel tempted to make another translation of the scenes i have changed. as the feeling for history gets stronger – and when the self-confidence of the masses is greater, it will be possible to leave everything pretty well as it is. the plebians are still very weak after the expulsion of the monarchy, and the existence of the nation (city state) is exposed to coriolanus's blackmail. it is the body of patricians which has to – and does – put everything below it in order, unless it itself wishes to be enslaved by the neighbouring states. coriolanus attempts to extort old and new privileges for his class during the constant wars, and he turns back in the interests of his class. (in west germany the play could today be performed just as it is.)

28 dec 52

the infallible sign that something is not art, or that somebody does not understand art, is boredom. it is as forceful as pleasure is elsewhere. art should be a means of instruction, but its aim is pleasure.

12 jan 53

even in poland MOTHER COURAGE AND HER CHILDREN was constantly described as pacifist. from an historical standpoint the play shows the experiences of a small trader who wants to do business in wartime and loses everything. the war does not strike her like blind fate, on the contrary, she recognises it as the profit-making wheeling and dealing of the mighty; she wants a piece of the action. her fate goes beyond the individual and achieves symbolic significance. this conjures up the picture of germany, waging wars of conquest, destroying itself and others, learning nothing from all these catastrophes. resistance to this sort of war is not overlooked. (dumb kattrin.) but all this does not satisfy the impatience of our new socialist society which is obsessed with getting things done.

20 jan 53

in my view the elaborate exercises stanislavsky prescribed for actors may have become necessary because only with extraordinary means, with almost yoga-like concentration, could they shore up figures from the private bourgeois sphere. only by immersing himself in himself could the individual build himself up from within in opposition to the 'rest' of society.

27 jan 53

stanislavsky opened the art theatre with a dramatisation of THE SUFFERINGS OF WERTHER. werther and lotte's tragic love consisted, according to him, in their betraying their love instead of offering themselves up to it. it is a nice thought: but i would like to know how s[tanislavsky] got it over the footlights if resistance to love was presented as a phenomenon of nature.

as for the 'message' of the work, there's nothing simple about it. like molière's L'AVARE in this respect. he is ridiculing the avarice of an age in which the bourgeoisie has recently discovered how to put money to productive use. avarice has become quite impractical, stands in the way of making money and is thus ridiculous (and also earns the laughter of the feudal class which is generous and does not stint with the product of the labour of the oppressed classes). and yet avarice is of long standing, basically, as the compulsion to save, as the aim of productivity, as the bad side of capitalism, throughout its career. (and is, if captured at the right time, a really deeply rooted bad quality.) – in TURANDOT the will to formulate, to think unproductively is captured at a time when the (capitalist) mode of production does not permit productive forces to develop any further; it presents itself as impractical, therefore ridiculous. and it will carry on like this for a while, until the intellectuals are no longer outside and in opposition to the rest of the population, and the whole population, on the contrary, has been intellectualised.

15 to 30 oct 53

travel to vienna with helli to direct the MOTHER at the scala. boarding-house on the karlsplatz. wekwerth is preparing the production excellently. the scala actors good, but accustomed to psychology and discussion. eat a cassata in the hotel sacher, see the brueghels and a bosch. am once again impressed by the cuisine. unfortunately, like all the arts it can't survive without constant praise. – much time with eisler. his productive crisis continues. he is living off film and theatre music. promises to compose an act of his FAUSTUS; i promise to put it on. writes a letter to the c[entral] c[ommittee] in which he regrets his west berlin escapade – he got drunk at the zoo station. was involved in an argument with a taxi-driver and arrested – and explains at the same time how chicanery had dried up any impulse to compose. he drinks nothing, takes anti-alcohol pills and is so edgy that he runs to the door each time the bell rings to see who has come to visit. when it was difficult to find a trumpeter for the orchestra for the MOTHER – they demand more money from the communist scala than from other theatres – he calmed down very quickly, happy, in fact, that the rousing jazz character of his music was being toned down a little. but then the music becomes a lament rather than an accusation; so i intrigued until a trumpeter was found. we discuss a GARBE, in the style of DIE MASSNAHME or THE MOTHER, to be written in march or april, with a full act on 17th june.

4 nov 53

bukharin: economic theory of the leisure class.

1953–4

my present girl-friend, who may be my last, resembles my first. like her she too is light-hearted; as in the former's case, deeper sentiments surprise me. these women weep when scolded, whether justly or unjustly, simply because they are being scolded. they have a kind of sensuality that needs nobody to arouse it and that isn't much good to anybody either. they want to please everybody, but are not pleased to accept everybody whom they please. my present girl-friend is, like that earlier one, at her most affectionate when she is being pleasured. and i don't know whether either of them loves me.

coming into my study today i came upon my girl-friend with a young man. she was sitting beside him on the sofa, he was reclining, somewhat sleepily. she stood up, with a rather strained joke about it being 'a situation that could very easily give rise to misunderstanding', and during the work that followed she was embarrassed, even shaken. it was only two days later, after we had been working together more or less in silence and without the usual intimacies, that she asked if i was angry with her. i accused her of fooling around at her place of work with any available man. she said she had sat down beside the young man for a few minutes without thinking, that there was nothing between them, etc. i laughed.
    i find i have lost my respect for her; she seems cheap to me. not without relief i note the total disappearance of love in me. she however is still distressed, does not defend herself, behaves as if she had just been surprised in a silly and unnecessary affair. she can only think of one thing to do: whenever it is at all possible she asks my advice. advice is something i can neither refuse nor keep to myself.

7 feb 54

roles like grusha and azdak cannot be shaped in our times by the work of the director alone. no less than 5 years at the BE were necessary to give angelika hurwicz the right foundation. and busch's whole life, from his proletarian childhood in hamburg via the struggles in the weimar republic and the spanish civil war to the bitter experiences after 45, was necessary to bring about this azdak.

4 jun 54

evening rehearsal in the big rehearsal building in the max reinhardt strasse. we are rehearsing the scene where they pour out wine in the CHALK CIRCLE with busch and weigel. the doors are open, suddenly we hear a nightingale. listening to it from time to time we discuss weigel's view that mother grusinia might be naive (you don't have to say that saint banditus is her brother-in-law). in the end we still find that mother grusinia is innocent only in the eyes of azdak.

7 jul 54

it is curious that the weaker works of shakespeare and molière, which still ought to stand above the best of lesser authors, are less appreciated than theirs. things can therefore be successful on different levels, and this is what it all turns on. – lovers can't tone down their requirements either, and make do with partners who are less than was originally assumed.

7 jul 54

this country still gives me the creeps. recently when i went out to buckow with young people from the dramaturgs' office, i was sitting in the pavilion while they were working in their rooms or chatting. it suddenly occurred to me that, had i fallen among them ten years ago, all three of them, whatever they had read of mine, would instantly have handed me over to the gestapo . . .

8 jul 54

steff sends me, through very indirect channels, oppenheimer's long and thorough piece written in his own defence. this unfortunate man helped to make the first atom bomb when american physicists in world war 2 heard that hitler had people working on an atom bomb. he and his colleagues were then appalled to find that it had been dropped on japan. he had moral objections to the hydrogen bomb and now he has been packed off to the wilderness. his document reads as if it was by a man who stands accused by a tribe of cannibals of having refused to go for the meat. and then claims by way of excuse that during the manhunt he was only collecting firewood for the cauldron. what darkness.

[may 55]

warsaw

worth imitating this annual book fair, an exhibition of new and old books, visited by schools etc.

town holidays for country dwellers. they come to the big city for their holidays and are looked after there.

the circular lawn among the tall buildings, grass.

children's fountains with funny animals, spouting water in short arcs, with a pleasant sound resulting. rectangular basins, not too small for paddling.

kulisiewicz's little animal drawings on tiles would be good for kindergartens. important: their smallness.

two open letters to henselmann are needed. 1) the rendering on the buildings, boring cement which masks the brickwork with its dull sameness and never improves with age. is it impossible to devise a transparent material that is weather-resistant and leaves the beauty and the variations of the brickwork visible? 2) the linear basis of our building work is open to question. harmony does not depend on regularity. where are the courtyards, the twisting streets, the overlapping buildings, where have all the contrasts gone, the surprise of a vista that suddenly appears, the specific quality of a block that makes it stick in the memory and stay attractive over the years? we are letting our children grow up among geometry, in identical stalls. in the anarchic building practices of the past, chance (and the pressure 'by external forces' to fit in just here, to make the best of a restrictive site etc) produced both ugly and beautiful things. how can we keep those beautiful things in a planned environment?

questioned infeld about einstein. he stresses how withdrawn he is. 'we have to talk more quietly today, my wife is dying in the next room.' infeld: 'einstein is no subject for a play, he has no partner, who are you going to make him talk to?'

i am however interested in a questionnaire relating to conditions in poland which einstein is supposed to have sent to poland via the physicist nathan.

moscow

the new university, the emblem of moscow from afar, a jolly building in grand lines with beautiful detail, of which photos do not convey a proper impression. the building is unprofessorial, built as if for the arts (which is what the sciences will one day turn into again).

saw mayakovsky's BATHHOUSE in the theatre of satire. a vital chamber mystery, with very lively acting by excellent actors. realistic acting, alienation effects everywhere, comic pathos.

in the art theatre the same evening, where mostly younger actors are performing MUCH ADO ABOUT NOTHING under a pupil of stanislavsky's. 'traditional' (within the bad tradition of the 80s), with hollow emotions, petty bourgeois inwardness, garden-gnome comedy and the usual coarse jibes at a major-domo who believes he has to love his mistress. of stanislavsky's sense of naturalness and truth, no trace.

laxness's BARTERED LULLABY in the LITTLE THEATRE. disappointing play from this extraordinarily good prose writer, old fashioned in content and form. coarsely performed by moderate actors, pathos-ridden naturalism. exactly what stanislavsky was fighting against.

hear that akimov wants to put on THE VISIONS OF SIMONE MACHARD in leningrad and savatzky COURAGE in moscow. recommend an eleven-year-old for simone. see the actress savatzky has cast as courage in a good revolutionary play, STORM. she is extraordinary, a walking a-effect. large piece of womanhood, full of surprises, very bold virtuosity.

in the art theatre saw ostrovsky's THE PASSIONATE HEART with enormous pleasure. all stanislavsky's greatness made apparent.

18 jul 55

sketching a few examples for DIALECTICS IN THE THEATRE, i analyse CORIOLANUS's first appearance again and wonder whether a performance could be done without the additions (which i wrote two years ago), or with very few of them, relying solely on good direction.

Editorial Notes

References to Brecht's letters are to our 1990 volume *Letters 1913–1956.*

Denmark
1934 to 15 March 39

1934
Brecht visited London (for the first time) from October to December, to work on a film project with Leo Lania. He stayed in lodgings at 24 Calthorpe Street, WC1. His friend Fritz Kortner was meantime starring in the Capitol Films production *Abdul the Damned*, directed by Karl Grune, with music by Hanns Eisler.

On age and workmanship see the poems 'When I was rich' and 'On reading "When I was rich"'.

1935
This slightly flippant statement appears to have been written on the occasion of Brecht's spring visit to Moscow at the invitation of Piscator's International Organisation of Revolutionary Theatres (MORT). He broadcast on Moscow radio, and a 'Brecht evening' of his songs and poems, featuring Carola Neher and Gustav von Wangenheim, was organised by German émigrés and attended by Sergei Tretiakov and the Comintern members Wilhelm Pieck, Vilis Knorin, and Béla Kun. The USPD to which he had briefly belonged at the end of the First World War was the Independent Social-Democratic Party of Germany. It broke up in 1921/2.

1936
Brecht was once more in London, where Fritz Kortner had got him a job as a scriptwriter on Richard Tauber's *Bajazzo* film, of which Eisler was again the musical director. According to Eisler Brecht's contributions were so unwelcome that the producers paid him off.

1938
Three notes of uncertain origin.
July 38
Georg Lukács's forty-page article 'Marx und das Problem des ideologischen Verfalls' was published in *Internationale Literatur – Deutsche Blätter*, 1938, no. 7. Its argument is that the ideology (or whole system of thought) of the rising bourgeoisie in Germany, France and England was declining from 1820 on, and that this 'Verfall', after bringing about the collapse of the revolutionary movements of 1848, still distorted people's view of reality ninety years later. The greatest realist writers – from Balzac to Thomas Mann – could overcome this by forgetting their preconceptions and faithfully reflecting their own experience.

But writers must not dismiss the realist tradition itself as an outdated part of bourgeois ideology or try to supplant it by new avant-garde approaches such as Lukács associates with the Surrealists and specifically with such other opponents of capitalism as Dos Passos, Ehrenburg and Brecht (whom the article names).

This particular essay was the latest shot in Lukács's campaign against 'formalism', by which he meant any preoccupation with new artistic forms that might replace those of mid-nineteenth-century tradition. He had been arguing this case ever since the Comintern first sent him to Berlin in mid-1931, and in 1933 he had paved the way for the so-called 'expressionism debate' among the emigration with an article called 'Grösse und Verfall des Expressionismus' in a Soviet Russian magazine. Such activities disturbed Brecht primarily because they occupied much of the space in *Das Wort*, the Moscow literary monthly of which he himself was a co-editor (see his letter no. 366 to Willi Bredel written soon after this entry). At the same time he could not help noticing how they coincided on the one hand with the Nazi campaign against 'degenerate art' and on the other with the official Stalinist denunciation of formalism and proclamation of Socialist Realism as the only correct creative method.

The protestant Pastor Niemöller, a former submarine captain, was arrested on 1 July 1937 for preaching against the Nazis, tried, found not guilty and promptly put in a concentration camp. He was the subject of Ernst Toller's play *Pastor Hall*.

Equites = knights; plebs = the people; patres = patricians.

20 July 38

Brecht was writing his unfinished novel *The Business Affairs of Mr Julius Caesar*. Lucius Sergius Catalina led a conspiracy against the Roman republic in 63 BC. Brecht uses the English word 'City' and has in mind a great commercial and financial centre.

22 July 38

The Poems in Exile should have gone into volume four of Brecht's *Gesammelte Werke* or *Collected Works*, which were being published by Wieland Herzfelde's Malik publishing house, nominally from London. This was the imprint on the first two volumes of plays, which appeared in spring 1938. Herzfelde himself was then an exile in Prague, where the books were printed by the firm of Heinrich Mercy. Volumes three and four were in proof when the Germans occupied that city in March 1939, and never appeared. The *Poems in Exile* section was renamed *Svendborg Poems*, then separately printed in Copenhagen in May 1939 under Ruth Berlau's direction and seemingly at her expense, after Brecht had left for Sweden.

'Gleichschaltung' was a common Nazi term for forced conformity – political, ideological or artistic. One of the key concepts of Hitler's Third Reich. All must move as one.

25 July 38

Brecht uses the French word 'décadence'. The idea relates to the German 'Verfall' or decline, likewise to 'Entartung' or degeneracy (a more biological version of the same thing). Trimalchio's Feast in the *Satyricon* of Petronius is a classic literary instance of Roman decadence.

25 July 38
The critic Walter Benjamin was living in Paris. He had arrived on 22 June. Grete = Margarete Steffin, Brecht's chief aide from 1933–41, who had been lodging in Skovsbostrand since 25 April and had learned both Russian and Danish. Their German translation of Martin Andersen-Nexö's early memoirs *Die Kindheit* would be printed in Switzerland and published in Moscow in 1940.

Benjamin's account of his two-month visit (in *Understanding Brecht*, London, 1973) reports Brecht describing Lukács and his Moscow associates (specifically Andor Gábor and Alfred Kurella) as 'enemies of production'. 'They want to play the *apparatchik* and exercise control over other people. Every one of their criticisms contains a threat.' Brecht was aware of Ernst Ottwalt's arrest in November 1936 – in 1931–32 he had collaborated on the script of *Kuhle Wampe* – while Steffin said she thought Tretiakov 'was no longer alive'. They told Benjamin it would be risky to send Asya Lacis a pair of gloves; somebody might imagine it to be a reward for 'espionage services'. Around this time Lacis was arrested and deported for ten years to Kazakhstan.

27 July 38
Julius (Gyula) Hay wrote his play of Hungarian village life while in Soviet exile. It was published in *Internationale Literatur – Deutsche Blätter* and lavishly praised by Johannes R. Becher in the June 1938 number. Lion Feuchtwanger, Brecht's fellow-editor at *Das Wort*, wrote a laudatory foreword. See letters 312–314 and 328 and the corresponding notes, showing Brecht's earlier objections to Hay's criticisms of the Soviet German director Bernhard Reich, friend of Brecht and common-law husband of Asya Lacis. (She and Reich were arrested at the same time.) In the secret Party meeting of the German Commission of the Soviet Writers' Union, where the Moscow German and Hungarian writers met on five nights of September 1936 in order to exercise their 'vigilance' at the beginning of the Soviet purges, it was Hay who reported on the 'utterly wretched defeatism' shown by Brecht and Weigel in some remarks about KPD policy three years before.

'The clique' for Brecht was the 'Moscow Hungarian clique' who, for obscure reasons, were particularly prominent in the affairs of the German Communist writers-in-exile. They comprised Lukács, the Gábors, Sándor Barta and Hay, who acted as party watchdogs along with Becher from 1929 till after 1956. Only the Hungarians (not the Poles or the Czechs) had this special footing in German cultural/political affairs.

3 August 38
This entry is also included under the title 'Underrating the formal aspect' in the Notes to our edition of *Poems 1913–1956* (London and New York, 1976). It was surely stimulated by the conversations with Benjamin which resulted in the latter's 'Commentaries on Poems by Brecht'.

13 August 38
For the short stories Ruth Berlau used the pseudonym Maria Sten. They appeared

in Danish in 1940. In America Brecht later told her (letter 445 of spring 1942) that they 'might be acceptable for a women's magazine, if at all'. The Brecht Archive has three pages of fragments in Brecht's hand.

15 August 38

The Moscow edition of *Fear and Misery of the Third Reich* appeared in 1941. It was the play's first publication and contained thirteen scenes, of which 'The Spy' had appeared in the March issue of *Das Wort* and six more in those of June, July and the ensuing March. The Bulgarian Slatan Dudow (who had directed Brecht's film *Kuhle Wampe*) directed the Paris world première on 21 May, under the title 99%. The essay 'The Street Scene', ascribed to June 1938 but unpublished at the time, is in *Brecht on Theatre*.

16 August 38

The 'Tui Novel' was a long-term project of Brecht's, which was never completed. Its subject was the 'Intellectuals', an ill-defined but widely spread community of liberal thinkers, writers and other pundits who used to be seen as a political force in the 1930s and 40s. With the word 'Tui' (for 'Tellect-Ual-In') Brecht stood the concept on its head.

Koloman Wallisch, an Austrian Socialist leader hanged by Dollfuß in 1934, was the subject of a fine novella by Anna Seghers (in *Neue Deutsche Blätter*, Prague, 1.10), that same year. In late 1949, Brecht sent Eisler the text for a cantata about Wallisch which seems never to have been composed (see letter 620). This text is in *Gedichte aus dem Nachlass* (*GW* Supplement 2, 1982). For the unrealised plan for a Lehrstück (didactic piece) about 'Bad Baal' see our notes to *Collected Plays Volume 1*.

16 August 38

The seventeenth instalment of Heinrich Mann's *Henri IV* appeared in the same number of *IL* as Becher's essay on ideological decline. Exceptionally, Mann was always paid in hard currency for his contributions. 'Lenin's Attitudes' remained an idea.

10 September 38

Compare the terms used on 24 July and the entry following. This time Brecht uses the words 'Decadenz' and 'Abstieg' for our 'decadence' and 'decline'. Everything following 'My first book of poems . . .' was included in our notes to *Poems 1913–1956* under the title 'On the *Svendborg Poems*'. When Brecht wrote, the latter were still unpublished.

11 September 38

The complete works. Presumably the Malik *Collected Works*, volume 3.

12 September 38

Stanislavsky of the Moscow Art Theatre, whose reputation and popularity had greatly revived during the 1930s, had now become the model for Socialist Realism in the theatre. Aged seventy-five, he died some five weeks earlier. The *DZZ* was the *Deutsche Zentral-Zeitung*, Moscow's German-language daily, whose staff had nearly all been arrested in mid-February; it would cease publication in July 1939.

25 September 38
This was just before the Munich agreement by which Neville Chamberlain and Edouard Daladier signed over the German-speaking ('Sudeten') areas of Czechoslovakia to Hitler. Friday, when the social philosopher Fritz Sternberg arrived, was the 23rd; Chamberlain's visit to Hitler at Godesberg was on the day of this entry. The deeply humiliating agreement, with Hitler's quickly-flouted guarantee of the rump Czechoslovakia, was signed in Munich on Thursday the 29th.

Idola (plural of Latin idolum) means fantasies, false ideas. Francis Bacon defined four main types. Brecht seems to take this as a singular word.

5 October 38
The reference is presumably to Gide's *Les Nourritures terrestres* of 1897, an ultra-'literary' work most unlikely to be found in the kitbag of a French private. V-zones must be the Sudeten (or 'volksdeutsche') districts now being assimilated by Hitler's expansive Reich.

23 November 38
The original version of *Life of Galileo* was also known as *Die Erde bewegt sich* – 'The Earth Moves'. Brecht's American friend Ferdinand Reyher, who had become a Hollywood script writer, saw him in Copenhagen between 28 October and 4 November, discussed the Galileo theme, and encouraged him to write a film story – apparently for submission to the director William Dieterle (for whom see note to 9 August 41). Brecht returned to Skovsbostrand and instead wrote the play. This was the version first performed in Zurich in 1943. (See letter 373 of 8 December to Reyher after his return to New York).

Saint Joan is of course Brecht's Chicago play *Saint Joan of the Stockyards*. For the 'a-' (alienation) or 'v-' (Verfremdungs-) effect, see *Brecht on Theatre*.

January 1939
Mikhail Koltsov, a leading Soviet journalist and associate of Mayakovsky and Tretiakov, had been chairman of the foreign relations committee of the Writers' Union and head of the Zhurgaz group of magazine publications. It was Koltsov and his German wife Maria Greßhöhner (known as Osten, a former editor at the Malik-Verlag), who had effectively founded *Das Wort* as a Zhurgaz product in winter 1935/6. He was arrested on 12 December after his return from Spain, where he had been reporting the Civil War. He figures in that capacity as a fictional character in Malraux's *Days of Hope* and Hemingway's *For Whom the Bell Tolls*. He is thought to have been shot in 1942.

Letters 346 and 347 show Brecht already to have been aware of the earlier arrests of Carola Neher and Sergei Tretiakov, by late November 1938 at the latest. For Reich and Lacis see notes to 27 July 38 above; they survived. Béla Kun, leader of the Hungarian Soviet in 1919, was one of Brecht's contacts on the Comintern. Kun was shot, as was his Latvian colleague Knorin (whom Brecht had also met). For evidence of Wilhelm Pieck's nervousness see his letter of 8 October 1936 to Piscator in Paris, advising him not to return. This followed Pieck's other letters of that autumn to the KPD foreign section, included in Reinhard Müller's *Die Säuberung*, pp. 564–70, where the dissolution of Piscator's office is foreseen.

Pravda's attack on Meyerhold ('An Alien Theatre') appeared on 19 December 1937 and was followed on 8 January by the closure of his theatre. He was arrested in June 1939 and shot the following winter. No political pretext is known to us.

12 February 39
The three 'novellas' are short stories subsequently included in Brecht's *Tales from the Calendar* and the Methuen/Minerva *Short Stories*.

February 39
Karl Korsch (1886–1961), formerly a philosophy professor at Jena University, was a neighbour of the Brechts in Denmark before emigrating to the USA in winter 1937/8. His book *Karl Marx* was first published by Chapman and Hall in 1938 in a series called 'Modern Sociologists'. Expelled from the KPD in 1926, he was one of the handful of friends whom Brecht referred to as his 'teachers'.

25 February 39
The one-acter *Señora Carrar's Rifles*, like the individual scenes of *Fear and Misery*, was conventional 'empathy-drama'. *Fatzer* and *The Breadshop* were unrealised projects of around 1930.

5 March 39
Cain = James M. Cain, author of *The Postman Always Rings Twice*. Coy (so Michael Morley suggests) could very plausibly be Horace McCoy, author of *They Shoot Horses, Don't They?*
By 'second spirit' Brecht presumably means second wind.

15 March 39
This was the day of the German annexation of Bohemia and Moravia. A 'protectorate' over Slovakia was established one day later. 'The housepainter' is Brecht's term for Hitler (who never actually was one). Hradčany is the old castle in Prague, which became the presidential palace when the Czechoslovakian republic was established in 1918.
'Love is the Goods.' The German is 'Die Ware Liebe', where 'Ware' – meaning a commodity – is pronounced the same as 'wahre' – meaning 'true'.

Sweden
23 April to 19 March 40

4 May 39
The lecture 'On Experimental Theatre' is included, in a shortened version, in *Brecht on Theatre*. Within weeks he delivered it again to members of the amateur theatre movement. The following year he would repeat it in Finland. 'Short Description of a New Technique of Acting' too is in *Brecht on Theatre*. Karl Valentin (1882–1948) was the great Munich clown whom Brecht much admired. He did not emigrate.
The Brecht's move to Sweden was due to their fear of a Nazi occupation, though this only took place a year later. It coincided with the closing-down of *Das Wort*, leaving Brecht now without any rôle in Moscow (though the journal

says nothing about this). The move itself appears to have been organised and guaranteed by the social-democratic senator Georg Branting (whom Brecht had probably met in Paris in 1937) and the Swedish committee for aid to Spain. As part of this operation the national association of amateur theatres ATR invited Brecht to work with its members.

He was already known as the author of *The Threepenny Opera*, which had been seen twice in Stockholm before his emigration. In 1938 there were two further productions of that work, one in Ernst Eklund's Oskarsteatern, and the other that autumn by the travelling Rijksteatern under the direction of Per Lindberg. In the second of these Mrs Peachum was played by the actress Naima Wifstrand, who had visited Brecht at Skovsbostrand to discuss her part. Now she was able to help the Brechts find somewhere to live.

25 May 39
Herman Greid (1892–1975) had been artistic director of the Düsseldorf agitprop group Truppe im Westen before 1933 and thereafter was based in Sweden , where he became naturalised. Like Brecht, he was living on Lidingö Island.

Greid had worked with Maxim Vallentin's travelling theatre in the Ukraine in 1934–6 (i.e. prior to the purges). A relative of Branting by marriage, it was he who had directed the Swedish production of *Señora Carrar's Rifles* with Wifstrand as Carrar. This opened at the Odeon theatre, Stockholm on 5 March 1938, and toured to other centres that spring. Brecht came from Denmark for the rehearsals. Meantime Curt Trepte, another German actor of the Ukraine group, had arrived in Sweden and was asked to direct an amateur production of the play in Västerås for the local committee for aid to Spain. This opened that October, with the print worker Lisa Looström as Carrar, and likewise went on tour. Brecht, Weigel and Ruth Berlau saw the final performance on 6 August 1939, by which time the Spanish Civil War was over.

'The book of change' – a title misleadingly suggestive of the *I Ching* – was an ill-defined project of Brecht's which for a time came to embrace the *Me-Ti* aphorisms that he had begun to write. For these see *GW* 12.

May 39, Whitsun
The long 'Speech to Danish working-class actors on the art of observation' is in *Poems 1913–1956*, p. 253. It had been written in 1934.

A special group was organised by the ATR to work with Brecht on a production. However, he delegated the director's tasks to Ruth Berlau, who came over from Denmark, and helped him to write the topical one-acter *How Much is Your Iron?* under the pseudonym John Kent. A typescript is dated 2 June. It was performed in the Tollare public high school. They also wrote a Danish counterpart called *Dansen*, but it was not performed. These were among his feeblest works.

There is no mention of the death of Brecht's father in Germany on 20 May.

15 July 39
The characters' names in *The Good Person* were changed later (see notes to our edition). The house on Lidingö Island near Stockholm belonged to a friend of Naima Wifstrand, the sculptress Ninnan Santesson, who also had a studio in the city.

1 September 39
The German invasion of Poland began that day, which also saw a lunch for Thomas Mann given by the mayor of Stockholm, where Brecht was one of the guests. Mann was to have delivered a lecture for the PEN Club, but this had been forbidden by the Foreign Ministry. The Soviet-German pact had been signed on 23 August, the Anglo-Polish treaty on the 25th. After two days' hesitation Britain and France declared war on Germany, but without distracting Hitler from the Polish campaign.

11 September 39
Brecht's not-so-little essay about their hostess's head of Weigel is in *GW* 18, pp. 272–8.

18 September 39
Here Brecht refers to 'Soviet Russia' rather than to the 'Union'. Stalin's invasion of the formerly Russian-ruled areas of Eastern Poland, following the Soviet-German pact, has determined Poland's Eastern frontiers up to the present day (1992).

19 September 39
The English empire. In the poem '1940', the section starting 'My young son asks me' (p. 348 in *Poems 1913–1956*), it was originally the British, not the French empire that Brecht said was 'going under'.

7 November 39
Hilding Rosenberg (b.1892), a leading Swedish composer, had a symphony performed at the 1937 Paris ISCM Festival. He discussed the Lucullus project with Brecht on Lidingö, but never saw more than an outline of the play and wrote no music for it. According to Jan Olsson, the Swedish radio took an option, for which they paid 400 crowns on 21 November, but turned down the finished play. It was first broadcast (without music) by the Swiss Radio Beromünster on 19 May 1940. The text, which largely differed in length and pace from the postwar opera version, was published in the Moscow *Internationale Literatur* 1940, no 3.

It is worth noting that Brecht as yet makes no mention of the work on *Mother Courage*, his great World War 2 play, which had occupied him and Margarete Steffin since late September. He sent copies to Switzerland and to Hanns Eisler in the US as well as to several Swedish theatres, and in December gave one to Naima Wifstrand inscribed 'to my Mother Courage'. He was hoping for a Swedish-language production with her, in which Weigel could play dumb Kattrin. Per Lindberg aimed to set up a 'People's' ensemble to this end.

Dr Waldemar Goldschmidt, whom the Brechts met through the Viennese architect Josef Frank, chose the pseudonym of Koch. Brecht reputedly made some use of his stories in his subsequent *Conversations Between Exiles*. See for example section XII of that work, where Ziffel reads out a long story told him by a biologist friend.

13 November 39
The SAP or Socialist Workers' Party was a left socialist group formed in 1931. Its leading members included Fritz Sternberg, Jakob Walcher, August Enderle and the post-1945 mayor of Leipzig Max Seydewitz. The young Willi Brandt, then

also an exile in Sweden, contributed to one of its pamphlets. Otto Strasser and his brother had headed the socialist wing of National Socialism.

7 December 39
This amateur performance of *Lucullus* was directed by Herman Greid (see note on 25 May 39)

8 December 39
'The Lord of the Fish' = an early Brecht poem (*Poems 1913–1956*, p. 94). The *Baal* drawing may be that reproduced in *Caspar Neher, Brecht's Designer*, p.11, which later hung in Brecht's East Berlin flat.

    Neue Zeit = theoretical journal of Marxism, founded by Karl Kautsky in 1883 and edited by him in Germany and (between 1875–90) in London for 34 years. It closed in 1923.

    Me-Ti = the work of Mo Tse or Mo Di, in a German translation by Alfred Forke (1922).

    Versuche = seven grey paperbound instalments of Brecht's current writings, published by Gustav Kiepenheuer, Potsdam from 1930–33 (here presumably rebound in two volumes. They were continued and re-published after 1945).

    Brueghel pictures = *Brueghels Gemälde* and *Das grosse Brueghel-Buch* by Gustav Glück, Vienna.

9 December 39
The Russians invaded Finland on 30 November, without enhancing their military or political reputation.

1 January 40
For Enderle see footnote to 13 November 39.

14 January 40
Naima Wifstrand had set up a private acting school in a disused architects' office in the Drottninggaten, Stockholm. Weigel found that the students were overawed by the classics, and needed loosening up. This led Brecht to write them the set of five 'practice scenes' included in *GW* 7 and vol. 6 of the Random House (Vintage) *Collected Plays*, giving alternative views of Shakespeare's and Schiller's characters. A sixth, based on *King Lear* V. 3, was not published. The course was resumed for another semester after the Brechts' departure.

16 January 40
Pär Lagerkvist (1891–1974) was a leading poet, playwright and novelist.

26 January 40
The story is in Brecht's collected stories under the title 'Esskultur' or 'A question of taste'. He had met Jean Renoir, the film director, in France, perhaps in 1937. Carl Koch, husband of the film animator Lotte Reiniger, was a Berlin friend, working at that time as an assistant to G. W. Pabst. He later settled in Watford, following Pabst's return to Germany in 1940. The story would be published in Swedish in the *Göteborgs-Posten* at the end of 1943. For Tombrock see next entry.

29 January 40
Hans Tombrock (1895–1966) was the sixteenth son of a Westphalian miner's family, who had joined Gregor Gog's International Brotherhood of Vagabonds. A self-taught artist, he exhibited with its art group in 1929, then left Germany under the Nazis and arrived in Sweden in 1937, where Brecht helped and encouraged him, notably by writing short poems to accompany his pictures. He remained in Sweden and returned to Germany after 1945.

29 January 40
Arnold Ljungdal was a Swedish Marxist. The History of the Bolsheviks is presumably the official *History of the Communist Party of the Soviet Union (Bolsheviks)*, published from Moscow in 1939, with a section on 'Dialectical and Historical Materialism' supposedly written by Stalin.

10 February 40
In a note Werner Hecht points out that a nine-volume German edition of Macaulay had appeared in the 1850s. Since Brecht however gives the English title and quotes in English he must surely have had an English edition before him.

19 March 40
In Brecht's scattered aphorisms 'Mr Keuner' (or Mr Naobody) was a thin disguise for the author. Interesting that he has nothing to say about the ending of the Soviet-Finnish war a week earlier.

Finland
17 April 40 to 13 July 41

17 April 40
Less than a month after the Soviet-Finnish treaty had eased the frontier around Leningrad, the German campaign in the West began in earnest on 9 April with the invasion of Norway and Denmark. Sweden managed to remain neutral, but the German troops were given transit rights, the Lidingö house was searched by the police, and in Werner Mittenzwei's view Brecht panicked. Branting for one advised him to leave for Finland while he could; so Brecht wrote to the Finnish playwright Hella Wuolijoki (1886–1954) to ask her for an invitation. The family, including Steffin, left furniture, books and papers with the Santessons and took the ship. A formal invitation to lecture at the New School in New York had come from Piscator the day before they left. Hoping to be able to sail from the northern port of Petsamo before the winter, Weigel booked passages to North America for 5 August.

It was a year before they got the necessary visas; by June Petsamo had been taken over by the Germans, and meanwhile it was mainly Wuolijoki who looked after the Brechts. She had been married before 1914 to a leading Finnish revolutionary, a victim of alcoholism; then became an outstanding business woman in timber and oil, knew John Reed and Joseph Losey, was a friend of Ivan Maisky and Alexandra Kollontai (Soviet ambassadors respectively in London and Stockholm), and wrote *The Women of Niskavuori* which was performed in theatres all over Europe including Nazi Germany. Ruth Berlau, who had a part in the Copenhagen production in 1938, met her then and would claim already to have spoken to her about Brecht and his need for asylum. Another intermediary was the English-born Mary Pekkala, wife of a socialist politician.

6 May 40
Elmer Diktonius (1896–1961), Finnish writer and critic. The Brechts had moved into a small flat in the Töölö district of Helsinki, near the harbour, which Mary Pekkala had helped them find. He had a workroom there. Weigel curtained off half the kitchen to make a room for herself, while the children seem to have slept in the entrance hall.

8 June 40
In less than a month the Blitzkrieg or 'lightning war' had defeated the French and British in Flanders; the Germans would enter Paris on the 14th and make an armistice with Pétain's Vichy government on the 22nd.

11 June 40
Compare Brecht's 'Finnish epigram' – 'To a portable radio' – in *Poems 1913–1956*, p. 351.

20 June 40
The changing of the *Szechwan* characters' names (li gung becoming Shen Teh, etc.) seems to have taken place in August–September.

Because Brecht only makes one mention of Ruth Berlau since he and his family left Denmark, we should briefly outline her activities. By her own account in Hans Bunge (ed.) *Brechts Lai-tu* (Luchterhand, Neuwied, 1985) she arrived in Helsinki when Brecht was working on *The Good Person of Szechwan*. This was in answer to an earlier letter from him which is not in the collected *Letters*. While he was in Sweden she had come over from Denmark occasionally when not acting, and had certainly collaborated on the two one-act plays (see note for Whitsun 1939). Now, however, the Nazis were in Copenhagen; her windows had been broken, and as Brecht wrote to Wuolijoki in letter 419, her personal safety was at stake.

His letter to Berlau, written (she says) before leaving Sweden but sent 'by roundabout channels', told her to go to Wuolijoki; she could count on him to organise her further travel, and meantime she herself was to apply for a US visa. He advised her to destroy that part of the letter; however, she kept the last few lines assuring her of his intention to wait for her, and of his eternal love. This appears more or less to have coincided with her divorce from her doctor husband, and she says she was left with enough money to pay for her passage and keep her for six months in the US.

She took lodgings in Helsinki near to the Brechts. Then when they went out to Marlebäk she and Steffin stayed with Wuolijoki in the main house until her hostess learnt of her relationship with Brecht and asked her to leave. So she camped nearby but (says Werner Mittenzwei) was forbidden access to the house. Neither Weigel nor Steffin – the main collaborator on all Brecht's work at this time – welcomed her presence, it seems, and at first she was not included in the family's travel plans.

24 June 40

Guernica, so called after the Spanish village destroyed by Nazi bombing in the Civil War, was painted for the Spanish pavilion at the Paris International Exhibition of 1937.

28 June 40

Lion Feuchtwanger emigrated to the Mediterranean town of Sanary-sur-Mer in 1933. He and his wife were separately interned by the French, but she escaped after the armistice, and with the help of the US consulate in Marseilles, Ben Huebsch of the Viking Press, a Unitarian Minister called Sharp and Mrs Roosevelt, she got him out that autumn via Lisbon and on a ship to New York. (See entry for 27 August below.)

2 July 40

Brecht's 'Ballad of the Widows of Osseg' (in the *Svendborg Poems*, GW 9, pp. 643–4) was based on a Czech mining disaster of 3 January 1934, when 142 miners from the Sudeten-German town of Osseg or Osecha were killed in a pit and 200 women and children came to Prague to demonstrate outside the parliament building.

5 July 40

Wuolijoki had bought her house with its 1200-acre estate in 1920, when she was at the height of her business success. It was in the Tavast country some 120 km north of Helsinki, not far from Lahti, and already she was finding it difficult to keep up. In fact this would be her last summer there. The Karelians must have been from the area ceded to the Russians in March.

7 July 40

The first of these plays was never written, but slightly recalls Brecht's early one-acter *The Beggar or the Dead Dog*. The second would be realised when he got to America.

30 July 40

The three poems are in *Poems 1913–1956*, pp. 427 and 352. (But the first of them is there ascribed to 1950 and may have been updated.)

2 August 40

The *Messingkauf Dialogues* (Methuen, 1965) were intended by Brecht as a 'four-sided conversation about a new way of making theatre', somewhat on the model of Galileo's *Dialogues*. They were never finished, though he worked on them in 1939–40 and would return to them later (e.g. on 11 August 42). He also used the label 'Messingkauf' for his theatre poems and other theoretical fragments, and for the 'practice scenes' referred to in the entry for 14 January 40 above.

4 August 40

Lenin's parable occurs in his 'Left Wing Communism, An Infantile Disorder' (1920), where he points out that climbers often have to take a zigzag route and sometimes to retrace their steps. See also entry for 17 October.

5 August 40

Hašek, Silone and O'Duffy – authors of *Schweik*, *Fontamara* and *The Wasted*

Island. It is possible, as the German editors suggest, that by 'O'Duffy' Brecht really meant Sean O'Casey. But there is no reason to suppose that he had yet come across the Irish playwright (who was not a novelist anyway); and Michael Morley points out that there was indeed a real Eimar Ultan O'Duffy (1893–1935), a satirist-economist who also wrote the enticingly titled *The Spacious Adventures of the Man in the Street* (1928), which has echoes of Butler's *Erewhon*. (There are two essays on Butler by Brecht.)

10 August 40
The 'Battle of Britain' was then at its height, night-time bombing of London about to begin. It is worth noting how Brecht was turning to English literature at this time.

19 August 40
Bernhard von Brentano, a correspondent for the liberal *Frankfurter Zeitung*, was a Berlin friend of Brecht's and had emigrated in 1933. It was not long before they became political opponents.

The stay in Finland had two marked effects on Brecht's writing, seen best perhaps in his poems. One was, as he says, the impulse to write epigrams, though this was not so wholly limiting as he here suggests. The other was a new interest in the landscape and the life of the countryside, such as he had barely expressed since moving to Berlin in 1924. This also permeates the writing of *Puntila*, a play of great freshness which reflects the character not only of his hostess but also of her estate.

Dirtschild ('dschädschild'), a mixture of Churchill and Rothschild, mocks the Nazi belief that the British leadership must be partly Jewish.

21 August 40
The moors. Dachau, Bögermoor and other concentration camps were on moorland. Cf. the internees' song 'Wir sind die Moorsoldaten' ('We are the peatbog soldiers').

27 August 40
For the *Puntila* collaboration and its different stages, see the introduction and notes to our edition.

29 August 40
English translations of the epigrams by Hugh Rorrison.

6 September 40
Kalle was later renamed Matti. See 1 October 40

14 September 40
Slatan Dudow, later better known as a film director, directed the Paris premières of *Señora Carrar's Rifles* and *Fear and Misery of the Third Reich*. (See entry for 15 August 38.) He was deprived of his film archive and expelled by the Vichy government.

25 September 40
Yuzo Yamamoto was a living Japanese playwright. Brecht planned a version to be called *The Judith of Shimoda*. There are some ninety-odd pages of fragments

22 January 41

John Steinbeck's (1902–68) novel was published in 1939. The film was directed by John Ford for 20th Century Fox, and featured Henry Fonda as the returning son. It can be seen as a swansong of the New Deal. Brecht's note virtually coincided with the US première.

25 January 41

That the *Good Person* could be made shorter would be shown by the Santa Monica version which Brecht made, apparently, for Weill.

26 January 41

The 'Song of the Smoke' was adapted from 'The Song from the Opium Den' which Brecht had written around 1920.

27 January 41

See 5 March 39 for 'second spirit'; i.e. a tank doesn't need to get its second wind. General Gamelin (1872–1958) was the elderly French Commander-in-Chief whose name, now almost forgotten, was associated with the fatal myth of the impregnable Maginot Line.

30 January 41

Rise and Fall of the City of Mahagonny is omitted, as (less surprisingly) are all the Lehrstücke and the disowned *Happy End*.

4 March 41

Max (Mordecai) Gorelik designed the sets for the Theatre Union production of Brecht's *The Mother* in New York in 1935 – the only aspect of that production that Brecht praised. From then on Brecht saw him as an ally, and tried to recruit him for the 'Diderot Society' plan and for Piscator's proposed new theatre journal in Moscow. In turn Gorelik tried to expound Brecht's ideas in the New York magazine *Theatre Workshop* (of which he was an editor) and a letter to the *New York Times* (7 Feb 1937). During 1936 he visited Europe on a Guggenheim grant in connection with his book, which appeared in New York in 1940, and Brecht got Piscator to help him with visas for the USSR. In late summer 1936 he spent a fortnight with Brecht in Skovsbostrand, and was also in Copenhagen with him to watch rehearsals of *The Round Heads and the Pointed Heads*.

8 March 41

For Diderot's *Jacques le Fataliste* and the origin of the *Refugee Conversations* plan see 1 October 40. *Mandragola*, play by Machiavelli, c. 1520. Luther's wife, a former nun, was Katharina von Bora, who bore him six children. Her portrait by the elder Cranach is in the Basel Museum.

28 March 41

The gangster play became *The Resistible Rise of Arturo Ui*.

7 April 41

Having abandoned all intention to invade England, the Germans attacked Greece and Yugoslavia, both of which were defeated within a fortnight. British, Australian and New Zealand troops were moved into Greece, where they conducted a steady withdrawal. The Germans meantime had come to the rescue of their Italian allies in Libya; and the British began to be pushed back there too.

12 April 41

Tasso: play by Goethe. Pasting up: Brecht's typescripts prior to retyping became a kind of montage, as he shifted lines or whole sections from one place, or one version of the play, to another.

Ui part 2 was not written.

13 April 41

The Schutzbund was the combined Austrian equivalent of the German Reichsbanner and Roter Frontkämpferbund – i.e. an illegally armed private force of the Left. It was suppressed in 1934 by Dollfuss, after which its members were also arrested by the Nazis.

15 April 41

Erkki Vala, a left-wing writer and editor, often met Brecht in Helsinki. Brecht translated this short poem (*GW Gedichte*, p. 1066), 'Sotakoira' ('The Dog of War') by Arvo Turtiainen, then used its theme in the concluding stanzas of his own 'The Children's Crusade', written in November after reaching the US.

16 April 41

André Maurois's *Tragédie en France* appeared in German in 1941. See entry 7 July 40 for the first mention of this project, whose relation to the fall of France now becomes clear. It can hardly have progressed far, as there is no material listed in the Brecht Archive catalogue of 1969.

New Masses was the American Communist magazine, competing with the *New Republic*. John Howard Lawson contributed to it and to *Theatre Workshop*, helped to organise the League of American Writers in 1935 and published his book *The Theory and Technique of Playwrighting* the following year.

18 April 41

Cassandra. There are seven pages of fragmentary ideas in the Brecht Archive.

21 April 41

For instance, since the Brechts' arrival in Finland on 17 April 40 he has only once (on 3 January 41) mentioned Ruth Berlau.

22 April 41

The Zurich Schauspielhaus, under the direction first of the wine merchant Ferdinand Rieser and then of Oskar Wälterlin, was the outstanding German-speaking theatre outside the clutch of the Nazis. Among its many great achievements – for which see Werner Mittenzwei's monograph in the Henschel-Verlag series 'Deutsches Theater im Exil' (Berlin, 1989) – the *Mother Courage* première was the most famous, not least because it came just as Hitler was about to make a fatal mistake. See also our introduction to the play in the Methuen edition.

23 April 41

The weakness of the flesh. There seems to be no known material for this project.

24 April 41

'gestarium' may well be a one-off, a word invented by Brecht (on the analogy of 'bestiarium') for a play which displays a wide variety of gests (or concretely depicted social attitudes). 'Different works by an author': the first three are by Schiller, the other three by Goethe.

9 May 41
Andreas Streicher ran away from school with Schiller and wrote about their journeyings in 1782–5. He became a piano-maker.

12 May 41
Vala. See 15 April 41, above. Rudolf Hess's flight was on 10 May. Brecht makes no allusion to his (possibly self-imposed) mission.

29–30 May 41
For a later account, given to her sister in 1947, see Letter 541. For the rôle of Mikhail Apletin, see letters 427–429.

13 July 41
As Werner Hecht points out, this entry was written in retrospect, and actually the Brechts left Finland two days later than it says. Note the confidence of their Moscow friends that the USSR would not be invaded, even though Churchill had warned Stalin in April that this was Hitler's plan. In the event the invasion by the Germans and the Finns began on 22 June, nine days after the Brechts and Ruth Berlau had sailed from Vladivostok on the 'Annie Johnson', a recognised refugee ship which was subsequently torpedoed.

Alexander Fadeyev was secretary of the Soviet Writers' Union, Mikhail Apletin the deputy chairman of its foreign department. Maria Greßhöhner was Maria Osten, Koltsov's widow. After Koltsov's arrest her party membership had been suspended following interrogation by a KPD Commission consisting of Ulbricht, Philipp Dengel and Herbert Wehner, who found her guilty of consorting with Carola Neher and such 'conciliators' as John Heartfield, and circumventing the Party by personal wire-pulling. She was arrested within days of Steffin's death, and shot on 8 August 1942.

1941
Alwa Anderson. A Mrs Anderson or Andersen was the Brechts' housekeeper in Denmark. Jerome was Victor J. Jerome of the US Communist Party, who was Brecht's political contact at the time of the New York *Mother* production in 1935. This table is undated.

America
21 July 41 to 5 November 47

21 and 22 July 41
Lion Feuchtwanger, former co-editor of *Das Wort* with Brecht and Willi Bredel, was now established in Pacific Palisades (LA) where he would live with his wife Martha until his death in 1958. He had put his Russian earnings at Brecht's disposal for travel expenses (greatly supplementing Brecht's own).

Elisabeth Hauptmann was first and foremost of Brecht's dramaturgical collaborators. She remained in Germany for a year after Hitler came to power, and according to Brecht her Berlin flat was searched more than twenty times before she was briefly arrested. She then went to her sister in St Louis and became a teacher. Margarete Steffin took over her rôle. At this time she was living in Greenwich, Connecticut.

1 August 41
The Dieterles' secretary, Erna Budzislawski, rented the Brechts a house at 1954 Argyle Avenue, Hollywood. Later that month they moved to 817, 25th Street, Santa Monica, where their rent was $48.50 a month.

9 August 41
William Dieterle was one of Max Reinhardt's former Berlin actors. In 1932 he had gone to Hollywood, where he became a leading director and producer for Warner Brothers, known especially for his biographical films of the 1930s about Pasteur, Zola, Juarez and Ehrlich. He had signed an affidavit for Brecht's immigration, and with his wife Charlotte is thought to have helped in a hundred or more such cases. With Liesl (wife of Bruno) Frank and her mother Fritzi Massary she set up the European Film Fund, which supported the Brechts among others.

August 41
Benjamin's death had occurred almost a year earlier, on the night of 26 September 1940. He was on his way to the US, after having been interned by the French for three months at the start of the war. He was forty-eight.

The Frankfurt Institute for Social Research headed by Benjamin's friend Max Horkheimer moved to the US in 1934 and was given hospitality by Columbia University. In 1941 Horkheimer and Adorno moved it out to California, where regular seminar-like meetings were held at the former's house. According to Werner Mittenzwei Brecht had not previously met the two men, though Benjamin would have told him about their work. Horkheimer has pointed out that he was neither a millionaire nor a professor, and that the relative wealth of the institute came from the funds provided by the German-Argentine Weil family (who had also helped finance Herzfelde's Malik-Verlag and Piscator's Berlin theatre). He had ensured that such funds were paid from 1930 on into a Dutch bank and not a German one. Otherwise they would have been confiscated by the Nazis.

4 October 41
For Reyher see 23 November 38.

20 October 41
The première of *Citizen Kane* was on 1 May 41. It was directed by Welles and conceived and written primarily by Herman J. Mankiewicz. Ben Hecht had been in Berlin in the early 1920s, when he was on the fringe of the Dada avant-garde.

21 October 41
Lang = Fritz Lang (1890–1965), director of the *Mabuse* films, the *Nibelungen*, *Metropolis* (with Weigel in a small part), *M* (starring Lorre). Emigrated in 1933 despite invitation from Goebbels to head the Nazi film industry. 1934 to US and

MGM, where he established himself with *Fury* (1936). He had subscribed to help bring Brecht to the US.

25 October 41

Alfred Döblin (1878–1957), a respected older friend of Brecht's from the 1920s, was a doctor in the East End of Berlin and author of the novel *Berlin Alexanderplatz*. He emigrated to France in 1933 and became a French citizen, then escaped to San Francisco after the French collapse, when he became a Catholic. Like Heinrich Mann, the elder brother of Thomas, he was not successful in the US.

26 October 41

Hans Reichenbach (1891–1953) was a professor at Berlin Technical University till 1933. After emigrating via Istanbul, he had been given a chair in philosophy at UCLA.

27 October 41

For Korsch see under February 1939. Hecht lists four articles by him to date in *Living Marxism* for 1940 and 1941.

Salka Viertel was living in Maybery Road, Santa Monica Canyon. She was the wife of the Austrian theatre and film director Berthold Viertel and mother of Hans and Peter, all good friends of the Brechts. Her brother was the pianist Eduard Steuermann, one of the Schönberg circle. He was the teacher of Alfred Brendel.

Ludwig Hardt (1886–1947) was a well-known reciter, then living in Pacific Palisades. The Goethe quotation comes from 'Selige Sehnsucht', which is not one of the Hafiz poems.

14 November 41

The persons here are Fritz Kortner the actor who played Shlink in 1923, Oskar Homolka the first Baal in 1926, Bruno Frank the Austrian novelist and dramatist (*Sturm im Wasserglas*, 1930), Fritz Lang, Rolf Nürnberg, a former Berlin theatre critic, and Peter Lorre who played Galy Gay in 1932.

16 November 41

There are about fifty pages of notes and fragments relating to the 'God of Happiness' project, which developed into a scheme for an opera with Paul Dessau.

This seems to have been the first 'Künstlerabend' given by the Los Angeles Jewish Club on 15 November. It was presided over by Leopold Jessner, formerly of the Berlin Staatstheater, Bruno Frank and Leo Reuss. Ernst Deutsch and Helene Thimig (Mrs Max Reinhardt) were among the most distinguished of the exiled actors in the US. The 'German War Primer' poems written in 1936–8 are in *Poems 1913–1956*, pp. 286–9. Eisler in 1936 set fourteen of them for unaccompanied chorus under the title *Gegen den Krieg* ('Against War'). They are not to be confused with the later *Kriegsfibel* epigrams.

17 November 41

In *Poems 1913–1956*, pp. 368–73. Brecht's *The Three Soldiers*, a long 'children's poem' illustrated by George Grosz, was published as *Versuche 6* in 1932.

20 November 41

Elisabeth Bergner, another outstanding German actress, also found little employment in Hollywood. Brecht had known her in Munich in the early 1920s.

21 November 41

The 'Naughty Boys' (Die bösen Buben) were a pre-1914 Berlin cabaret act by Meinhard and Bernauer. There is no report of any 'Brecht evening' taking place.

22 November 41

Clarence Muse, an American black actor, was aiming to start a National Negro Theatre with Paul Robeson's support. For the unrealised *Threepenny Opera* project, see notes 439xx and 441x, xxx and xxxx in our edition of Brecht *Letters 1913–1956*. Briefly, Weill was against it and Brecht saw that he was right.

2 December 41

The 'subject for a film comedy' was called 'Bermuda Troubles', and was not developed further. The German actor Robert Thoeren, now working as a script-writer for MGM, was one of Brecht's most successful acquaintances.

3 December 41

Having been driven back to the Egyptian frontier in the spring, the British Western Desert Force, now renamed Eighth Army, attacked Rommel's Afrika-Korps on 18 November and embarked on a three-week battle before advancing to Benghazi again. Meantime the Red Army had pushed back the Germans from Rostov-on-the-Don and outside Leningrad and Moscow. Hitler now made himself Supreme Commander.

5 December 41

Lilli Laté was Fritz Lang's secretary. Barbara is Brecht's daughter, then aged eleven. For the Viertels, see note 27 October 41.

8 December 41

Boyer = the French film star Charles Boyer. That day Brecht took out his first papers (the initial step towards naturalisation, which he never followed up). The Japanese had bombed Pearl Harbor and Malaya the previous day. The US and Britain declared war on Japan; then on the 11th Germany and Italy declared war on the US. On the 9th, Brecht wrote to Archibald MacLeish, asking to take part in broadcasts to Germany. He got no reply.

17 December 41

There is no material in the Brecht Archive for the Kortner and Boyer projects. 'Bermuda Troubles' occupies two pages in *GW Texte für Filme II*, 'The Snowman' one page in the Archive and 'The Bread-King learns to Bake' fifteen.

The Jeanne d'Arc plan was already in Brecht's mind on 7 July 40. It would now fill it for the next few weeks, under the title first of *The Voices*, then later *The Visions of Simone Machard*.

25 December 41

The director Paul Czinner was Bergner's husband.

26 December 41

Colonel-General Walther von Brauchitsch had been commander-in-chief of the German army since 1938.

28 December 41

Hans (John) Winge was an Austrian friend of the Brechts.

31 December 41

Erich Maria Remarque (1898–1970) was the author of *All Quiet on the Western Front* (1929), possibly the most famous novel to come out of the First World War. It was filmed by Lewis Milestone in 1930. Its Berlin première was followed by a ban, as being injurious to national prestige. Hanns Heinz Ewers was an early twentieth-century writer with some claim to decadence. He wrote a life of Horst Wessel.

6 January 42

Education for Death, by Gregor Athalwin Ziemer, was published in New York in 1941.

9 January 42

The long poem 'To the German Soldiers in the East' is in *Poems 1913–1956*, pp. 373–7. It is not known if it was actually sent or broadcast. It was published in *Freies Deutschland*, Mexico, no. 5, March 1942. Earlier it bore the title 'Lament for the Dead, 1941', which Brecht discarded. In 1943 Eisler set section 6 for voice and piano under the title 'And I shall never again see'.

14 January 42

The Soviets in World Affairs, by Louis Fischer, was published in 1930. Fischer was an American of Russian descent who was a reporter in the USSR for many years from 1922 on. He and his family were close friends of the Friedrich Wolfs in Moscow. Unlike them, he would become openly critical of Stalin.

16 January 42

Bergner (says James Lyon) meant the hypnotised girl to commit 'certain radical political acts'. She and Czinner asked Brecht to help with the plot, and the three would meet frequently during February and March. Then – see 11 April 42 – Czinner told the story to Billy Wilder, one of the makers of *Menschen am Sonntag* (the classic film to which *Kuhle Wampe* had been a riposte), who reputedly sold it to a friend. Brecht reacted with the poem 'Die Schande' (*GW* 10, p. 858).

17 January 42

For Hardt see 27 October 41.

18 January 42

Theodor Wiesengrund-Adorno (1903–69), philosopher, musicologist and (eventually) all-round pundit, emigrated to the US in 1934. He was Walter Benjamin's editor and Hanns Eisler's collaborator on *Composing for the Films* (OUP, New York, 1947); he advised Thomas Mann on *Dr Faustus*, and became Horkheimer's closest collaborator at the Institute for Social Research after World War 2. In 1938 he was a guest at New College, Oxford. He wrote a number of essays and reviews about Kurt Weill's works with Brecht. For the Institute, see entry and note for August 1941.

Ernst Bloch (1885–1977), who emigrated to the US from Czechoslovakia in 1938, was an independent Marxist of a utopian bent, an old friend of Lukács and of Hanns Eisler. Günther Stern (ps. Anders), another philosopher of the Frankfurt circle, had a job as cleaner in a Hollywood costume warehouse. In 1938 he had written a notable essay on photomontage in connection with a New York exibition of John Heartfield's work. Like Bloch he would become a founder of the Aurora-Verlag.

Lukács never lived in America; and he never visited that continent. But the others of this group – whom Brecht would come to identify with the 'Tuis' (see entry and note for 16 August 38) – held discussion meetings which not only Reichenbach and Steuermann (26 and 27 October 41) but also Brecht himself and Eisler might occasionally attend.

24 January 42
Frank Warschauer (1892–1940) was a good friend to Brecht in Berlin in the early 1920s. He was a subeditor on Universal Edition's music magazine *Anbruch* and a contributor to *Mass und Wert* and the *Weltbühne*. He emigrated in 1933 to Czechoslovakia, thence in 1938 to Holland where he killed himself.

7 February 42
Herbert Kline (b. 1909) made some well-known documentaries, including the Steinbeck film mentioned here (*The Forgotten Village*, 1941), *Heart of Spain* (with Henri Cartier-Bresson, 1937) and *Crisis* (1938–9) about the Munich Agreement. It was he who, during 1942, introduced Eric Bentley to Brecht.

13 February 42
For Reyher, see 23 November 38. The battleships *Scharnhorst*, *Gneisenau* and *Prinz Eugen* had managed to leave Brest and reach home waters in the Baltic. Two days later, Singapore would surrender to the Japanese. In Africa Rommel had begun the offensive which would push the Eighth Army back to El Alamein by the end of June. In the US William S. Knudsen became president of General Motors in 1937, then served Roosevelt as Director-General of the Office of Production Management from 1941 till the end of the war. He died in 1948.

19 February 42
Ludwig Renn, president of the Mexico Free German Committee, was author of the World War I novel *Krieg* (1929) and had fought in the Spanish Civil War as Chief of Staff of the 11th International Brigade. A member of the Saxon aristocracy as well as the KPD, his real name was Vieth von Golssenau. The editor of *Freies Deutschland* was Alexander Abusch, who would later play a leading part in East German cultural affairs.

Kisch = the Prague-born journalist Egon Erwin K. (1885–1948). The Saarland writer Gustav Regler (1898–1963) also served in the International Brigades, but subsequently left the KPD; he emigrated to Mexico in 1941.

20 February 42
Blimp: cartoon figure by David Low, often depicted in the London *Evening Standard*, clad in a moustache and a towel, pontificating from a Turkish Bath.

26 February 42
See Brecht's poem 'The fishing-tackle' (*Poems 1913–1956*, p. 386) for evidence of his sympathy with the interned Japanese.

15 March 42
Arch Oboler (b. 1909) also wrote scripts for MGM.

16 March 42
Cas = Caspar Neher, Brecht's schoolfriend and preferred designer. He had remained in Germany.

22 March 42
Potsdam = the Prussian royal palace just south-west of Berlin. Schwabing = the Munich artists' quarter. The reference is to Hitler's ambitions as ruler and as artist.

24 March 42
Dieterle's film was called *Syncopation*. It cannot have been very widely shown.

25 March 42
The Times presumably = the *Los Angeles Times*. The curfew (says James Lyon) was imposed during this month, and lasted for under a year. It called for 'enemy aliens' to be off the streets between 8 pm and 6 pm.

27 March 42
Eisler had started giving his course on film music at the New School in New York on 4 February. This sprang from the Film Music Project set up by the Rockefeller Foundation two years earlier. Another Rockefeller-financed undertaking, the Princeton Radio Research Project, had engaged Adorno; it later transferred to Columbia University. As the two men were both members of the Schönberg circle, and had been familiar with one another from the mid-1920s, it seemed natural for them to pool their ideas on these closely related subjects, and they therefore collaborated on a book which according to Eisler was written – i.e. partly written – during 1942. Since Eisler himself would not arrive in California for another month, it is not unlikely that Adorno was giving Brecht a first idea of their joint conclusions, which would eventually appear in (improved) English in 1947 under Eisler's name only.

The original MS material having vanished, the unattributed quotation given here, with such odd neologisms as 'hear-stripe' (for soundtrack) may well have come from it. Their original joint foreword of 1944 underlines 'the affinity of many of [our] thoughts with those of the writer Bert Brecht. He was the first to set down theses about the gestic character of music which – while deriving from the theatre – have proved highly fruitful with regard to the film'. See also 2 May 42 below.

29 March 42
Oboler. See 15 March 42.

April 42
This entry dated '1942' is from the 'Autobiographische Aufzeichnungen' appended to *Tagebücher 1920–1922* (Suhrkamp, 1974).

8 April 42
'Might be possible to forecast'. The British employed an astrologer to tell them what Hitler's astrologer might be predicting to him.

11 April 42
See 16 January 42. Werner Hecht points out that this film story is not among Brecht's papers.

14 April 42
The then Dean of Canterbury (Hewlett Johnson) and Joseph Davis, US Ambassador in the Stalin era, both wrote uncritically about the USSR.

15 April 42
See the notes referred to under ours of 22 November 41, when this project originally cropped up. The *Neue Volkszeitung* appeared weekly from 1933–49. Seger, a journalist of Brecht's generation, arrived in the US in 1934 and became editor two years later.

Neither end of the Brecht-Weill correspondence from February on has been published except as summarised in our notes to the *Letters*. But it is clear that Brecht's paranoid remarks here need not be taken very seriously. Weill's reponse was to Brecht himself, not to Adorno, and the reason he gave for writing in English was so that Clarence Muse, the would-be producer, could be shown his objections to the project. On the 20th Brecht followed by replying that he had not acted one-sidedly, nor led Muse to think that Weill's agreement could be taken for granted. He wanted to resume the old collaboration and not to lose friends. Then on the 26th Weill wrote a conciliatory letter which seems to have closed the matter.

16 April 42
Otto Bauer was leader of the Austrian Socialist Party (SPÖ). The 'southern railway' is presumably the Southern Pacific.

20 April 42
See note 27 March above. Eisler's quintet *Fourteen Ways of Describing the Rain* (not 'fifteen') was composed in 1941 to Joris Ivens's film *Rain*, and dedicated to Eisler's teacher Schönberg for his seventieth birthday.

21 April 42
The *stories*. These were the numerous ideas for films, culminating in the fiasco with the Bergner-Czinner story (see 11 April 42). Ruth Berlau helped with some of them, and evidently she had also discussed early notes for the *Voices* plan (17 December 41) with Brecht. But clearly she was no replacement for Steffin, and it must have been at least in part her sense of frustration and uncertainty that discouraged her from returning when she went to Washington in May for a vaguely-described 'women's congress'. What made this decision possible was a combination of factors. First, it seems that from Washington she was able to get a job in the Danish section of the OWI, the Office of War Information in New York. And around the same time the Danish Ambassador told her that, following the promulgation of her divorce from Robert Lund, he could now pay her the maintenance for which Lund was subscribing: $75 a month.

2 May 42
The Russian film *Deputy of the Baltic Fleet* was made by Heifetz and Zarkhi in 1937. The Rockefeller Music Fund paid Brecht $250 on 13 May for helping Eisler in his researches.

7 May 42
Erwin Kalser had been one of Piscator's actors in Berlin before 1933, when he

emigrated to Switzerland. In the US he had acted in the Fritz Kortner/Dorothy Thompson play *Another Sun* at the National Theater, New York in the spring of 1940, but had gone back to Zurich.

9 May 42

Brecht's song, for which Weill, Dessau and Eisler all composed settings, was published in *Freies Deutschland*, Mexico on 5 March. It was included in *Schweyk in the Second World War* for which Eisler would compose the music. For details, and an English version under the eventual title 'Song of the Nazi Soldier's Wife' – the SA wasn't the army – see *Poems and Songs from the Plays* no. 135.

11 May 42

For the different versions of *Man equals Man*, see our edition. The Malik *Collected Works* text of 1938 is not the final one.

15 May 42

Max Reinhardt and his wife had come to LA after the fall of Austria in 1938, and started a Hollywood Workshop for Stage, Screen and Drama which failed after two years, leaving them living in what Kortner termed 'slightly damaged splendid isolation'.

16 May 42

The book was Charles Singer: *Short History of Scientific Ideas* (expanded edition, London, 1960).

20 May 42

For the various versions of this play, pre-war and wartime, see our edition of *Fear and Misery of the Third Reich*. Brecht here is speaking of the wartime 'Private Life' framework, which he had elaborated for Max Reinhardt. Reinhardt however abandoned his idea of staging it, leaving Berthold Viertel to produce five scenes at the Fraternal Clubhouse in the following month. *Woyzeck* is Büchner's early nineteenth century play which Berg used for his opera *Wozzeck*. Reinhardt had staged it in sets by Heartfield at the Deutsches Theater in April 1921, with Klöpfer and Dieterle.

28 May 42

Heydrich, the 'Reich Protektor' of Bohemia and second-in-command to Himmler, was wounded by an SOE agent's bomb in Prague on the 27th, and died in hospital on June 4th. M. R. D. Foot reckons that the Nazis retaliated by murdering over 2000 Czechoslovaks, including virtually the whole population in Lidice and Lezháky (who were unconnected with the two London-based agents).

30 May 42

Brecht had written a poem (*Poems 1913–1956*, p. 260) after seeing Odets's *Paradise Lost* staged by Harold Clurman and the Group Theater when he was in New York in 1935. It had not been published.

31 May 42

John L. Lewis, president of the United Mineworkers since 1920, had helped to found the CIO, more radical of the two great trade union organisations.

5 June 42
Alexander Granach, a leading actor of the pre-Nazi theatre, emigrated to the USSR, became director of the Jewish National Theatre in Kiev, then was arrested in the purges of 1937 and released on intervention of Feuchtwanger and Mrs Molotov. He went to the US in 1938, and had many supporting parts in films. Brecht may well have regretted his playing in Lubitsch's *Ninotchka* (1939), which satirised the USSR, but this does not seem to have stopped them from remaining friends (up to the actor's death in 1945).

Klabund's *Chalk Circle*, based on the fourteenth-century Chinese story, had been directed by Reinhardt in Berlin at the Deutsches Theater in October 1925, with Bergner in the lead. It inspired Friedrich Wolf's 'counter-play' *Tai Yang erwacht* which Piscator directed in 1931 with sets by Heartfield, which in turn has echoes in *The Good Person of Szechwan*, then finally would become re-functioned and stood on its head in *The Caucasian Chalk Circle* in 1944.

8 June 42
Hermann Kesten had been chief editor at the Kiepenheuer Verlag, who published Brecht's *Versuche*. In emigration he worked for Allert de Lange, the Amsterdam publisher for whom he and Walter Landauer had set up a German-language branch. There they seem to have kept in close touch with Fritz Landshoff, the exiled manager of Kiepenheuer, who was now running the other main Dutch-based German-language publisher, Querido. Despite Brecht's manifest dislike of Kesten, he was responsible for taking on the original edition of the *Threepenny Novel* in 1934.

9 June 42
Stefan George (1868–1933) was a high aesthete and disciple of Mallarmé, with a significant circle of friends.

18 June 42
Paul Henried (b. 1907, real name Von Henreid) emigrated to England in 1935 and came to Hollywood in 1941. He played a resistance leader in the film *Casablanca* (1942).

20 June 42
It was during this month that Brecht wrote letter 446, showing extreme exasperation with Ruth Berlau and asking if she wished to turn exile 'into an endless lovestory'.

27 June 42
By Lang's own account in an interview (1971) with James Lyon, he had been free-lancing since making *Manhunt* for 20th Century Fox. The Brechts were living a few minutes away from him in Santa Monica; his friend and secretary Lilli Laté had helped raise money for them, and he and Brecht often took walks together on the beach. An émigré producer, Arnold Pressburger, had been sounding him about making a film, and the Heydrich assassination (see 28 May 42) struck Lang as a good theme where Brecht too could be involved. 'Brecht instantly accepted; in a matter of days – four or five at the most – we produced a short outline between us. I was sure I could sell Arnold Pressburger the idea of making such a film. . . .' Having convinced Pressburger that Brecht was essential

to it, he got him a scriptwriter's contract for $7500, which was more than twice what Brecht had asked for. After eleven months in the US, this was Brecht's first serious Hollywood job.

28 June 42
This was just when the Eighth Army reached its last defensive position inside Egypt between El Alamein and the more or less impassible Qattara Depression.

29 June 42
Until the House Un-American Activities Committee (HUAC) hearings were reactivated in 1946 Eisler would regard Clifford Odets as a good friend, even if he could not understand Brecht. Eisler would shortly be writing music for one of his scripts, *None But the Lonely Heart* (1944), and earning an Oscar nomination in the process. Meantime the composer's settings for a 'Hollywood Songbook' multiplied, without ever leading to a complete, revised and rounded-off collection. They were not confined to the Finnish poems, nor only to poems by Brecht, but broadened out to embrace settings of Shakespeare, Goethe, Heine, Hölderlin, Mörike's Anacreon versions, Berthold Viertel and others, often of great beauty. Retrospectively in the 1960s Eisler would realise how astonishing it was that these should have been written and composed by political exiles. And later still we can see that they confirm Brecht's poems of 'the Dark Times' as world classics.

2 July 42
'The Face of Fascism' was another title of Pudovkin's film *The Murderers are on their Way* (1942), based on five scenes (not 'short stories') from *Fear and Misery of the Third Reich*. This project had run into trouble, initially because of the Soviet-Nazi pact and then, following the German invasion, because (said Jay Leyda) 'it seemed too gentle a treatment of an enemy that the audience was now desperately protecting itself against'.

8 July 42
This will have been the Serbian resistance movement led by General Mihailo-vitch, which in 1943 would become discredited for its compromises with the German and Italian occupation. Thereafter it was replaced in Allied favour by the multinational Partisan movement under Tito, himself not a Serb.

15 July 42
'Candel' has not been identified. By 'Petroleum' Brecht must mean Leo Lania's play *Konjunktur* about the oil business, which Piscator had staged in April 1928. Brecht had been involved in this as a member of the 'dramaturgical collective', as also in Hašek's *The Adventures of the Good Soldier Schweyk* which immediately preceded it. *The Last Days of Mankind* was Karl Kraus's epic documentary play about the First World War, which Kraus withheld from the stage in his lifetime: a work that Edward Timms has called 'the submerged masterpiece of the twentieth-century theatre'.

18 July 42
Gabriele d'Annunzio (1863–1938) was a one-man Hollywood epic – romantic, rhetorical and highly poetic – a magnificent self-concoction of words and actions

far too easily dismissed as 'Fascist'. His mystery play *Le Martyre de Saint-Sébastien*, with music by Debussy, was denounced by the Archbishop of Paris in 1911, his private invasion of Fiume secured that city's annexation to Italy; even today he still asks to be made into the super-film to which he and his life approximate. Brecht's view of him was not fashionable.

26 July 42
The poems set by Eisler can be found in *Poems 1913–1956* on pp. 303, 304 (these were pre-Finnish) and 347, where they are partly included without individual titles in the composite poems 'Spring 1938' and '1940'.

27 July 42
Ulm is a Swabian town on the Danube with a population of some 75,000 in 1930. From 1929–34 the theatre's conductor was Herbert von Karajan (who then moved to the more important post at Aachen).

29 July 42
Schönberg's house was actually in Brentwood. The unfinished opera will have been *Moses and Aaron*. A competition for completing Schubert's Unfinished Symphony had been held in 1928.

12 August 42
Ernst Toch (1887–1964), a self-taught Viennese composer, took part in the 'Neue Musik' festivals of the 1920s, writing a cantata called *Das Wasser* with Döblin. He emigrated in 1933 to England, where he composed film scores for Korda and for Viertel's *Little Friend* (the *Prater Violet* of Isherwood's novel), but soon moved on to the US. Having taught first at the New School, he became a professor at University of Southern California and wrote film music for Paramount and Columbia. *Mrs Miniver* (1942), MGM's sentimental picture of wartime Britain, starred Greer Garson in the title part.

14 August 42
This is the first mention of the *Messingkauf Dialogues* since 2 June 40. See also 10 October 42.

19 August 42
According to Lang he and Pressburger had offices in the former Chaplin studios.

21 August 42
Gina Kaus, a friend of Vicki Baum, was a successful if unremarkable scriptwriter.

22 August 42
According to David Pike, Klara Blum had been expelled from the German Section of the Soviet Writers' Union in 1939 for 'lack of discipline and hysteria'. Then it seems that her accuser was arrested and she was reinstated.

14 September 42
See Note 27 June 42. The Communist John Wexley, who scripted the brilliant Warner Brothers film *Confessions of a Nazi Spy* (1939), had been brought in to work with Brecht, because Lang wanted him to have an English-speaking collaborator with a good knowledge of German. At first, says Lang, the two men worked well together, putting new scenes before him every four or five days.

Then Brecht discovered (by 5 October 42) that Wexley was getting paid more than he, and asked for the same treatment. Pressburger grudgingly agreed. When the two writers discovered that Lang was also dealing with yet another writer (called Henry Gunzburg or Ginsburg) behind their backs, they seem to have agreed to make an 'ideal script' which they would not immediately tell Lang about. Of this document there is now no trace, and Lang says he never knew of it. Ginsburg, he claims, was only brought in because the still imcomplete script was twice as long as he wanted, so that he and Ginsburg had to cut it in the last week before shooting began.

20 September 42
For the 'Hollywood Elegies' see *Poems 1913–1956*, pp. 380–2, along with the relevant notes on p. 586. They formed only part of the notional 'Hollywood Songbook', for which they seem to have been the only texts that were specifically written. See the next entry and Eisler's own later remarks to Hans Bunge in *Reden Sie mehr über Brecht* (Munich, 1970). There is no mention of Brecht's meeting with Kurt Weill – their first since 1935 – which took place (according to David Drew) on 1 October when Weill was in Hollywood trying to interest Marlene Dietrich in what became *One Touch of Venus*.

17 October 42
This is the journal's first mention of Ruth Berlau since she left for Washington some six months earlier. Her typed letter to 'liebe Bertolt' is in erratic German, and reports her impressions of a public 'mietung' attended by Chaplin and Orson Welles. The latter, who read his short speech, struck her as looking unwell, 'fatpale'. Chaplin however spoke spontaneously and made a very good impression; he was, he said, 'eine citizens der welt', and made the V-sign. There is no reference to the nine cheerful women in overalls (and one man) whose photo Brecht has stuck in on the same page of the original.

17 October 42
Mission to Moscow (1943) was based on the book by Ambassador Davies and directed by Michael Curtiz. Maxim Litvinov was the Soviet Foreign Minister from 1930 to the spring of 1939. The line 'the dinghy which might save us' comes from the first scene of *The Good Person of Szechwan*. The Langnam association was a Westphalian industrialists' lobby.

18 October 42
For the *Versuche* see 8 December 39. The *Kriegsfibel* epigrams, first collected in 1955, were written mostly in 1940 and 1944 to accompany photographs from Scandinavian, British and US illustrated magazines. Some examples are included in the *Journals*; see pp. 106, 107, 320, 429.

20 October 42
See the poem 'Of sprinkling the garden' (*Poems 1913–1956*, p. 382) which Brecht developed from this idea and Eisler set for the 'Hollywood Songbook'. Werner Mittenzwei quotes Helene Weigel's saying that Brecht would on the contrary turn off the water if he thought she or the children were wasting it.

22 October 42
Starting around 1880, the Rose family ran a large theatre of that name in Berlin's East End, where classics were performed for a popular audience.

24 October 42
Murmansk in the extreme north of the USSR, close to the Finnish frontier, was the chief port for Allied convoys to Russia.

30 October 42
This is the plan last mentioned almost a year earlier, on 17 December 41, which would now develop into the Brecht/Feuchtwanger play *The Visions of Simone Machard*. Thomas Heywood's *A Woman Killed with Kindness* was the Jacobean play in which Brecht had tried to interest Elisabeth Bergner; there are some twenty-six pages of typed projects and fragments in the Brecht Archive.

4 November 42
From Goebbels's diary for 12 December it appears that some German prisoners of war in Canada had been fettered, to which Germany had responded by fettering English. The former had now been unshackled, leading Goebbels to hope that by the 15th 'we, too, shall be out of this loathsome affair'.

16 November 42
Finn was the author of Mezhrabpom-Film's *Okraina* ('Outskirts' or 'Patriots') which Boris Barnet directed in 1933. A German soldier called Müller III is one of the characters; Brecht would use a name like this in *Schweyk in the Second World War*. Borchardt = Hans Hermann Borchardt (1888–1951), friend of George Grosz, Brecht and Elisabeth Hauptmann, who had been arrested by the Russians when teaching in Minsk and deported to Germany. He was put in Mauthausen and Dachau. Thanks to Brecht among others, he had been freed and helped to reach the US. In 1939, living in New York on $12 a week from a Jewish charity, he had accused Ernst Toller of plagiarism over *Pastor Hall*.

19 November 42
Gustav Glück and his wife were also living in Santa Monica.

20 November 42
Brecht's essay 'On rhymeless verse with irregular rhythms' was published in *Das Wort* no. 3, 1939. It explains his 'gestic' way of writing free verse, and can be found in *Poems 1913–1956*, pp. 463–71.

24 November 42
Lang later assured James Lyon that he had never thought of giving any part to Helene Weigel, since no actor with a German accent was to play a Czech character. The part of Mrs Dvořák was therefore played by Sarah Padden. What is not clear is whether this would have been so if, as Brecht intended, it had remained a non-speaking part. In any case, however, Lang would feel that the real breakdown in his relations with Brecht had other reasons, for which see 20 January 43.

25 November 42
Konstantin Simonov's poem evidently suggested the verse 'Go calmly into battle,

soldier' which Brecht put into scene 2 of *The Caucasian Chalk Circle* two years later.

8 December 42
'The Angry Woman'. This title figures neither among the play nor among the film projects in the Brecht Archive. Perhaps it refers to *A Woman Killed with Kindness*.

10 December 42
Trotsky's *Über Lenin* was published by the Neuer Deutsche Verlag (a Muenzenberg firm) in Berlin in 1924. Lenin had died that January. Trotsky by now was an un-person whom Communists were not supposed to read.

11 December 42
Herbert Jhering (1888–1977) was Brecht's chief supporter among the Berlin theatre critics before Hitler. He remained in Germany after 1933, but was expelled from the official Chamber of Writers and sometimes banned from publication. In 1942 he became chief dramaturg or literary adviser at the Vienna Burgtheater under Lothar Müthel, then in 1945 returned to help re-found the theatres in East Berlin.

13 December 42
By the 'KI-song' Brecht presumably means Eisler's Comintern Song, which he wrote for the Red Megaphone agitprop group in 1929, on a text by Franz Jahnke and Maxim Vallentin. But it is not easy to see how the new song would fit the notes.

17 December 42
The 'hitparademan' was Sam Coslow – known, says Lyon, for the hits 'Cocktails for Two' and 'My Old Flame'. Ludwig Ganghofer (1855–1920) was a Bavarian popular novelist and playwright.

5 January 43
François de Wendell, mineowner, president of the Comité des Forges and a governor of the Banque de France, was in fact neither pro-Nazi nor uncritical of Pétain. But he favoured the old order in France.

20 January 43
In his interview with James Lyon, Lang blamed himself for not having understood the worsening relations between Brecht and Wexley. At the same time he saw Brecht's demands for more pay as having antagonised Pressburger, the producer, who felt he was being blackmailed. Accordingly Pressburger refused to give the Screenwriters' Guild evidence about the extent of Brecht's contribution to the screenplay, though both Lang and Eisler argued that he was at the very least entitled to be given a credit as co-author. The arbitrators appointed by the Guild then found in favour of Wexley on the grounds (says Lang) that Brecht would be returning to Germany in due course and could therefore do without the credit, whereas for Wexley a solo mention would be professionally vital. Their meeting a day earlier was the last occasion when Lang saw Brecht.

12 February 43
There is no indication in this journal or in Brecht's letters that he would now be

going to New York for a three months' visit. But according to James Lyon he had written in November to Berlau asking her to get him an invitation from Piscator, as he needed official permission to make the trip. Piscator then obliged with the suggestion of a production of *The Good Person of Szechwan* at the New School, along with an accompanying lecture. This was just after the surrender of Field-Marshal Paulus and the German army at Stalingrad.

16 February 43

Karl Wittfogel (1896–1988) had begun in Germany as a KPD member and playwright. Piscator staged one of his short plays in 1920 at the 'Proletarian Theatre' in Berlin. Though he was now a US citizen and a committed anti-Stalinist, Brecht more than once went to see Chinese theatre with him in New York. His *Oriental Despotism* was first published in 1957. Heinz Langerhans had already met Brecht as a friend of Korsch's in Berlin. Like Wittfogel, he had been in a Nazi concentration camp. 'The housepainter' = Brecht's expression for Hitler.

March, April, May 43

Dr Horst Bärensprung had been governor and police president of Magdeburg before 1933; he was prominent in the exiled SPD. Wieland Herzfelde had for the first time ceased publishing since emigrating from Czechoslovakia in 1939; his bookshop was called 'Seven Seas Books'. Oskar Maria Graf, one of his collaborators, had been arrested after the Bavarian Soviet in 1919, emigrated to Vienna in 1934, then to New York in 1938 where he was president of the German-American Writers Association; his *Wir sind Gefangene* was published in 1927; his *Reise in die Sowjetunion 1934* includes letters from Tretiakov.

Ernst Josef Aufricht, lessee of the Theater am Schiffbauerdamm from 1928–31, had been the producer of *The Threepenny Opera* in Berlin and Paris as well as other works by Brecht, Fleisser, Horváth and Lampel; likewise the film *Menschen am Sonntag*. Erna von Pustau was a colleague of Fritz Sternberg, the economist who was expecting Hitler's state to collapse. Paul Dessau had written music for 99%, the 1939 première of scenes from *Fear and Misery of the Third Reich*, but had not yet met Brecht. On March 6 the FBI would open a file on Brecht.

Though Piscator's letter of invitation had spoken of a production of *The Good Person of Szechwan* at the New School, he and Brecht now aimed rather at *Fear and Misery of the Third Reich* in a version to be made by Hofmann Hays; and during Brecht's stay a certain amount of work seems to have been done, till Hays dropped out and the project collapsed. On 6 March the 'Tribüne' group (with Herzfelde, Graf and others, and F. G. Alexan as secretary) organised a Brecht evening at the school, with readings by Bergner and Lorre; on 3 April a programme organised by Aufricht at Hunter College called 'We Fight Back' featured Lotte Lenya in some Brecht-Weill songs (including the new 'And what did the mail bring the soldier's wife?') as well as a staging of Brecht's war epigrams by Piscator and a Schweyk sketch with the Czech clowns Voskovec and Werich; this was broadcast by the Voice of America. Another Brecht evening staged by the Tribüne at the Hecksher Theater on the 16th had Brecht himself reading new poems, and he seems also to have been marginally involved in the Tenth

Anniversary of the 'Burning of the Books' at Piscator's Studio Theatre on 10 May.

But Brecht's main concern during his eleven-week visit (which represents a blank also in his published correspondence) was his production prospects. These he pursued from Ruth Berlau's flat at 124, East 57th Street, where her OWI chief and flatmate Ida Bachmann had moved out to make room for him. And certainly their private relationship was decisively reestablished, so that Berlau became to a great extent his plenipotentiary in New York, reporting on directors and translators and making suggestions and fair copies of his plays. *The Good Person of Szechwan* had just had its première at the Zürich Schauspielhaus when he arrived, and he was no longer so anxious for Piscator to stage it, particularly at the now declining Studio Theater. However, Kurt Weill was interested in doing something with the script that Brecht had sent him from Finland, and at the end of April Brecht and Berlau spent a week at the Weills' in New City, where they discussed *Schweyk* and evidently made the new *Szechwan* outline that would become that play's shortened and toughened 'Santa Monica version' (for which see the notes to our edition, pp. 121–6 and 132–47).

The *Schweyk* project, for which Aufricht was arranging finance, was at once more urgent and more tangled. Hašek's great novel had many enthusiasts, and memories of the 1928 Piscator-Grosz Berlin production were still vivid throughout the emigration. Two Schweyk schemes therefore were in the air when Brecht left for New York: first, Piscator hoped to update the 1928 script with Brecht's assistance and stage it for the Theatre Guild, while secondly Aufricht was trying to bring Brecht and Weill together to make a musical version. These two producers were old rivals, as Brecht must doubtless have known, and he unwisely kept each in ignorance of the other's moves. During the visit to New City, by which time Lenya had experienced the success of the 'Soldier's Wife' song in Weill's setting, Brecht was able to hand over a *Schweyk* outline headed 'The Story' which can be found in our edition (paperback, pp. 184–93); moreover he appears to have hoped that Piscator would be able to direct it. As a translator he and Berlau had in mind the poet Alfred Kreymborg, who chaired the book-burning programme at the Studio Theater. Not unforeseeably, the same idea occurred to the unwitting Piscator for his own scheme.

A fourth doomed project was initiated by Bergner and her husband, who commissioned Brecht to make an English-language adaptation of Webster's *The Duchess of Malfi* for the former to play on Broadway. Work on this seems to have begun during that spring, with Brecht making his changes and additions in a mixture of English and German, which Hofmann Hays was engaged to turn into Webster-compatible blank verse; they worked together for about a month. Unfortunately Paul Czinner was unable to raise enough money for a production in the 1943/4 theatre season, and the delay would not only upset the collaboration but also put a stop to any idea of Brecht himself directing the play.

27 May 43

It is not clear if the 'old Schweyk' was Grete Reiner's three-volume German translation of Hašek's novel and its conclusion by Karel Vaněk or the shortened (and bowdlerised) English single-volume version by Paul Selver. The Chalice

(Ư Kalichû) is Mrs Kopecka's pub in Prague. However, the first thing Brecht did on getting back to Santa Monica was to revise *Simone Machard*. Less than a week before, the Comintern had been dissolved.

9 June 43
For 'German Miserere' and 'Sheep March' see *Poems and Songs from the Plays* nos 138 and 113. Both were later taken into *Schweyk in the Second World War* along with their Eisler settings. For 'Im Sturmesnacht', which Eisler had set five days earlier for broadcasting to Germany, see *GW Gedichte* 3, p. 843. It was also called 'Lied vom Juli 1942'. Two lines of it were quoted from a speech by Stalin.

24 June 43
Brecht is not quite accurate in saying that he 'wrote' Piscator's *Schweyk* version. It was based on a stage adaptation by Max Brod and Hans Reimann (to whom it was credited) and the surviving script bears the names of 'Brecht, Gasbarra [Piscator's chief dramaturg, later a collaborator with the Italian Fascists], Piscator, G. Grosz' pencilled in Brecht's hand. What the new version would be, undoubtedly, was much more conventional in form.

26 June 43
That day a finished script of *The Duchess of Malfi* was sent to New York to be copyrighted in Brecht's and Hays's names.

Anna Seghers, the greatest German Communist novelist, emigrated to Paris in 1933, and thence in 1941 to Mexico, where she spent the Second World War. Her husband was László Radvanyi (also known as Johannes Schmidt) who had run the Marxist Workers' School or MASch in Berlin; they were close friends of Lukács. In 1934 Piscator directed a Russo-German cast, including Lenya and Leo Reuss, in a version of her first novel *The Revolt of the Fishermen* (German, 1928; English, 1929) for Mezhrabpom: his only film. With Herzfelde and O. M. Graf she edited the short-lived *Neue Deutsche Blätter* from Prague, the precursor of *Das Wort*. She was badly injured in Mexico in what appears to have been a hit-and-run accident, and took several weeks to recover. Her best-known book *The Seventh Cross*, soon to be filmed by Fred Zinnemann, had been published in German and in English in 1942.

28 June 43
'A revue' seems likely to have been Weill's musical *One Touch of Venus*, which would open on Broadway that October. The visit allowed the two men to discuss contracts for both Brecht plays.

3 to 6 July 43
Nothing is known of the 'Crouching Venus' project.

7 July 43
A. W. Ward's three-volume work, published in 1899, goes up to the death of Queen Anne. In the Mediterranean the British and Americans were now launching the invasion of Sicily. *Schweyk* was evidently finished, and was about to go off to Weill. Brecht was hoping that Kreymborg would make the translation by mid-August.

17 July 43
John Howard Lawson was a contributing editor to *Theatre Workshop*, along with Gorelik, Losey, Strasberg and Herbert Kline. See 4 March 41 and 6 April 41.

19 July 43
Souvarine's book on Stalin appeared in French in 1935.

20 July 43
Nine 'Songs of the God of Luck' are in *GW Gedichte* 3 pp. 889–94, of which Dessau composed four for tenor voice and guitar. Thereafter he and Brecht began planning an opera on this theme, but made little progress. For the god's first appearance, see 4 December 41.

20 July 43
The Free German Committee was set up on 12/13 July in Krasnogorsk near Moscow, where there was a centre for the retraining of German prisoners of war. This was run, and the committee formed, by the émigré KPD (notably the poets Erich Weinert and Becher, the politicians Ulbricht and Pieck, and the latter's son Arthur who had been Piscator's aide at MORT); these people had distinguished themselves in front-line psychological warfare with the Red Army, and were supported by the Russians. Many Wehrmacht officers joined, followed the next year by Field-Marshal Paulus himself. There was no comparable organisation in the other Allied countries. In the US the exiled theologian Paul Tillich, a professor at the University of Chicago, played a leading role in setting up the Council for a Democratic Germany in 1944. Heinrich Brüning, a Catholic centrist now at Harvard, had been Chancellor of the German republic from 1930–2. Both preferred to remain clear of the Moscow-sponsored movement.

21 July 43
Brecht's list omits *Lucullus*, *Carrar* and *The Horatians and the Curiatians*. (The ballet *The Seven Deadly Sins* falls just outside the ten years.) He no doubt drew it up, feeling that he had finished with *Simone Machard*, *Schweyk* and *The Duchess of Malfi*, which last had now been copyrighted and sent to Czinner by Hays.

25 July 43
Kaus: see 21 August 42

26 July 43
There was an even heavier raid on Hamburg two nights later. 'A city of a million inhabitants', wrote Goebbels in his diary, 'has been destroyed in a manner unparalleled in history'.

1 August 43
The Frankfurt parliament of 1848 failed to unify Germany and was dissolved in the following year.

8 August 43
Robert (Lord) Vansittart (1881–1957) was Chief Diplomatic Adviser at the Foreign Office from 1937–41. A Francophile, he became famous for his refusal to draw a distinction between Hitler's régime and the German people.

9 August 43
The poems are on pages 382 and 392 of *Poems 1913–1956*. Both were set for voice and piano by Eisler.

14 August 43
Blandine Ebinger (wife of the composer Friedrich Holländer) was a cabaret singer whom Brecht had known since the early 1920s. Döblin had become a Catholic. Thomas Mann had written an essay called 'Brother Hitler'. The ceremony took place in the Play House, Montana Avenue.

25 August 43
Gorelik's report: i.e. his book *New Theatres for Old*.

30 August 43
Hermann Budzislawski (b. 1901) had worked for the *Weltbühne* before 1933, and became editor of its successor the *Neue Weltbühne* in Prague and Paris. He arrived in the US in 1940 and was assistant to Dorothy Thompson, columnist of the *New York Herald-Tribune*, an influential supporter of the Roosevelts and generous helper of the anti-Nazi emigration. He would function as secretary of the new Council for a Democratic Germany (see entry for mid-November to mid-March). In 1949 Dorothy Thompson would write an article about him for the *Saturday Evening Post* headed 'How I was duped by a Communist'.

4 September 43
The 'Song of the Moldau' (German name for the Vltava, the river which flows through Prague) was to be the theme song of *Schweyk in the Second World War*. See *Poems and Songs from Plays* no. 139. This was the second day of the Allied invasion of Italy. The Salerno landing by the US Fifth Army began on the 8th.

6 September 43
Georg Branting, the Swedish senator, had helped the Brechts move to Sweden in 1939 and thence to Finland, where Wuolijoki had looked after them. Already in the Soviet-Finnish war of winter 1939/40 she had tried to promote peace negotiations through her friendship with Alexandra Kollontai, the remarkable Old Bolshevik who was Stalin's ambassador in Stockholm. After the Brechts had left and Finland had joined in the German invasion of the USSR, the Russians parachuted-in the daughter of an old friend of hers to reopen discussions through her. As a result, Wuolijoki was arrested and accused of high treason. Louis Lochner, a senior AP journalist who edited the 1948 selection of Goebbels's diaries, together with the journalist Willi Frischauer, must have been involved with organising the American movement to free her, in which Brecht joined; she herself wrote that three former foreign ministers gave evidence as to her deep concern for Finland's interests. The upshot was that she escaped the death penalty by one vote, but spent a further ten months in gaol (having already served eight since her arrest).

20 September 43
Christopher Isherwood emigrated to the US at the beginning of the war and moved out to California in 1940. He had translated the *Threepenny Opera* songs included in Desmond Vesey's version of the *Threepenny Novel* (published in

1937 under the title *A Penny for the Poor*). His Berlin stories were turned into a play by John van Druten under the title *I am a Camera*, which in due course was transmuted into the musical *Cabaret* and the film of the same name. Before leaving England he had worked with Berthold Viertel on a film called *Little Friend*, starring Nova Pilbeam: an experience beautifully related in his novel *Prater Violet* (1945).

26 September 43
This small selection differs both from the photocopied 'Poems in Exile' of winter 1944 and from the last part of the bilingual *Selected Poems*, edited and translated by H. R. Hays and published in 1947. All apart from 'On a stormy night' and 'Aurora' are in *Poems 1913–1956*. The second of these relates to the new publishing house which Wieland Herzfelde was planning and for which Brecht suggested this name.

27 September 43
It is charitable to presume that Brecht meant 'scrape the bottom of the barrel'.

30 September 43
Franz Werfel, whose work Brecht seems always to have disliked, wrote the foreword to Borchardt's novel. (For Borchardt see 16 November 42.)

2 October 43
Naples was taken on 30 September. For an earlier meeting of Brecht with Jean Renoir, see 26 January 40.

15 October 43
Granach's *There goes an actor/Es geht ein Mensch* was published in Sweden and New York in 1945, shortly after his death. It deals with his life up to 1920, when he played Shylock in Munich.

16 October 43
During this month Brecht met Clifford Odets's wife, the actress Luise Rainer, and discussed making an adaptation of Klabund's *The Chalk Circle* for her. She had a would-be backer in New York, but meantime was off to entertain the Allied troops in the Mediterranean.

The controversy is probably that originally conducted in the Moscow journal *Literaturnyi kritik* with relation to the 'Socialist Realism' proclaimed somewhat vaguely at the 1934 First Soviet Writers' Congress and later thrashed out in a meeting at the Home of Soviet Writers in March 1936. According to David Pike, Isaac Nusinov of the Institute of Red Professors argued that the new dogma could only be implemented by writers of proletarian origin; Mikhail Lifschitz, an ally of Lukács at the Marx-Engels-Lenin Institute, attacked this 'vulgar sociology', as he termed it, in favour of the 'cultural heritage', populism (or accessibility to a mass public) and the avoidance of 'formalism, naturalism and left-wing radical foolishness'. His line was backed up by *Pravda* in a leader of 8 August 1936, from which would flow the condemnation of these features of all avant-garde arts, first by what Brecht called 'the Moscow clique' of German and Hungarian exiles, and later by right-thinking party members throughout the world. This was only a month before the four secret 'vigilance' sessions of the German writers reported in Reinhard Müller's *Die Säuberung*.

1 November 43

Reinhardt's production of Strindberg's *The Dream Play* at the Deutsches Theater, with Werner Krauss and Helene and Hermann Thimig, opened on 13 December 1921. See Brecht's *Diaries 1920–1922*, entries for 11 and 12 December, which show that he was authorised to see just two rehearsals. It was not till 1924 that he had a job at that theatre, and could see Reinhardt rehearsing Pirandello's *Six Characters* and Shaw's *Saint Joan* (with Bergner).

11 November 43

The historian Golo Mann, Thomas Mann's son, reacted to this and other criticisms by Brecht of his father in an article for the Hamburg weekly *Die Zeit* where he denied the '4–5 cars', said that since Heinrich Mann's contract with Warner Brothers ran out (in autumn 1941) he was getting an allowance of at least $150 a month from his brother, and maintained that there was no question of his being allowed to starve. Certainly Brecht's dislike of Thomas Mann is generally agreed to have been far from rational, even though some of his views may have come from Döblin.

The Socialist Friedrich Ebert was the first president of the Weimar Republic.

7 January 44

At its 12th Congress the American Communist Party dissolved itself. This followed within a week of the Teheran Conference at which Roosevelt and Stalin met for the first time. It was at a dinner there on 29 November that Stalin called for the physical liquidation of between fifty and a hundred thousand German officers; Roosevelt thought it too many, and Churchill walked out.

Mid-November 43 to mid-March 44

Originally Brecht seems to have hoped that Ruth Berlau, who had lost her New York job with the OWI, would come to California in the late summer, but for reasons of expense this fell through. Accordingly he set out by train around 15 November, and this time stayed in New York for some thirteen weeks. The first task, it seems, was to revise *The Duchess of Malfi* with Hays to meet Bergner's demands (the Czinners now being in the East). Hays, however, dropped out on hearing that W. H. Auden was being asked to join the collaboration, and although Brecht went on working sporadically at the Czinners' apartment it does not seem that Auden was as yet all that closely involved or that the revision was finished. In any case no production was now planned.

The *Schweyk* project was still alive at the end of September, when Brecht and various friends (none of them entirely Anglophone) had been trying to improve Kreymborg's translation, which had then been returned to him and Berlau for further revision. It looked as if Peter Lorre, who had provided the translator's advance, might want to play the name part. Then Weill arrived in LA and visited Brecht just before he left, when he made clear that the script was by no means what he wanted – which was an accessible American version, with Brecht as a librettist and somebody like Ben Hecht as a fixer – moreover Aufricht thought poorly of it. But what really torpedoed the original plan was Piscator's discovery on 12 August that he had been by-passed; Aufricht had got the rights and the translator, on both of which Piscator had counted for his own plans with the

Theatre Guild, and it was moreover unlikely that he would be asked to direct. The result, aggravated by the threat of a lawsuit, was that not only Weill but also the two rival producers lost whatever interest they had once had, and Brecht was left cradling the script.

As for *The Good Person of Szechwan*, Brecht had completed the 'Santa Monica' version discussed with the Weills at the end of his previous visit, but Weill was not yet interested to tackle it; evidently he mentioned it to Moss Hart in LA around 17 December, but Hart had been put off. Then on 30 January, so David Drew tells us, Weill asked his lawyer to make a contract with Brecht for a six-month option and a $600 advance. This was for what Brecht termed a 'semi-opera'. Part of Weill's object was to 'help a very talented (and very difficult) man a little bit'.

This left Luise Rainer's proposal for a new *Chalk Circle* version as the one prospect which might have some life in it, and when Brecht saw her backer Jules Leventhal in New York he evidently suggested something like the play's eventual medieval Georgian (or *Caucasian*) setting. On her return to the US Rainer was not pleased to hear this. At the same time there was good news in February from California, where Feuchtwanger had sold the film rights of his novel *Simone*, based on the *Simone Machard* collaboration, and very generously proposed to divide the sum of $50,000 between himself, Brecht and Berlau (who had been included in the play contract). The condition was that there should be no stage production without MGM's permission for three and a half years. The film however was never made.

The Council for a Democratic Germany came about partly as a result of the discussions in which Brecht and other Hollywood exiles took part, e.g. at the Viertels' house on 1 August 1943 (see the entry above) when both Mann brothers were present. See also the note on the Moscow Free German Committee (20 July 43). One of the points of controversy was the new movement's relationship to this, which led Thomas Mann to withdraw his name. From New York, where (so Lyon reports) he attended at least seven relevant meetings, Brecht wrote on behalf of the founding committee to Heinrich Mann asking him to be a member of the executive, to which the elder Mann promptly agreed; then on returning to Santa Monica Brecht wrote to Paul Tillich (Letter 482) to report a number of other acceptances. The formal birth of the movement, with Tillich as chairman and Budzislawski and Elisabeth Hauptmann as secretaries, was announced on 2 May 1944, and its policy statement next day was supported not only by eminent exiles but also by such Americans as Ben Huebsch, Alvin Johnson, Louis Lochner, Reinhold Niebuhr and Dorothy Thompson. The FBI regarded it as a Communist 'front', and according to Budzislawski the State Department tried to limit its influence.

We do not know when (or even whether) Brecht heard of the death of his first child Frank Banholzer with the German army in Russia, but it took place on 13 November while Brecht was travelling to New York. It is not mentioned in these journals.

6 April 44
Thornton Wilder had seen and been impressed by the Zurich *Mother Courage*,

and in 1945 Weill would send Cheryl Crawford a script of *The Threepenny Opera* for him in the hope that he might translate it. Wilder called it 'superb' but thought it too cool for him. The première of *Galileo* had by now taken place – also in Zurich – on 9 September 1943, and Brecht's 'I am given to understand' must refer to Swiss reviews such as that by Bernhard Diebold which gave what he felt to be the wrong interpretation.

29 April 44
Brecht met Charles Laughton, one of the outstanding English actors of his time, at Salka Viertel's house soon after returning from New York. He and his wife Elsa Lanchester had a house not far away at 14954 Corona del Mar, Pacific Palisades, looking out to sea from above the Pacific Highway.

8 May 44
The figure of Azdak in *The Caucasian Chalk Circle* was derived from Brecht's earlier story 'the Augsburg Chalk Circle' and intended for Oskar Homolka. It seems that Luise Rainer had not been told about this. See the introduction and notes to volume 7 of the Methuen *Collected Plays* for the play's evolution in the next few weeks. The first script was finished by 5 June, a revised version in early September, a third script before the end of the year.

22 May 44
Characters noticeably omitted:- Anna Balicke, Kragler, Macheath, Polly, Mr and Mrs Peachum, Ackermann/Mahoney, The Young Comrade, Señora Carrar, Lucullus, the Jewish Wife, Schweyk.

6 June 44
Karin = Karin Michaelis. During the month Ruth Berlau, now pregnant by Brecht, arrived from New York. The social science teacher = at Santa Monica Girls' High School.

12 June 44
See item 35 in *Brecht on Theatre*: 'A Little Private Tuition for my Friend Max Gorelik'. It is followed by a comment from Gorelik to the editor.

The lower picture on p. 318 which follows, captioned 'Nazi abbatoir in Russia', appears to be from *Time* magazine, and bears a footnote locating the scene 'outside Pyatigorsk' in the foothills of the Caucasus, 'where retreating Germans butchered 200 Russian prisoners of war and civilians'. It goes on to add that 'In Katyn Forest, similar pits held 12,000 bodies,' but without mentioning that these comprised Polish officers deported from Eastern Poland and shot by the Soviet NKVD. Katyn is near Smolensk in the Western Region.

15 June 44
It must have been around now that Brecht wrote his notes on Brueghel (item 34 in *Brecht on Theatre*, where there is also a reproduction of *Mad Meg* (*Dulle Griet*). At some point he gummed this image into all three versions of the *Caucasian Chalk Circle* script.

20 June 44
These are the *Kriegsfibel* (or War Primer) epigrams mentioned on 18 October 42.

After Brecht's death Hanns Eisler would set fifteen *Bilder aus der Kriegsfibel* for soloists, male chorus, wind, percussion and double-bass. Twenty-eight, accompanied by projections of the relevant pictures, went to make up the second section of Dessau's cantata *Deutsches Miserere*, on which he was currently starting work. An example follows.

25 June 44
Franz Werfel's play *Jacobowsky and the Colonel* was adapted for Broadway by S. N. Behrman, who thereafter figured (in its many English-language productions) as the principal author. 'Saint Frunzis' is presumably a side-swipe at Werfel's Lourdes novel, *The Song of Bernadette*, one of the greatest successes of the entire emigration.

21 July 44
The day before, Colonel von Stauffenberg had made his unsuccessful attempt to blow up Hitler at his Prussian HQ. The Herrenklub was a Berlin gentlemen's club with strong right-wing associations; it dissolved itself within the year. Its members would have included Junkers (or Prussian landowners). The Russians meantime were advancing into Poland and would take Brest-Litovsk on the 28th. They installed the 'Lublin Committee' as a Polish administration and gave no support to the Polish Rising in Warsaw.

30 July 44
See 26 June above. Dessau had moved out to the West Coast following his meeting with Brecht in New York the previous year. This was the beginning of a collaboration which would last the rest of Brecht's life, supplementing rather than replacing those with Weill and Eisler, who unlike Dessau had no shortage of other composing jobs. Dessau was working partly as a gardener.

July 44
The conductor Otto Klemperer had emigrated to the US in 1933.

14 August 44
The US Seventh Army was breaking out of the Normandy bridgehead. A day later the Sixth Army would land in Southern France

20 August 44
The first (limited) edition of Gide's short novel appeared in 1902.

28 August 44
For 'Garden in progress' see *Poems 1913–1956*, p. 395, and the note on p. 591 of that book. For a photograph of the garden see entry for 17 December 45, below.

1 September 44
For the new optional epilogue and the first (shorter) version of the prologue see our edition vol. 7, pp. 324–5.

3 September 44
This was the premature birth of Brecht's short-lived son Michel. See Lyon: *Bertolt Brecht in America*, p. 224. On leaving hospital Berlau stayed at Salka Viertel's in Santa Monica. She would return to New York on 31 March 1945.

12 September 44
FFI = the French Resistance (Forces françaises de l'intérieur).

16 September 44
Romania had been knocked out of the war, the Americans were into Germany near Trier, the British were about to make their unsuccessful attempt to seize the Rhine bridges at Arnhem and Nijmegen.

20 September 44
Bruno Bettelheim, an Austrian psychoanalyst some five years younger than Brecht, had arrived in the US in 1939 after leaving a Nazi concentration camp. He was now teaching in the University of Chicago.

5 October 44
Brecht's 'Ballad of Marie Sanders, the Jew's whore' was written in 1935 on the occasion of the Nuremberg Laws codifying Nazi anti-semitism. Eisler composed a setting for voice and small orchestra at that time. The opera project now discussed with Dessau does not seem to have got beyond six pages in Brecht's handwriting (in the Brecht Archive).

19 October 44
'Joseph' = Thomas Mann's four-volume roman-fleuve, whose last instalment, *Joseph der Ernährer*, had come out the previous year.

October 44
Anna Seghers's novel (see note 26 June 43) was filmed for MGM by Fred Zinnemann, with another émigré, Karl Freund, as cameraman. Spencer Tracy played the central figure Georg Heisler; Granach and Felix Bressart had supporting parts; Helene Weigel had a small non-speaking rôle – her only film appearance in her five years in LA.

End October 44
Arnold Schönberg lived at Brentwood Park, LA from November 1934 to his death in July 1951. From 1936–1944 he was professor of composition at UCLA. Eisler had been his private pupil for four years after the First World War.

6 November 44
Brecht and Eisler appear to have worked on the *Goliath* opera project for much of their time together in Denmark in the spring and summer of 1937. The first act (out of four) was allegedly completed, and the material in the Brecht Archive amounts to around 150 pages, which are sprinkled with evidence of Steffin's involvement. The two collaborators do not seem to have resumed work on it after Eisler left for Prague that October. He emigrated to the US at the start of the new year.

7 November 44
Roosevelt was re-elected for a fourth term by a good majority against Thomas Dewey. Pascal = Ernest Pascal, a producer.

27 November 44
Strasbourg had been taken by the Americans and Free French. The Red Army

had advanced into Hungary. The Eighth Army was entering North Italy. US troops were fighting in the Philippines. The port of Antwerp had been cleared.

29 November 44

For the relationship of Waley's and Brecht's versions with the Chinese originals of this and the following poem, see Antony Tatlow's *Brechts chinesische Gedichte* (Suhrkamp, 1973) pp. 105–16. This furthermore cites the Chinese ideograms, along with their phonetic transcription, and gives an exact character-by-character translation into English.

10 December 44

For an extensive account of the *Galileo* collaboration (which would go on for the next two and a half years) see vol. 5 part i in our edition, which draws mainly on the work of Werner Hecht and Ernst Schumacher, as well as the 'model book' *Aufbau einer Rolle/Laughtons Galilei* with Berlau's photos (Henschel, 1956). It also prints the Laughton text of the play.

December 44

Photographic experiments. Ruth Berlau had taken a three-month photographic course before leaving New York, and henceforward it would be her photography that would be her most tangible contribution to Brecht's work. It would prove to have two main purposes: first to form an archive of his writings, and secondly to record what he saw as 'model' productions of the plays, starting with the Laughton *Galileo*. The *Poems in Exile* photocopies would be sent to various recipients. They are virtually all in *Poems 1913–1956*, in some cases as parts of composite poems under other titles: 'Spring 1938' and '1940'. For details of this, and their relation to the later collection under the same name, see pp. 512–13 in the notes to that volume. The *Studies* were his 'literary sonnets' of various dates, of which those on Villon, Hamlet, Dante and Lenz's *The Tutor* will also be found there on pp. 180, 214, 311 and 312.

22 December 44

The popular rising in Warsaw which started on 1 August and lasted two months had been allowed to fail by the Russians; its chief was General Bór-Komarowski, who was supported by the London Polish government-in-exile but not by the Lublin Committee. In Greece a conflict was building up between the Communists and other elements of the Resistance, and the Russians had recognised that it would be Britain's responsibility to deal with this.

19 January 44

The meeting was in connection with forming a postwar international trade union confederation. Konrad Heiden, a Swiss socialist, had written a widely-read biography of *Hitler*.

20 January 45

Quatrain: from the *Kriegsfibel* epigrams, for his oratorio *German Miserere*.

23 January 45

God of Luck. For this project see also 20 July 43.

28 January 45

Brecht will have had hopes of the meeting between the invading Red Army and the Silesian miners. Like its principal city, Breslau (which became Wrocław), the area would be annexed to Poland.

11 February 45

The manifesto = the *Communist Manifesto* of Marx and Engels (February 1848). Brecht now began turning this into German hexameters on the model of Lucretius's philosophical epic *On the Nature of Things* (c. 55 BC). The result forms part of the incomplete 'Didactic Poem on Human Nature', whose German text is in *GW*, pp. 895–930.

4 March 45

Paul Muni, a fine actor used by Dieterle in his biographical films, was formerly for several years an actor with the New York Yiddish theatre. The film may have been *A Song to Remember (Polonaise)* 1944. Chaplin was talking about his own plans for *Monsieur Verdoux*.

end of April 1945

Besides collaborating on *The Duchess of Malfi*, Brecht hoped that Auden would translate *The Caucasian Chalk Circle*. Already during the previous summer the English poet had passed this suggestion on to his friends James and Tania Stern, who translated the dialogue while he concentrated on the songs. By then Luise Rainer seems already to have rejected the idea of playing in it, but Leventhal and Robert Reud, the would-be producers, signed a contract on 12 March for a production within a year. However, Auden evidently was reluctant to continue with Brecht's play, and in the event no further progress was made. The translation (now in our Collected Plays Volume 7) was shelved, and within three years had been supplanted by a new version by Eric and Maya Bentley which had a number of college and university productions.

Master Race: the wartime version of *Fear and Misery of the Third Reich* (see 20 May 42 and June to mid-July below), for whose production by Piscator Brecht would shortly visit New York.

8 May 45

As a result of Franklin Roosevelt's death at the age of sixty-three on 12 April, the president now was Harry Truman. The Red Army had taken Berlin and Vienna (where they installed a provisional government under the Socialist Karl Renner); Hitler and Goebbels had committed suicide; Mussolini had been killed by the Italians, and the SS commander-in-chief in Italy had surrendered. The capitulation followed.

Mid-May 45

The 'epistle to the Augsburgers' is in *Poems 1913–1956* in Lesley Lendrum's translation (as here) but with two lines added. Brecht had not been in his home town for over twelve years.

June to mid-July 45

Following the two German-language performances of four scenes by the Tribüne in New York in 1942, with Viertel as director, all plans for *Fear and Misery of the Third Reich* had gone wrong. Reinhardt, for whom Brecht had made the *Private Life* version, was taken by Ruth Berlau to see the second performance, but his interest evaporated not long before he died. Hays was commissioned to complete his translation for a school production at Piscator's Studio Theatre in spring 1943, but stopped work on hearing that Bentley, who had been shown a script by Viertel, was being encouraged by Berlau to translate it too. This he did that winter in consultation with Elisabeth Hauptmann, who was living in New York and had been brought back into Brecht's team. When the producer Ernest Roberts approached him a year later Bentley unilaterally gave permission for an off-Broadway production by Roberts's 'Theatre of All Nations'.

Brecht's somewhat reluctant agreement was no doubt due to the engagement of Piscator as director, along (says James Lyon) with the promise of the best available actors and a first-rate production. Leo Katz was to be the designer; the music was Eisler's. However, the budget was low, some of the cast were Piscator's students, others were émigré professionals (including the eminent but ageing Bassermanns) whose English was none too intelligible, and within a week of Brecht's arrival from California he had rejected Piscator's ideas along with his new framework, so that the latter resigned. Unable to cancel the production as he would have liked, Brecht got Berthold Viertel to take over for the last ten days of rehearsal; but it seems that the result was catastrophic. One obvious reason was that the 'master race' had been defeated. As Hallie Flanagan said of the play earlier in that year, 'five years ago it would have been very strong – ten years from now it would have great historical significance, but definitely the moment is not now' (cited by Lyon).

Brecht's enthusiasm for Laurette Taylor was evidently based on her performance in *The Glass Menagerie* (not a play he admired). One of the 'two publishers' was Reynal and Hitchcock, who would publish the bi-lingual *Selected Poems* translated by Hays in 1947 and also considered undertaking a volume of plays (to include *Galileo* and *Chalk Circle* under the editorship of Bentley and Hauptmann); the other was probably New Directions, who had published *The Private Life of the Master Race*, containing Bentley's important introductory essay on the writer. For the 'Didactic Poem', see 11 February 45 above. The audience for it consisted of three politicians from the left wing of the Council for a Democratic Germany: Albrecht Schreiner (KPD) who had been chief of staff of the 13th International Brigade in Spain, Jakob Walcher, a founder member of the KPD who went over to the Socialist Workers' Party, and Hermann Duncker of the MASch in Berlin.

Wieland Herzfelde had started his new publishing business at the end of 1944 as a successor to the Malik-Verlag. This was called Aurora and was jointly sponsored by Brecht, Viertel, Oskar Maria Graf, Döblin, Feuchtwanger, Heinrich Mann, the Marxist philosopher Ernst Bloch, the playwright Ferdinand Bruckner (who taught in Piscator's school), the Austrian poet Ernst Waldinger and the Czech-German Communist writer F. C. Weiskopf. Weiskopf's contribution *Die Unbesiegbaren* was a selection of reports on episodes from Nazi Germany. Herzfelde's list also included the first publication of Brecht's *Furcht und Elend des Dritten Reiches*, Anna Seghers's *Ausflug der toten Mädchen* (one of her finest stories) and a book of Viertel's poems of exile *Der Lebenslauf*. (After Herzfelde's postwar return to Germany his Aurora list would be absorbed into the East Berlin Aufbau-Verlag as a distinctive series.)

With Auden away in Europe, Brecht visited the Czinners in their summer place near Woodstock, Vermont to revise the *Malfi* version with Bergner; the Viertels and the Zuckmayers were in the same neighbourhood. Letter 502a, written to Viertel soon after Brecht's return to Santa Monica on 18 July, asks him not to discuss that play with Bergner, in case she gets the idea that it may need more work.

3 August 45

During the Potsdam conference of the victorious allies (UK, US and USSR), which met from 17 July to 2 August, the British general election was won by Labour, and Churchill and Eden were replaced by Attlee and Bevin. The question of a future German government was left unsettled, but since the Warsaw Polish government had just been recognised the Polish-German frontiers were agreed, with Pomerania and Silesia now going to Poland (up to the Oder-Western Neisse river line) and East Prussia to the Russians. German reparations to the USSR and Poland would come from the Soviet occupation zone, plus 25 per cent of surplus industrial capital from the rest of Germany.

Moabit. A working-class district in West Central Berlin, to the north of the Tiergarten.

10 September 45

The first atomic bomb was dropped on Hiroshima on 6 August. The second, on Nagasaki, on 9 August. The USSR declared war on Japan, and on the 14th Japan surrendered, thereby ending the Second World War.

20 September 45

The film story was *All Our Yesterdays*, a transposition of the Macbeth plot to the stockyards of Chicago, with a Duncan who recalls Puntila and a detective called Inspector Duffy. The twenty-five episodes of the English text are given in *Texte für Filme II*, with a German translation (not by Brecht); clearly it was written by Reyher. The role of Machacek, 'a slightly superstitious steercutter', was designed for Lorre, who seems to have been in on the scheme at the start, though his name as one of the authors was deleted. There appear to have been negotiations with Columbia and signs of interest from Lewis Milestone, but nothing more. As with Shakespeare, there was rather a lot of blood.

25 September 45

The Threepenny Opera, directed by Karl Heinz Martin, opened the first postwar season at the Berlin Hebbel-Theater in the American sector, the former Theater in der Königgrätzerstrasse. It seems that Brecht himself had not been consulted; and it was he who tried to stop it, writing to the American Theatre Officer and to Martin to that effect on 14 October. But it was still being performed in January, and there is no record of any ban. Macheath was shared between Hans Albers and Hubert von Meyerinck; Kate Kühl was Mrs Peachum. It was said to be a success.

2 October 45

This was an old scheme for which the Archive catalogue lists four pages of brief notes.

15 October 45

Pierre Laval became Pétain's prime minister in Vichy from 1942–4, and was responsible for Unoccupied France's collaboration with the Germans: notably the payment of occupation costs, the supply of forced labour to the Reich, and the policy of modified anti-semitism. He was sentenced to death by de Gaulle's government on 9 October.

20 November 45

The poet Ezra Pound, friend and collaborator of T. S. Eliot, had lived in Italy since 1924 and supported Mussolini's Fascist regime. Tried for treason by a US court, he was sent to a mental hospital for thirteen years. The other poets mentioned by Brecht, and certainly respected by him, had died in 1933, 1936 and 1938. (See 9 June 42 and 18 July 42 for Brecht's remarks about George and d'Annunzio; *Brecht in Context* chapter 3 for his debt to Kipling.)

1 December 45

Morton Wurtele, a friend of the Brechts in Santa Monica, would become professor of meteorology at UCLA. Albert Brush, a poet friend of Laughton, is supposed to have helped with the English verses. The Prologue is not known to have been used or translated before our edition.

2 December 45

See Note below. The news clearly related to Ruth Berlau.

5 January 46

William Joyce, 'Lord Haw-Haw', broadcast to the British from Germany. He and John Amery were executed as traitors.

At this point there is a break of thirteen months in the typescript of the journal, though the page numbering of the Archive's copy goes straight on. The German editors give no reason for this apparent black-out of the year 1946. However, James Lyon tells us that Ruth Berlau's flatmate Ida Bachmann called a doctor to her in New York on 27 December 1945, and Berlau responded by attacking both of them. This was reported to Brecht by Fritz Sternberg. The next day Ferdinand Reyher brought another doctor and a policeman who escorted her to Bellevue Hospital. On 31 December she was transferred to Amityville hospital on Long Island, where she was given electric shock treatment. In Brecht's subsequent letter to Reyher (letter 511x) he asks that the doctors should be told that she had 'done some stupid things, and thought I was going to pack her off'. They should know that 'certain psychic disturbances' had preceded her breakdown. Brecht's previous entry suggests that these were under way by the beginning of December. There are no published letters from him to her during November; then he wrote her the poem 'The writer feels that he has been betrayed by a friend' (*GW* 938) which he dated 'Dec. 45'.

According to the letter to Reyher Brecht had influenza in January, and it was not till 10 February that he could get to New York and visit Berlau, together with Bergner and Paul Czinner, who were partly paying for her medical treatment. Bergner, she would write later in *Brechts Lai-tu* (p.175), 'helped me more than anybody'. During March she was released into Brecht's care and allowed to return to the 57th Street apartment. In May he took her back to California in Laughton's car. According to Lyon, Czinner subsequently deducted the amount of the doctors' bills from sums due to Brecht from the receipts for *The Duchess of Malfi*.

Evidently Brecht devoted part of his stay to working on that play with Auden, who had done some revising on his own in Chicago during the previous November. A final text was copyrighted before Brecht left New York. The *Duchess* had run her course before Brecht's journal entries resume, though the story can be followed in the *Letters*, the notes to Volume 7 and Lyon's *Bertolt Brecht in America*. In brief, a production was mounted, and opened in Providence, Rhode Island in September 1946. Czinner however had decided to infuse various elements of the H. M. Tennant production from the Haymarket, London – notably George Rylands as director of the Webster text, music by Benjamin Britten and the essentials of the Haymarket sets. Brecht removed his name (while Auden remained credited as 'adaptor') though it is possible that he had some say in the New York run (15 Oct – 16 Nov) after Rylands had gone home. But at least the critics, who generally found the production a bore, did not associate Brecht with it. And its failure appears not to have affected the long-drawn-out negotiations for the production of *Galileo*.

For the plans for a Brecht edition see Note on June–mid July 1945. Brecht signed a contract for the plays with Reynal and Hitchcock during February 1946, Hauptmann's involvement presumably being due to Berlau's illness. Brecht wanted *Galileo* and *The Caucasian Chalk Circle* to be in the first volume, and it was also planned to include *The Threepenny Opera* in Desmond Vesey's pre-1939 translation, which Bentley would revise. Bentley himself (*The Brecht Commentaries*, p. 286) says he 'jibbed at' the idea of collaborating with Hauptmann. Nothing was ready for the publishers by the time when Brecht left for Europe, however, after which the firm was taken over by Harcourt, Brace, who were apparently not interested in publishing Brecht.

Otherwise, the letters show Brecht making touch again with old friends in Germany and finding out about theatre prospects in that country. Already on 26 January 1946 Helene Weigel had written to Hella Wuolijoki to say that she and Brecht were waiting to return. During the rest of that year they became increasingly interested in what to expect, as their letters to Neher, Reyher and Piscator make clear.

20 February 47

Sonntag was the weekly paper of the Kulturbund, or League of Culture, of which Becher was president. Both were based in the Soviet sector of Berlin, where the Moscow exiles had become the arbiters of the arts. The League aimed to appeal to all parties in all four sectors, but during the following autumn it would be stopped from operating in the West. Becher's nationalism was in accordance with the new Socialist Unity Party's line on German reunification, which the Western powers were then opposing.

The figures for deaths on the map on p. 364 came from *World Report*, and need to be revised. In 1974 Hecht cited a later estimate giving nearly twice as many Germans – 6.5. million – 20 million Soviet citizens (as against 7 million 'Russians'), and 6 million Poles. It will be noted that no figures are given for Italy, the US or Japan. The map's barely legible figure for Norway is 11,000.

20 March 47

For the poem and its relation to Shelley's original, see *Poems 1913–1956*.

Shelley's influence can also be seen in Brecht's 'On thinking about hell' (1941). With its leitmotiv of 'Freedom and Democracy' it has lost little of its significance since the incorporation of the former Soviet Zone in the German Federal Republic.

24 March 47

Since the Soviet Writers' Congress of 1934 A. A. Zhdanov (1896–1948), Stalin's right-hand man and leader of the Party in Leningrad, had dictated policy in the arts. Mayakovsky, editor of *LEF* and close colleague of Tretiakov and Koltsov, had committed suicide in April 1930. Among the reasons was the campaign mounted against him by the 'proletarian' writers and critics. These had their counterpart in the German League of Proletarian-Revolutionary Writers who published *Die Linkskurve* with its critiques of Piscator, Brecht and Tretiakov. See Brecht's 'Epitaph for M', dated 'New York, autumn 1946' (*Poems 1913–1956*, p. 405).

24 March 47

Brecht wrote an outline from Gogol's story with Elisabeth Hauptmann. It is in *Texte für Filme II*, p. 598ff. 'Two sons' is in *Short Stories 1921–1946*; it originated in his note of 12 May 45 about a film 'which one might make for germany'. Dudow, his old collaborator on *Kuhle Wampe, Carrar* etc, had become a director for DEFA, the Soviet-sponsored successor to UFA. The story was eventually filmed as part of a series in 1969.

30 March 47

Eric Bentley's influential *The Playwright as Thinker* was published by Reynal and Hitchcock in 1946. In later editions he would change 'naturalism' to 'realism'. See Letter 521. Brecht's comparative table shows his prescriptive rather than historical approach to these terms, which would make him accessible to the idea of 'Socialist Realism' even though he disliked the use which the Party aestheticians had come to make of it.

3 April 47

Again there is a sizeable unexplained gap in the entries, this time lasting five months. No doubt this was due in part to the *Galileo* preparations, through the beginning of rehearsals at the end of May till after the last performances at the Coronet Theatre, Beverly Hills on 17 August. About all this the journal says nothing, and there is nothing to suggest any new development in Brecht's personal affairs. But there must also have been the worry in connection with the new witch-hunt associated with the reactivation of the House Un-American Activities Committee (or HUAC) at the end of 1946. Gerhart Eisler was one of its first targets, particularly once his sister Ruth Fischer had begun publicly denouncing him that November, along with his brother Hanns and (more marginally) their friend Brecht. In May, Hanns had to appear before a subcommittee, and the FBI reopened its file on Brecht. In June–July, Gerhart was twice prosecuted, once for contempt and once for making a false visa declaration. Sentenced to three years' imprisonment, he was released in July on $20,000 bail. Hanns was ordered not to leave the country, only to be officially deported to Prague on 26 March 1948. (This was one of the rare occasions when Stravinsky joined in a public protest.)

15 September 47

The *German Stanislavsky Book*, compiled and published under Soviet auspices, was evidently to be the bible of Socialist Realism in the East German theatre: the new orthodoxy. Maxim Vallentin (so christened after Gorki) had led the old Kolonne Links agitprop group in the Ukraine before the purges, was arrested in 1937 and spent the war in the USSR. With Gaillard and Otto Lang he founded a new acting school in Weimar which now developed into the 'Institute for Methodical Renewal of the German Theatre'. In 1952 he would take over the new Maxim Gorki Theatre in East Berlin.

30 October 47

This is all that Brecht has to say about his own HUAC hearing. Cole and Lardner were two of the so-called 'Hollywood Nineteen', along with John Howard Lawson, Albert Maltz and others not exactly attuned to Brecht. Stripling was the committee's chief investigator. Senator Joe McCarthy was not involved in these hearings. The chairman was J. Parnell Thomas, later sentenced to eighteen months in prison for a payroll swindle. Losey and Hambleton were respectively director and producer of *Galileo*, which would open in New York on 9 December.

After his subcommittee hearing in Hollywood, Hanns Eisler had been summoned on 12 July to Washington to testify before the full committee. He was heard there on 24–26 September. For Brecht the summons came on 19 September and the hearing (in Washington) was on 30 October. Clearly it was only as a matter of public relations that this was treated as part of the inquiry into 'the motion picture industry'; the FBI's interest in Brecht being due primarily to his friendship with the Eislers, and in the second place to his role in the Council for a Democratic Germany. He had never – formally at least – been a member of the Communist Party, and the citation of *Die Massnahme*, his 1930 Lehrstück with Eisler, may have been due to Ruth Fischer's obsession with that work, which the committee was hardly equipped to understand. But it is wrong to regard his discussion of 'the japanese model' as a subtle camouflage. *Die Massnahme* from the first was conceived as a 'counter-play' to the original *Taniko*, which Weill had made into a Lehrstück under the title *Der Jasager*. In Berlin before 1933 Brecht had wanted them to be performed together.

1 November 47

Donald Ogden Stewart, winner of an Oscar for his script of *The Philadelphia Story*, was one of the same generation of American humorists as James Thurber and Robert Benchley. He and his Australian wife Ella Winter, previously married to Lincoln Steffens and once secretary to Justice Frankfurter of Roosevelt's Supreme Court, were neighbours of the Viertels in Santa Monica till they fell foul of the Un-American Activities inquiry and emigrated to England. They were among the Brechts' few intimate non-German friends in California.

3 November 47

Jean-Louis Barrault, now famous for his performance in the wartime film *Les*

Zurich in mid-February. Ernst Glaeser (1902–63) was a novelist who emigrated in 1933 to Switzerland but returned to Germany at the beginning of the Second World War.

21 April 48

Hans Albers (1892–1960) was a blond actor whom Aufricht had described before 1933 as 'the heart-throb of the time to come'. He played the lead in UFA's nationalistic film about the Volga Germans, *Flüchtlinge*, to which Goebbels awarded the State Prize in 1934, for embodying 'spirit of our spirit, power of our power and will of our will'. This appears to have been no handicap after 1945. Liliom was the rakish hero of Ferenc Molnár's sentimental fairground piece of that name.

13 April 48

Friedrich Meinecke (1862–1954) was a neo-Hegelian philosopher who (in Lukács's view) saw nineteenth-century German thought as a progress towards Bismarck. Heydrich's assassination provided the theme of *Hangmen Also Die*. Ernst Kaltenbrunner, his Austrian-born successor, was hanged at Nuremberg for crimes against humanity.

15 April 48

This was at the Schauspielhaus. Steckel had acted in Piscator's productions before 1933, when he emigrated to Zurich. He directed the premières of *The Good Person of Szechwan* and *Galileo* (where he also played the title role). Walter Richter has left little trace; Käthe Gold however (who played Marie) had been an outstanding actress of the Third Reich. Meanwhile Neher was visiting Salzburg to discuss Brecht's possible involvement there with Schuh, Von Einem and the civil service head of the Austrian theatres, Egon Hilbert. Einem then wrote to tell Brecht that he must get immigration documents through the Austrian consulate in Zurich.

20 April 48

Brecht and Neher at this time were discussing a plan for an 'aristophanic revue' to be called *Ares's Chariot*. This promising scheme for following the adventures of the god of war after a military fiasco had been conceived before Brecht left California, but never got beyond a short ballet scenario and a dozen pen and gouache drawings of possible situations (see for instance 'The Goddess of Trade acquiring an egg on the black market' on p. 30 of *Caspar Neher: Brecht's Designer*).

10 June 48

Evidently the production of *Puntila* had been one of Brecht's main objectives in coming to Switzerland, and certainly it was his chief requirement of the Schauspielhaus management. Details were discussed at the end of April, when Neher's doubts about that theatre's capabilities may have helped Brecht to entrust the designing to Teo Otto. The direction had, for appearance's sake, to lie with the chief dramaturg Kurt Hirschfeld, since Brecht could not officially be employed. Only one song, it seems was included, the 'Plum Song' sung by Therese Giehse as Sly Grog Emma. Steckel was Puntila, Gustav Knuth Matti, Helene Vita Eva, Blandine Ebinger the Chemist's Assistant, Regine Lutz the Milkmaid Lisu. The first night was on 5 June.

11 June 48
The Swiss novelist and playwright Frisch was then aged thirty-seven. At the time when he met Brecht (whose *Fear and Misery of the Third Reich* he had already reviewed in the 1947 Basel production) he was primarily working as an architect. Brecht's poem of 1919 is in *Poems 1913–1956*, p. 29.

This, the last entry for another two months, was a week before the West German currency reform which had the double effect of bringing about the 'economic miracle' in the West, and dividing the country for the next forty years. The Russians quickly retaliated by cutting all land communications between the western zones and Berlin – which by some oversight had never been formally guaranteed in the occupation arrangements – so that the western sectors of that city could only be maintained by a massive, mainly American airlift. Clearly this would affect Brecht's travel plans, which already had been delayed by the non-arrival of his papers for Salzburg, where he was now expected.

19 August 48
No doubt the propaganda of which Brecht complains was stimulated by the Soviet blockade of Berlin and the resentment of Western intellectuals at the dictatorial attitude of the USSR at the impending Wrocław Congress under the leadership of Alexander Fadeyev of the Union of Soviet Writers.

3 September 48
This was one of the later and lesser trials at the International Military Tribunal convened three years earlier.

25 September 48
Gustave Geffroy, writer and art critic, was a friend of Monet and president of the Académie Goncourt. He died in 1926. Cézanne's portrait of him, painted in 1895, was then in the collection of René Lecomte; it is now in the Musée d'Orsay. Wilhelm Hausenstein and Gotthard Jedlicka were current art critics, the latter writing for the *Neue Zürcher Zeitung*.

17 October 48
Barbara Brecht was remaining in Zurich, where she was attending acting school, while her parents planned to go via Salzburg and Munich to Berlin. There Brecht (so he had told Herzfelde) would stay for two or three months before returning to Switzerland. In Salzburg he further discussed Festival plans, hoping also to bring in Berthold Viertel, who had been directing a Shaw play at the Zürich Schauspielhaus. The journey to Munich proved impossible, since the US military government would not let Brecht into their Zone. This meant going through Prague up into Saxony (in the Soviet Zone) and thence into Berlin.

19 October 48
E. F. Burian, composer and leader of a 'voice-band', had revived his prewar experimental theatre. He had directed a visually brilliant, very freely adapted and physical production of *The Threepenny Opera*, but we do not know if Brecht ever saw it.

Berlin
22 October 48 to 18 July 55

22 October 48

Wolfgang Schreker: no information. For Ludwig Renn see 19 February 42; this fine novelist had returned from exile in Mexico, and wrote a number of books of reminiscence that were published by the Kulturbund's house, Aufbau-Verlag. Alexander Abusch, also from Mexico, was a rising arts administrator, a 'Kulturpolitiker' who headed the Kulturbund's ideology department. Its president was Becher. The Adlon Hotel, Unter den Linden, now badly bombed, had been Berlin's most famous hotel. Hanns Eisler, Arnold Zweig (author of *The Case of Sergeant Grischa*, 1927) and the Hungarian Julius Hay were also the Kulturbund's guests there in connection with its forthcoming Peace manifestation.

23 October 48

Heinz Kuckhahn had worked on the film *Kuhle Wampe*, and got in touch with Brecht before his return. He acted as an assistant until the formation of the Berlin Ensemble. Gebrüder Weiβ, in West Berlin, published *Antigonemodell 48* and the *Kalendergeschichten* short stories (1949). Hay's play *Haben* was well received except by Brecht. See note to 25 July 38 for their previous encounter. Colonel Alexander Dymshitz, a German-speaking Mayakovsky specialist seconded to the Soviet military government, had interpreted Zhdanov's cultural edicts of 1946 in four articles in the official *Tägliche Rundschau*, laying down the doctrine of Socialist Realism for Germans. He appears to have supported Brecht before returning to the USSR in March 1949.

24 October 48

Jakob Walcher, whom Brecht knew from New York, held various political posts in East Berlin, and was closely associated with Wilhelm Pieck. Otto was Otto Müllereisert, a medical doctor who had been a schoolfriend of Brecht's in Augsburg.

26 October 48

Breslau = the now Polish city of Wrocław. See 19 August 48.

3 November 48

The Deutsches Theater, which had been Max Reinhardt's till 1933, had agreed to Brecht's proposal that he and Erich Engel should jointly direct *Mother Courage* with Weigel in the title part.

Wolfgang Langhoff, who had played Eilif in the Zurich production, was now the theatre's Intendant. Brecht hoped that Caspar Neher would come to Berlin from Salzburg to design the play, and on 1 December Neher was given an Austrian passport; but it seems that his travel arrangements broke down (Letters 567 and 572). At the same time Brecht, despite his inability to stop off in Munich, was still trying for a *Threepenny Opera* production with Hans Albers which would start at the Munich Kammerspiele, with slightly updated songs, and tour West Germany. This scheme was largely frustrated by Kurt Weill, who had not been properly consulted and did not want his music rearranged. See April 49.

8 November 48
Engel, a contemporary and colleague of Brecht's, had remained in Germany throughout the Third Reich, working mainly as a film director. He had staged the original *Threepenny Opera* at the Theater am Schiffbauerdamm in 1928.

11 November 48
Werner Hinz had worked at the Nazi-run Volksbühne under Eugen Klöpfer and Karl Heinz Martin. He had also appeared in many films.

25 November 48
For the changes in the play see notes to our edition.

9 December 48
Hand-over of goods. Unfortunately the 'goods' were capital goods – the machinery allocated to the Russians under the Potsdam agreement (see 3 August 45). Peter Huchel was editor of the Academy of Arts magazine *Sinn und Form* from 1948 to 1962. Walter Felsenstein the conductor was Intendant of the Komische Oper in East Berlin. The 'pajoks' were additional rations given to special classes of workers.

10 December 48
Gerda Müller, a leading Expressionist actress whom Brecht had known in the 1920s, had returned to the Berlin stage after being barred since 1934. She had confirmed her reputation at the Deutsches Theater as Mrs Kepes the midwife in Hay's *Haben*. Now she played the small part of the Old Woman.

12 December 48
Curt Bois, a leading performer in cabaret and musicals before 1933, had played comic parts in many Hollywood films (such as *Gipsy Wildcat*); Langhoff brought him back, and Hollywood friends raised the fare. Käthe Gold had played leading parts for Gründgens at the Staatstheater, till the closing of the Berlin theatres in 1944. One of Margarete Steffin's 'children's plays', *If he had an Angel*, is in her posthumous collection *Konfutse versteht nichts von Frauen* (Rowohlt, Berlin 1991).

   Paul Bildt had been at the Staatstheater till 1944, and before that was in Viertel's short-lived 'Die Truppe' (1923/4).

14 December 48
Aase Ziegler was the sister of Lulu Ziegler, who in 1936 had played in the Copenhagen *Round Heads and Pointed Heads* under the direction of her husband Per Knutzon.

14 December 48
The 'Möwe' or Seagull was a club for actors, writers and other artists close to the present Bertolt-Brecht-Platz in East Berlin.

17 December 48
Hermann und Dorothea (1796) is by Goethe.

18 December 48
Goethe's discussion in letter form 'Der Sammler und die Seinigen' is in Part One of his *Schriften zur Kunst*. Mrs Kasprowiak would become one of Helene Weigel's secretariat at the Berliner Ensemble.

21 December 48
Brecht at this point seems to have wished to rejuvenate the militant 'Kampflied' (or fighting song) of pre-Hitler times. The 'Aufbau' and 'Zukunfts-' (Reconstruction and Future) songs here referred to are in *GW Gedichte* pp. 953–8 and would be composed by Paul Dessau in the new year. Eisler, who had just arrived from Vienna, felt on the other hand that the time for such songs had passed. The Nazis, so he told Hans Bunge, had debased the genre, 'and I was so sick of marching of any kind . . . that I preferred something like Mao Tse-tung's Ode. . . . We needed time to get over this. Unfortunately the time was much too short'.

22 December 48
The refrain of the 'Song of the Future' ends each stanza with the line 'A marvellous flag, coloured red'.

The cutting which Brecht pasted on this page reads 'Court adjourns because of cold. Last Thursday the rooms of the Second Main Criminal Court in the Moabit Lawcourts were too cold to permit any conclusion to the trial of Neukölln borough officials for the misappropriation of ration cards. The case had to be adjourned until the following noon.' This was in Berlin.

29 December 48
Brecht's version of the Mao 'Ode' – nowadays given the title 'Thoughts while flying over the Great Wall' (*GW Gedichte*, pp. 1070f.) – was based on a misleading translation by Fritz Jensen; see Antony Tatlow's analysis in *Brechts Chinesische Gedichte* (1973). Mao's original was actually called 'Snow', and was written in February 1936, and not while flying.

1 January 49
Brecht here copies his letter 573 to Dessau explaining the decision to cut 'The Song of the Hours' in scene 3 of *Mother Courage*. This long and slightly monotonous song, based on a sixteenth-century hymn, had been recently added for the Berlin production.

3 January 49
Mies van der Rohe's memorial to the murdered Spartacist leaders in the Friedrichsfelde cemetery was originally commissioned by the KPD and unveiled by Wilhelm Pieck in 1926. According to Werner Hecht, Walcher's information was wrong: the decision had been taken to restore it, and a 'provisional monument' erected in 1946. The restored 'memorial to the Socialists' would be dedicated by Pieck in 1951. Presumably this was the Mies van der Rohe memorial as we now have it.

6 January 49
As a result of the blockade, the civil administration of Berlin was now split. Ernst Reuter, a former Communist, became Lord Mayor of West Berlin on 5 December, while the old 'Gross-Berlin' town hall now ran East Berlin only, with the Socialist Friedrich Ebert, son of the Republic's first president, as its Lord Mayor. Brecht had hoped to get the Theater am Schiffbauerdamm (near the Deutsches Theater) for the proposed Ensemble which he had been discussing with Langhoff, but it was decided to leave it in the hands of Fritz Wisten, the

former concentration camp inmate who had been Intendant for the Nazi-licensed Jewish League of Culture from 1939 till its closure in 1941. Wisten was to move to the Volksbühne's old Bülowplatz theatre once it had been rebuilt, and meantime the Ensemble would share facilities with the Deutsches Theater and its adjoining Kammerspiele, spending half the year on a tour of the Soviet Zone. Ackermann and Jendretzky were from the Socialist Unity Party (SED) Central Committee; Kurt Bork headed an 'Amt für Kultur'. It seems that final agreement was only reached some 3–4 weeks later, after the young Party journalist Wolfgang Harich had set himself to mobilise outside support for Brecht (see Pike, *The Politics of Culture*, pp. 621–2.)

18 January 49
The Chinese Communists took Tientsin on the 15th. Chiang Kai-shek would resign as President on the 21st, leaving Mao to take over until the People's Republic was formally set up. For Mao's poem see Note 21 December 48 above.

26 January 49
Hans Mayer, the Marxist literary historian, had been an exile in France and Switzerland. He would head the Literary-Historical Institute at Leipzig University until 1963. Then he went West to the technical university at Hannover.

28 January 49
Friedrich Wolf, leading Communist playwright before 1933, had spent much of his exile in Russia, whose language he spoke, and was author of the wartime play *Professor Mamlock*. His critical dialogue with Brecht about *Mother Courage*, dated 1949, is item 42 in *Brecht on Theatre*. Fritz Erpenbeck, the former Piscator actor who had been one of the grave-diggers of *Das Wort* in Moscow, had been editing the East German magazine *Theater der Zeit* since its foundation in July 1946. He had just been appointed to the new 'Bureau for Theatre Questions' which later (November 1950) would develop into a 'Repertory Commission' controlling choice of plays throughout East Germany. He consistently supported the Socialist Realist establishment against Brecht, and now raised the question whether Brecht was moving towards 'Volkstümlichkeit' (populism) or 'volksfremde Decadenz' (alien decadence). This harks back to the debates of the Moscow emigration, for which see journal entries of July 1938.

10 February 49
This 'motto' became the poem 'Observation' (*Poems 1913–1956*, pp.416f) in which the word 'excitement' was altered to 'travails'. ('Aufregungen' and 'Mühen'.)

12 February 49
Eduard Stichnote would print Brecht's *Versuche* numbers 10 and 11 for Suhrkamp-Verlag in 1950–1. Erich Wendt, former German director of the Vegaar (or Foreign Workers' Publishing House) in Moscow, then for a time under Soviet arrest, had returned to become head of the Aufbau-Verlag, set up in the first place by the Kulturbund and subsequently the GDR's main literary publishing house.

20 February 49

More or less according to plan (as of 17 October) Brecht was now about to fly back to Zurich via Prague, having made contracts in West Berlin with his friend Suhrkamp (head of the aryanised S. Fischer firm under the Nazis) for the resumption of the *Versuche* series and an eventual Collected Works, which Wendt at Aufbau could then publish under licence, and with Weiss for the *Kalendergeschichten* short stories. He had added his voice to those of Jhering and Wolf, who hoped Piscator would return from New York to head a revived Volksbühne, suggesting to him that he first direct a play for the new Ensemble, preferably Nordahl Grieg's Paris Commune play *The Defeat*. (The Norwegian Grieg had been a war casualty with the RAF.) Meantime Helene Weigel would stay in Berlin to prepare for the formal establishment of the Ensemble. This was voted by the SED Politbüro at the end of March, then passed on a month later to the (East) German Economic Commission to put into effect.

In Zürich (where Brecht appears to have made no diary notes) he recruited a number of important actors for the new company, and had also to secure travel documents for the return to Berlin of himself and his daughter, once again via Salzburg and Prague. With the idea of the 'Salzburg Dance of Death' in mind he went to the Basel Carnival celebrations, then in April wrote to Von Einem in Salzburg suggesting that if he was to contribute to the Festival perhaps he might be given an Austrian passport, since his wife (like Neher's) was an Austrian. Probably Brecht's main concern during this visit was to decide whether Nordahl Grieg's Commune play could be made into a major, politically significant work with which to launch the Ensemble that autumn. By the time he had finished adapting it on 21 April he saw that this was not feasible; it would therefore need to follow after *Puntila* and Gorki's *Vassa Shelesnova* to give time for further work on it. On the 27th *The Threepenny Opera* directed by Harry Buckwitz eventually opened at the Munich Kammerspiele, with Hans Albers playing Macheath, Trude Hesterberg Mrs Peachum, and Erni Wilhelmi Lucy; the sets were by Neher, who would come to the New Berliner Ensemble after the end of the 1949 Salzburg Festival. Brecht had hoped vainly that his elder daughter (by his first wife Marianne) Hanne Hiob would be given a part in this production.

7 May 49

'A new house' in Michael Hamburger's translation (as here) is in *Poems 1913–1956*, p. 416. The house was 190, Berliner Allee in the Weissensee district of Berlin, where the Brechts would live for the next four years. Five days later the Berlin blockade was lifted. This would be followed on the 23rd by the formation of a German Federal Republic with its capital in Bonn. Movement between the former Western zones would be free.

18 June 49

There was however a prize for the 'actors' collective' who performed *Mother Courage*, headed by Helene Weigel.

28 August to 4 September 49

During the three (unchronicled) months after Brecht's return to Berlin he seems to have been concerned with the Salzburg project and the plans for setting up a supposedly all-German Academy of Arts in East Berlin, with Arnold Zweig as president. In June, when Brecht was in hospital with a kidney infection, Paul Wandel, the Zonal education chairman, appointed him a member of the Academy's organising committee. This held its first meeting on 4 July.

Hearing that the Zurich Schauspielhaus wanted to do *The Threepenny Opera* in the next season, with Steckel as director, Brecht proposed that Albers should play Macheath; Weill however, who wanted to make a new agreement about the rights, was holding up further productions. Elisabeth Hauptmann arrived from the US, and would join the board of the Ensemble. Meanwhile Eisler that spring had made a new cantata version of *The Mother*, which the Russian-backed radio in Vienna broadcast on 29 May with Ilona Steingruber and Karl Paryla; it is not clear how much Brecht had to do with this, or indeed knew about it.

Freilassing is a village on the frontier near Salzburg. Jakob Geis was an old friend, now working mainly in the cinema. George Pfanzelt (the Orge of Brecht's early poems) still lived in the town of their childhood. In Munich (where he had been at the university) Brecht agreed to direct *Mother Courage* at the Kammerspiele the following spring.

12 October 49

Theodor Heuss had become president of West Germany, Konrad Adenauer his Christian Democrat chancellor. Military government was finished. The airlift ended on 30 September after more than a quarter of a million flights by US, British and French aircraft. On 7 October the old Soviet Zone became the German Democratic Republic, with (East) Berlin as its capital. Wilhelm Pieck was president, Otto Grotewohl his prime minister. Pieck enjoyed the theatre, and would see all the Berliner Ensemble's productions, starting from its inauguration on 12 November with the Brecht-Engel production of *Puntila*, designed this time by Neher and with the Dessau songs.

14 November 49

On returning from his trip to the south, Brecht had come to terms with DEFA about a film version of *Mother Courage*. Engel would direct, R. A. Stemmle write the script, Neher provide designs. See the introduction to our edition of the play for a résumé of what happened.

The 'Short Organum' was published the same year in the Academy magazine *Sinn und Form*.

22 December 49

The Tutor by Goethe's contemporary J. M. R. Lenz is a highly original but also muddled play written in 1774 which had been rediscovered shortly before the First World War. *The Robbers* was by Schiller. Brecht and his young collaborators Egon Monk and Benno Besson, plus Berlau and Neher, tidied up the story and introduced scenes from student life in the age of Immanuel Kant. Neher sketched episodes and movements before they were rehearsed. Brecht's reason for the further postponement of *The Days of the Commune* (final title of the play based on Grieg) was not the whole story: the official repertory planners thought its approach too defeatist for a middle-class audience. Meantime the Gorki play *Vassa Shelesnova*, directed by Viertel and designed by Teo Otto, would open next day as the Ensemble's second production.

6 March 50

P. M. S. Blackett's *Military and Political Consequences of Atomic Energy* appeared in the UK in 1948 and in German translation in 1949.

2 April 50

Berlau had been in the Charité hospital since the beginning of March, when she was thought to have taken an overdose of sleeping pills. For the Ensemble she had three main rôles: compiling an archive; photographing certain productions to make 'model' accounts of them, some of which would be published in book form with the aid of another young collaborator, Peter Palitzsch; and going out herself to direct or supervise provincial performances. She was not always easy to work with. Letter 637 will have been written to her around now.

The Tutor was in rehearsal, under the joint direction of Brecht and Neher. It would open on the 15th, to an excellent reception. Mittenzwei indeed counts it as the most widely applauded of all the Ensemble's productions. Meanwhile Brecht will have heard of the success of his application for Austrian nationality the previous spring – See Note 20 February 49 and Letters 591 and 597–599 – though he would not actually get his new passport till some months later.

23 April 50

Carl Hofer, then aged seventy-one, was a middle-of-the-road Expressionist artist who had been dismissed as 'degenerate' from the Berlin Academy by the Nazis, and was now director of the Hochschule für bildende Künste. He was active in the Kulturbund, and Stichnote in Potsdam had made him the first of a series of 'Present-day Art' booklets edited by Adolf Behne.

28 April 50

The composer Rudolf Wagner-Régeny (1903–69) wrote four operas with Neher under the Third Reich. The new project (title: 'Persian Legend' or 'The Gut-Cleanser') included three or four songs contributed by Brecht, notably 'Lucifer's Evening Song' from *Mahagonny* and the otherwise unpublished 'Oil Song'. Its completion seems to have been hindered by official objections.

29 April 50

Boris Blacher, a contemporary of Wagner-Régeny, composed a number of operas. In 1953 he would become director of the West Berlin Conservatoire.

25 May 50

An all-German youth festival was held in East Berlin from 27–30 May, with numerous foreign guests. Michael Tschesno-Hell was an East German writer, evidently with Soviet affiliations. (See the reminiscences of Hans Mayer.)

10 June 50

There were fifteen such songs in all, of which Eisler set one group of three as a 'Children's Cantata'. He also planned a 'Children's Songbook'. Six are in *Poems 1913–1956*, pp. 420–3. Eisler had now settled in East Berlin, having moved into 9, Pfeilstrasse, Pankow during March. Most of his collaborations this year were with Becher, including the setting of the GDR national anthem.

From 26–30 June a Congress for Cultural Freedom met in West Berlin under the local presidency of Ernst Reuter, Otto Suhr and Ernst Redslob (rector of the

Free University), with the American editor Melvyn J. Lasky as its secretary-general. Conceived as an anti-Stalinist version of Muenzenberg's conferences of 'Intellectuals' in the 1930s, and given additional force by the invasion of South Korea on the day before it met, this was funded by the US military government and led to the establishment of a permanent – covertly CIA-backed – CCF which would be widely influential in Cold War propaganda over the next twelve years. Its magazines in Germany, France, England and Italy would print a number of attacks on Brecht, starting with one by Herbert Luthy sneeringly called 'Of Poor BB'.

Beginning of August 50
Ahrenshoop: a seaside resort on the Baltic, not far from Rostock. The 1949/50 theatre season was over, and Brecht would leave for Munich soon after his return to Berlin; Weigel and her daughter had left for Vienna almost at once.

4 September 50
Brecht was starting to rehearse the Munich Kammerspiele *Courage* production arranged a year earlier, with Giehse as Courage. It would open on 8 October. He also wrote to DEFA after talking to Engel and Burri (who had succeeded Stemmle as scriptwriter) about the film project, which he hoped could now get moving. Five weeks later he would hear from Sepp Schwab (an old Munich Communist who had run the German section of the Soviet Radio and was now head of the GDR Film Committee) that no decisions could be taken till they knew how Brecht meant the story to end. The question for DEFA was 'can a film for peace be effective only in a pacifist sense, or can it contribute to the active struggle against war'?

October 50
Kurt Desch the Munich publisher was at one point to have published a four-part selection of Brecht's 'Poems in Exile' in partnership with Herzfelde. After returning to the GDR the latter made a different selection of *Hundred Poems* which would be published by Aufbau-Verlag, but not in the Federal Republic. Ernst Schumacher was a young Munich scholar who was preparing a substantial dissertation on the early plays; he later became a professor in East Berlin and a leading German authority on Brecht.

October 50
Peter Lorre had taken a house at Garmisch-Partenkirchen in the Bavarian Alps, but would not return to the theatre as Brecht had hoped. He did however direct and co-script a German film, under the Pabst-like title *Der Verlorene* – The Lost One.

8 October 50
Friedrich Domin, Hans-Christian Blech and Erni Wilhelmi were some of the best West German actors.

9 October 50
Biberpelz und Roter Hahn was to be a conflation of two plays by Gerhard Hauptmann: *The Beaver Coat* and *The Red Rooster*. Brecht had been hoping that Berthold Viertel would again come to direct this for the Ensemble, with Therese

Giehse in the part of Frau Wolff/Fielitz. See Letter 649 explaining his intended adaptation. Kurt Hirschfeld seemingly could not help, and although the play would be performed under Egon Monk's direction in March the rights holders would not let it be published. Vera Poliakoff was the Group Theatre's 'manageress' who negotiated (inconclusively) about *Mother Courage*; she was married to Gerald Barry and later to John Russell. Brook was Peter Brook.

29 December 50
Kurt Weill, whose death is reported in the cutting which Brecht stuck in at this point, had died on 3 April. It is difficult to believe that Brecht had not heard about it before.

10 January 51
The Ensemble's fourth production was directed by Brecht with Weigel as the Mother, Ernst Busch as Lapkin the old worker, and the young Käthe Reichel in Steffin's old part as the servant-girl. For all three it was their first appearance with the company. Sets and costumes were by Neher, projections by John Heartfield and his brother. Widely though this more conventional staging and theatre differed from the original 1932 production, with its minimal set and agitational character, it represented (in the East German context) a notable attempt to introduce a changed audience to actively political theatre.

15 January 51
For the radio play of 1939 see 7 November 39. In 1946, when Brecht was already looking for a likely composer, the American Roger Sessions decided to make this into a school opera, using the text of H. R. Hays's translation which Brecht had sent him. The result was a major work which was performed at Berkeley on 18 April 1947, then seems to have been abandoned by Brecht, who hoped that Stravinsky might be interested. Dessau's role at this point was to approach Stravinsky on Brecht's behalf, and there the matter rested until after Brecht had returned to Germany. It was now Dessau who wanted to compose the work, which appeared to gain fresh relevance with the new arms race and the inclusion of West Germany in NATO. Serious collaboration began in 1949, and by the summer of 1950 the East Berlin State Opera had planned a production in the coming season, with Neher as designer and Hermann Scherchen as conductor. Unfortunately the sudden alertness of the ministry was followed by the appearance of a virulent anti-'formalist' article in the official *Tägliche Rundschau* (21 and 23 January) by a Soviet pundit called Orlov.

25 March 51
The planned première was treated as a single trial performance, after which the opera was withdrawn for revision. This entry was written on the day following the meeting with the Council of Ministers, where Brecht had insisted on his contract with the State Opera Intendant Ernst Legal. Part of the official hostility to *Lucullus* was due to its performance coming only a week after the adoption of a resolution to combat 'Formalism in Art and Literature' by the 5th conference of the SED Central Committee. Attention had already been drawn to *The Mother* and its breaches of Socialist Realism. Subsequently Paul Wandel, the popular minister for education who had supported Dessau, would be relieved of his

responsibility for the arts. He had been a senior KPD figure in Moscow and spoke Russian, but was said to be disliked by Walter Ulbricht, the SED Secretary.

5 May 51
The work on *Coriolanus* with Brecht's young colleagues would continue sporadically over the next two or three years. Hecht says he was planning a production with Ernst Busch in the title role.

4 June 51
Ernst Barlach, outstanding German sculptor and playwright, had died in isolation in 1938, a year after the Nazis had banned his work. Brecht would use his position in the Academy to support him against criticisms by Wilhelm Girnus in the Party paper. For Girnus see Hans Mayer's *Der Turm Von Babel*, pp. 58f: 'Girnus was a Stalinist, quite definitely.'

4 June 51
The revised *Courage* production would open the new season on 11 September. This was the first under the name of the Berliner Ensemble, with Brecht as the sole director. The two Deutsches Theater actors who had to be replaced were Hinz as Chaplain and Bildt as Cook. They were succeeded by Geschonneck and Busch respectively, both from the old world of agitprop. Angelika Hurwicz took over Kattrin, Regine Lutz the whore Yvette.

1 July 51
FDJ = Freie Deutsche Jugend, the (Communist) Free German Youth.

3 July 51
Brecht and Dessau wrote this minor work for the impending World Youth Festival, taking its theme from an episode the previous year (see 25 May 50) when young West Germans returning from East Berlin were held up by the Federal police at the Herrnburg frontier crossing. The initiative was Dessau's. The FDJ organisers had proposed to perform this throughout the Festival, but found it too simplistic. Only five performances were given.

10 July 51
Hans Garbe was an East German Stakhanovite, or record-breaking worker. Brecht thought of writing a play about him, to be called *Büsching* after a character in his early *Fatzer* project, of which a fragment had been published in the first issue of the *Versuche* (1930). There are about twenty pages of sketches in the Archive and twelve more outlining the story. In 1952, Brecht's assistant Käthe Rülicke would publish some of her interviews with Garbe himself under the title *Hans Garbe erzählt*.

11 July 51
Three stories by Anna Seghers were published under this title by Aufbau-Verlag.

4 August 51
Theaterarbeit was the illustrated volume describing the first six Ensemble productions, from *Puntila* to the revamped *Mother Courage*, with excellent photographs and a variety of notes and essays by many hands. The basic book on

the company's work, it was first published by the Dresdner Verlag, Dresden. Later editions would contain further material relating to other productions. The designer was Peter Palitzsch. See the account given in section 46 of *Brecht on Theatre*.

17 August 51

Wandel, who had been personally committed to *Lucullus* (and to Dessau's work in general), would be relieved of his responsibility for the arts in the course of the month. Two new bodies were founded outside his ministry: the State Commission for Art Affairs and the Office for Literature and Publishing. The former was chaired by a former schoolmaster called Helmut Holtzhauer, who became the bane of the artists by his rigid application of the party resolution against 'formalism'. The new system and its officials would subsequently be much criticised by Brecht and others.

22 August 51

During the four-month gap in the entries following this date Brecht wrote the first of his widely publicised open letters against the danger of another war. He was awarded a GDR National Prize (1st Class). A campaign against his being given Austrian citizenship led to Von Einem's leaving the Salzburg Festival board. Elisabeth Hauptmann and Suhrkamp began planning the edition of his early plays. The revised version of Dessau's *Lucullus* opera (see pp. 432–3) was included in the new season at the State Opera, where it had its première on 12 October. It bore the changed title of *The Condemnation of Lucullus*. None of this is referred to in the journal.

5 January 52

The Broken Jug. A standard classic by Kleist. This Ensemble production would open on 21 January, with Therese Giehse as director and Hainer Hill as designer. Dessau's *Appeal*, on a text by Vera Skupin(a) of the Ensemble, was a work for soloist, chorus, children's chorus, speaker and orchestra, directed against West German rearmament. The 'press night' was for Curt Bois's first performance of the Puntila part in succession to Steckel, who had left the company.

6 January 52

Vera Skupina's play was called *Das Tiergericht* (The Animals' Tribunal). Ernst Busch was to direct the Ensemble in Nikolai Pogodin's *Kremlin Chimes*, a recent Soviet play which would be designed by Heartfield and his brother. Heartfield was not in favour with the SED arts arbiters, who disapproved of photomontage.

1 February 52

These two Berlin papers were respectively the Soviet and the SED daily organs. For Brecht's reply see *GW* 19, pp. 511–16. Two days previously *Lucullus* had been performed in Frankfurt-am-Main under Scherchen and well received.

2 February 52

The *Urfaust* is Goethe's early version of the two-part *Faust* play by which he is best known. Brecht saw Langhoff's production of the latter for the Goethe bicentenary in 1949, found it wanting (10 September 49) and now planned to give his own interpretation of the Faust figure in a theatre outside Berlin, with young performers and Monk as director. Kurt Palm and Hainer Hill would be responsible for costumes and set. Meantime Eisler was aiming to write a Faust opera on his own libretto, which he would later discuss with Brecht. He attended several of the *Urfaust* rehearsals.

3 February 52
Fritz Cremer was a leading sculptor who had studied, among a group of other active anti-Nazis, in the sculpture department of the Hochschule für Kunst. The Buchenwald memorial would be unveiled in 1958. Brecht's suggestions are in *GW* 20, p. 331.

14 February 52
Märkische Schweiz. Roughly = 'The Brandenburg Alps' or 'Prussian Switzerland': a hilly area some 50 km east of Berlin. The Brechts would acquire this pair of houses, where the 'Buckow Elegies' would be written.

18 February 52
See Eisler's draft 'Remarks on the draft resolution of the SED Central Committee on the 125th anniversary of Ludwig van Beethoven's death'. A devastating critique, which Eisler slightly shortened before sending it to Egon Rentzsch of the SED, who had asked for his views. The Committee's eventual statement, somewhat amended, would be published in the March issue of *Musik und Gesellschaft*, pp. 8–10.

24 February 52
Hans Marchwitza, a former miner, had joined the League of Proletarian-Revolutionary Writers, fought in Spain and emigrated to the US. He was now a GDR diplomat. The Brechts were going to discuss a visit of the Ensemble to Poland during that autumn. Leon Schiller was a leading Polish director, and a man of the left.

26 February 52
Fernando de Rojas's fifteenth-century Spanish *Celestina* may already have been in Brecht's mind. There are three pages of typewritten notes in the Archive, which are tentatively dated around 1948.

6 April 52
Lines from Goethe's *Faust* taken from the translation by Barker Fairley (University of Toronto Press, Toronto and Buffalo, 1970). Brecht in fact directed the original *Urfaust* version, but these quotations survive in *Faust* Part 1.

15 July 52
Again, a gap of nearly four months. The entries only resume once the Brechts are installed in Buckow. In the interval *Kremlin Chimes* has opened in Busch's production; Neher sees this conventional Soviet drama as 'the end of the Berliner Ensemble'. Brecht is again working on the *Courage* film project, whose second script (written by Emil Burri) is completed by the end of February; Engel however drops out and is succeeded by Wolfgang Staudte as the designated director; evidently it was Staudte who introduced the idea of using some non-German stars. A third version is finished in mid-June, but Brecht's hopes of

shooting during 1952 have to be abandoned. As for *Urfaust*, Brecht once again says nothing about its opening (on 23 April, in Potsdam) nor about Erpenbeck's decision (30 June) on behalf of the new Arts Commissions that the production must not go into the Ensemble's repertoire. This because of its slightly flippant undercutting of the Faust figure, whose affront to national susceptibilities would blow up into a major controversy with Eisler's opera libretto the following May.

22 July 52

Erwin Strittmatter (b.1912) was a novelist of unpretentious origins who had come to maturity in the GDR and could write about its rural and provincial problems. Brecht rated him highly, and spent much time working with him on his play *Katzgraben* which the Ensemble would stage in the following spring. Georg Lukács, now somewhat withdrawn from political life following criticism during the First Hungarian Writers' Congress, had visited Buckow on 6 July.

25 to 30 August 52

The title of Eisler's opera was *Johann Faustus*. No music had been written as yet.

30 August 52

Beside the work on *Coriolanus* and *Katzgraben*, Brecht was about to go over Anna Seghers's radio play with Benno Besson, who was turning it into a stage work. On 4 October he would ask Holtzhauer, of the new Commission for Art Affairs, not to ban *The Mother* from the Ensemble's forthcoming Polish tour (as had apparently been intended).

2 November 52

Anna Seghers's *The Trial of Joan of Arc at Rouen, 1431* was first broadcast in Flemish in 1935, then published in German in the Moscow *Internationale Literatur*. In 1950 it was broadcast in the GDR. The Ensemble's stage version would be directed by Besson with Käthe Reichel as Joan and sets by Hill. Neher now left the company, having been told by the Austrian government that further work for the Ensemble would be inconsistent with his citizenship oath. He was not prepared to move house to East Berlin.

3 November 52

Brecht was miscalculating. He was 54.

November 52

Lusatia or Lausitz was the Slav-speaking area round Cottbus. The 'Soviet farce' was by Tokaev. The Ensemble cast included Barbara Berg (stage name of the Brechts' daughter) and Ekkehard Schall.

15 November 52

Brecht's long told-to-the-children ballad on 'How to bring up millet' was written in 1950 under the influence of the (generally discredited) biological theories of Michurin and Lysenko – which were backed by the authority of Stalin. Dessau set it as a 'Musikepos' for baritone, speaker, two choruses and orchestra; it had its première at Halle on 29 October. It contains Brecht's unique flattering allusion to Stalin, calling him 'the Soviet people's great harvest-leader'. Meyer = the composer Ernst Hermann Meyer, who had been a refugee in the UK.

16 November 52
Harry Buckwitz directed, Teo Otto designed costumes and set. This was the day of the Frankfurt opening. In Berlin that evening, the Ensemble presented *Señora Carrar's Rifles*, directed by Monk with sets by Hill, and Weigel as Carrar. Of all Brecht's plays this lone example of 'aristotelian (i.e. empathy –) drama' was the most often performed in the GDR.

17 November 52
See 2 November 52 above. The première would be on the 23rd. The 'Tui story' is Brecht's first mention of such inverted intellectuals since leaving the US.

28 November 52(?)
Hermann Henselmann (b. 1905) was the city architect of East Berlin from 1954–9, designing buildings on the Stalin-Allee (the former Frankfurter Allee) which introduced a style termed 'national tradition'. Later the street was renamed 'Karl Marx-Allee', which part of it has remained to this day.

About 1952
This vaguely dated entry comes from the 'Autobiographische Aufzeichnungen' appended to the *Tagebücher 1920–1922* published in 1975.

15 December 52
Albert Schreiner was one of the refugee group on whom Brecht had tested his 'Manifesto' hexameters in New York (June to mid-July 45). He subsequently discussed *The Days of the Commune* with him. Ernst Thälmann had been the KPD secretary during the rise of the Nazis; he was imprisoned and eventually killed in Buchenwald in 1944. The film was written by Bredel and Tschesno-Hell and directed by Kurt Maetzig.

12 January 53
The Ensemble Polish tour took in Cracow, Lødz and Warsaw. Weigel went, though Brecht evidently stayed behind. There were performances of *The Mother* after all. As for *Mother Courage*, Brecht now thought that the film project was 'hopelessly bogged down'.

20 January 53
If Brecht was reading Stanislavsky it may have been because of the impending Stanislavsky Conference, to which Brecht and Weigel would be invited by Kurt Bork on behalf of the State Arts Commission on 20 February. This would be held in mid-April.

4 March 53
With the date of the conference fast approaching, Brecht was concerned about the position of his slightly heretical theatre. A day later, Stalin died and was succeeded by the fifty-two-year-old Georgi Malenkov. Brecht wrote a message of non-committal sympathy in the Academy's magazine *Sinn und Form*.

20 August 53
Again, over five months had passed without Brecht recording anything in the journal. They were particularly eventful ones, first forcing Brecht and Eisler to make some kind of obeisance to party aesthetics, then jolting Brecht out of much

of his optimism about the GDR, then giving him a new degree of authority in its art affairs and a permanent theatre in which to work. All this within the growing climate of 'Thaw' (a term adopted by Ehrenburg) which began to be felt in Soviet arts policy following Stalin's death.

At the Stanislavsky conference, which was held at the Academy from 17–19 April, Brecht said little, while Weigel was diplomatic. The Ensemble's position did not worsen, but this was at the cost of paying some cautious lip-service to Soviet 'Realism' and Stanislavskyan principles. Then came three Wednesday sessions in a private series of the Academy's own, when Eisler's (rashly published) libretto for *Johann Faustus* was attacked by a group of Kulturpolitiker led by Abusch, Girnus, Ernst Hermann Meyer and a certain Walter Besenbruch, with Becher's slightly evasive support. The Austrian communist Ernst Fischer, now married to Eisler's former wife, had provoked this by writing (in *Sinn und Form*) that it promised to be 'the German national opera' even though not a note of music had yet been written. The fact that Eisler too was Austrian, and that both of them presented Faust as a 'renegade' intellectual rather than a national hero, was an outrage to the German academicians. Such a view (and by implication Brecht's of a year earlier) was not merely an offence to the memory of Goethe; it was anti-national, anti-social, contrary to the 'cultural heritage' and to the principles of Socialist Realism. Party resolutions were cited, and so (by Girnus and Meyer) was the authority of Stalin's lieutenant Zhdanov (see 24 March 47). Wilhelm Girnus (1906–85), a former concentration camp prisoner, was deputy editor of *Neues Deutschland* from 1949–55.

Brecht was Eisler's one effective supporter, and attended all three meetings. The prospective conductor Felsenstein also spoke against such 'aggressive and personal' criticism, though he was less versed in the jargon. But the effect was to throw Eisler into the deepest depression of his life, so that he returned to Vienna and stopped work on the opera's composition; nor was it ever really started. Meanwhile *Katzgraben* opened on 23 May, just before the second Eisler session, in Brecht's production with grey, 'daguerreotype-like' sets by Karl von Appen, the company's new designer from Dresden.

A week after Eisler had been dealt with there was a crisis in the affairs of the GDR, when East Berlin building workers refused to accept the increased work norms (or quotas) decreed for the end of June. On the 16th they demonstrated outside the ministries and in the Stalin-Allee; then next day more widespread rioting began, notably on the border with West Berlin and in some other cities, after which the Russians declared a state of emergency and brought out the tanks. With Weigel away in Budapest, the immediate reaction of Brecht and the company – a mixture of criticism and support, expressed in a number of letters and statements – clearly improved its position with the authorities, who most notably reacted by confirming that they would indeed get the Theater am Schiffbauerdamm. More broadly, the Central Committee of the SED agreed that in future its arts policy must not be 'administratively enforced', after which Brecht was able to head the open attack on those philistine arts commissions which had been doing the enforcing for the past twelve months. (See his *Neues Deutschland* statement of 12 August, in *Brecht on Theatre*, pp. 266–70.)

As he now wrote on returning to Buckow, the events of 17 June – most particularly the evidence of the workers' hostility to 'their' government – had 'alienated the whole of existence', or turned his world on its head, with visible effects on his writing. This was less evident in the long-projected *Turandot* (which would take him back to the 'Tui' theme) than in the Elegies that he would be writing off and on at Buckow from now till December. If Eisler's attitude to life, work and politics had been shaken, so now had Brecht's.

12 September 53
Werner Mittenzwei suggests that Helene Weigel had temporarily moved out in protest against Brecht's love affairs and the overhanging problem of Ruth Berlau, who no longer had any clear rôle with the Ensemble. The Weissensee house however could now be given up altogether, when friends found the Brechts two storeys much closer to the theatre and the Academy, at 125 Chausseestrasse (a northward prolongation of the Friedrichstrasse where the Brecht Centre and Archive now are). Brecht moved in during October, and Weigel followed after their return from Vienna.

13 September 53
To the Germans *Turandot* is primarily a play by Schiller, and only secondarily an opera.

15 to 30 October 53
The Neues Theater in der Scala, in the Soviet Fourth Bezirk of Vienna, was Communist-run from 1945 till after the signing of the Austrian Peace Treaty in 1955. In November-December 1948 it mounted a 'Brecht-Abend', with Giehse, Karl Paryla and Wolfgang Heinz (the Intendant), followed by a production of *Mother Courage* directed by Lindtberg with Giehse in the title part. The Berliner Ensemble came in mid-September 1950 and performed *The Tutor*. Now, three years later, the Soviet-licensed firm Wien-Film were proposing to make a film of *Puntila* starring Curt Bois, while the Scala had commissioned a translation of *Volpone* from Besson, who consulted Brecht and Hauptmann; this had opened on 2 September.

  The Mother followed on 31 October. The non-Communist theatres were now boycotting Brecht, since the campaign against his Austrian citizenship had been intensified by news of his support for the GDR government in June. None the less, aside from Weigel and Busch the actors were drawn from Vienna. Manfred Wekwerth directed, following Brecht's 1951 model.

4 November 53
Nikolai Bukharin was editor of *Pravda* from 1917–1929 and of *Izvestia* in 1934. Originally written in 1914, and published five years later, this book was widely translated, an English-language version first appearing in New York in 1927. Primarily an economist, he was shot in the purges of 1937. On 17 November Brecht would start the long process of rehearsing *The Caucasian Chalk Circle*, with music by Dessau, sets and costumes by von Appen. In the new year the arts commissions were replaced by a Ministry of Culture under Becher, and the anti-formalist campaign was quietly dropped.

1953–4
The 'present girl-friend' might be any one of three people.

7 February 54

Angelika Hurwicz played Dumb Kattrin in the Ensemble's *Mother Courage*; she had started at the Deutsches Theater in 1945. Busch's bitter experiences were surely before that: he was arrested in Antwerp in 1940 and interned in the Pyrenees, was caught trying to escape over the Swiss frontier, then handed over to the Gestapo in Paris. Imprisoned in Berlin-Moabit, he was tried for high treason, but escaped the death penalty thanks to lawyers provided by Gustav Gründgens, the Intendant of Goering's State Theatre. Badly wounded in the head when the prison was bombed, he was later transferred to Brandenburg gaol till the Red Army arrived and he could identify himself by singing the old Party songs.

8 July 54

This was J. Robert Oppenheimer. In the first half of 1954 (for which there are only two entries) the Ensemble launched three productions: the early German comedy *Hans Pfriem*, directed by Rülicke in a studio; Molière's *Dom Juan*, adapted and directed by Besson; and a modern Chinese play called *Millet for the Eighth Army* adapted by Elisabeth Hauptmann and Wekwerth and directed by the latter. *Dom Juan* inaugurated the Theatre on the Schiffbauerdamm (today called Bertolt-Brecht Platz) into which the company had just moved. In January Brecht had been put on the advisory board of Becher's new Ministry for the Arts. In June he was made vice-president of the Academy, and at the end of that month he and Weigel took the Ensemble to Paris to play *Mother Courage* in the Paris international festival. After the announcement in December that he had won a Stalin Peace Prize, he and Becher took part in a discussion with Congress for Cultural Freedom members headed by Melvyn J. Lasky. GDR policy still favoured a reunited Germany.

[May 55]

On 15 May Brecht flew to Moscow to receive his Stalin Prize, stopping in Warsaw en route. Tadeusz Kulisiewicz was the Polish artist who made pen drawings of the Ensemble's production of *The Caucasian Chalk Circle*, which finally opened in Berlin on 7 October 1954. Leopold Infeld the physicist had met Brecht on his previous visit. Brecht thought of writing a play about Einstein (about whom he had mixed views) to complement his *Galileo*. There are some ten pages of notes in the Brecht Archive. The Icelandic novelist Halldor Laxness won the Nobel Prize for Literature that year.

18 July 55

See *Brecht on Theatre*, item 54, for a note on Brecht's ideas for 'Dialectics in the Theatre', the collection of theoretical writings included in *Versuche 15*.

Select Bibliography

The following is primarily a list of books which have been found useful, informative and suggestive in the preparation of this English edition of the *Journals*. It takes for granted standard reference books in English and German, and the principal German editions: that is, the first Suhrkamp hardbacks of 1973, the two supplementary volumes to the softback 'Werkausgabe' (or '*GW*') of 1974, and volumes 26–7 of the 'große kommentierte Berliner und Frankfurter Ausgabe' which were still being worked on when we went to press. It does not pretend to completeness.

Brecht in German

Bertolt Brecht, *Kriegsfibel* (new edition). Eulenspiegel-Verlag, Berlin, 1968.

Bertolt Brecht, *Tagebücher 1920–1922. Autobiographische Aufzeichnungen 1920–1954*. Herausgegeben von Herta Ramthun. Suhrkamp, Frankfurt am Main, 1975.

Brecht/Neher, *Antigonemodell 1948*. Redigiert von Ruth Berlau. Gebrüder Weiss, Berlin, 1949.

Brecht et al. (eds), *Theaterarbeit*. Sechs Aufführungen des Berliner Ensembles. Dresdner Verlag, Dresden, 1952.

Brecht in English with variant versions and relevant notes

Bertolt Brecht, *Plays, Poetry and Prose*. Edited by John Willett and Ralph Manheim. Methuen, London. Notably vol. 5 i, *Life of Galileo* (1980); 6 i, *The Good Person of Szechwan* (1985); 6 iii, *Mr Puntila and his Man Matti* (1987); 7 i, *Schweyk in the Second World War* & *The Visions of Simon Machard* (1985); *Poems 1913–1956* (with the cooperation of Erich Fried, 1976); *Poems and Songs from the Plays*, (1990); *Letters 1913–1956* (1990).

Bertolt Brecht, *Collected Plays*. Edited by Ralph Manheim and John Willett. Random House/Vintage Books, New York. Volume 9. *Adaptations* (these are not in the Methuen edition, which otherwise has progressed further).

Bertolt Brecht, *The Private Life of the Master Race*. A Documentary Play. English Version and An Essay on the work of Brecht by Eric Russell Bentley. New Directions, New York, 1944.

Brecht on Theatre. Edited and translated by John Willett. Methuen, London, and Hill and Wang, New York, 1964.

Other publications in German and English

Ernst Josef Aufricht, *Erzähle, damit du dein Reicht beweist*. Propyläen, Berlin, 1966.

Elisabeth Bergner, *Bewundert viel und viel gescholten*. Bertelsmann, Munich, 1978.

Ruth Berlau, *Brechts Lai-Tu, Erinnerungen und Notate*. Herausgegeben und mit einem Nachwort von Hans Burge. Luchterhand, Darmstadt und Neuwied, 1985.

Albrecht Betz, *Hanns Eisler Political Musician*. Translated by Bill Hopkins. Cambridge University Press, Cambridge, 1982.

Hans Bunge, *Fragen Sie mehr über Brecht; Hanns Eisler im Gespräch*. Rogner & Bernhard, Munich, 1972.

Hans Bunge, *Die Debatte um Hanns Eislers 'Johann Faustus'. Eine Dokumentation*. Herausgegeben vom Brecht-Zentrum, Berlin. BasisDruck, Berlin, 1991.

Simon Callow, *Charles Laughton: A Difficult Actor*. Methuen, London, 1987.

Humphrey Carpenter, *W. H. Auden: A biography*. Allen and Unwin, London, 1981.

Wolfgang Gersch, *Film bei Brecht*. Henschel, Berlin, 1975.

David Drew, *Kurt Weill: A handbook*. Faber, London and Boston, 1987.

Fritz Hennenberg, *Dessau-Brecht Musikalische Arbeiten*. Henschel, Berlin, 1963.

Fritz Hennenberg, *Paul Dessau: Eine Biographie*. Deutscher Verlag für Musik, Leipzig, 1965.

Klaus Jarmatz, Simone Barck, Peter Dietzel, *Kunst und Literatur im antifaschistischen Exil 1933–1945* in sieben Bänden. Reclam, Leipzig. 1: *USSR*, 1979; 2: *Switzerland*, 1981; 3: *USA*, 1983; 4: *Latin America*, 1980; 5: *Czechoslovakia, UK, Scandinavia and Palestine*, 1980; 6: *Netherlands and Spain*, 1981; 7: *France*, 1981.

Fritz Kortner, *Aller Tage Abend*. Kindler, Munich, 1959.

Joachim Lucchesi, *Das Verhör in der Oper: die Debatte um die Aufführung 'Das Verhör des Lukullus'*. Basis Druck, Berlin, 1993.

Georg Lukács, Johannes R. Becher, Friedrich Wolf u.a., *Die Säuberung*. Moskau, 1936: Stenogramm einer geschlossénen Parteisitzung. Herausgegeben von Reinhard Müller. Rowohlt, Reinbek 1991.

James K. Lyon, 'The FBI as Literary Historian'. *The Brecht Yearbook*, vol. ii, 1982.

James K. Lyon, *Bertolt Brecht in America*. Princeton University Press, Princeton, 1980

James K. Lyon, *Bertolt Brecht's American Cicerone*. With an Appendix Containing the Complete Correspondence Between Bertolt Brecht and Ferdinand Reyher. Bouvier Verlag Herbert Grundmann, Bonn, 1978.

Hans Mayer, *Ein Deutscher auf Widerruf, Erinnerungen*. Suhrkamp, Frankfurt, vol. 1, 1982; vol. 2, 1984.

Hans Mayer, *Der Turm von Babel: Erinnerung an eine Deutsche Demokratische Republik*. Suhrkamp, Frankfurt, 1991.

Werner Mittenzwei, *Das Leben des Bertolt Brecht oder Der Umgang mit den Welträtseln*. Suhrkamp, Frankfurt am Main, 1987.

Werner Mittenzwei, *Das Zürcher Schauspielhaus 1933–1945 oder Die letzte Chance*. Henschel, Berlin, 1979.

Jan Esper Olsson, *Bertolt Brechts schwedisches Exil*. Dissertation, Lund University, 1971.

David Pike, *German Writers in Soviet Exile, 1933–1945*. The University of North Carolina Press, Chapel Hill, 1982.

David Pike, 'Brecht and Stalin's Russia: the Victim as Apologist (1931–1945)'. *The Brecht Yearbook*, vol. II, 1982.

David Pike, *The Politics of Culture in Soviet-Occupied Germany 1945–1949*. Stanford University Press, 1992 (imprint), 1993 (date of publication).

Bernhard Reich, *Im Wettlauf mit der Zeit. Erinnerungen aus fünf Jahrzehnten deutsche Theatergeschichte*. Henschel, Berlin, 1970.

Ernst & Renate Schumacher, *Leben Brechts in Wort und Bild*. Henschel, Berlin, 1978.

Margarete Steffin, *Konfutse versteht nichts von Frauen*. Nachgelassene Texte. Herausgegeben von Inge Gellert. Rowohlt, Berlin, 1991.

John Russell Taylor, *Strangers in Paradise. The Hollywood Emigrés 1933–1950*. Faber, London, 1983.

Theater im Exil 1933–1945. Exhibition catalogue, Akademie der Künste, Berlin, 1973.

Klaus Völker, *Brecht-Chronik. Daten zu Leben und Werk*. Hanser, Munich, 1971

John Willett, *The Theatre of Erwin Piscator. Half a Century of Politics in the Theatre*. Eyre Methuen, London, 1978. Holmes and Meyer, New York.

John Willett, *Brecht in Context. Comparative Approaches*. Methuen, London & New York, 1984.

John Willett, *Caspar Neher Brecht's Designer*. Methuen, London and New York in association with the Arts Council of Great Britain, 1986.

Hella Wuolijoki, *Und ich war nicht Gefangene. Memoiren und Skizzen*. Herausgegeben von Richard Semrau. Hinstorff, Rostock, 1987.